What's It Worth?

A Guide to Valuing a Small Business

SUCCESSFUL BUSINESS LIBRARY

What's It Worth?

A Guide to Valuing a Small Business

Lloyd R. Manning

The Oasis Press®
Central Point, Oregon

Editor: Sheila Bean
Interior design: Last Impression Publishing Service
Cover design: Steven Eliot Burns

Please direct any comments, questions, or suggestions regarding this book to:
    The Oasis Press®/PSI Research
    Editorial Department
    P.O. Box 3727
    Central Point, Oregon 97502-0032
    (541) 245-6502
    info@psi-research.com e-mail

The Oasis Press® is a Registered Trademark of Publishing Services, Inc., an Oregon corporation doing business as PSI Research.

Manning, Lloyd R., 1930-
    What's it worth? : a guide to valuing a small business / Lloyd R. Manning.
        p. cm. -- (Successful business library)
    ISBN 1-55571-504-4 (pbk.)
        1. Business enterprises—Valuation. I. Title. II. Series.

HG4028.V3 M326 2000
658.15--dc21
                                                        00-023830

Printed and bound in the United States of America

First Edition 10 9 8 7 6 5 4 3 2

Printed on recycled paper when available

Table of Contents

Chapter 3:

LOOK BEFORE YOU LEAP   23

Chapter 4:

THE APPRAISAL OF REAL ESTATE: A CRASH COURSE   39

Chapter 5:

INTRODUCTION TO THE VALUATION MODEL   69

Chapter 6:

INTERPRETING FINANCIAL STATEMENTS

(A Fast Walk Through the Jungle) 79

Chapter 7:

MACHINERY AND EQUIPMENT 109

Chapter 8:

RISKS OF AND RETURNS ON INVESTMENT   127

Chapter 9:

CAPITALIZATION AND DISCOUNT RATES   135

Chapter 10:

THE COMPARATIVE SALES APPROACH TO VALUE   151

Chapter 11:

INTRODUCTION TO THE EARNINGS APPROACHES   167

Chapter 12:

WHAT IS GOODWILL AND HOW DO WE MEASURE IT   187

Chapter 13:

THE ASSETS APPROACHES TO VALUE   197

Chapter 14:

THE CASH-FLOW APPROACHES TO VALUE 227

Chapter 15:

VALUING THE FRANCHISE 237

Chapter 16:

THE VALUATION OF SHARES 253

Chapter 17:

THE APPRAISAL OF A FRACTIONAL INTEREST   261

Chapter 18:

THE APPRAISAL REPORT   271

List of Figures

List of Primary Tables

VALUING a small business can be a confusing process. If you were to listen to a collection of business people, you might reasonably assume that they all know how to value a business. But if you were to examine the various transactions they've made, you'd probably conclude that no one knows how to establish a fair and marketable value for a going concern. This applies to buyers, sellers, and at times, even real estate appraisers and lenders. Appraisers are supposed to be unmotivated and neutral, but buyers and sellers often set aside good judgment because they're so desperate to make the deal. They don't make level-headed decisions based on supportable facts, and instead rush into deals based on guesswork and wishful thinking.

In over thirty years as a professional appraiser, business and investment real-estate broker, and business analyst, I have seen, again and again, businesses being sold to unsuspecting souls who asked all of the wrong questions to all of the wrong people. They overlooked or glossed over nitty-gritty, life-and-death issues, yet confidently concentrated on irrelevant aspects of the venture. Before making the purchase, they didn't have a clear idea of the business's prospect for making or losing money, and they wouldn't listen to advice.

This book has two purposes: first, to help both buyers and sellers determine a fair price for a small business; and second, to be a guide for the practising real-estate appraiser.

Although much has been said about business valuation over the years, little has been written about it. Several very good books do address buying or selling a business, but most come up short on establishing a fair price, and on how to assess the value of the assets and the income and profit.

This book will not turn a novice business buyer into a professional appraiser, but it will simply show you what to do and how, what to look for and what to disregard, and even if and when to consult a professional appraiser.

For the practising real-estate appraiser, the intent is not to break new ground, but rather only to build on what you already know and do every day. Anyone with an MAI, SREA, AACI, or equivalent, or at or near the Certified General Level will have no difficulty with the text, or with conducting the professional practice that follows. I am not an academic. I am a country appraiser who learned my skills from the school of hard knocks and the university of experience.

Throughout this manual, in many places, I could have said much more. For these shortcomings, I do not apologize. No guide can cover every possible type of enterprise or address every conceivable situation. Some topics are so complex that I can only hit the high spots, outline the common denominators, and describe the more popular procedures. I don't have the space for in-depth analysis or endless arguments about specific situations. At the same time, I have explained complicated or intense procedures in several ways. In controversial situations, or where the experts do not agree, I've tried to present both sides, the pros and cons, and the viewpoints of the financial community.

There are no pat answers or quick fixes. Every situation is unique, and so is every solution. Appraisals are not created from formulas nor packed in boxes. Many situations call for different approaches or procedures. They might come to conclusions that seem foreign but are also logical and acceptable.

A wise seer once said that if a writer borrows or steals from another, that is plagiarism; but if from many, it is research. To all of those who were researched, I express my thanks. To those who directly contributed to this project (every appraiser, every author, and every academic who has added to the science of real-estate or business valuation—and there are many), I give thanks.

I especially thank John A. Crozier, B.Comm, C.A. Chartered Accountant (equivalent to the American C.P.A.), of Edmonton, Canada, for his review and advice on the financial and accounting sections; and Darrell Manning, B.Comm, M.B.A., for his help with the original manuscript.

For the eager student of this subject, I recommend that you read the work of several learned theorists and practitioners in this field, many of whom were researched. Many varied and excellent texts are available, including some that are more highly technical or theoretical, particularly those that look at the valuation of shares and fractional interests.

For the buyer, all that I can say is, "Look before you leap." The universe if full of businesses for sale, but most of them are past their prime and overpriced. Should you become a little lost in the more difficult and material sections, read them several times. They show the way.

For the appraiser, I hope to give you the confidence that most real-estate appraisers lack in the field of small business valuation. Appraising a small business isn't all that complicated. You might not need any new skills, and instead merely need to broaden the basic appraisal sciences that are improving every day, thanks to conscientious appraisal practitioners. Most important, I hope to provide the groundwork so that we can learn still more and become more professional.

Lloyd R. Manning
Lloydminster, Saskatchewan
December 1999

Chapter 1

WELCOME TO OUR WORLD: WHAT THIS BOOK IS ALL ABOUT

Over the next several days, weeks, and months, many people will make unwise business purchases. Many should not buy because they should never go into business for themselves in the first place. Others will:

- pay far too much for the business,
- overpay for goodwill that is not all that good,
- buy a business that has absolutely no potential,
- buy a business that is on the decline,
- buy a business that is, by every standard, obsolete.

With this manual, you will not learn what to buy, because that is too tough a call. You will learn, however, what to look for, how to separate the golden opportunities from the dead dogs, how to avoid some obvious pitfalls, and how to calculate a purchase price.

Perhaps you are a real-estate appraiser. If so, your job is to interpret the forces that propel the marketplace, and to give the buyer a purchase price that jibes with its value. Sometimes your client will be the seller, or perhaps a third party, such as a banker or an attorney. Yet you are most concerned with the actions and reactions of buyers, those who spend hard cash. These are the people who set the market.

This book will help you to:

- determine what the other person is trying to sell,
- sort out profitable businesses from those that are certain to fail,
- measure sales and profit potential,
- check out the competition,
- establish and measure the value of a going concern, using the methods of professional appraisers,
- measure and value goodwill,
- value a franchise.

You will also quickly look at:

- valuing shares,
- valuing fractional interests,
- what professional appraisers do, and what business buyers can expect in appraisal reports when employing one.

Throughout, you will hear this so often that you will tire of it:

Is it reasonable? Is it logical? Does it make sense?

This is what business valuation is all about. At the end of every step, you must ask yourself these questions. And, you must always answer, "Yes."

*Is it reasonable?
Is it logical?
Does it make sense?*

This is what business valuation is all about. At the end of every step, you must ask yourself these questions. And, you must always answer, "Yes."

THE URGE TO OWN A BUSINESS

In today's economic and political climate, anyone who buys or starts a business probably has a poorly developed sense of fear. Still, small business is the backbone of the western economy and, because of layoffs in major corporations and government, is becoming more tempting to the workforce each day. Our society includes a vast army of middle-aged clerks, tradespeople, artisans, and laborers who want to buy or start a business. No matter how skilled they are, many of these people do not know how to select an appropriate business, much less how much to pay for it. Few can distinguish between a poor enterprise and a successful one that will provide a good living and a proper return on the investment. Still fewer can tell if a business is on the upswing, has potential, or cannot be saved from bankruptcy, even by God.

Each year in the United States and Canada, about four million businesses are sold and another one million or so started. We are an entrepreneurial people. Those of us who are entrepreneurs share an inborn need to do our own thing, be our own boss, be independent, take charge of our own destiny. Working for someone else, despite its many advantages, seldom fulfills this end. Large companies, who were once major employers, are now reducing their labor forces through attrition, permanent layoffs, mergers, developing offshore plants, and building greater efficiency that requires fewer people. The big players are becoming lean and mean. Many employees with years of seniority, who once enjoyed good wages and expected lifetime security, are unemployed. Their jobs have disappeared and their skills are obsolete. As a result, many people look at buying a business.

Still more want to sell. The ratio is probably about four sellers to one buyer. Very few sellers have more than a vague idea of their business's worth. They seldom know what price to ask, how much negotiating room is practical, or how to market the enterprise. Too often, they base their price on a totally unrealistic notion of its market value. They always want top dollar and all cash. As they are not likely to get either, most have to consider the trade-offs between total price and terms. On the other side of the deal, the buyer needs to measure the seller's willingness to negotiate — maybe the seller is desperate — and capitalize on that.

Just look the annual number of listings that pass through the offices of Realtors and business brokers. What percent ever sell? Two, three, four? Definitely not over five. The same businesses keep coming back, constantly relisted, often with different offices, but with their inherent faults uncorrected. Read the classified ads for "business opportunities" in any local newspaper to see how often the same ones reappear. The words might change so that the reader will think this is something new. Most offerings are grossly overpriced or not in a marketable condition, or else the seller has failed to leave something behind for the next owner. How is the buyer to tell? A plain, old-fashioned gut feeling will often suffice, but before launching into a future of high investment and huge risk, the sophisticated buyer will leave as little to chance as possible.

> Each year in the United States and Canada, about four million businesses are sold and another one million or so started.
>
> As a result, many people look at buying a business. Still more want to sell.

KEY QUESTIONS

Every buyer needs to answer the following questions:

1. What is a fair price for the business? How can that be determined? Why does the seller want to sell? What are the rules of the game?

2. How can you tell if the business is a genuine going concern or if it is someone else's discard and just "blue sky"? What should you look for? How do you check it out?

3. What should you offer for the business? What are the trade-offs between price and terms? How can you tell if the owner really wants to sell, is just testing the waters, or hopes to catch a fool?

This book will address these questions in the context of small businesses. Larger corporations and the stock market will be mentioned only in passing or to make a point. So if you have bought, borrowed, or stolen this book to learn how to do a leveraged buyout on General Motors, you have made a poor choice. But both the publisher and I thank you.

WHAT IS A SMALL BUSINESS?

Not that many years ago, a small business was defined as one with fewer than one hundred employees and a sales volume of less than one million dollars a year. The number of employees may still be valid, but the sales ceiling for a small business would now extend to five or even ten million dollars. You can also consider the services offered, products made or sold, number of owners, and so forth.

To simplify the discussion, this book will concern itself only with such enterprises as service stations, restaurants, dry cleaners, neighborhood convenience stores, small-town hotels, and motels. They will be valued at much less than a million dollars, there will be fewer than twenty-five employees, and the sales volume will be lower than five million dollars. This is the type of business that most unsophisticated sellers sell, inexperienced buyers buy, and real estate appraisers appraise.

WHY BUY AN ESTABLISHED BUSINESS?

Is it not easier and cheaper to start a new business from scratch? Yes, no, maybe, sometimes, and all with qualifications. What are your personal motives and constraints? Are you a capable business pioneer? How long can you withstand the pangs of hunger and frustration? New businesses die because of bad management, but also because of lack of capital. Starting a business and nurturing it to the break-even point costs more than most folks realize.

Although franchises are improving the statistics, about sixty percent of all start-ups still fail within the first five years and fifty percent of the survivors fail during the next five. Of course, everyone who founds a business is certain of being among the twenty percent who survive long-term. I hope that you are. But if you were truly certain, you would not be reading this book. From that perspective, let us consider the advantages and disadvantages of buying an established business, because if you are going to invest all of your time and money in this gamble, should you not consider the alternatives?

> …about sixty percent of all start-ups still fail within the first five years and fifty percent of the survivors fail during the next five.

Advantages

1. An established business has a known and recorded financial history. The profit and loss statements, if properly prepared, (you can safely assume that those prepared by any bona fide accounting firm are), accurately record past income, expenses, and profitability. An interpretation of the statements relates how well or poorly the business is doing which indicates how well it will probably fare in the future. A start-up owner, on the other hand, relies heavily on educated guesswork, most often buoyed up by her or his own

optimism. It is much easier to predict future sales and profitability based on a track record, even with poor management, rather than in an uncharted universe.

2. A going concern usually offers an established market, or at least a foundation, from which to build or expand. Those who start new businesses soon find out that patrons do not flock to their doors. A loyal customer base builds slowly, and most customers must be wrested from the competition. The customer's business must be bought and paid for, one way or another. Despite the higher up-front cash outlay of buying an existing business, this is probably less expensive than paying for a fresh start.

3. A going concern could have a unique site that generates patronage. You might not have this advantage with a new business. An old adage says that only three things really count in business: location, location, location. An equally old adage spouts that all of the good locations are already gone. And this might just be true for your specific enterprise. You might find a terrific location with the ideal land and building. You might, though, find an appropriate location with a building that needs to be upgraded or demolished, and both options cost wads of cash. The initial costs might outweigh any return on the investment.

4. Because it is more likely to succeed, even under new management, the purchase of an established business is easier to finance. It is a safer bet for the investment community. The very best analysts and crystal ball gazers cannot predict how well a new venture will do, nor can they properly estimate its ability to carry debt. There are too many what-if questions. All the investor, or the banker, can do is very roughly predict sales and profitability, perhaps guess at expenses, and basically give little-better-than-nothing odds on your success. No one wants bad news, however. No one willingly pays a professional analyst for a pessimistic, even if correct, report. So some analysts tend to gloss over negative aspects, overestimate the revenues, underestimate the expenses, and make everyone happy.

5. An established business may have exclusive lines, distribution rights, a sought-after franchise, a protected marketing or distribution territory, or a competitive advantage not readily obtained by a new entrant. It may have obtained a market or product penetration that would take a newcomer years to develop. A manufacturing company, even a very small one, could own valuable patents, modern technology, processes, or equipment that is impossible to duplicate. You may choose to buy this company strictly for the perks in the package.

6. Starting a new business adds a new competitor. Buying an existing one does not. The universe remains undisturbed, the competitive position unchanged.

New entrants are always the most vulnerable to the contortions of the marketplace, and usually the first to fail.

Some years ago, the oil marketing companies practised the philosophy that where there was room for one, there was room for four. The objective was a service station on every corner. As a result, every town and city in North America has vacant, abandoned, and converted-to-another-use gas stations or empty sites. All of these companies would now agree that any community, whatever its size or economic wealth, can support only so many of any particular type of business. New entrants are always the most vulnerable to the contortions of the marketplace, and usually the first to fail. Although a going concern normally shrinks at first when the ownership changes, the survival chances are greater than for a new venture. Yet we never learn. We now try to put a fast-food restaurant on every corner.

On the Other Hand, There Are Disadvantages

1. You need a lot more money up-front to buy an existing business. This, many first-time entrepreneurs simply do not have and cannot raise. Building any business to an economic unit level takes time and money. This level is the point at which the business can pay its bills, faithfully offer its product or service, provide the owner with a reasonable standard of living, and earn a return that competes with alternative forms of investment. Any additional value, such as goodwill (reputation), is always a bonus. Still, you have to compensate the seller for his or her cash and sweat equity in building the company's financial health and goodwill. In contrast, starting anew resembles paying on the instalment plan. A small down payment and so much per month, usually a combination of lower earnings and more hours. If the entrepreneur has the choice and the seed capital, it is still probably preferable to buy, rather than start from the ground up.

> …you have to compensate the seller for his or her cash and sweat equity in building the company's financial health and goodwill.

2. When buying an existing enterprise, there may be no goodwill. In fact, the previous owner's reputation might not be good, and that is tough to erase. In other words, when you buy the pond, you get both the princes and the frogs.

3. If your target is a manufacturing, service, or supply company, you may have to honor warranties and guarantees. This could prove very costly, particularly if the previous owner was too liberal with their issuance. You would probably be legally entitled to walk away from many of them, but you would guarantee that those customers will never return.

4. When you buy an existing company, it is difficult to create a fresh image. Signs and banners proclaiming "Under New Management" do not always do the trick. Although you may have innovative ideas that improve the business, customers and even the staff might be reluctant to change the status quo.

5. The company's goodwill, for which you pay a lot of money, might not be very good. If you pay money for the company's potential reputation, and must invest still more money to achieve that reputation, you are paying twice for the same thing.

6. No matter how carefully you investigate a business, no matter how much the seller reveals, there could still be undisclosed items or problems with the selling company. You might not discover the seller's real reason for selling until well after consummating the purchase. Only the vendor knows exactly what is being sold. The purchaser must always spend her nickel and take her chances, relying on the seller's honesty, the correctness of the disclosures, the accuracy of the financial statements, and her own sharp observations and intuition.

7. In the purchase of any going concern, redundancy is always a factor. Maybe the location, staff, equipment, or some other aspect of the business needs to go. Obsolescence probably will not show on the income or profitability statement but it soon will if the business cannot stay competitive.

The Final Test

Should you buy an existing enterprise or start a new one? Well, it always comes down to the money in your pocket, the unfilled opportunity in the marketplace, and your personal perseverance. You can buy a business by paying one lump sum or through a deferred payment plan—usually longer hours and minimum take-home pay for a long time. It is always a trade-off, benefits vs. costs, the advantages and disadvantages of each. This is well worth repeating: you must pay for your business one way or the other. It is just a test of which is best.

PRICE AND VALUE

Although often used synonymously, the terms price and value really mean totally different things. It is important not to mix them up.

Price

Price is the cost at which something is obtained; something which one ordinarily accepts voluntarily in exchange for something else; the consideration given for the purchase of something — a good or service; the amount which a prospective seller indicates as the sum for which he is willing to sell; market value; the amount of money given or set as the amount to be given as a consideration for the sale of a specified good or service.

The term may be synonymous with cost, and with value, as well as with consideration, although price is not always identical with consideration.[1]

Value

Value is the utility of an object in satisfying directly, or indirectly, the needs or desires of human beings; called by economists as "value in use" or "value in exchange" in terms of a power to purchase other objects; also the estimated or appraised worth of an object, or property, calculated in money; to estimate the worth of; to rate at a certain price; to appraise or to place a certain estimate of worth on something, based on a declared scale of values.[2]

Simply stated: Price is what the buyer will pay for something; value is what it is actually worth. They are not necessarily the same.

OBJECTIVE AND SUBJECTIVE VALUE

Seldom would two individuals buy or sell a business for the same reason. In every buy-sell decision, it is important to know why both the seller and the buyer want the deal. What is each person's true purpose? The answer is always a blend of both objective and subjective motives. The objective is what is actually there, the tangible, the physical, that which is real and measurable. The subjective is the logical or illogical rationale that is a fundamental part of the decision, a value created in the mind of each participant to the transaction. It is what you think and hope is there for you, or perhaps to some other person, but in actuality may not be. It is the intangible.

Because you will encounter these two terms frequently throughout this manual, let us thoroughly define them and discuss how each applies to the science of valuing a small business.

Price is what the buyer will pay for something; value is what it is actually worth. They are not necessarily the same.

all business buy-sell decisions include two elements: the objective, which could be interpreted as the head, and the subjective, which is the heart.

Objective Value

When you set aside your personal bias, prejudice, and feelings, and instead look at the business's value in relation to the market, you are being objective. You are considering only the facts and observable conditions.

Subjective Value

You might buy or sell for a specific reason totally unrelated to the market. The business might hold a certain personal value for you and nobody else, a value based on your opinions, attitudes, and thoughts, a value that depends solely on the benefits that you expect to receive.

This means that all business buy-sell decisions include two elements: the objective, which could be interpreted as the head, and the subjective, which is the heart. Even though you might not be able to separate them, you can only ever value a business by measuring the objective. This is what an average, knowledgable, willing buyer will pay and an average, knowledgable, willing seller will accept. Each will weigh the identifiable and measurable tangible assets, normally real estate, equipment, and working capital; the intangible is usually limited to goodwill. Whatever price a singular individual will pay, or accept, because of some special reason or motivation, simply cannot be measured and therefore cannot be taken into account. You may pay your father-in-law more than the business is worth just to get him out. You may pay him less because you have worked there for twenty years for nothing. Those are not value considerations. They are strictly subjective.

Appraisal, in theory and practice, leans towards central tendency or most probable market value. It recognizes that while other values could exist under differing circumstances or to a specific party, two-thirds of all buyers and sellers usually transact within a given price-value range. Why the remainder trade above or below this range does not concern us. Professional appraisers do not know why and make no effort to find out.

Here lies a problem: You want to calculate a reasonable price for a business. But this manual cannot, nor can any text, steer you towards that specific price, because it cannot weigh the unique, subjective factors that affect every price. It will only help you calculate the value, which is based on objective factors.

This value might not seem that accurate All that you can reasonably expect is a number obtained by analysing the financial statements, the operating history of the business, the marketplace, a variety of assumptions, and, hopefully, a levelheaded interpretation of related and supportive data. The resulting value could be correct in most situations if based on logic, mathematical exactness, and calculated by following proper appraisal procedures. Yet neither the buyer or seller can completely separate logic from emotion, the objective from the subjective, thus the calculated value could appear to be too high or too low.

The bottom line is that this manual will address objective motives only. We will discuss value, not price. No attempt will be made to suggest what price you should pay, or accept, for any specific enterprise. From the most probable market value, you must add or subtract any bonus or penalty to come up with a price that makes the deal work for you.

> most probable market value …recognizes that while other values could exist under differing circumstances or to a specific party, two-thirds of all buyers and sellers usually transact within a given price-value range.

GOING CONCERN VALUE DEFINED

Without exception, any business is a blend of tangible and intangible assets, plus the management's skill in using them to produce a reasonable profit. Each business requires a different amount of capital and expertise. Although two businesses' earnings could be similar, created by different capitalization techniques and rates, their values could vary considerably. One business might seem more, or less, valuable to certain individuals because of buy-sell motivation, financing capability, operational know-how, or tax considerations. Going concern value is the value to an average buyer or seller, not to a specific individual.

Let us break down, clause by clause, a standard definition used by professional business appraisers:

Going concern value is defined as:

> "The most probable market value, expressed in terms of money, available in the open market for a proven business enterprise that has established patronage, exclusivity, or uniqueness, which results in demonstrated earnings or profitability."

In layman's terms, this means that when you buy or sell a business, there must be an inherent value. It must be viable, perceptible, and realizable, not just blue-sky. The enterprise must be able to attract venture capital in preference to alternative forms of investment. No one pays out good money for a dead horse, at least not knowingly.

The definition continues by describing the tangible assets:

> "It incorporates the value of real estate, machinery and equipment, working capital, and all other assets that are in place, operating within that are a part of an established business."

And then there are the intangible assets, essentially goodwill:

> "Included is the excess of value over cost that arises as a result of earnings capability in a complete and well-coordinated operation. The present value of surplus earning after the costs of capital, labor, management, and real estate have been attended to."

This is followed by the nuts and bolts of the whole matter, which starts with the real estate portion:

- land and the improvements (buildings) placed thereon,
- the quality and utility of the building(s),
- location including access and visibility, neighborhood, and surrounding amenities.

The business portion includes:

- machinery and equipment (or furniture and fixtures), the quality and use thereof,
- efficiency of plant (how things work as a coordinated unit)
- working capital.

The intangible, or goodwill, portion includes:

- management expertise and ability,
- existing customer attitudes and patronage,
- stability and capability of business aspects that generate earnings,
- probability of continued profit.

The definition presupposes that:

- the seller is knowledgable, experienced, and willing,
- a reasonable time is allowed to find an informed, experienced, and willing buyer,
- sufficient sellers and buyers exist to form a market,
- adequate financing is available at equitable rates,
- all parties are informed (there is full disclosure),
- no party is acting under duress (this is not a fire sale),
- other or special values may exist that are not acknowledged or considered.

That is it. When you put it all together, it is called "Going Concern Value." Estimating Going Concern Value is what this book is all about.

METHODS OF APPRAISING SMALL BUSINESSES

Accepting Book Values as Correct

According to this method, the going concern value of a business is the summation of: current and capital assets, less liabilities.

This is one of the more common methods, yet it only estimates what is called book value, which seldom represents market value. It shows only what was initially paid for the business, plus any additions, less depreciation from all sources. You really have to be stuck before appraising a business this way.

Adjustment of Book Values to Reflect Current Market Values

This is the same as above, except that in this instance capital assets are valued according to their value in the open market. This usually involves obtaining a market value estimate for the real estate. Machinery and equipment value is usually taken at cost, less accumulated depreciation. All else is taken at book value.

The Comparative Sales Approach to Market Value

Primarily used in real-estate appraisal, this approach determines the value of a business by directly comparing it with similar enterprises recently sold or currently held for sale. These market value indicators or comparables are adjusted towards the subject based on similarities and differences.

Sum of the Assets

When capital assets represent a high proportion of the business value, real-estate appraisers usually choose this method. Each asset, including goodwill, is individually appraised. The going concern value is the summation of the respective value contributors.

Capitalizing or Discounting of Net Profits

Basically the income approach to market value, this approach discounts or capitalizes historical average or pro forma net operating profit, producing a single estimate of going concern value. It always uses stabilized income and profitability.

Discounting Projected Net Earnings and Cash Flows

This is the same as discounting or capitalizing the stabilized historical or pro forma net operating profit, which is now projected into the future. Although history may still form a backdrop, the future is the more important consideration.

Price-Earnings Ratio

This procedure is mainly reserved for the stock market and larger companies. It differs from the capitalizing or discounting of profits in that it uses a multiplier, rather than a rate. A stock sells for the earnings multiplied by a certain number. Do not confuse this with the dividend ratio, which is based on what the shareholders actually receive.

S.W.A.G. (Scientific Wild-Assed Guess)

Commonly used by the nonprofessional, this is usually more wild-assed than scientific. The seller sets a price or value based on what he would like to get, rather than what the company is logically worth. He adds up his years of unpaid or poorly paid labor, his sentimental attachment, how much it cost him to buy or build the company, plus appreciation and worldly advice from well-meaning but uninformed friends and relatives. The business will never sell until he attaches a realistic price tag and leaves a little on the table for the next guy.

FORMS OF BUSINESS ORGANIZATION

The target enterprise's organizational style does not really affect its going concern value. You might have your own personal requirements based on the advice of an attorney and tax accountant, and this book cannot presume to know the personal requirements of every reader. Still, you might feel more comfortable knowing the basic organizational forms.

The Single (or Sole) Proprietorship

Here, an individual owns the business and everything in it, personally holding title to all assets. He or she claims all profits and is personally responsible for all debts. As the financial exposure and the potential for lawsuits is so great, this form of organization is becoming less and less common. Although many small businesses start out as single proprietorships, most owners soon seek greater personal protection and tax benefits by incorporating.

The Partnership

This is basically the same as the sole proprietorship, except that now two or more people share ownership. They are often registered on the title to any real estate and personal property as "Tenants in Common". Each benefits from the assets based on the percentage owned, and each accepts a proportional responsibility for the risk and the losses, if any. The legal and financial ramifications are the same as for the single proprietor, but shared. The same danger exists: personal liability for all indebtedness.

In the increasingly popular incorporated partnership, two or more incorporated companies join together in a partnership or joint venture, which itself is not incorporated. Take, for example, the professional practices of lawyers and accountants. Many of the partners are professional corporations, but the practice is a partnership. The legal, tax, and financial benefits and limitations revert to the individual partner's incorporated status.

The Limited Liability or Incorporated Company

Identified by Limited (Ltd.) or Incorporated (Inc.), synonymous terms after its name, this is the most common form of business organization. The owner (or owners) create a legal entity known by name or by number. The individual owner's equity is represented by so many shares in the incorporated company. The company — not the individual shareholder — transacts all business, owns the assets, and holds responsibility for all debts. Although this concept often offers income tax considerations, the principal advantage is the limitation of liability. Personal guarantees excepted, the term "limited" implies that liability for losses is limited to the amount of the financial contribution, or equity, of the individual shareholder/owner. In the event of bankruptcy, the owner loses her investment, plus any retained earnings in the company, but that is all.

Limited liability companies can be registered as either private (the term — closely held — is used in some jurisdictions) or public. The terms "private" or "closely held" mean that the ownership of the shares is restricted to a few friends and invitees. The maximum number is usually fifty. The law prohibits the company from offering its shares to the public. Any potential investor, particularly one who owns a minority of shares, is not very well protected because he has no right to public disclosure or a Securities and Exchange Commission prospectus.

A public company is merely an extension of the private company, and shares the same principles, except that it must provide certain public disclosure. Its shares can be sold to the public, dealt with by brokers, and traded on the stock exchanges. This involves filing an SEC prospectus, which details the company's purpose, organization, history (if any), contributions from the promoters, and capital base. This ensures that the company is legitimate and has a reasonable chance of succeeding.

The S Corporation

One of the problems of owning a corporation is that the income is taxed at two levels: first as income to the company, and second as dividends to each shareholder. The S corporation allows small businesses, under certain circumstances, to avoid this double tax. With its limited liability, its profits are taxed only as income to the shareholders. This model works well for small, established, and profitable companies, but not for larger or growth situations. Some states do not recognize the S corporation.

The Cooperative

Examples are coop stores, wheat pools, and credit unions. The owners, known as members, usually invest a relatively small amount of cash. Equity increases are then based on purchases or patronage, rather than on financial contributions. In theory, coops are break-even enterprises, with the profits (called savings) returned to the members based on the volume of their purchases.

The Limited Partnership

While some argue that this is a form of business organization, I see it more as a method for promoters to acquire debt, not equity capital. This concept is seldom employed in the ownership of going concerns, although it comes up on the occasional levered buyout but is more commonly used for passive investment purposes. Such investments could be real estate, but they could also be highly speculative schemes. The procedure is to sell interests, known as limited partnerships, usually in one specific venture. The general partner, most often the promoter, theoretically takes all of the risk and the limited partners make all of the money. Somehow it seldom works quite like that. Most are promoted as income-tax deferral vehicles, which they are. Few come up to expectations. Paper losses often become real ones. If promoters could raise sufficient equity and debt capital through more traditional sources, probably limited partnerships would never exist in the first place.

Throughout, our concerns and valuation exercises will be directed to the incorporated, privately held company, and, as necessary, the proprietorship and partnership. Neither the cooperative nor the limited partnership will be mentioned again anywhere in this text, except in passing or to make a point.

THE FLIP-FLOP

Throughout this manual we will follow a flip-flop procedure. You will first learn the background requirements and theoretical aspects of small business valuation, then apply them to the model, a fast-food restaurant, one at a time. You will learn what and why to do something, then how to do it.

References

1 Black, H.C. (1991). *Black's law dictionary*, Abridged Sixth Edition. St. Paul, MN: West Publishing Co.
2 Ibid.

Chapter 2

WHY BUSINESSES ARE FOR SALE: THE REAL REASONS

N EVER ask why a business is for sale; you just might believe the answer." Even if you believe that old axiom, you will still ask. Every buyer does (and so does every appraiser). The reason is that few sellers tell the whole truth. They probably will not lie outright, but most disguise their true motives and will never knowingly volunteer any negative information. If you are looking for the truth, the whole truth, and nothing but the truth, do not rely solely on the seller.

A case in point: A few years ago one of my clients bought a larger country hotel that was running close to 100% occupancy. Why did the owners, Frank and Herman, say they wanted to sell? Because of their nonstop bickering. Frank told everyone — that Herman was incompetent. And Herman openly accused Frank of stealing. One month later my client knew the truth. This was a union hotel in a single-industry solid-union town. The labor cost were over 40% of sales, when it should have been 25%. The union, not the management, ran the hotel, and nothing could be done about it. The hotel prospered in the past because of several large construction projects, but now those projects were drawing to a close. Within one year, the hotel was way too big and way too empty, and it could not pay its mortgage. Frank and Herman, who had earlier given an Oscar-winning portrayal of enemies, were now the best of friends. It was all an act. My client, now in receivership, had not looked hard enough. He had foolishly accepted Frank and Herman's performance at face value.

When you buy any business, only the seller knows exactly what is being sold, and why. You, the buyer, must determine, by fair means or foul, what is being offered. You must extract full disclosure, because the seller will not offer it up. The true reason for selling will often tip you off as to whether the enterprise is on the uptick or going into the toilet. Before you can confidently figure out what you had have to shell out for the business, not what it is worth, you must know the seller's motivation. This, more than any other single factor, indicates the seller's anxiousness to deal. Anxiousness decrees price and terms or, more often, true value.

Sellers range from the owner who wants out, not now but right now, all the way through to the person who advertises her business for sale about once a year, just to fish around for bites and test how serious she really is. With the first group, all of the red flags are flying; with the second, usually, you will never make a deal. A minor exception occurs when the owner believes that if you are stupid enough to pay that price, she would be stupid not to take it. Having said all that, there comes a time for every business and owner to pass the torch to someone else. Of course, that might mean that it is time to dump your mess on the next sucker, but on the other hand, it could mean that it is time to let a healthy company grow with someone new at the helm.

Why sell? The possible reasons are numerous. There is a natural process in the life of any commercial enterprise — birth, growth, maturation, decline, and often death. The success or failure of any business relates fundamentally to the owner's motivation, age, health, managerial capability, position, desire to continue, and financial resources. Many managers cannot maintain the same drive that has propelled them for so many years. Others cannot, or will not, adapt to changing times and circumstances. Some simply close shop, others offer their companies for sale, and others liquidate piecemeal. What may be the end of the road for a seller could be an excellent opportunity for a buyer.

...few sellers tell the whole truth. They probably will not lie outright, but most do disguise their true motives and they will never knowingly volunteer any negative information.

There is a natural process in the life of any commercial enterprise — birth, growth, maturation, decline, and often death.

A POINT IN PASSING

This chapter, seller motivation, has nothing whatsoever to do with the topic of this book, which is how to determine a fair value for a small business. This chapter deals with price. Remember: price and value are seldom the same thing.

Most for-sale businesses scream, "Opportunity of a lifetime!" This implies, "Grab it, quick, before the next guy gets it!" Never believe this. It is definitely not true. Opportunities outnumber the persons seeking them. The exact ratio of offerings to completed sales has never been recorded, but one statistician has suggested that, of all going concerns for sale, only one-third ever sell. Of those sold, over eighty percent demonstrate goodwill. Real estate boards accurately track the residential sales market, while other agencies follow investment properties. Good luck finding this kind of data on small businesses.

The ratio of listings and offerings to sales indicates the multitude of opportunities and the difficulty of selling a going concern. It gives the buyer a better feel for the market, enabling him to make a more appropriate selection, negotiating for the one that meets most objectives and overcomes most constraints.

> Opportunities certainly outnumber the persons seeking them. The exact ratio of offerings to completed sales has never been recorded, but one statistician… has suggested that, of all going concerns for sale, only one-third ever sell. Of those sold, over eighty percent demonstrate goodwill.

WHY OWNERS SELL

Losing Money

Usually, whether she fesses up or not, the owner wants to sell because the business cannot earn a profit, or continually operates at a loss. The causes could be anything — declining markets, high overhead, employee theft, an unfortunate business decision, excessive competition, price cutting, or old-fashioned bad management. Look for clues. A business going broke cannot:

- pay its taxes, either income and property,
- maintain its property and equipment, or else repairs them in the cheapest possible manner,
- pay its accounts (watch for bouncing checks, kiting checks, or a COD situation with all suppliers),
- keep up with mortgage payments or rent,
- pay staff.

While the crises may occur in any order, there is a natural progression. The business does not pay its bills according to who is easy to put off, who has the weakest legal position, and who is out of town.

You will see these problems in the financial statements. If you cannot skillfully read and interpret those statements, hire a professional accountant to conduct a detailed review and critique. The accountant's bill — and good ones are not cheap — will be repaid several times over. Insist on at least three years' statements, preferably five. In a cyclical industry, get the documents for seven or preferably ten years. Do not let the seller tell you that the statements are not available, or they are not proper, or they are confidential, or some other nonsense. This is a sure sign of a cover-up. When a seller will not provide proper financial data, for whatever reason, do not walk from the deal, run. Completely discount any malarkey about money made under the table, kitty, sluff, side pocket, or whatever nickname the owner uses for unreported income. That the statements are prepared only for government's tax department, or that they understate the income and overstate the expenses, is absolute nonsense. If you believe this, never buy a business, any business, because you are far too gullible. Accept only the information supplied to the IRS or Revenue Canada and nothing else. Moreover, anyone who lies to the tax department will also lie to you.

During the 1970s, I rented aircraft from a small company that gave me a very hard time, despite the fact that I paid them about $10,000 a year in rent. They seemed to want to see their airplanes circling directly overhead, rather than taking the long trips that I preferred. One bright morning this company declared bankruptcy. In a subsequent TV interview the owner blamed all of his problems on the economy, the falling oil prices, and so on. No one could afford to fly any more, etc., etc., etc. I was greatly tempted to phone the station and ask, "What ever happened to old-fashioned bad management?"

I relate this tale for two reasons. First, to show that the given reasons for bankruptcy are rarely accurate. The same goes for the reasons for selling a business. Coming to one's senses too late in the game often propels a bankruptcy or a sale. Second, I want to suggest that this airplane company's owners should have looked inward to find the root of their problems. If they constantly mistreated a customer who paid them a $10,000 a year, which they did, how did they treat their smaller customers? If they had corrected their problems or sold the company before it was too late, they could have either saved the business or reaped some cash from the sale. At some point, not that far from the end, an astute manager could have rescued this company, even if it was losing money at the time. Of course, they would have had to blame themselves, not the economy, for their problems. As it turned out, they got to blame everyone and everything else, but they lost the chance to make some money.

When an owner sees no way out of a financial dilemma, the business will be offered for sale, usually plugged as the opportunity of a lifetime. The onus is on the buyer to establish, before making an offer, why the business is in this sorry predicament and whether the problems can be reversed. The price range and terms will depend on how long and how badly the business has been losing money and how far the owner will bend before dumping the whole mess.

Now, here is a curious quirk of human nature: In a potential bankruptcy situation, there is often a negative psychosis at work. Many owners would prefer to see the bank or mortgage company foreclose, rather than bail out and salvage something for themselves. I cannot explain this foolishness to myself, let alone explain it to you. Perhaps we all still believe in miracles, both in health and in business. If one holds on, something positive will happen. Or perhaps if one ignores a problem long enough, it will fade away. Or maybe a motivated buyer with deep pockets will suddenly appear and all the world will be a better place for it.

> …the given reasons for bankruptcy are rarely accurate. The same goes for the reasons for selling a business.

> The onus is on the buyer to establish, before making an offer, why the business is in this sorry predicament and whether the problems can be reversed.

Failing Health

A majority of owners say they are moving on because of failing health. At times, a spouse's or partner's ill health is the motivator. This may be fact or fiction. If the seller looks like a candidate for the morgue, maybe it is fact. If he is just talking about his aches and pains, maybe it is nothing.

The leading cause of failing health, physical and mental exhaustion, is often prompted by a business's poor performance. The owner might be slaving away, fifteen hours a day, 365 days a year, just to pay the bills. Time eventually takes its toll. People burn out. Still, never overlook a major possible cause of the owner's failing health: starvation, as a result of continually losing money.

Retirement

Many owners say they are selling because they want to retire. This could be true, and easy to verify, even if the seller is still young. Look at the seller's house, her car, her cabins at the lake, her holiday cruises, and so forth. The seller's lifestyle indicates how well the business has done, and how well you probably will do. Some retiring people want to gallop off into the sunset, with their health and wealth still intact. Others are burned out. You can negotiate easily with the burnout, while the energetic, unharried retiree will hold out for more cash.

Often, the retirement-bound owner will set an unrealistically high price that is the sum of years of TLC, intimate attachment, and the owner's belief that the business should have a special value to all others. Only if it sits on the market for a long time or if negotiations with several potential buyers drag on, will the owner realize that the price is out of line with the market.

In nearly all cases of owner retirement, a business is worth its orderly liquidation value and nothing more. This is the market value of the capital assets of real estate, fixtures and equipment, and inventory or current assets. The business will be stagnating or in decline. Goodwill, if it ever existed, is by now totally exhausted.

The retiree might also be keen to escape the cold, hot, wet, or dry climate. People often feel the need to be somewhere else.

> Some retiring people want to gallop off into the sunset, with their health and wealth still intact. Others are burned out.

Partnership and Shareholder Disputes

Although many partnerships and active shareholders of closely held corporations have buy and sell agreements, a surprisingly high percentage do not. And if they do, these disposition agreements commonly fail to address the possibility that one day the partners may hate each other.

Most partners initiate a joint enterprise when all are very good friends. Up to a certain point, the relationship is amicable. But problems inevitably arise. Sure signs of a failing business are bickering and blaming amongst the partners. If the business is failing and the working partners have overlapping areas of responsibility, similar talents and personalities, but differing objectives, trouble will always occur. It is only a matter of time. If their skills are different and complementary, and if the business makes a profit, you will not see many confrontations.

Some partners honestly feud, but others, such as Frank and Herman, put on an act. You must put your antennae up to detect whether the conflict is real. Watch for unprovoked fights, switching roles, and inconsistencies as each partner relates what is wrong with the other. Meet with each partner individually to discuss his other interests, goals, and ambitions. Watch the operation and see who does what. If a fifty-percent owner of a supermarket is bagging groceries, you know the problem is real. If the partners have different areas of managerial responsibility and each in his own area appears competent, it may be just show.

Sometimes the spouses or families, not the actual partners, duke it out. Sometimes the families goad the partners. "You are working harder than the other guy. He has getting a better deal. You are just being jerked around. You are being had," and so on. In most of these cases, as spouses seldom back down or kiss and make up, the problems cannot be solved and corporate divorce proceedings commence. In shareholder disputes, the majority shareholder usually buys out the minority holder(s). If one partner cannot or will not buy out the other (or others), then the entire enterprise must be sold.

Although minority shareholders, whether active or silent, have little legal protection, they can bring about extreme pressure.

Excessive Competition

Everyone loves competition, just so long as it affects the other fellow. A little is good, too much is ruinous. Unrestrained competition, either now or looming on the horizon, can spell disaster. Businesses slash their prices or extend generous credit, just to survive.

Before buying, you must ensure that you can live with the opposition, meet it head on, and at least survive, if not win. Never assume that the competition will shrivel up just because you have bought or started a business. The competition will remain, and usually be a lot tougher than you first expected. Its chances are better than yours, as it is better established and may have more market clout.

Poor Management

Although few ever admit to personal ineptitude, not even to themselves, poor management is pretty common. Often, through no fault of their own, a business will simply outgrow the owner's management know-how. An expert small-business manager might not be able to handle the sales volume and staff as the business grows. This is called the Peter Principle: a worker is promoted (in this case, by himself) until he reaches a level at which he is no longer competent. If the competitive market heats up, the owner might not know how to react; he will not know how to increase sales, control expenses, and turn a profit.

Many larger concerns are run by people who never wanted to run a major enterprise. They lack both interest and aptitude. A chain of events, often beyond their control, has propelled them into this position. It just happened. Perhaps they inherited or repossessed a business. Maybe they thought they could manage a big company, but now they realize that, they cannot.

Take my own situation. I never wanted to be in the hotel business. Managing an appraisal and consulting practice was bad enough. Along came a former business partner, who thought he was God's gift to the hospitality industry, but even with another partner could not cough up enough money to buy their first property. He offered me half of his half. A week later I owned twenty-five percent of a country hotel. This was just a sideline for me. I was just going to be a very silent, silent partner. Seven years later I owned a controlling interest in four hotels and was six million dollars in debt. I still did not want to be in the hotel business. What happened to my sideline?

To find out if an owner wants to sell because of her own incompetence or loss of interest, you must do some detective work. Listen to the staff and the customers, and note their genuine complaints. But keep in mind that old army slogan: "If the troops are not bitchin', they are not happy." Watch for the owner's obvious mismanagement, lost opportunities, excessive drinking, predictable morning headache, temper tantrums, reluctance to come to work, very long vacations, and lack of interest. The price here may be inflexible, but you might be able to negotiate great terms.

Too Much Ability or Ambition

A business might outgrow its owner, but in some rare cases the owner outgrows the business. The business is still growing, but the owner wants to sell it for maximum dollar so he can reinvest in something larger.

Redundancy

There comes a time when every business reaches its maximum economic value. All tangible assets produce a return comparable to other forms of investment, and goodwill is generated, but the company cannot grow any more. Like an old car, the business has a few miles left, but is worn and tired and needs to be traded off. And like an old car that can be spiffed up with some new parts and elbow grease, a tired business might be revitalized with fresh ideas, improved marketing, up-to-date equipment, modern methods, and improved management. Some businesses, though, cannot be revived. The source of raw materials — logs, minerals, or the marketplace — could be exhausted. Beware of failing single-industry communities, declining neighborhoods, out-of-date stock, antiquated or worn-out machinery, changing tastes, and changing fads.

High profits and goodwill cannot continue indefinitely. As a company flags, competition will surge, and production or sales volume and profit curves will flatten. An astute owner tries to sell while her company is still on the uptick. A wise investor buys at the beginning of the upswing, or will negotiate price and terms if the business is already nearing its peak. But it is tricky to determine whether the business is steaming ahead, stable, or starting to slow down. I cannot overstate the importance of this information. That is why Chapter Three is so vital.

Many rusty businesses have hidden strengths, but the gold in these old derelicts is buried deep, very deep. If you are a real gambler and want to buy, pay only for what is actually there, not what can be made out of it. Never buy potential, because you also have to pay to develop that potential, and you will be paying twice for the same thing.

End of a Line

Think about the longer-term potential, especially if you are considering a service company, small manufacturer, distribution company, contractor, or specialty marketer. The prospect company might have an excellent track record and is capably managed and very profitable. But maybe the contracts are nearing completion or must be renegotiated. The production of a hot item is approaching the end of a cycle. The spinoff benefits from the construction projects are drawing to a close (remember Frank and Herman). The writing on the wall will suggest that substantial changes must be made to survive, that lower prices will probably prevail, and that future profitability will be much less. At this point, an owner will try to dump the whole company on some naive soul. The unwary might see only the rosy short-term: the profits, the good track record, the uptick. But you must look under the skin and into the future.

Inability to Expand

Sometimes a business has peaked. Income and profitability have remained stable for years. But longer-term stability does not exist. As the old axiom says, either you move ahead or you go backward. You must at least grow at the rate of inflation just to stay even. If an owner forecasts only level or declining fortunes, particularly coupled with any other reasons to sell, it could well be bailout time. Maybe the product line or location is obsolete, maybe the management or the economy is falling down on the job, or maybe the owner's spouse is balking.

What if the business cannot cope with a declining or changing community? Most of North America's rural communities are failing, some faster than others. When their economic base crumbles, they crumble, too. Urban neighborhoods also change. It is easy to have the wrong business in the wrong place at the wrong time.

More Money Needed

A business commonly (but quietly) needs more investment capital. The owner does not want to pour in more money, and so he tries to sell before this problem turns into a crisis. For a buyer, it might be worthwhile to invest some extra money, provided the business can earn back a reasonable return. There is no point in investing only to maintain the status quo. Sometimes the business needs additional capital to update equipment or premises, or to meet the competition. When this situation is discovered, the prospective buyer should ask herself: Will the extra money sufficiently boost business volume and/or improve profitability sufficiently to justify the expense? Often it will not. For example: one of our clients owned a motor hotel that needed about one million dollars' worth of renovations and upgrading. That owner did not think the expenditure would increase revenues or improve the motel's profitability. At best, the maintenance costs would drop, and this was not enough gain to warrant the expenditure. The hotel was sold on the strength of its respectable track record. The buyer spent the million dollars, which did not result in more sales or profit. Many a restaurateur has renovated, only to do less business than before.

Capital Gain

Some owners want to sell so they make a big profit. That is why most of us go into business in the first place.

Just Plain Tired and/or Fed Up

Owning your own business is not always all that it is cracked up to be. Not all independent business persons are truly independent — or rich. In fact, few are. They do not work shorter hours or make more money than anyone else, but rather, longer ones at less pay per hour. Like employees who are subject to the whims of their boss, business owners have to please not just one boss, but all of their employees and customers. Few enjoy the paid vacations granted to government and large-corporation employees.

After some years, many owners conclude that it is just not worth it. So they offer for sale what was once thought to be a golden opportunity. They will, of course, tout it as just that — but for someone else. Before buying or starting a business, you have to accept that very few owners earn sufficient profit to pay all of the bills, enjoy a good standard of living, and receive a financial return comparable to alternative forms of investment. In a small business, therefore, goodwill value seldom exists. Some owners' expectations are low because they know they are simply buying themselves a job. Others, after enduring the long hours, risk, headaches, and other baggage of ownership and success, are ready to sell out and work for someone else. A buyer could find a real bargain from this kind of seller, but look for hidden motives as well.

Even in our fabulously enlightened age, many folks still think small-motel ownership is the ideal way to semi-retire: easy work, good hours, living quarters in the building, and the opportunity to meet fascinating guests. A reality check: the hours are cruelly long, as most small motels do not make enough money to pay for more than a bare-bones staff. Thus the owner is the desk clerk, the chambermaid, the bellboy, and the repair man. The motel is open 24 hours a day, 365 days a year, so holidays…do not exist. The pay, considering the investment and risk, is very poor. If one's dream is to own a small motel, it is a bad one. (Neighborhood pubs are an equally popular dream/nightmare, but even more exhausting, both physically and financially.)

Court-Ordered Distress Sale

This happens if the owner simply cannot make payments on a debt owing to a financial institution or to the previous owner. The present owner, or the court, offers the business for sale. Sometimes, in what is called Chapter Eleven in the US or Soft

Receivership in Canada, the financial institution or court controls the enterprise but gives the legal owners time to sell or rearrange their affairs. These businesses are often offered at what appears to be a bargain. That does not mean this is the opportunity of a lifetime. Before making any offer, a prospective buyer should always ponder: If the present owner could not make a go of it, what makes me so smart?

Not that many years ago, a client — despite our advice to the contrary — bought a larger motor hotel, the replacement cost of which was over six million dollars. The previous three owners had gone broke. After each bankruptcy the mortgage company resold the hotel for a still lesser amount. The first distress sale was for $3,900,000, the second $2,800,000, and the third, $1,600,000. We told our client not to buy this property at any price. But he did anyway, for $500,000. The problem was, this hotel was so overbuilt in relation to its community that it only broke even. It could not service one dollar's worth of long-term debt. The past management might not have been perfect, but the real culprits were a host of external problems beyond each owner's control. The hotel was big enough to produce over five million dollars of yearly revenue, but that market would never generate over two million and would never enlarge. It was a single-industry town and the industry was in trouble. Still, the owner had to pay taxes, insurance, utilities, repairs and maintenance, staff wages, and all of the other costs that come with a hotel. Being four or five times too large for its market, this hotel could never hope to make money.

Before buying a distressed company, you should carefully consider why the previous owner is in receivership. Did he go into bankruptcy voluntarily or was he forced into it, and for what reason? Establish exactly why the business was lost. Agents, brokers, and especially financial institutions always cite bad management, because they want to resell the thing. And most times this reason is correct — sort of. But bad management might be too simple an explanation. In some business situations, even God could not make a dollar.

You will find, sometimes, that three owners in succession lose their shirts, but the fourth one will turn the business into a winner. It can happen. Maybe the property was overbuilt, or built at too high a cost for the market, or else the initial owners had too much debt. The next guy could buy the ailing property at far less than its replacement cost, with a much smaller mortgage, and (a hotel is a good example) do very well. Still, proceed with caution. What looks like a genuine bargain may not be so genuine.

The Spinoff

A larger company, rather than a smaller ma-and-pa enterprise, often amalgamates with or buys another, and wishes to sell, or spin off, an operating division or subsidiary. Here, haggling over price and terms is very minor. Negotiations should occur, though, regarding the benefits to both seller and buyer, such as longer-term contractual supply or material purchase agreements.

The corporation will say it wants the spinoff because it wants to use its capital elsewhere or because the division is inappropriately staffed, ineffectively managed, a poor corporate fit, or not meeting expectations. Always, the true reason is this division's profits are lagging behind the performance of other divisions.

Nervous Anticipation

The future might not bode well for a business because of, say, a declining community, a changing neighborhood, relocation of traffic arteries, rezoning, the advent of a nearby superstore, or a related and much-needed business about to shut down. If an owner sees a negative force on the horizon, she will try to sell out in advance — for cash, of course. In Chapter Three, you will learn more about predicting the future for a target industry in general, and a prospect business in particular.

Family Pressures

Managing a going concern is not necessarily a vocation, or an administrative occupation, or even what most would consider a normal business. It is a way of life. Operating a restaurant is a perfect example. A successful restaurateur must devote twenty-four hours a day, seven days a week to the venture. After the cafe closes, and some never close, the owner preps meals, makes repairs (and there is always something broken), does the books, pays the bills, interviews staff, and plans for the next day's operation. Forget about a home life, watching the tube on a quite evening, dining out at a different restaurant, or visiting with friends. Of all enterprises, restaurant operators have the highest historic rate of alcoholism and divorce.

If the restaurateur does not finally say it is time to throw in the towel, his family does. The cafe is offered for sale. But the restaurant biz is a disease, it gets into one's blood. Almost all former owners soon return to it.

The owner might also want to sell because of peer pressure, perhaps rooted in social or religious convictions. Southern Baptists do not like to sell alcohol.

No Successor

This is quite common, particularly in medium-sized enterprises. In many sad cases, the entrepreneur has spent a lifetime building a prosperous concern or professional practice, hoping that one of her children will continue, only to find that no one's interested. Equally often, the children lack the ability to manage the operation. Children do not always inherit their parents' foresight, skills, or ambition. Very few princes inherit the kingdom.

Farmers and farm families are often embroiled in succession dilemmas. Many a farm couple have sent their children, at great personal expense and sacrifice, through university to become doctors, lawyers, or teachers, and then expect them to come home to feed the hogs. It does not work this way. The children will always do their own thing, even if it frustrates the parents. In these situations, as the owner is in no hurry to sell, the buyer needs superior negotiating skills.

Sometimes the owner, having no one to grasp the torch, hangs on to the business and dies. In this case, you might be able to find good value for a good price.

Labor Problems

I am not saying this to union-bash, but unionized businesses are often put on the block when management becomes fed up with fighting with the union. It is difficult or impossible for a smaller concern to make a profit while trying to meet many of the nonsensical demands and whims of shop stewards and union labor. Unionization, which has helped the working person immeasurably, has developed into an adversarial system. It is about what exorbitant demands the unions can extract from management, versus how little the owner will give away. The continued survival and prosperity of the employer is seldom a union concern.

Related to bad management, employee theft has placed many companies in jeopardy. As some can no longer pay their debts, insolvency and sale is the only way out. Although not related to our topic, industrial espionage is a big business.

Etcetera

Of course, there are other reasons for selling, there will always be others (genuine or not). No list is ever complete. The reasons range from aging neighborhoods, to labor or family problems, to not having enough money to expand and beat the competition. Most important, before you start to negotiate with an owner, you must figure out why the owner is selling. Only then can you place a proper value on the business, predict the owner's flexibility on price and terms, and ensure that you do not pay too much. You can bargain from a position of strength.

Psych out the seller at every opportunity. Ask the same question several times, each time differently phrased. Choose your words and your timing carefully. Talk to the owner's spouse, or to senior employees who know that the business is for sale, which they always do. Be the best Hollywood lawyer, lead the witness, be ambiguous, evasive, and at times insistent. Always let the other person answer your question. Never volunteer information yourself, or try to confirm someone else's opinion. Watch for reaction, hesitation, fumbling for words, and inconsistent responses. Listen for what is not said. Look for clues pointing to the real motive. Yet bear in mind that, as you are analysing the seller, he is doing exactly the same thing, trying to determine what price and what concessions he can get from you.

Failure rates are very high in business. Many buy a dream and lose everything. Yet crises can often be avoided if the buyer takes more time and does better detective work. Before signing the sale agreement, always find out why the business is for sale—not what the seller says, but the real reason. Then negotiate.

Chapter 3

LOOK BEFORE YOU LEAP

THE FIRST STEP

BEFORE placing a monetary value on any business, and definitely before making a purchase offer, the buyer must establish that:

- the business is profitable or can be made profitable,
- it can continue to earn a profit,
- there is room for positive growth.

To this end, the first step is a logical investigation, examination, and analysis of its economic environment. That is, you must take a hard look at why the business exists, what role it plays in the scheme of things, and why. Only then can you establish its longer-term potential. Take into account changing technology, marketing methods, and increasing competition. The seller wants to sell. The agent wants a commission. Even the lender wants the deal. Thus, the gathering and interpretation of background data, good or bad, is left to the purchaser. Because businesses are often bought more on the basis of subjective feelings, than cold, hard facts, this process is most often short-circuited. Yet it is vital to the selection and valuation process. If you want to buy a business that fulfills your objectives, you must do your homework. There are no shortcuts.

Some bits of information, by themselves, might seem unrelated or inconsequential, but when collectively considered will always provide a more accurate assessment of the business. If nothing else, often this intelligence will reveal the seller's actual motives. If diligently acquired and correctly interpreted, they can indicate future direction and pinpoint less evident shortcomings.

In the collection of data, you will probably do well to follow the real-estate appraiser's traditional procedure. That is, start with the broader spectrum and work towards more specific influences or situations. Segment by segment, gather and analyse your findings in ever-diminishing circles. Move from the external to the internal. First, consider how international and national political policies and economic trends will affect the industry and the prospect business, then reduce your focus to the state level, the municipal, the local, the immediate neighborhood, and finally the target business itself. A detailed competitive analysis is probably the most important element in the entire process. More judgmental errors are made by underestimating the competitor's desire and ability to survive, than by any other factor.

The value of any business is the present worth of future expectations and benefits, be they monetary, personal, or other. You should buy in only if you predict the business will meet your anticipated objectives and overcome your constraints. History serves merely as a guide. You need to properly understand the external factors that affected the history and will affect the business's future income and profitability—and your personal ambitions. First of all, everyone wants to make money, so pay most attention to factors that directly influence, now or will in the future, the health of the target company.

> The value of any business is the present worth of future expectations and benefits, be they monetary, personal, or other. History serves merely as a guide.

The necessary requirements have been subdivided into three categories:

1.

   National, regional, and location-specific economic data and trends,

2. The subject industry and business,

3. Competitor analysis.

I have tried to cover as many small industries and businesses as feasible. Still, not all possibilities are explored. Thus, much of the following cannot be applied to certain situations, nor does everything said apply in every circumstance. The size of the target company relates directly to its vulnerability to change and thus the required intelligence. For example, the data required to fully analyse the purchase of a neighborhood dry-goods store would differ from the relevant data for a movie theater or a manufacturing or service company. And, as always, there is a distinct overlap and some classifications would apply to all three categories.

NATIONAL, REGIONAL, AND SITE-SPECIFIC ECONOMIC DATA AND TRENDS

The Money Trends

Consider the money supply and the general trend of interest rates. Is this the time to buy and take on debt? Are interest rates going up or down? What will they do in the near future? Is the economy experiencing a recession, a boom, or a period of stability? A high percentage of businesses and real estate are sold at a time of increasing interest rates. What are buyers thinking? That they should jump in now, before the cost of money soars any higher? Conversely, when rates fall, buyers hold back, waiting for rates to bottom out thus creating a lag in the market. At this same time, for the most part, as the cost of debt financing increases, cash on cash returns to equity decrease, and vice versa. (The term "cash on cash" means spendable income, or net operating profit. It does not include equity gain through debt reduction or inflation, nor does it consider depreciation.)

The stock market does not usually affect smaller businesses, or if so, only in the most extraneous way. Still, you might wisely consider any longer-term market trends or activities that could directly affect the prospect company.

The Political Climate

Think about the political climate, the attitude of government at all levels that affects industry and business in general, and the target business in particular. Although it would be unfair to consider all politicians as antibusiness, or anti-capital, the concept of profit-making offends many (unless, of course, they are the ones making it). Take into account the effect of political support, or the withdrawal thereof, and if this is a requirement for continuing a healthy enterprise. The political climate could be of little concern if you are buying a corner convenience store. Yet, it could be most important where community stability relies on manufacturing or distribution, resources, or a single industry. We have all seen how political favoritism, or its withdrawal, can affect the birth, growth, and death of specific regions and communities.

An example: During the early 1980s, the British Columbia government, along with

The term "cash on cash" means spendable income, or net operating profit. It does not include equity gain through debt reduction or inflation, nor does it consider depreciation.

indirectly, to develop the Quinette and Bull Moose Mines at Tumbler Ridge. This political intervention, intended to make British Columbia a major player in the world coal market, helped Tumbler Ridge, but devastated the towns of Sparwood and Elkford, which are several hundred miles away, but also in British Columbia. Tumbler Ridge siphoned off any lucrative coal contracts held by the five coal companies in the Sparwood-Elkford area. Masses of people lost their jobs and left the area, bankrupting many of the business people there, including me. Both are single-industry, coal-mining towns, with most of the output sold to Japan.

The National Scene

Does, or could, anything on the international or national scene directly affect the general area or the particular community or neighborhood?

Although this could be construed as repetition of the political influences just detailed, nonpolitical groups and forces can also provide or withhold impetus in a community.

Lobby and Ethnic Groups

Pay attention to pressure and lobby groups. If you are venturing into the hospitality industry, groups might be concerned about drinking and driving, excess traffic, risqué entertainment, lounges open on Sundays, and the noise created by late-night crowds.

Local ethnic or religious groups could, under certain circumstances, present problems. All nationalities, without exception, prefer to live among and patronize their own, and outsiders are often treated with suspicion. Although many preach equality, they do not practise it. I am not suggesting that this is wrong, or that every city has its own Harlem or Alpine County, but this influence exists.

Consider overall community attitudes towards the type of industry or business you want to buy. Although most small communities welcome new industries, many really do not warm up to outsiders, especially those who would compete with their own, or who would plug up the golf courses, parking lots, malls, or church pews.

Changes in the Population Base

Take a close look at the population base of the local neighborhood and the general area. Is it changing according to age, earning capacity, and lifestyle?

Drug stores and corner convenience stores do better in older neighborhoods, where senior citizens need them more and do not wish to walk too far or spend too much money at one time. If the prospect enterprise depends on local patronage, consider occupations, income levels, disposable incomes, and spending habits. Even if the business does not depend on local patronage, give these topics a look anyway, but on a much larger scale and covering a greater geographical area.

Examine any factor that will change the population levels and character of the area, such as factories closing, the development of a new office building, the awarding of new contracts, or contracts winding down. Look at the area's potential for growth or decline. If a basic industry changes or diversifies, that could be good or bad. A major industry might be expanding or cutting staff. The community might be prime for a mass immigration or a mass exodus.

Changing Neighborhoods

Where does the community sit on the lifestyle curve? Very few districts, least of all residential neighborhoods, remain static. Is your prospective community on the wax or the wane?

All neighborhoods, whatever their status, start out as unimproved land, usually farmland, and are then subdivided into blocks and lots with roads and utilities. In a residential district, actual life commences when homes, shopping centres, schools, churches, and community centres are constructed. Locales reach equilibrium when all lots are built on, lawns planted, driveways paved, and the boulevard trees are growing. The next stage is disintegration, a normal process as the houses and community amenities age and deteriorate. As the citizens age, school enrolment falls, the population drops, and patronage at the local stores declines. Yesterday's fashionable districts become seedy. Meanwhile, new neighborhoods spring up with new and different traffic generators and interceptors, and the cycle renews itself.

This same lifecycle applies equally to industrial, commercial, retail, central-core, apartment, and all other areas of any town or city. The question then becomes: what is the present stage of your prospective business's district? In particular, can the target enterprise survive any changes? Can it grow and prosper amid the changing backdrop, or will it ultimately be downsized or permanently closed? As a district converts, such as from single-family residential to apartments or multifamily units, the district's businesses are affected.

Is the business on the upswing or on its way down? If the district is converting from younger families to senior citizens, it might be too early for a business that caters to the older set, yet too late for a children's clothing store. Pioneers seldom get rich.

What is the impact on the business's going concern value? Think about property values, which increase during the community's development stage, level off at the point of equilibrium, then fall as the area declines, but increase again as a change of use comes into play. A business value follows this same general pattern. Like a neighborhood, it too becomes old and redundant. As business value and patronage are directly related, the same cycle occurs. No retail store holds the same market value when a district is in decline as when populated by young families.

Sources of Patronage

Consider the type of community or district, its economic base, sources of clientele for the business, potential for this source changing, positive and negative influences, and trends. Once again, how will any drastic change or evolution affect the target enterprise?

The retail store probably provides the best example. I am oversimplifying here, but retail stores can be placed into four main groups. The required background analysis, and its importance, would differ for each. I will start with the first three:

The Destination Store: This is the freestanding megastore, such as Wal-Mart. Customers go there strictly to patronize this store, and for no other reason, because nothing else is there.

The Generator: This can also be a destination store, but it is normally surrounded by a cluster of smaller parasitic outlets of various types. Shoppers go there specifically to patronize this particular establishment, and while there, also visit the adjacent outlets. For instance, a major department store, will anchor either a regional shopping centre or a cluster centre. This store, if for no other reason than its size, generates traffic for itself and spinoff sales for the smaller stores and services within close proximity.

Parasitic or Secondary: This smaller or specialty store receives that spinoff traffic created by the generator. Retail and specialty outlets line the malls of major shopping centres or surround the freestanding supers. Although some create their own customer base, most rely heavily on the anchor tenant and each other. Their prosperity often relies more on the capability of the generator than on their own merchandising abilities.

How would various happenings affect these different types of stores? How would changes in the generator affect the parasitic or secondary retail store be affected by the changing styles, prices, and policies of the generator? What is each store's position in the retail lifecycle? How do the new superstores affect the traditional traffic generators? In many situations, these generators, particularly the major department stores, are gradually losing their influence.

Traffic Flows

The fourth class of retail store is the Interceptor, which stops, or intercepts traffic that is on its way from A to B. The typical corner convenience store or a service station would be good examples. Several smaller stores could be considered interceptors if they are clustered in a neighborhood shopping centre where none has more drawing power than any other. Yet the entire centre could equally be categorized as a generator, as each occupant creates business for the others. To this type of store, location is ultra-important, as is traffic flow, visibility, signage, ease of entering and exiting, and adequate on-site parking.

What would be the consequence for any of these types of retail stores if the traffic pattern were to change? What about a new highway, a median, or one-way street? The store might suddenly find itself buried on a sleepy side street, or thrust out onto a busy thoroughfare, or placed behind a service road for which the entrance is half a block away.

Suppose a new highway bypasses a small community. This could be the death knell for service stations, cafes, and convenience stores that rely on travellers. Others that rely on local patrons might happily carry on as before.

New Developments

Will local employment skyrocket or drop with the opening or closing of mines, military bases, or factories? What about regional or neighborhood sites that generate traffic or patronage? What is the spinoff? Is a new business short-term or long-term? What are the longer-term economic and locational trends and qualities?

Consider the spinoffs from other local developments, including competitors adding to or subtracting from their premises. A growing competitor might not be bad. The theory of cumulative attraction holds that when several stores, each selling approximately the same line, operate within a confined area, business improves for all. Together they attract patrons to the area and thus to each other. Several competitive automobile or farm-equipment dealerships often locate side by side on purpose.

Technological Changes

How important is technological change? Will new inventions, developments, products, or processes render your prospective business obsolete overnight? Or will they make it better, easier to manage, able to cater to a wider market, and more profitable? You need to broaden your concern here to include related and competitive industries, particularly suppliers and customers.

Suppose you want to purchase a dry cleaning business. You would want to know how new equipment affects the dry-cleaning process and the operating costs. Can dry cleaning work on the new synthetic fabrics? Can people just wash these popular fabrics at home?

Will customers' product preferences change? Should one buy into some of the new products resulting from technological developments? How much will this cost?

What about environmental problems or concerns in the industry or the community? A case in point. We recently appraised a photo lab, one of those one-

Will new inventions, developments, products, or processes render your prospective business obsolete overnight?

hour developing and processing businesses. The equipment, which initially cost over $75,000, was now about eight years old. It was good, efficient, and adequate for this lab. But here is why the lab was for sale: due to environmental rules, the processing chemical now used would not be available after two years. In other words, this equipment and this process would have no value whatever. The present owner or a buyer would have to purchase new equipment, to the tune of about $100,000.

Legal Concerns

The business's present or future growth could be affected by licensing laws, early closing bylaws, restrictive trade practices, non-competition laws, zoning bylaws, etc.

Do Not Restrict Your Investigation

Never restrict the investigation solely to the prospect business, or its locale. Consider the total community or market area, and what is happening at all levels, from international to local. Consider the outcome for the general industry and the specific business.

You could considerably expand this investigation, depending on the type of enterprise, its stability, and its potential. Do not just pore over the micro-economics of the target enterprise, but also focus on the demographic and political aspects that affect this type of operation, the market area, and its longer-term prospects. How has the business reacted to current changes? How will it react in the future?

THE SUBJECT INDUSTRY AND BUSINESS

History of the Business

You need to know who started the business, and when. Is this the original location? Does it have branches? Has anything occurred that affects its present market value or its future potential? Have there been any prior transfers or sales? Any sellouts by a majority or a minority shareholder? Any foreclosures or distress sales in the past? What will probably happen to it if the business is not sold?

Supply and Suppliers

Does the subject company rely on a single supplier, or does it have many? Can it freely buy from any supplier, or is it restricted by purchase contracts or anything else?

A major supplier might not be able to, or want to, continue to supply. Maybe its prices will shoot through the roof, or its quality control or delivery will take a severe nose-dive. What if its workers go on strike? Where else can you readily find the same raw materials or goods at a competitive price? If the supplier swallows up, or is swallowed by, its own supplier or customer, will that hurt the business? Does your supplier rely on a single source of supply? If it went bankrupt, would it destroy your business too?

To maintain its supply or market position, does the target enterprise need to buy out a supplier or customer? (This is vertical integration.) Does it need to buy out its competitors? (This is horizontal integration.) Can it continue indefinitely the way it is?

If the raw materials are far away, transportation can be very expensive. Extractors of raw materials, without exception, harvest those closest to home and of the best

The margin note reads:

> Never restrict the investigation solely to the prospect business, or its locale. Consider the total community or market area, and what is happening at all levels, from international to local. Consider the outcome for the general industry and the specific business.

quality first. At times a company is offered for sale because the supply of low-cost inventory is nearly exhausted. Be extra-cautious here. The prospect's historical profit may not reliably indicate its future prospects.

Assuming all else to be equal, compare a sawmill with a fifty-mile log haul to one that has all of its wood within twenty miles. Or suppose that the hauling distance is the same, but Mill A's logs have twenty-four-inch butts and Mill B can only find logs with ten-inch butts? No, the values are not the same. They will not have the same profits, if not in the past, then definitely in the future.

Customers and Clients

Now repeat these considerations on the client or customer side. How far away is the customer base? Is it buoyant and prosperous?

The business might have to slash prices to attract patrons. It could achieve high sales volume but low or inconsistent profits. Does it make money, or just friends? At this profit level, can it continue and prosper?

Does it need to carry extensive credit lines to attract or maintain sales volume? What are the credit granting policies, the average collection period, and the inventory turnover time?

Do any customers receive preferential treatment, such as lower prices or delayed payment? Relatives and close friends are notorious for this. Who and where are the customers or clients? Are they concentrated? If you lose a few small accounts, how would that affect the total business? Do a few key customers monopolize the sales volume?

Assume that the target company makes blue jeans, most of which are sold to the ABC Retail Chain. One day ABC advises that it is changing to a cheaper supplier. If you match the other supplier's price, you will not make a profit. What will you do?

You simply cannot overlook or underestimate the importance of the customer's changing wants and needs. If you sell a dress that is all the rage, and no one else carries it, then you can charge as much as you dare. When it is out of style, top price is twenty five cents on the dollar at the Salvation Army Thrift Store.

Franchises

Many franchises and other agreements are personal to the owner and cannot be assigned or transferred in any way, including a transfer of shares in the vendor company. Often this refusal to assign is little more than a ruse by a franchisor to extract another up-front franchise fee. In other cases, assuming that the franchisor did not exercise its option and on buying the franchisee's store (first right of refusal is standard in almost every agreement), the franchisor can appoint a new franchisee, or can itself now compete with this newly independent outlet.

In some cases, for business continuance, the transfer of the franchise is a must, regardless of the value of the franchise itself, which could be nothing. In others, especially in the distribution or installation of hard goods, there really is no franchise in effect, merely a supply and purchase agreement, often unwritten. This type usually asks for a minimum performance which, if met, the supplier will not appoint another dealer or outlet in this territory. No money is normally paid for this type of arrangement. Yet some less than honest vendor, in selling you on the fine qualities of the business, might suggest that this is a very valuable intangible asset and a high value should be assigned to this non-exclusive, unsecured distribution right.

Others must be reapplied for every time the business sells—with some, even when managers change. Although no one would buy a restaurant without acquiring a liquor licence, that licence is not a part of the package.

Working Capital and Inventories

Must the business carry excessive inventories at peak seasons, or when supplies cannot be shipped? Some years ago, we considered buying a hotel in Canada's Northwest Territories. This hotel received all of its food and alcohol shipments twice a year: first boat up the river after the spring breakup and the last one before freeze-up. Normally, a hotel of this size in a more populated area would have carried an inventory worth $25,000 to $35,000. For this particular hotel, each semiannual purchase totaled over $200,000. We did not buy this hotel because, among other reasons, we could not afford to carry this inventory.

Some specialty manufacturing or distributing companies need a high working-capital-to-sales ratio, and it is common in professional practices. Although few would admit to it, lawyers are very poor collectors, perhaps not of their clients' accounts, but of their own.

Poor Contracts

You might be locked into contracts or agreements that could trip you up:

- noncompetitive purchase or transportation agreements,
- unprofitable agreements or contracts to supply to others,
- useless patents, franchises, timber berths, running rights,
- union agreements or labor contracts.

The Labor Situation

Consider the kind of staff you will need, their availability and cost:

- Does the business require a highly skilled staff?
- Can the staff do most jobs with a minimum amount of training?
- Does the staff include deadwood? What are you going to do with the old guys who have been there for thirty years, but have not produced anything for the past ten and probably will not in the future?
- Is there unusually high staff turnover? Why?
- Does this company pay competitive wages?
- Is staff morale good, fair, or poor? Can it be improved?
- You might need a union, or maybe the existing union is detrimental. If the competitors are nonunion, you probably cannot afford to pay union wages. But if you are in a solid union town, you do not want to be the only company running a nonunion shop.
- If you lost a key employee and her irreplaceable technical skill, how will you be able to operate and turn a profit? What if she dies or was hired away by a competitor?

Obsolescence

Are the product lines, manufacturing equipment, or marketing or distribution methods becoming obsolete? Does anyone want or need the business's product? Is its equipment out-of-date, costly to operate, possible to maintain?

Look at the physical condition of the plant or premises. How does the subject compare with competition and the industry as a whole? Developments in the industry could create a need for newer or more modern machinery, or a cash injection just to remain competitive. Technological, marketing, or distribution changes could affect the product.

Look at the physical condition of the plant or premises. How does the subject compare with competition and the industry as a whole?

30

Is the company developing new products or processes, or acquiring new lines to sell? Will any be discontinued, and if so, will this create an excess of dead inventory?

Profitability Levels

Have the gross income margins remained consistent during the past few years, or have they fluctuated? What is the inventory turnover time? How do these, and all ratios, compare with industry averages?

As the external economy and population statistics change, how does the business react? Customer patterns and preferences shift according to the population's age, occupation, and income level, as well as adverse influences.

The analysis should include the lifecycle of trends and themes, particularly if you are tempted to buy a theme, fashion, or impulse-oriented business. Many of these have more than an ample supply of dead stock.

If a local factory or larger employer were plunged into a prolonged strike, major layoff, or boycott, could you lose business and still survive?

Is the business holding its own? Is it expanding, contracting, or what? Any business must increase according to the rate of inflation just to remain even. If you keep the same or similar management, will the business increase? Can you see any particular difficulties, now or in the future? Is there room for expansion? Are the projected growth rates realistic in view of the economy and the competition? Or must it be reduced in size to preserve the assets?

Can you identify new markets, or else existing markets that are not fully developed? How easy would it be for someone to set up competition across the street?

Are government grants part of the package? If certain production goals or other conditions are not met, do you have to repay the grants?

You cannot automatically assume that you will keep the same customers forever. As their income levels, interests, desires, and wants change, will they take their spending money elsewhere?

You need to gauge whether the target business can continue, and indeed prosper, in the face of change.

> Customer patterns and preferences shift according to the population's age, occupation, and income level, as well as adverse influences.

Neighborhood Considerations

As the community and neighborhood change, can the subject remain, or become profitable? Or is the owner continuing to flog the dead horse until he finds a sucker to take it off his hands?

What is the business's geographic and economic position in the industry? Should it be relocated within the neighborhood or within the city, or should it move elsewhere? Most successful enterprises are close to either their supply sources or their markets; very successful ones are near both. The choice depends on the comparative transportation costs for the raw and finished products.

Some enterprises are located in a certain place because of their origins, the directors' desire to live there, or some reason unrelated to economics. Some would thrive closer to their suppliers, or to their customers, in a more centralized distribution point, or in a friendlier political climate. Sometimes a new business springs up at a specific site because the land is cheap. But when the location hurts the company's performance, the choice of site may turn out not to have been economical after all.

Watch for any unusual risks that may be created by the industry's location. Is it foreign to this area?

How do the citizens regard the business or the industry? Would the local residents be happier if your company moved elsewhere? An abattoir, a chemical plant, or a salvage company here? Never!

Litigation

Are there any lawsuits in progress or pending? This may not effect the market value, but could hurt the business's reputation. If you are just buying the assets, you can refuse to accept responsibility for the liability, but still make the deal. On a share transfer, you could be liable for the outcome of the litigation and the cost of settling it. The vendor might guarantee to pay for any unsettled claims, but if she cannot afford to honor the pledge, or has joined the Foreign Legion, then you cannot collect. You will be stuck with the bill.

A couple of years ago, one of our clients contracted to buy a patent for a revolutionary transmission for stationary industrial engines. He agreed to an initial price of $250,000, plus a royalty after so many transmissions were sold. The buyer agreed to produce a minimum number each year; that way he could not go to sleep on the inventor, nor wait until the patent expired, then manufacture without paying a royalty. He paid $100,000 to the inventor up front. Several transmissions were manufactured and sold. Unfortunately, they did not work as promised. My client apologized to his customers, refunded their money, then gathered up all of the duds. He then told the inventor where to go. Legally, however, he may still be indebted for $150,000. This potential liability does not appear anywhere on the books of the company. There is really no way a new buyer, or her attorney, could ever find out about this unless she asked, and was given an honest answer. Conversely, does my client have a case against the inventor for a refund of the $100,000? If so, should he sue to recover? These are questions of law, not valuation. Still, this potential capital loss or recovery should be considered. Either way, it could change the value of this small company by several thousands of dollars. There is always the potential for a buyer to be hung by this type of arrangement if dealing with a seller who is less than honest.

> The vendor might guarantee to pay for any unsettled claims, but if she cannot afford to honor the pledge, or has joined the Foreign Legion, then you cannot collect. You will be stuck with the bill.

Personal Factors to be Considered

- general reputation of the business,
- reputation for paying bills and honoring commitments,
- warranty and service policy (Does it already owe money for guarantees?),
- claim service and refund policy,
- goodwill (In professional practices, often goodwill cannot be transferred. If the owner dies, does the business also die?),
- what proportion of the business is conducted with friends, relatives, and insiders.

Some years ago I bought a small insurance agency for only about $10,000. Usually seventy-five percent of policy holders stay on with the new owner, but in this case it was less that ten percent. What I soon found out that almost all of the policy holders were relatives or personal friends of the previous owner and scattered far and wide? (This was my first acquisition.) Almost all started to deal with other friends, or other agents closer to home, when Howard sold out. The next time I bought an insurance agency — a larger and more costly one — I was determined not to fall into the same trap twice. The seller was an elderly gentleman who wanted to retire. I made sure the price paid included his services for at least six months. During this time he was to provide a personal introduction to all of the policy holders, most of whom lived close by. Unfortunately, the old gent passed away that night—not even the next day, but within twelve hours of me signing the purchase contract, and him getting paid.

Is the business personal? Can the profit continue without the previous owner? What about the goodwill — is it transferrable?

Are the customers satisfied? Has the customer list grown or shrunk over the past five years? Find out why any customers came or left.

What is the company's main drawing card? Is it unique, or is the same as all the others in the industry? Is, say, a restaurant special because of location, easy parking, price, service, credit extended, more attractive table attendants, or a superlative hamburger? What if one of these qualities changed?

Toxic Problems

Waste disposal can be a problem, especially if it is toxic. An ecological problem could haunt a new owner like a mummy from the tomb. This modern-day concern applies particularly to anyone buying a business or property that has processed or stored a hazardous material, such as an old service station site or chemical warehouse. Thanks to a leaky gasoline tank years ago, the soil could still be contaminated and the cleanup cost high.

The present owner is usually responsible for cleanup, even though you may obtain a cleanup contract and innumerable guarantees from the seller. If you can keep the seller to his word, if he honors his pledges and guarantees made at the time of sale, everything is fine and dandy. But if he has no money or has left the country, then you, the buyer, are left holding the bill.

Lease Provisions

In the case of leased premises, what is the status of the lease? Has the lessor kept up her mortgage payments? Although you may not think this concerns you, it often does. If the mortgage company forecloses on the leased premises, you might be required to vacate. You may be legally right, but financially dead. Will your business be dispossessed at the end of the lease period? Although a sale does not terminate a lease, foreclosure sometimes does.

What does the lease say about leasehold improvements at the end of the lease term? Does equipment, installed by the lessee at great expense, become the property of the building owner at time of vacating, or can the lessee sell it?

Prepaid rent sometimes appears as either a current or capital asset. Some leases stipulate that if the lease is abandoned or assigned, prepaid rent will not be refunded or transferred. Unless the business will outlive the lease with the current owner, if this prepaid-rent clause exists, you may be about to pay good money for an asset that is worth nothing.

Management Philosophy

Look at the overall attitude with the prospect's industry. Is it optimistic or pessimistic? What has been the philosophy of past management? If negative, can it be corrected in staff and remaining customers?

Etcetera

I could go on and on. I just want to hammer home that the prudent buyer must carefully scrutinize all data and judiciously analyse the community, the area, the market, and the existing business including its history and its potential. Examine the economic conditions as they are, not as you want them to be. Throw away the rose-colored glasses. Set aside your subjective motives and be objective. Do not dismiss negative details, even if you think they are unimportant.

SURVEY OF THE COMPETITION

I will say it again: most business buyers make mistakes, not in their business or data analysis, but in their analysis of the competition. Competitors will always be there. They want to survive. They do not go away just because you have come along.

Study the competition with the greatest of care and accuracy. If you short-circuit anything in this chapter, do not let it be your assessment of the opposition.

Direct and Indirect Competitors

Detail all competitors in both the primary and secondary trading or market area. When counting hotel rooms, or restaurant seats, or square feet of retail store space, or whatever, always consider your target company as a competitor. It is easier to keep track of this way.

Direct competitors operate the same kind of business and essentially offer the same product or service. Indirect competitors are not in the same business, but they compete for the same dollar. Take a restaurant. All other restaurants of the same general class and type would be direct competitors. Indirect competitors would include all outlets that sell ready-to-consume food—hotels, supermarket delis, home delivery services, cocktail lounges, snack bars in department stores, and convenience food vendors. A pizzeria might be considered either a direct or an indirect competitor to a chop suey parlor? It is a matter of opinion, and perhaps their relative proximity.

> most business buyers make mistakes, not in their business or data analysis, but in their analysis of the competition. Competitors will always be there. They want to survive. They do not go away just because you have come along.

Separate competitive outlets according to their trading areas: the primary areas within easy walking or driving distance, and the secondary that are further away.

For a corner drug store, for instance, this delineation is vital. Not so for a manufacturing plant. In the secondary area, focus on the possibility of the patrons switching to a closer competitor, once the business changes hands.

Competitive Advantage

Can your target business match the amenities or advantages of the competitor, such as off-street parking, better visibility, special attractions, a better product, and better prices?

Does the competitor's neighborhood give it an edge, or is it a disadvantage?

Objectively consider your competitor's:

- facilities and capacities, including condition of property and equipment, technological advantages and disadvantages,
- levels of service,
- staff (Are they capable, courteous, well-trained, efficient, unionized?),
- management capability,
- hours of operation,
- discounts, and their ability to endure a price war (Could we?), national franchise (if applicable), which creates a profit advantage.

Sources of Competitor Patronage

Does your competitor cater to or appeal to an ethnic or other special group? Is it important to be similar, or different, from your competitors? Being the only Asian restaurant in an Italian district could be a good thing.

Consider the competitor's clientele. Are they local folks, or do they come from across town? The farther it is from its clientele, the more vulnerable it is to new competition.

A competitor catering to a specific segment of the population, such as a much-needed clothing shop for oversized women, could thrive even if it is tucked away in an obscure industrial area.

Stability of Competitors

Can you accurately estimate your competitor's sales, service levels, income, expenses, operating profit, debt, and capacity to service that debt? Do not automatically assume that you cannot.

Often it is tricky to make anything other than an educated guess. Yet you need to measure the opposition's strength. So if you are buying a hotel, spend a night at the one down the street. If you really want to know the occupancy rate, ask the maids.

If the competition is stable and financially capable, you could be in for a long fight, which may take the form of deep discounting or a price war.

A case in point: A nearby small town has three hotels, each of which boasts a large lounge, and each of which should sell a reasonable amount of beverages. Of the three hotels, two have large mortgages and the third is owned free and clear. The owner of the clear-title hotel is not bankrupting his competitors on purpose, but he sells table beer, the highest revenue producer in a country hotel, at slightly above his cost. Despite pressure from the other two hoteliers, he steadfastly refuses to raise the prices — most of the customers are his old friends. They have been patronizing this pub since time began. The other two hotels must charge full retail price to show a profit, which they require to service their debt. So who does all the business in this community? Who has all the friends? And which two hotels are constantly in the red? The pricing policy of the one, created almost exclusively by its lack of debt, markedly influences the other two.

> If the competition is stable and financially capable, you could be in for a long fight, which may take the form of deep discounting or a price war.

Competitors' Intentions

Does a competitor plan to expand or renovate? Does a new guy plan to open shop near your target's location? Is this good or bad? If you are buying a neighborhood flower shop and a new one is about to start across the street, ponder how that could increase or decrease your patronage. Remember that cumulative attraction works for furniture stores and food courts in shopping malls.

Measure the gain or loss resulting from the new competition. Thanks to fickle patronage, this is tough to predict. Perhaps it is best to calculate how much trade the target can lose and still survive.

Are any competitors closing, or being converted to a different, noncompetitive use?

Franchises

Sometimes a competitor gains a distinct identity or marketing advantage by being franchised, or by belonging to a particular group. Although franchises will be extensively discussed in Chapter Fifteen, consider the possible benefits for a franchised competitor. Now apply the same benefits to your target enterprise, if it is now or soon to be franchised.

Is Any Competitor for Sale?

If any competitor is for sale, why? For what price and terms? Have any competitors recently been sold? Analyse the asking and selling prices of similar, or competitive, businesses, particularly if they have actually sold. I will delve into this extensively in later chapters, but for the present purpose of analysing the competition, determine which businesses are for sale and at what price. Establish their volume, profitability, and reason for selling.

Potential

Is the target business doing better or worse than any competitor? Why?

Detail each competitor's market share, major products, location, pricing policies, and distribution methods. Does a competitor demonstrate an above-average growth rate? Has anyone recently introduced a revolutionary new product or process? Will anyone do so?

How easy is it for a new kid on the block to enter the marketplace? Can the market support all of the participants in a profitable way?

Is a branch-plant competitor weak but with a strong parent, or vice versa?

Who sets the prices in your market area? Can you do your own pricing, or must you follow your competitor's lead, no matter what?

How does the subject business stack up against the competition? Be objective. It is important.

> Can the market support all of the participants in a profitable way?

The Bottom Line

Survey the competition this way:

1. Determine the size of the total market, both primary and secondary, for your product or service.

2. Measure the competition's percentage of that market. Can it keep a grip on its market share? In the future, will it gobble up less or more? You get the remaining share of the market. Unless you have a revolutionary product, a hot fad, or an untapped market on your side, you just have to chip away at the competition's sales. Thus, it is ultra-important to size up the market and the potency of the competition.

SOURCES OF INFORMATION

In some circumstances, you might not need all of the data mentioned above. In others, it is crucial. I am trying to suggest the information required for many types of small businesses — everything from the neighborhood day care through to a trucking company. Of course — and I realize this — every case is different.

Before making an offer to buy a business, you must obtain and interpret the relevant background knowledge. It can make or break you. Additionally, it should underline the seller's, and the industry's, present or future dilemmas.

Business buyers often rightly claim that it is easy for high-priced consultants and authors to call for all this information, but where do buyers obtain it in the first place?

The sources are numerous and are often free. Many agencies, pleased to be asked, will literally pass out armfuls of paper.

Every town's Chamber of Commerce is chock full of demographics and other statistics about its community and area. Populations, relative ages, income levels, occupations, spending habits, growth statistics — it is all there. What the chamber cannot provide, you will find at the town's industrial development department. Engineering departments can provide traffic counts and proposed roadway changes, and can tell you who goes where and when. Legal and building departments will outline what you can and cannot do.

The federal and state governments can provide countless books, booklets, and pamphlets on whatever your heart desires, from financing advice to general industry background.

Innumerable commercial publishers, trade journals, professional consulting services, and statistical data gathering services will supply information of all types, usually at a reasonable cost.

Almost all trade journals, and you are sure to find one that applies to your business, publish annual statistical updates. These highlight many of the happenings in their area.

The local real-estate agent probably knows more about any business in the area than any other outsider. Eager to earn a sales commission, he will likely volunteer lots of pertinent information, particularly about the competition. If he does not have it at hand, he will find it. To a qualified agent, earning a commission involves much more than tramping a potential buyer through a property.

Statistics are collected by all banks and by most credit unions and savings and loan associations. Some of this is both analytical and critical. If they want your account, they will be most cooperative. In fact, most are quite helpful even if they think you will deal elsewhere. Banks are excellent sources of broader-based statistics and interpretations of longer-term trends at the local, state, and national levels.

Do not be afraid to employ a professional appraiser. They are expensive, but this could be the best investment that you have ever made. Although I will talk much more about professional appraisers and their reports later on, their valuable font of knowledge extends beyond estimating the value of a business.

It is all out there, and it is easy to find. Ask and you shall receive. If you knock on the right doors and ask the correct questions, you will need a truck to haul away all of the books and papers you gather. Still, the interpretation and application is left to you.

NOTES

Chapter 4

THE APPRAISAL OF REAL ESTATE: A CRASH COURSE

IN any going concern, its value is based on the underlying or tangible assets, real estate, fixtures and equipment, and current assets. The intangible assets, essentially goodwill, which is largely a creation of good management, can disappear overnight. Thus, in determining what any business is worth, after analysing the supportive data and market base, you must value the principal asset, the real estate. When the real estate is owned and is part of the deal, this is crucial; if rented, it is still not a bad idea to give it a thorough perusal.

With an assets valuation approach, which is the most commonly used method for most small businesses, first divide the going concern into two distinct components: the real estate as the first and the business as the second. Regard the real estate as if owned by a third party and leased to the business element. To this end, I will talk in this chapter exclusively about the valuation of real estate. It is only a crash course, however, and therefore much will be left unsaid.

The real estate portion includes:

- land and the improvements on it, such as buildings,
- the quality and utility of the building(s),
- location, including access, visibility, and neighborhood.

The business portion includes:

- machinery and equipment, or furniture and fixtures,
- efficiency of the plant,
- current assets,
- intangible assets, such as goodwill.

Where the property is leased, not owned, it is nice to know what the property is worth so you can determine if you are paying too much rent or if you have a leasehold interest. In this event, leasehold or tenant's improvements would be part of the business portion.

> In any going concern, its value is based on the underlying or tangible assets, real estate, fixtures and equipment, and current assets. The intangible assets, essentially goodwill, which is largely a creation of good management, can disappear overnight.

MOST PROBABLE MARKET VALUE DEFINED

The market value of the real estate could basically be described as its orderly liquidation value. What would someone pay for this property, in order to rent it to a third party or, in the case of a strip mall, to several tenants, such as a restaurant, convenience store, insurance office, and drug store? The property owner wants to earn a competitive return on the investment capital. He pays no attention to the business operation, other than its ability to pay rent. Considering only the land and the structures thereon.

Market Value of Real Estate is defined as:

The standard USPAP (Uniform Standards of Professional Appraisal Practice) definition sets out in detail what is sought.

"The most probable price which a property should bring in a competitive and open market under all conditions requisite to a fair sale, the buyer and seller each acting prudently and knowledgably, and assuming the price is not affected by undue stimulus. Implicit in this definition is the consummation of a sale as of a specified date and the passing of title from seller to buyer under conditions whereby:

1. buyer and seller are typically motivated,

2. both parties are well informed or well advised, and acting in what they consider their best interests,

3. a reasonable time is allowed for exposure in the open market,

4. payment is made in terms of cash in United States dollars, or in terms of financial arrangements comparable thereto,

5. the price represents the normal consideration for the property sold unaffected by special or creative financing or sales concessions granted by anyone associated with the sale."[1]

> Market value is…what the average, willing buyer will pay to the average, willing seller, neither under any undue pressure and both being fully aware of all circumstances and conditions?

In other words, what would the average, willing buyer will pay to the average and willing seller, neither under any undue pressure and both being fully aware of all circumstances and conditions?

You will note that I am using the term "most probable market value," rather than "market value," or "fair market value," or "estimated market value." No one can predict to the penny what any property will sell for. The best that anyone can ever do is come close. The term "most probable" recognizes that some will pay more and others will accept less for the same property, each governed by their own dictates and requirements.

IMPORTANT PRINCIPLES TO CONSIDER

Substitution

The fundamental principle of substitution simply states that you will not pay more for anything if you can buy something equally desirable for less. This principle assumes no unreasonable delay in acquiring the substitute; it also assumes that, all else being equal, the lowest-priced product will attract the greatest demand and have the widest distribution.

Supply and Demand

When a sufficient number of buyers and sellers negotiate prices obtained or paid, they are said to be market driven. If demand exceeds supply, prices will rise; if supply exceeds demand, prices will fall. Thus you must consider the number of comparable or competitive properties for sale and the number of potential buyers for each.

Balance

The principle of balance maintains that value is created and sustained when supply and demand balance out, or achieve a state of equilibrium. In any given place or time, market forces dictate a proper allocation of various land uses, a proper mix of occupancies, who survives, and who does not. In some businesses the age-old perception, where there is room for one there is room for four, seldom works in the long run. Neighborhoods and shopping centres find their own balance, eliminating those that are surplus or do not measure up.

If you are buying a business that is domiciled in a leased property, such as a neighborhood shopping centre, you need to ensure that the centre works, that each tenant attracts patronage for each other, that the mixture is balanced.

Contribution

Property comparison is based on each component's relative contribution to the value of the whole. Here, you look at neighborhood influences, location, visibility, land, building, site improvements, accessibility, and competition, etc.

Externalities

Outside economics or influences can harm or help a property's value. A house overlooking a beautiful park will have more value than the identical one located beside a busy highway. In commercial properties, this could be extended to regional and local economics.

Anticipation

Value is created by the expectation of benefits that accrue to the property owner.

Change

Ben Franklin said that only two things are certain: death and taxes. Let us add a third: change. Nothing is static. As the market changes, and as the forces that create the market change, so do property values. Any meaningful market value estimate must be tied to a specific point in time.

MARKETABILITY STUDY

Before actually determining the value of the subject property, you should undertake a marketability study. This differs from a feasibility study, which is always conducted before construction commences. A marketability study can be done anytime. This study answers only one question: Is there a demand for this property, at this time, without considering the business of the tenant(s)? It then categorizes that demand by considering possibilities for resale, rental, or site redevelopment for some alternative use. A shopping centre could be for sale because it cannot attract a proper balance of rent-paying tenants. A personal service business in the centre may be for sale because it cannot garner sufficient patrons and hence does not earn enough return on the investment to support the capital assets. Despite your management ability, you might not be able to make it work, either. The steps of a study are:

- Estimate the demand for rental space of all types in this area. Interview leasing agents and property managers. Extrapolate population and occupancy statistics from comparative neighborhoods and apply them to the target enterprise's area. Record interest from pre-construction advertising signs. Measure the amount of vacant space in the primary trading area. Determine what type of stores and services are missing.

- Estimate the supply of space that competes with your subject. Include what is now available or is proposed, both for rent and for sale. Take inventory of the each space's location, type, age, condition, amenities, present occupancy, rental rates, rental concessions, etc.
- Is the market growing, declining, or stagnant?
- Is more demand being created, or does the forecast suggest a glut?
- Is the competitive space offered at an equitable price and on competitive terms? What are the prevailing rental rates? How many square feet will be needed to satisfy the projected demand?
- If any tenant fails or vacates, can the empty space be leased at or near market value? Is the centre readily resalable? Can you make a capital gain or must you take a bath to bail out?

METHODS OF APPRAISAL

You can choose from three traditional methods for gauging the value of real estate:

- the cost approach,
- the comparative sales approach,
- the income approach.

Although this is a crash course, I will explain all three approaches. Still, a full narrative-type appraisal, as prepared by a professional appraiser, will contain a lot of detail that I will not cover in this chapter. In other sections of this manual, however, I will touch on everything that an appraiser considers, analyses, and reports on.

Select only one or two approaches, depending on which makes you feel most comfortable, based on your training and experience. Select whatever provides the most meaningful answer for your specific purpose. Real-estate valuation theory and practice focuses solely on what an average buyer will pay and an average seller accept. It does not particularly address the unique problems or standards of a single buyer or seller. Thus, you should modify your appraisal methodology to suit your specific situation. If you follow only one approach to value, make it the income approach. For a commercial or investment property, this procedure is the most significant of the three. Although both the cost and comparable sales methods add much to the exercise, the income approach is superior.

With these constraints in mind, let us consider the theoretical and practical aspects of a commercial property appraisal, step by step.

> Select only one or two approaches, depending on which makes you feel most comfortable, based on your training and experience. Select whatever provides the most meaningful answer for your specific purpose.

THE COST APPROACH TO VALUE

What Is It?

With this approach, value is a synthesis of the physical components of the property. To find the value, add up:

- the market value of the land or site as if vacant,
- the reproduction or replacement cost of the building, less depreciation,
- the contributory value of the site improvements,
- the contributory value of any other capital asset.

Although this procedure is most applicable to new properties, and does not always indicate market value, the cost approach value estimate often plays an important part in the investment decision.

Always bear in mind that this approach may not produce a credible estimate of market value. It may only reliably estimate the cost if developing the property, exactly as is, less accrued depreciation. Most times it provides only an orderly liquidation value. That is, it ignores the sales and profitability of the business domiciled there. A property housing a very profitable business would, by this procedure, holds the same value as a property housing one on the verge of bankruptcy. Also, it does not measure reproduction or replacement cost and depreciation very well. In an older building, this is often little more than guesswork.

Recommended Cost Approach Procedure

1. Determine the market value of the site as if vacant. Although there are other methods, the easiest way is to compare the site with any vacant land sales, or those currently held for sale that are located in the immediate area.

2. Determine the reproduction or replacement cost of the building(s) by one or more methods. For a larger or more elaborate building, use at least two procedures so that you can cross-check your findings. (Except for quantity surveying, no single cost method is really all that accurate.)

3. Measure accrued depreciation — physical, functional, and external. Deduct total depreciation from the reproduction or replacement cost of the building, and you will come up with the building value, often termed as the depreciated replacement cost.

4. Measure and add in the contributory value of the site improvements, such as landscaping, paving, or overhead lights, etc.

5. Measure and add in the contributory value of any additional capital assets, such as advertising signs, unloading hoists, ramps, or anything of a physical nature so far not included.

6. Sum up the values found. The total is the physical replacement or cost approach value estimate.

Market Value of the Site as if Vacant

First, estimate the market value of the land or site without considering any of its improvements. Think of what would be paid for the land in an open market transaction, were it vacant, by a willing buyer to a willing seller. What would an equally desirable alternative site cost?

In site valuation, you must take extra care to ensure that the land is adequate for its use and that all comparisons are made from this perspective. In some forms of investment real estate, such as an apartment block or a warehouse, probably moving a block here or there is not material. Location is ultra-important, however, for a fast-food restaurant, retail store, strip mall, or many service businesses. Even half a block, or around a corner, or on a blind side of a traffic artery can spell the difference between success and failure.

Compare sites that are the same size and shape, in the same neighborhood, of similar zoning, and with a corresponding optimum use capability. In addition to this, establish the upside of the market by looking at listing and asking prices. If in a fully developed area where no sales have occurred for some time, you may need to go well

In site valuation, you must take extra care to ensure that the land is adequate for its use and that all comparisons are made from this perspective.

out of the district. Examine relative locations, size, zoning, and physical attributes in ever-increasing circles.

Obtain and consider this data on a comparable site:

- date of sale (the market is never stable),
- size and shape,
- topography,
- visibility,
- municipal zoning (do not compare residential with commercial sites),
- safety and ease of entry and exit,
- level of utility servicing,
- usable improvements, if any,
- the selling price (do not just count on rumors from your neighbor),
- any special terms on the sale, such mortgage, equity, or payments,
- demand (How long was it on the market?),
- the unit price per square foot or per front foot.

Compare as many sites as you can, keeping in mind that quality is always preferable to quantity. Three good sales are better than ten listings.

Compare as many sites as you can, keeping in mind that quality is always preferable to quantity. Three good sales are better than ten listings.

Adjustments to Comparable Land Sales

The comparable sales, or listings, selected are adjusted towards the subject based on any differences between the comparable sale and your subject site, point by point. Consider anything that would make your target site more or less valuable than the comparable. Note each of the several possible reasons that would alter market value.

Adjustments are preferably based on a percentage of value, whole dollars, or dollars per square or front foot. They would include, but not necessarily be limited to:

- time (Is the market going up or down?),
- differences in the general neighborhood or area value,
- size and shape, frontage vs. depth,
- corner influence,
- differences in municipal zoning or land classification,
- any development restrictions,
- easements, transmission, or pipelines that limit site use,
- comparative topography, percentage of usable area,
- amount and contribution of existing landscaping,
- visibility from what distance, what directions,
- relationship to traffic patterns,
- proximity to public transportation, if relevant,
- soil conditions, subsoil bearing capacity,
- value of usable preexisting surface improvements,
- availability of utility connections,
- utility services, prepaid or paid by local improvement taxes,
- proximity to population base and patrons,
- potential for toxic or environmental problems,
- effect of special or beneficial financing,
- a discount for a longer marketing time,
- a downward adjustment if only a listing.

You will want to know if the seller sold for more or less than market value for this or that reason. If you use this qualifier, be careful. Some developers, for specific lessees, pay a seemingly exorbitant price for a particular site, but often no other property will do as well for this specific use, such as a fast-food restaurant or gasoline kiosk. The price paid may not always reflect market value.

Be extra-cautious if you are comparing listing or asking prices. In fact, do not use them at all if you can get away with it. Even a poor sale beats an unrealistically priced listing, which so often no one — including the owner — ever really expects to get. If you must use a listing price, ensure that it is in line, then apply a substantial discount to the price. Every seller juggles three prices: what he would like to get, what he wants, and what he will settle for.

Next do the arithmetic. The value of your subject site is the price of the comparable, plus any adjustments for superiority and minus any for items of inferiority, based on each sale or individual listing.

Next, select the median value of the several individual comparable sales values found. This is the number that occurs in the centre of the array when arranged from the highest to the lowest, number two of three, or number four if seven are used, or number five if nine are used, and so forth. It is not, as some believe, halfway between the highest and lowest. Sometimes the median and the best value indicator are the same comparable. This substantially increases the comfort level. When several sales are used, particularly when they are not all that comparable, or several adjustments must be made to each, or when quite large, the median provides the best indicator of value. It is not unduly affected by the extremes and largely tends to minimize the error factors and personal bias in the adjustment process. It best represents market value to the average seller and the average buyer. Never use an arithmetic average. In real-estate and business valuation, this is a no-no.

> ...select the median value of the several individual comparable sales values found. This is the number that occurs in the centre of the array when arranged from the highest to the lowest...

Value of the Building(s)

Next estimate the value of the building(s), step by step:

1. Estimate the reproduction or replacement cost of the building(s) new, at the applicable date,

2. Estimate the amount of accrued depreciation,

3. The value of the building is the reproduction or replacement cost less accrued depreciation from all causes.

Before continuing, we need to clear up a popular misconception. Although often used synonymously, the terms "reproduction cost" and "replacement cost" mean two quite different things. Reproduction cost means duplicating the building exactly as is, replacement cost means reproducing the utility. This approach to value can start with either reproduction or replacement cost but it always ends with depreciated replacement value.

Reproduction or Replacement Cost Estimating Methods

The reproduction or replacement cost of a building can be estimated several ways:

- the actual cost of the building as abstracted from the financial statements of the owner, indexed to today by the amount of inflation that has occurred,
- an estimate provided by a building contractor active in this field,
- an estimate provided by a professional quantity surveyor,
- an estimate provided by a professional building cost estimator,
- construction cost services, such as Marshall-Swift, Boech, Landsdown's, etc.
- your own personal experience.

Frequently even contractors' prices are wrong. With the variable cost of materials, labor, and profit requirement, seldom can one measure reproduction cost to within a five-percent error factor. The superficial appearance of any building can be deceiving. Paint and plaster hide errors in construction, many of which can be very cheap or very costly to rectify. As with all costing methods, the resultant is only as good as the technician who provides the estimate.

Project development costs, known as soft costs, should be built into the reproduction or replacement cost estimate. They include, for example:

- architectural, design, and engineering costs,
- legal fees for contract preparation and examination,
- surveying costs,
- utility installations,
- taxes and insurance paid during construction,
- mortgage standby fees,
- cost of interim and takeout financing,
- developer's overhead and anticipated profit,
- appraisal reports.

Depreciation

The three forms of depreciation are:

1. physical deterioration, curable and incurable,
2. functional obsolescence, curable and incurable,
3. external obsolescence.

When calculating loss in value caused by depreciation, take into account the common overlap between physical and functional. Seldom is it simple to pigeonhole incurable depreciation as neatly as textbooks, and this outline, might suggest.

Physical Deterioration, Curable and Incurable: Physical depreciation would be best described as the loss in property value due to the physical action of time, the elements, and use; inadequate maintenance; or normal weathering and decay.

Buildings, like you and me (me for sure), simply become old and worn out and are not as good as they once were. Construction methods change, materials change, and all desire a more modern appearance.

This form of depreciation can be incurable and curable. If it is incurable, it cannot be remedied except at an exorbitant cost; if it is curable, you can simply upgrade or correct aspects that have not been maintained.

To be considered curable, the cost of correcting the flaw must be reasonable and feasible. You have to calculate how much it will cost to repair what is broken and to rectify what has not been maintained. This is upkeep that has been postponed, allowing the building to deteriorate faster than it should. You will want to bring the building up to the standard that is normal for a building of this age and use. The repair costs must make sense, that is, the structure cannot be so functionally obsolete that you would just be wasting your money by upgrading.

The effective age of a building does not mean its chronological age. It means that, all else being equal, the subject has an equivalent age of a building that is so many years old. This difference could have been created by higher-quality construction than most, better maintenance, and T.L.C. Conversely, it may have been badly abused and is thus older than its years. Always bear in mind that the economic life of any building can be continuously extended by modernization, renovation, and general upgrading.

To be considered curable, the cost of correcting the flaw must be reasonable and feasible.

Functional Obsolescence, Curable and Incurable: Functional obsolescence means the building is less or more than what you need in terms of size or efficiency. Functional obsolescence reflects loss in value brought about by such factors as overcapacity, inadequacy, and changes in the art that affect the property item itself, or its relation with other items comprising a larger property.

Like physical depreciation, functional obsolescence is subdivided into the curable and the incurable.

Functional obsolescence, incurable, is measured by loss of revenue or increased cost to operate. The principal criterion is a direct comparison with similar buildings, used for similar purposes that do not have these features of obsolescence. For example, in a shopping centre, incurable obsolescence could be rental loss for those out-of-the-way spots that lack visibility, or are out of the main traffic stream, or are far from the main entrance or patronage generators. In an office building, you should look at hallways that are too wide or narrow, wasted space in washrooms, overly large utility rooms, or hard-to-find, poorly designed, or inadequately lit office areas. The ceiling could be too high, wasting heat. The building might not have enough elevators. The kitchen might be located at the wrong end of a restaurant, causing the staff to spend too much time walking.

To measure the loss in value created by functional obsolescence, incurable, measure the net present value of lost revenue or the increased operating cost until the end of the economic life of the building. The annual amount is discounted at the longer-term midpoint or safe interest rate. For example, assume that the market rental rate is $10.00 per square foot per year, net, but because of a poor shape or some other quirk, a particular 5,000-square-foot store space will command only $7.50 per square foot. The interest rate is nine percent and the building has a projected remaining economic life of twenty-five years.

The loss in building value caused by the functional obsolescence, incurable, would be:

Net present value of $2.50 per sq. ft. per annum loss,
Times the area of 5,000 sq. ft. for 25 years,
Discounted at 9.0% per annum = $122,782

Since obsolescence and physical deterioration often overlap, take special care to ensure that the same depreciation is not measured twice. To avoid this mistake, deduct the percent already taken for physical deterioration, incurable, from the functional obsolescence, incurable.

Net present value of loss of $12,500 per annum for 25 years @ 9.0% = $ 122,782
Less: percent of physical depreciation already taken;
assume 25% (this would be 25% of $122,782) = ($ 30,695)

Amount of functional obsolescence, incurable $ 92,087

Always measure functional obsolescence, curable, like physical deterioration, by the cost to cure. The cost to cure must be economically feasible; if not, the depreciation must be considered as incurable.

External Obsolescence: This defect is caused by negative influences from outside the site. The owner, landlord, or tenant generally cannot cure it.

Plainly stated, external obsolescence is physical loss created by anything outside the limits of, and almost always beyond the control of, the property itself, its owners, or its occupants. It can never be fixed by structural or cosmetic modernization, such as a coat of paint. Almost always incurable, it is going to create a loss forever.

To measure the loss in value created by functional obsolescence, incurable, measure the net present value of lost revenue or the increased operating cost until the end of the economic life of the building.

Measure this form of depreciation just as you would for functional obsolescence. Loss in value is the net present value of the loss of revenue. The calculating procedure is identical, but unless very large, or very obvious, the loss is often difficult to assess accurately.

Summary of Building Costs and Depreciation Factors

Reproduction or replacement cost estimate
Less depreciation from all causes
Equals the depreciated value of the building

Site Improvements

A site improvement is mainly anything on the site that is not a building. This would include an asphalt parking lot, parking bumpers, painted parking stalls, curbs and gutters, site drainage, site electrification, etc. Many sites require substantial preparation work such as filling, levelling, compacting, removal of contaminated soil (an increasingly important and costly issue), grading, energizing, etc. To estimate these costs, use your own knowledge of the area or ask contractors who actually do this type of work.

Depreciation rates always vary substantially. In northern climates, frost causes asphalt heaves and concrete cracking, thus reducing the life of most parking lots to about ten years. In the south, seasonal heat can equally deteriorate asphalt, but concrete is relatively safe from high temperatures. Again, check local conditions and take a good look at the site, particularly the higher traffic areas, when the parking area is empty.

Miscellaneous Improvements, Fixtures and Equipment

This includes anything else connected with the physical aspects of the property, such as gasoline kiosk canopies, snow removal equipment, janitorial equipment, special chattels, and advertising signs, including those on the highway. You absolutely must determine if these are part of the real estate or the business. At this juncture, deal with real estate only; the fixtures-and-equipment part of the business comes later. These items can be separately identified, or included with either the building or the site improvements. It is not important how they are categorized, so long as nothing is missed.

In the cost approach, there is no variation from the tested formula. Take fixtures and equipment that are a part of the real estate, and add them at the current replacement cost, less accrued depreciation. Exceptions would be permanently attached equipment, such as air conditioners, hot water tanks, and plumbing fixtures.

Summary of Cost Approach Value Estimates

- Market value of the site, as if vacant, plus
- Depreciated value of the building(s), plus
- Contributory value of the site improvements, plus
- Contributory value of other improvements,
- Equals the cost approach value estimate

This is the only approach that breaks the value down by its input segments; all others give only a lump-sum value estimate.

THE COMPARATIVE SALES APPROACH TO MARKET VALUE

The Approach Defined

The comparative sales approach directly compares the target property with similar properties that have recently sold or are currently held for sale. They should contain as many similar or comparable features as possible. Listings and properties offered for sale set the upper limit of value.

The underlying tenet is that a property's value directly relates to open market prices paid for similar, competitive properties. Unfortunately, this approach is not very reliable when comparable sales or offerings are few and far between, or when those offered are not truly comparable.

The Procedure

1. Search out, as many as are feasible, properties that have been recently sold or are currently held for sale, which are as similar as possible to your subject property. Work in ever-increasing circles, as to location, date of sale, and comparability. Start from the target property and move outward. The more distant the location, time, and similarity, the less valuable the comparable. Start with the closest, most recent, and best, until a sufficient number of comparable sales have been established. All pertinent data must be available on these sales. You are using the same procedure as was detailed with the vacant land, except now you are searching out fully developed properties. There is no magic number as to the total to be used. Quality is always better than quantity. It is not necessary to use a hundred sales, yet one sale does not make a market. Most times, five or six good comparables is ideal.

   In rural areas, you might examine sales in other towns, or sales four or five years old. If you cannot find any appropriate sales at all — and this happens frequently — do not use the comparative sales approach, and instead rely exclusively on the cost and income methods.

   All sales must be bona fide arm's-length. Do not use intercompany transfers, interfamily sales, or value declarations by a continuing owner. Verification is important.

2. Find out almost as much about each comparable sale as you know about the subject property. This would include, but not necessarily be limited to:

   - date of sale (consider changes since date of sale),
   - confirmed selling price,
   - true consideration if a trade was involved,
   - down payment, equity,
   - amount and terms of financing, vendor take-backs,
   - any special financing terms,
   - a detailed description of the building(s):
     - size, gross leasable area,
     - age, chronological and effective,
     - type and style of building,
     - secondary structures, warehouses, compounds, etc.
     - construction materials, quality of workmanship,
     - condition, deferred maintenance, repairs required,

> The underlying tenet is that a property's value directly relates to open market prices paid for similar, competitive properties.

- areas of obsolescence,
- other improvements, serving windows, lifts, ramps,
- site size and description,
- site improvements (asphalt, gravel, landscaping, etc.),
- topography of site, visibility and accessibility
- excess land, parking lot,
- visibility and accessibility of site,
- location, neighborhood differences,
- use and occupancy of property,
- income and expense summary (if the property is leased),
- historical vacancy rate, present vacancy rate,
- legal difficulties, easements, caveats, encroachments,
- zoning and municipal ordinances that may affect value,
- any special motivating factors,
- intended use by the buyer,
- demand (How long was the property for sale?),
- other offers on the property,
- whether this was a sale or a listing.

> There is little point in gathering useless data. Yet you must not overlook any relevant details, particularly if they affect market value. ...ensure that the comparables used are comparable.

You cannot always collect all of the data I have suggested, and sometimes some of the points are not relevant to your case. There is little point in gathering useless data. Yet you must not overlook any relevant details, particularly if they affect market value. And — I cannot repeat this too often — ensure that the comparables used are comparable.

3. Equate each comparable sale with the subject, adjusting the value for each difference that you can measure. Adjust each difference individually so that a market value of the target property, based on each sale, one at a time, can be determined. You might consult the above list of possible differences and make adjustments on several details or, if the properties are very similar, on as few as two or three. Theoretically, identical properties will sell for identical prices, superior properties for more, inferior properties for less. The object of the process is to interpret the thinking of a typical buyer: how would she make the comparisons, adding for this, or subtracting for that? By making those additions to, or subtractions from, the selling or asking price, you can estimate a value for your subject. Most important, ensure that you do not make the same adjustment more than once, by calling it something different each time.

4. Adjust several comparable sales to come up with an estimated value for the subject property.

Adjustment Factors

To make adjustments, you can use:

- whole dollars for each measurable difference,
- percentage of value difference.

The choice is purely a matter of training and personal preference, but I prefer the percentage-of-value factor. Lots of times, though, such as in site value differences or building sizes, whole dollars are probably easier. The point is, do whatever makes you feel most comfortable, yet be consistent. If you throw around percentages here and dollars there, you will become confused and wind up adjusting the same difference twice.

When applying the adjustments, work from the comparable to the subject. That is, if the subject property is better than the comparable, add the difference to the subject, rather than deduct it from the comparable. If the subject is poorer, deduct the difference from the subject, rather than add it to the comparable. Again, be consistent. In the imperfect market, most adjustments are imprecise judgment calls. The several adjusted comparable sales will hardly ever fall within a narrow, or readily definable, value range. If they do, you are either reading a textbook or, if this happens in the real world, you may have inadvertently cooked the books. Always make several smaller adjustments, as opposed to a few large ones. You can easily justify a small adjustment of three or five percent, but it is almost impossible to rationalize a difference of forty, fifty, or sixty percent, unless you are talking about land or building sizes.

Throughout, all adjustments will be on, or converted to a percentage-of-value difference. Let us look at the differences one at a time:

Time (Changes in the Market)

No market is ever completely static, or if so, not for long. Economic pressures and other factors constantly drive values this way or that. When looking at time, you will inflate or deflate the price of the comparable sale according to the current market level. If the market has risen, increase the comparable's selling price according to the percentage of market change from the date of sale to the present. If the market has fallen, drop the selling price according to the change in the market since the sale date. It is often difficult to establish what percentage the market has changed during the interim period. The market value of two properties do not necessarily move up or down in tandem during a specific time frame, especially if there are many differences between them. And even though prices for investment properties move in a more synchronized fashion, thanks to the stability of longer-term leases and financial leverage, they still lag behind both the residential real-estate and the money market.

Other than knowing your marketplace intimately, the best statistical source is the sales and listings data gathered by companies that gauge commercial trends or by real-estate statistical publishing companies. Both have offices in at least every larger city in the United States or are on the internet.

The selling price of the comparable is altered to indicate the price for which it would be sold today. All other adjustments are then applied to this, not to the original selling price.

Quality and Appeal

Here, you rate the subject property against comparable sales and listings, based on how each fits in with the scheme of things. Consider the neighborhood location and appeal. Is the neighborhood progressive, dying, stable, or what? Is the subject a proper fit or out of character? How does it relate to the flow of vehicle traffic, ease of access, visibility, and safety? Is this a good place for the enterprise? How does the comparable's layout rate against that of the subject? Without getting into specific physical differences, consider how the physical attributes of the property itself, not that of a tenant, draws or discourages patrons.

The Property

Separate this topic into five areas:

- size and construction of the building,
- age and condition of the building,
- functional design and layout of the building,

- site size, parking ratio, and surplus land not used or required,
- ease of vehicle movement into and around the site.

In some circumstances, the first three and the last two could be grouped. Many appraisers do it this way. If you break it down into the five listed areas, make separate adjustments for each and do not duplicate anything.

Size and Construction of Building

Differing sizes are adjusted based exclusively on area. Masonry buildings usually cost about five percent more to construct than wood-frame buildings.

Age and Condition of Building

The normal economic life of most commercial buildings, if properly maintained, is fifty to sixty years. Some specific tenants, such as fast-food restaurants or dry cleaners, will reduce this to about forty years. The shell lasts longer than this but the interior usually less, because of high moisture content, specialized design, and high maintenance requirements. The building's lifespan could be longer or shorter, depending on the type and quality of construction and building materials, use and occupancy, climatic conditions, and level of maintenance, which directly affects the profitability of the property. Fifty years is a good base for most commercial-frame construction, sixty for masonry, forty for metal-frame and sidewalls or special uses. Still, because of the definite overlap between age and condition, depreciation progresses on a curve. Depreciation is relatively flat for a newer building, accelerates with age, then levels out as a building nears the end of its economic life.

As it is a tall order to thoroughly examine every nook and cranny in the subject, let alone every comparable, the condition rating is always arbitrary.

Site Size and Quality

When you buy an investment property, the price is always a combination of future benefits, including money. Investors seldom compartmentalize the varying value contributors, at least not to the same extent as do professional appraisers. When you look at site size and quality, you always need to ask whether this property should be evaluated as vacant land or if it should be included with the building. The same scenario applies to site quality and appeal. With investment properties, particularly those developed to a customer's requirements, the adjustment process is not as finite as for single-family dwellings, where physical and financial characteristics do not overlap.

Beneficial Financing

The effect of beneficial financing must always be weighed against the realities of the marketplace. Maybe the seller got a better price, or the buyer snapped up a good property with a lower down payment or with more attractive terms than available in the conventional market. You have to weigh these benefits against who was helped the most. Assuming conventional financing, what would a typical buyer have paid? (I will talk about this much more in Chapter Ten.)

Fixtures and Equipment

If the comparable sales did not provide anything similar, the depreciated value of the equipment lumped in with the real estate would be a superiority rating for the subject. But do not include fixtures and equipment that are part of the business.

Subjective Motives

When I introduced adjustment factors earlier on, I kept the list short for the sake of demonstration and simplicity. I did not list one common factor: motive. When you look at motive, you are first conducting a mini-appraisal of the comparable to see if it can even be used as a comparable. This also applies to aesthetic values, which are usually so subjective that it is difficult to adjust for them in a methodical way.

In situations of this type, I always wonder about the validity of the comparative sales approach. Does the marketplace really make accurate, levelheaded adjustments? Can anyone do so without substantial training and market knowledge? Probably not. Most of the time, even the pros have difficulty. Can anyone really defend his adjustment as being correct? Probably not. While this factor has merit in many situations, the resultant is only as good as the input data and the capability of the person using it.

> When you look at motive, you are first conducting a mini-appraisal of the comparable to see if it can even be used as a comparable.

Adjustments to Comparable Sales

Because adjustments are speculative, the nonprofessional will probably find comparative sales the most difficult of the three approaches to value. You must be extra-careful when performing this task. Wrong adjustments or improper comparisons produce an unreliable end value.

Comparative Sales Value Estimate

To determine the value of the property, you are left with one of three choices:

1. Use the best comparable, provided that its indicated value is in line with most or all of the other adjusted comparables. At times, the best comparable sits above the midpoint of the value range; other times, it hangs below the midpoint. And remember: No matter how similar to the subject, one sale does not make a market.

2. Select the median value, which occurs in the centre of the array. This value is usually unaffected by either the extremely high or low values found, and it tends to dampen any adjustment errors and areas of bias.

3. The mode value, if one exists, is the number that occurs most frequently in the array of adjusted values. Note that when comparing more than five sales, a mode can occur anywhere in the array — in the high end or the low end or the middle. As with the best comparable, the value must fall within the middle range and be supported by the other adjusted market values.

As I have said before, you should select the tactic where the data is most reliable and where you feel most comfortable. If the best comparable and the median are miles apart, go back to the drawing board. See what you have done wrong. Although seldom identical in value, they should be reasonably close.

THE CAPITALIZED INCOME VALUE ESTIMATE
(Income Capitalization Approach to Market Value)

Income, Income, and Income

When all is said and done, in investment properties and going concerns, there are three approaches to value: income, income, and income. Agreed, the cost approach estimates the cost to duplicate the capital assets, less depreciation from all sources. The comparative sales value estimate looks at sales for similar properties, adjusted for differences. In the final analysis, however, it is all for naught if the property cannot earn income or the business established therein make a profit and pay its rent.

Sure, it is alright for me to explain how to value a property by adding up the depreciated value of its parts, or by comparing it to other sales and listings. You might not have the foggiest idea of how to find the necessary basic information, or else you cannot make the adjustments that at times boggle even the professionals. If so, I understand. The cost and comparative sales approaches are tough to comprehend and apply without considerable time, practice, and frequently more instruction than I have provided.

But do not bomb out on the income approach. If you understand, or use, only one method to determine value, make this the one. Although traditionally left to the last, the income approach to market value is, in the end, the only one that counts in an investment property. To be really certain that you understand this, I will explain this procedure in detail, duplicating much found in subsequent chapters. That is how vital this is.

The Income Capitalization Approach to Market Value Defined

"A set of procedures through which an appraiser derives a value indication of an income-producing property by converting its anticipated benefits (cash flows and reversion) into property value. This conversion can be accomplished in two ways. One year's expectancy can be capitalized at a market-derived capitalization rate or at a capitalization rate that reflects a specific income pattern, return on investment, and change in the value of the investment. Alternatively, the annual cash flows for the holding period and the reversion can be discounted at a specified yield rate."[2]

Do not worry. I will explain all that. For starters, though, reversion means the remaining value of the property at the end of the lease period, or the economic life of the improvements, in which case it is only the value of the site, as if vacant.

Intertwined with the buying decision is investor motivation. Not all buyers share the same objectives. The decision to buy real estate instead of something else, or to buy this property rather than that one, or to buy anything at all, is based on one or more of the following:

...reversion means the remaining value of the property at the end of the lease period, or the economic life of the improvements, in which case it is only the value of the site, as if vacant.

- pride of ownership,
- ability to exercise a measure of control,
- self-use,
- diversification of portfolio,
- security of capital,
- return on investment,
- equity buildup through debt amortization,
- equity buildup through inflation,

- tax shelter,
- leverage.

The income approach to market value concentrates only on the monetary aspects of the investment, for which the bottom line is a competitive return on and the security of the money you invest. Let us put it this way: You want to receive a certain return on your investment through periodic payments. You also want to get back the original investment or ensure that it stays intact when the property can no longer earn money. How much will you pay for a property to achieve these goals?

Moreover, the capitalized income value estimate is the present value of all income that the property is expected to earn over its remaining economic life.

The Procedure

With these three steps, you can determine market value by the income approach:

1. Estimate the periodic cash flows from the investment. This is known as the income stream.

2. Obtain and apply the appropriate capitalization rate that will convert the income stream into an estimate of value.

3. Establish the indicated value of the appraised property by dividing the income stream by the capitalization rate. Or you can calculate the net present value of the income stream for its remaining life, then add the net present value of the reversion.

The best methods to abstract capitalization rates are:

- from the market (market-derived capitalization rates),
- the mortgage-equity concept.

The most probable market value is estimated by:

- capitalization of one year's stabilized income,
- capitalization of a variable income stream.

Pro forma Income and Expense Statement

When you are looking at income, it is always wise to develop a pro forma, or stabilized, income and expense statement. This composite statement is based on the operating history of the property and the probability of what will occur during the forecast period. It results in a relatively level, supportable net-income synopsis. This reconstructed statement, based on specific assumptions, eliminates the common flip-flopping between cash and accrual accounting systems, levels the humps and depressions, and projects what will probably occur at the end of the lease period.

Market and Contract Rent

First, determine the gross annual income to the property, which is usually stated as rent. If the owner occupies the property, or if it is part of a going concern, you must obtain a market rental rate for the property. In all cases, the real estate is considered from its investment perspective, divorced from the business or other

When you are looking at income, it is always wise to develop a pro forma, or stabilized, income and expense statement. This composite statement is based on the operating history of the property and the probability of what will occur during the forecast period.

interests of the owner. That is, it must be considered exclusively from its rental-earning capacity, no matter who owns or occupies it, as if it is rented to a third party.

Market rent refers to whatever rental fee the subject property could command in the open market, in competition with all other rentable spaces, if it were vacant and available for lease. This is usually calculated on the property as is. If the rent is based on renovations being completed, or the granting of special conditions, etc., these must be factored into the formula, or the net present value of the concession deducted from the final value estimate.

Although some folks think market rent and economic rent are one and the same, that is not always the case. Think of market rent as the rent obtainable for a property when compared with others up and down the street. Economic rent is the rent that a tenant can afford to pay as a part of the sales or income to the business. The two may not be synonymous.

Contract rent is the rent that a tenant is actually paying, usually as stipulated in the lease, or by agreement. You should check the contract rental against the market. If the rent is too low, the property is penalized; if too high, the tenant will move out or negotiate when the lease expires. Market corroboration is probably unnecessary if the property has been rented, long-term, to a top-flight company that you trust not to walk out of the agreement. But for other rental agreements, particularly with short-term or month-to-month tenants, you must compare contract rents with the market.

The procedure is the same as with other comparative market data approaches, valuing vacant land, adjusting capitalization rates, undertaking the comparative sales approach, and so forth. Search out as many comparable rental properties as possible, adjusting for differences such as:

> Think of market rent as the rent obtainable for a property when compared with others up and down the street. Economic rent is the rent that a tenant can afford to pay as a part of the sales or income to the business. The two may not be synonymous.

- market changes since the lease was executed,
- neighborhood influences,
- location of the comparable space,
- quality of the comparable space,
- size and shape (shape is often important but overlooked),
- traffic and visibility,
- ease of access,
- on-site or nearby parking,
- amenities included, allowances, bonuses, amortization,
- usable partitions, etc., from the previous tenant,
- whether this lease has been executed or is merely a listing,
- demand, appeal, time on the market.

When the comparable lease has a special clause that will vary the rent from one period to another, use the average rental for the lease term.

Always convert all leases, the subject property included, to net leases. This means that, in addition to the basic space rent, the tenant must also pay all operating costs connected with the property, such as taxes, insurance, utilities, normal repairs, and maintenance. This leaves the owner responsible only for property management and structural repairs. Never get into the great harangue about who pays what and why. Finally, be consistent throughout. What you do for one property, do for all, the subject included.

Income Analysis

Income is analysed separately according to quantity and quality. You must establish the effective gross annual income over the remaining economic life of the property. That is, for how many more years can the property be profitably and feasibly used?

Quantity of Income

Quantity, or gross income, always expressed on an annual basis, is the total revenue that a property can generate from all sources when it is completely occupied. The principal sources are:

- minimum or base rentals received,
- overage (percentage) rents received,
- common-area costs received,
- parking-lot stall rentals,
- sign rental,
- amortization of tenants' improvements,
- operating costs charged to the tenants,
- laundry income (in an apartment block),
- potential income from vacant areas,
- miscellaneous income.

Quality of Income

The essential components of income quality are:

- length of lease(s),
- strength of the tenant(s),
- rent obtained in relationship to the market,
- present, historical, and future probable vacancy.

Length of Lease

A longer lease is not necessarily better. Fixed-rent long-term leases provide no cushion for changes in interest rates or inflation. As the owner pays off the mortgage and inflation boosts the value of the property, the owner's equity grows. Meanwhile, the lease is locked in and the owner's return on this investment decreases proportionally. So long-term leases, even for strong tenants, should be tied to some form of escalator clause.

Long-term leases work for the owner in a declining or very stable market. Where the economy or rental rates are moving upward, the shorter lease is usually the better.

> A longer lease
> is not necessarily better.
> Fixed-rent long-term leases
> provide no cushion
> for changes
> in interest rates or inflation.

Strength of the Tenant

Triple A national tenants are always preferred to local independent entrepreneurs, particularly in a smaller centre where no individual tenant could be considered as an anchor. An investment's security improves with lessees who can afford to pay the rent during a downturn. Even with locals, drug stores are traditionally good, fad-type businesses bad. And it seems that every time the wind blows, three cafes open and four close.

Rent in Relationship to the Market

Rentals must always be related to the market. How does the rent compare to alternative locations? If the rent is relatively low, the lessor will not obtain a competitive rate of return on the investment. If the rent is too high, the lessee will negotiate for a lower rate at renewal time, driving down the investor's revenues. When forecasting rent after the lease expires or when the rent is revised or renewed, always use market rents, regardless of the rental presently paid.

Vacancy and Collection-loss Allowances

These fluctuate unpredictably and are often pure speculation. A fully occupied property does not necessarily stay that way. At the same time, high vacancy could be temporary, caused by poor marketing, high rent, sloppy maintenance, restrictive lease clauses, etc. In preparing a pro forma income statement, ignore most of these problems and introduce what is standard in the market area.

A vacancy rate should be inserted in an owner-occupied building. Owners go broke and vacate, as do the best of tenants. And not all tenants pay all of their rent. Tenants naturally turn over, and even if every space is filled immediately, you still need to allow for cleanup time, rental holidays, move-in allowances, partitioning allowances, and so on.

To estimate this rate, you must make one of four choices:

1. Use the annual average historical vacancy and collection-loss rate for the subject property, going back at least three years, preferably five.

2. Use a formula vacancy rate that may not apply to your market. Five percent is the all-time favorite. On larger, well-leased properties, some appraisers prefer to use two or three percent. Seldom is either correct.

3. Calculate a market rate. Consider the total area of the vacant spaces in the market area as a percent of the total leasable. While relevant, this takes considerable — perhaps too much — time and effort.

4. Develop a market vacancy rate that forecasts the future. Operating history provides only a guide.

Calculating Effective Gross Annual Income

Take the gross annual income, at a 100% occupancy level, based on a combination of market and contract rentals, for the full projection period. Then subtract the vacancy allowance expressed as a percent of the gross annual income.

The first part of the income and expense formula is:

- Gross annual income at the 100% occupancy level,
- Minus vacancy and collection loss allowance,
- Equals effective gross annual income.

Operating Expense Analysis

In the income and expense statement, particularly for the larger property, you may encounter expenses grouped under such headings as management, utilities, and maintenance.

Operating Costs

You must distinguish between operating costs and capital costs. Charge as an expense item only operating costs. These are:

Management:
- manager's salary,
- employees' salaries and benefits,

- auto and travel expense by property employees,
- management fees (other),
- payroll service charges,
- office expenses,
- office telephone and utilities,
- miscellaneous costs.

Fixed expenses:
- property taxes,
- insurance,
- leased areas' utility costs (heat, lights, power, water, sewer),
- common areas' utility costs,
- vacant areas' utility costs.

Building maintenance:
- all building maintenance and repairs,
- salaries and expenses of maintenance staff,
- damage repairs,
- painting and decorating,
- maintenance of mechanical systems,
- cost of service contracts on equipment,
- miscellaneous costs,
- janitorial and sanitary supplies.

Public area maintenance:
- parking lot maintenance,
- marking parking lot,
- paving,
- yard equipment repairs and maintenance,
- snow removal,
- traffic signal maintenance,
- police security,
- sign maintenance,
- trash removal,
- extermination,
- miscellaneous.

Advertising and merchants association:
- advertising and contributions,
- miscellaneous.

Administrative and general:
- legal and audit, other professional fees,
- office supplies.

Capital Costs (Not to be Included)

- Initial cost of construction
- Additions or major renovations to the building
- Acquisition of additional property
- Replacements and upgrading not considered as maintenance

Capital costs are either part of, or added to, the capital base. The operating or pro forma statement of the property does not consider them.

We are determining property value through a capitalization process. That means we will not look at debt service interest and principal and capital recapture or depreciation. In practice, except for comparative property analysis and feasibility studies, appraisers always work on a before-income-tax basis.

An important point that will be frequently repeated:

> ***Real-estate appraisal is always done before payment of income tax;***
> ***business valuation is always done afterward.***

Next, simplify the accounting process. It might seem impossible to reconcile different entries from different years, constantly jump back and forth from cash to accrual accounting, and stay on top of the general discordance that creeps in. But when comparing properties, consistency is a must. You need to group direct operating costs and disregard irrelevant expenses.

Property Management

Property management includes accounting and staff costs. Most professional property managers charge a standard fee of five percent of the rental amounts received. For this, they collect the rents, pay all bills, supervise repairs and maintenance, oversee the property, and regularly report to the owner. Some fees include leasing of vacant areas, while others charge another fee for this service. If the owner manages or occupies the property, you still need to insert this fee as an expense. Nothing is free.

Net Lease Chargebacks

In these cases, the property owner pays the building and common-area costs, but charges them back to the tenants. The property owner's only net expense is her fair share for unoccupied spaces. Use the same percent of the total annual cost as the vacancy and collection-loss allowance, plus any expenses that are identified for vacant areas only. The property pays its proportional share of:

- building heat, water, and sewer,
- property taxes,
- property insurance,
- parking lot maintenance,
- parking lot and sign power,
- trash removal.

Structural Reserves

Most leases contain clauses by which the lessor is responsible for structural maintenance. He must, for instance, repair the leaky or sagging roof and the exploding furnace. Still, most leases are pretty vague about what structural maintenance exactly covers. Read the lease. Who pays for painting and repairs to a space after a tenant has vacated? Although most leases stipulate that the lessee has to leave the premises as they were found, this seldom happens. New tenants almost always insist on some upgrading, or at least a paint job and clean rugs.

...most leases are pretty vague about what structural maintenance exactly covers. Read the lease.

Use the subject's historical average, or at the minimum a flat-rated annual amount. An annual rate of twenty-five cents per square foot of gross leasable area is popular. Still, this is the minimum and assumes a new structure in excellent condition. This amount should be doubled or tripled for an old or creaky building.

Expense Items Not Included

Disregard the final group, which can be capital costs or the expenses of the owner, both unrelated to the operation of the property. Valuation is made assuming no debt or depreciation, which is often a legal fiction. Do not include:

- bank charges and interest,
- depreciation,
- mortgage interest (and reduction of principal),
- professional fees,
- income tax.

The net operating income to the property is always based on so many dollars per annum, before long-term debt service, depreciation, or income tax.

The property's net operating income (NOI) is capitalized into an estimate of market value. Capitalization can be direct, on a yield basis, into perpetuity, or by use of a residual technique. It can be based on the NOI for one year only, or as the present net worth of the income stream for the projection period, plus the value of the reversion.

The income and expense formula is now expanded to:

- Gross annual income,
- Minus vacancy and collection loss allowance,
- Equals effective gross annual income,
- Minus operating expenses,
- Equals net operating income, before debt service, depreciation, or income tax.

Next, obtain and apply the capitalization rate to the net operating income.

> The net operating income
> to the property
> is always based on
> so many dollars
> per annum,
> before
> long-term debt service,
> depreciation,
> or income tax.

THE CAPITALIZATION PROCESS DEFINED

"The process of reducing to net present value a series of anticipated future earnings. Also defined as the process of estimating the value of an asset by the use of a rate that represents a proper relationship between the asset and the net earnings that it is projected to produce."[3]

This is the process of converting future income into current value. Here is the valuation formula:

$$\frac{I}{R} = V \text{ or } \frac{\text{Net Operating Income}}{\text{Capitalization Rate as a Percent}} \times 100 = \text{Value}$$

(Note: the $\times 100$ converts a decimal into a percentage.)

Capitalization Rates

The Capitalization Rate Defined

"The combination or sum of a discount rate and a capital recapture rate. Includes both return on and return of invested capital. Usually expressed over a finite term during which all invested capital will be returned to the owner."[4]

A capitalization rate includes interest (return on investments) plus recapture or depreciation (return of the invested capital) and/or debt amortization. "Recapture," means the return you can expect in the future. "Depreciation" refers to what is already happened. Accountants use the term "amortization" for both, but real-estate appraisers prefer "recapture" and "depreciation." That way this does not become mixed up with periodic mortgage payments.

A capitalization rate is both return on and return of capital, while a discount rate is only the return on, or interest. Many people confuse capitalization and discount rates, but do keep them straight. Capitalization, a mathematical process, finds value through a process of discounting cash flows.

Capitalization Methods

Although capitalization can be performed through either the direct or the yield method, we will consider only the direct.

Capitalization Rate Abstraction Procedures

The two most common ways to abstract a capitalization rate are:

- From the market.
  - use of a market-abstracted overall capitalization rate,
- the mortgage-equity concept (also called band of investment).

Although not really a capitalization rate, the gross income multiplier is frequently considered in the capitalized income approach.

Factors Affecting Capitalization Rates

Capitalization rates are based on both internal and external factors affecting the property. External factors are beyond the control of the owners or the property itself. You should look at, for example, governmental monetary policies, local economic conditions, demand, overbuilding, vacancy rates, and competitive rental structures. Management can control, or at least influence, internal factors.

These market influences, and others, can affect capitalization rates:

1. The prevailing interest rates of the day, primarily the bank prime lending rate, ease of obtaining credit, and the money market in general. In major investment properties and multimillion-dollar developments, changing foreign exchange rates and stock market trends are reckoning factors.

2. The general trend in interest and capital market rates. Are they increasing, decreasing, or stable? Long-term AAA Bond rates often provide a good directional guide.

3. General economic and market conditions. What is the current political climate? How will the rates be affected by a change of government, or government policies? Are we in an inflationary, disinflationary, or stable period?

4. Local economic and market conditions. What is happening in town? Are people building, buying, selling, or leasing? Is there a surplus of any type of property on the market? Are vacancy rates at an acceptable level? Can the present rentals service the debt and provide an adequate return on the investment? What is the future?

Capitalization rates are based on both internal and external factors affecting the property. External factors are beyond the control of the owners or the property itself.

Management can control, or at least influence, internal factors.

Subject property influences include, among other things:

1. The type, age, condition, location, and longer-term prospects of and for the subject property.

2. The stability of the tenants in the property. Length of leases from AAA tenants. A property leased to national AAA tenants will be smiled upon by financial institutions and investors alike. All others must necessarily follow.

3. Competition in the marketplace. How long does it take to rent a vacant space? Look at demand and vacancy rates.

4. Rentals being obtained per square foot. Are they competitive with alternative space? Are the tenants paying their rent?

Other Considerations

Market lag and trade-off are worth noting.

Market lag: Because of the stabilizing effect of longer leases, capitalization rates lag behind interest rates and the capital market by at least six months on mid-sized investment properties and up to one year on the larger ones. You cannot change rents in any investment property every time the interest rate changes.

Trade-off: When mortgage or bank prime interest rates increase, investors seem generally prepared to accept a lower equity yield rate. When rates decline, investors usually want more — or, as is said in the stock market, now is the time for profit taking. This constant trade-off creates a greater stability in real-estate capitalization rates than you will find elsewhere. Further, the theory of negative covariance states that stock and real-estate prices move opposite to each other. When one goes up, the other moves down. I will not delve into any more detail here, but there just might be something to it.

It all comes down to:

- current interest rates that will attract mortgage money,
- available ratio of mortgage money to fair market value,
- full mortgage amortization term available at the time,
- market conditions, demand, and vacancy rates,
- prospective yield that will attract equity investment,
- competition with other forms of investment,
- anticipated market changes during the projection period.

> Because of the stabilizing effect of longer leases, capitalization rates lag behind interest rates and the capital market...

> When mortgage or bank prime interest rates increase, investors seem generally prepared to accept a lower equity yield rate.

The Gross Income Multiplier

The gross income multiplier expresses the relationship between the gross annual income and the value, or selling price, of a property. This is to say that a property has a value of, or has sold for, so may times its total revenue.

This may be expressed as so many times the potential gross annual income at the 100% occupancy level, or it may be based on effective gross annual income, which is potential income less actual or allowed-for vacancy. In all cases, you do not consider the operating expenses or the net operating income of the property. The ratio is based on collections or projected revenues only.

Which to choose? Potential or effective gross annual income? Well, that depends totally on the structure of your comparative data. If your comparables' financial information is based on potential income at the 100% occupancy level, then this is how you should examine the prospect property. If your comparables use actual receipts, then start with the effective gross annual income. Just be consistent. What you do in one place, you must do in all.

The Procedure

Calculate the gross annual income and multiply it by the gross income multiplier. If the income stream varies, use the annual average for the projection period.

This method of determining market value produces only an approximate amount. You can never reconcile this method's fundamental weaknesses, all of which are important and reduce the element of accuracy. It does not consider, for example:

- the subject's actual or potential vacancy rate,
- operating expenses,
- the age or condition of the building,
- whether rentals meet the market rates,
- the property's income growth potential,
- any surplus land.

Although you might come up with a reasonably accurate value estimate, usually you have to accept that the gross income multiplier is an unreliable tool.

Market-Abstracted Capitalization Rates

For the average business buyer, who might not know what to look for or where, it is difficult to obtain comparable sales and then mine them for credible data. Even professionals struggle with this. If you do it only partly, or incorrectly, you will wind up confused and with bad information. On the other hand, if you can obtain all of the required data, this method is a breeze compared to the others.

With this procedure, you look into the marketplace, analyse several comparable sales, and pull out an overall capitalization rate. This rate is not subdivided, nor built up, as with the mortgage-equity concept. The resulting single, overall rate combines the equity dividend rate, equity gain through debt amortization reduction, and gain or loss through inflation or disinflation and changing market conditions, which together make up the total return to equity. To qualify:

- the comparable sale must be bona fide,
- it must be arm's-length (that is, no interfamily deals),
- it must be voluntary, not forced,
- it must be recent, particularly in an unstable market,
- it must be of substantially the same type of property, preferably in the same area, in the same town or city,
- the appraiser must be privy to all details concerning the sale including:
  - gross annual income,
  - vacancy, both in the comparable and the market,
  - stability of tenants,
  - operating expenses,
  - net, pre-tax operating income,
- the price is unaffected by deferred maintenance, beneficial financing, adverse or unusual conditions, etc.

Market Rate Strengths

- it is based on actual sales, making it more representative of the marketplace,
- it is easy to calculate,

> For the average business buyer, who might not know what to look for or where, it is difficult to obtain comparable sales and then mine them for credible data.

- it does not require forecasting of future income, future financing, or consideration of special deals.

Market Rate Weaknesses

- the required information from the comparable sales might not all be available or correct,
- the method does not account for existing or probable financing. (very few properties are bought for all cash, which this procedure assumes),
- the method does not separate return on capital from return of capital,
- it does not provide any investment analysis information,
- the method works only in an active market where you can find sufficient comparable sales (one sale does not make a market).

The Mortgage-Equity Concept

For all practical purposes, these common terms all mean the same thing:

- mortgage-equity formula,
- band of investment,
- weighted average cost of capital.

Here, the capitalization rate is the weighted average of the risk and recapture rates, divided between the debt service requirement and the required net return on the equity portion of the investment, the total equalling 100%. Some analysts prefer to use a cash-on-cash equity dividend rate, then add or subtract for other gains or losses.

Mortgage Constant Defined

"The capitalization rate for debt: the ratio of the annual debt service to the principal amount of the mortgage loan. A mortgage constant maybe calculated on the basis of the initial mortgage amount or the outstanding mortgage amount; also called mortgage capitalization rate."[5]

Simply stated, the mortgage constant is the repayment of one dollar, interest and principal, for the amortization period of the mortgage. It can be calculated on either the original amount or the outstanding amount of the mortgage.

Cash-on-Cash Defined

"The ratio of annual equity income to the equity investment; also called the equity capitalization rate, cash flow rate, or equity dividend rate."[6]

It is the return that the investor obtains on the cash investment. It does not include equity built up through amortization or inflation.

Do not confuse the equity dividend rate with the equity yield rate. Equity yield combines equity dividend, equity gain through debt reduction and inflation, and loss by disinflation.

Investment analysts, bankers, accountants, and most appraisers prefer the mortgage-equity method. Because it relies less on historical data, it can be made more current. It is also less speculative. Fewer unrelated factors and variables enter the exercise because only the equity yield rate is subject to personal judgment.

Investment analysts, bankers, accountants, and most appraisers prefer the mortgage-equity method. Because it relies less on historical data, it can be made more current. It is also less speculative.

Moreover, investors and lenders understand it. As a yield rate, additional to the cash-on-cash dividend, it considers equity built up through debt reduction, and gains or losses created by inflation or disinflation. The investment community seldom segregates these last two points, and accepts them as facts of life and factors them into the base rate.

The Formula

The debt portion is easy. Just phone several mortgage companies to obtain the current rate, longer-term rate forecasts, amortization periods, and applicable balloon dates. Use a longer-term more stabilized rate, which may not be the rate of the day. If interest rates are noticeably wobbly, take extra care.

The equity portion is more difficult. Examine completed and financed sales. As a buyer, a good guide is what you anticipate, not what others have settled for. Generally, equity yield rates are all over the map, so check with investors to see what they expect. Remember market lag and trade-offs. Investors assess risks individually, weighing the various factors that make up the capitalization rates. Still, it is always a trade-off between desired return and measured risk. The higher the risk, the greater the anticipated return. There is no pat formula. Often the equity yield rate is gut feeling, an overall reaction to the market, based on your experience, or because someone told you what is required for this or that property to make economic sense.

The Calculation

Assume that a first mortgage can be arranged for seventy-five percent of the value of the target property, at a 7.50% interest rate, amortized over twenty-five years. If the term or balloon date is shorter, always use the full amortization period. Somehow, although capitalization lasts into perpetuity, the market takes for granted that all properties are sold or refinanced every five years or so. As it is common for monthly payments to be made, use the monthly constant times twelve.

Assume that the equity yield rate, as determined from your investigation, is twelve percent. This will be for the remaining twenty-five percent of the investment.

Capitalization Rate:

Mortgage: Annual Constant	$0.088868 \times 75\% =$	0.06651
Equity Yield: Cash-on-cash	$0.120000 \times 25\% =$	0.03000
Rate Total:		0.09651
	$(\times 100)$ or	9.65%

Capitalization Methods

If one year's NOI is capitalized into an estimate of value, the procedure is quite simple. Remember the formula:

$$\frac{\text{Net Operating Income}}{\text{Capitalization Rate}} \times 100 = \text{Value}$$

Assume, for this demonstration, that the value of the appraised property is based only on the capitalization of the projected NOI for the next year. This assumes capitalization into perpetuity. As such, you do not have to worry about a specific reversionary factor.

$$\frac{\text{Net Operating Income \$ 100,000}}{\text{Capitalization Rate: 0.9651}} \times 100 = \$\,1,036,269$$

Rounded To: $ 1,036,000

A projected variable income stream complicates things a bit. You have two choices:

1. Discount the annual NOIs individually for the projection period and add to them the net present value of the reversionary factor.

2. Average the annual income streams for the projection period. This is direct capitalization into perpetuity.

Fixtures and Equipment

When determining the value of fixtures and equipment that are a part of the real estate, and not that of the business, you should probably prorate the rent between the premises space and the equipment. To establish value, the equipment rent can be capitalized using the same procedure as for the land and building; that is, separately capitalize its designated rental portion into an estimate of value. Due to a shorter economic life, thus a higher rate of depreciation, the equipment would carry an increased capitalization rate. If you continue with the same 7.50% interest and a 12.00% equity yield rate that was used to calculate an overcall capitalization rate of 9.65% for the real estate, then add a 6.67% recapture rate for the equipment, you come up with 16.17%. By this method, you can determine a separate value for the equipment. Unlike the other assets that are part parcel of the real estate, the equipment is a segregated portion of the whole. However, the 9.65% already included a portion for capital recapture. If we assume a remaining economic life of the property of forty years or so, as the land does not depreciate, the calculated rate should be reduced by approximately 2.00% to 14.17%.

If the equipment is being included with the value of the whole and you do not need to determine its separate value, then you must use the higher level of depreciation. Use the value found in the cost approach and deduct the appropriate depreciation, in dollars, from the NOI. Capitalize the residual income the same as before, that is, where no equipment is involved. Now the equipment becomes a part of the value of the whole, unsegregated from the other assets.

Now that you have seen how to do it the hard way, the easiest — and it works equally well except where equipment is a major value component — is simply to add the depreciated value of the equipment, in one sum (the same one you calculated in the cost approach), to the income value estimate.

Tenants' improvements, as supplied by the owner, would be a part of the building in the both the cost and comparative sales approaches. Include and amortize the installation costs in the rent in the income approach. In the Income Approach, though, these costs must be amortized during the first term of the lease agreement; the present tenant might not renew his lease, and you can never assume that the improvements will have any residual value to a subsequent tenant.

Tenants' improvements, as supplied by the owner, would be a part of the building in the both the cost and comparative sales approaches.

In the Income Approach, these costs must be amortized during the first term of the lease agreement;

RECONCILIATION OF THE THREE VALUE ESTIMATES

If you have completed all three approaches, you probably have three very different value estimates. In a declining market, the cost approach sets the upper limit of value; in a rising market, it is the comparative sales value estimate. Because of the stabilizing effect of longer-term leases and interest rates, the income approach is most reliable for commercial and investment properties. The other two add supportive and background data. Still, in the final analysis, all three only interpret the market, and the actual market should always be your final guide.

THE LAST WORD ON REAL ESTATE APPRAISAL — FOR NOW

There is no intention to make you an appraiser — just show you how it is done. If in doubt, and you probably are, it may be best to hire a qualified professional. Besides, most lenders insist upon it.

References

[1] The Appraisal Foundation. (1998). *USPAP*. Chicago, IL: The Appraisal Foundation.
[2] The Appraisal Institute. (1993). *Dictionary of real estate appraisal*. 3rd Edition. Chicago, IL: The Appraisal Institute.
[3] Ibid.
[4] Ibid.
[5] Ibid.
[6] Ibid.

Chapter 5

INTRODUCTION TO THE VALUATION MODEL

THE PURPOSE OF THIS CHAPTER

FROM this point forward, except for the last three chapters, a flip-flop procedure will be employed. First, I will introduce the theory and why it should be done, detail the methodology, then apply it to the model, step by step. I will also inject unique market conditions to help familiarize you with situations a business buyer or appraiser might encounter. The exercises are not made any more complicated than you would find in real life, nor so simple that it serves no purpose.

The model selected is a typical fast-food restaurant in a smaller city with a fluctuating local economy. This model is favored because it is often challenging to pinpoint the line separating a restaurant's real-estate value from its business value. And among small businesses, restaurants are frequently traded. Everyone wants to sell food. If you learn to place a proper value, or price, on an existing restaurant, then you should be able to place a value on any small business. Businesses differ only in their individual characteristics and contributors to value. They all follow the same pattern and use the same valuation methods.

In this chapter, only limited analysis is provided. That will come step by step, segment by segment, in future chapters, starting with Chapter Six.

AN OVERVIEW OF THE FAST-FOOD INDUSTRY

Born during the 1920s with the development of the automobile, the fast-food restaurant dominates today's food services industry. Still, it did not become a tangible market force until after the end of World War II. Fast-food restaurants have evolved from the 1950s drive-in hamburger-and-ice-cream stand, complete with car hops, gaudy buildings, and excessive noise, to a more sedate industry. Many of today's principal players, the drive-through and sit-down variety, cost more than a million dollars to develop. These businesses depend largely on location, visibility, ease of access, advertising, promotion, speed of service, and consistency of product from one outlet to another. While the chain owners often chatter about their product's nutrition, this feature is a matter of opinion. What the owner really cares about is a volume of sales, plus an operational environment and quality of management, which together yield an equitable return on the investment. That is, the restaurant's profit must compare well with other investments.

Historically, fast-food restaurants have been among the leading growth industries of the United States and Canada. Because the first twenty or so years after 1945 demonstrated the most rapid growth, some observers feel that the industry peaked around 1965. This could be true. Yet Wendy's, the third-largest chain in North America (McDonalds and Burger King come first and second), did not start until 1967. From the early 1980s on, expansion has slowed. New construction is chiefly restricted to new subdivisions and replacing or enlarging existing properties. During the past decade, only the pizza sector and soup-and-sandwich bars have recorded noticeable increases.

From this point forward, except for the last three chapters, a flip-flop procedure will be employed. First, I will introduce the theory and why it should be done, detail the methodology, then apply it to the model, step by step.

Restaurants are a romantic type of business. They seem to be nothing but fun to operate. Yet restaurateurs have the highest rate of divorce, alcoholism, and mental breakdown of all business people. Restaurants are not merely businesses; they are a way of life. Restaurant operations look simple, but probably no business requires more management skills and hands-on attention than food service. People skills, cooking skills, and exotic recipes do not guarantee success in this business. Very few restaurants make money. Most start-ups close during the first year of operation, making room for a new crop.

Statisticians place restaurants into three main categories: quick-service, mid-scale, and upscale. Quick-service restaurants dominate the market. They hold 72.7% of the total market, followed by the mid-scale at 18.5%, and the upscale at 9.8%. Of the quick-service, or fast-food, category, the hamburger sector holds 51.5% of the market, followed by pizza at 16.2%, chicken at 10.2%, ice cream at 6.0%, and all others classes combined at 16.1%.

Chains and franchises have transformed the market. Franchises, a network of independently owned restaurants, all offering exactly the same quality of delivered goods, marketing style, preparation methods, management controls, buildings, and prices. Chains are identical, except that the restaurants are usually company-owned. Customer cannot tell the difference, yet are attracted to both because they know what the fare is before they enter the premises.

Chains and franchises, together, comprise over fifty percent of all classes of the restaurant market. Fast-food restaurants set the pattern, not only for the remainder of this industry, but for franchising in general. Although the franchise landscape is dotted with failures, franchised owners are much more likely to succeed than independents. For the most part, their sales volume is greater and profit margin higher.

Drive-in restaurants originally catered to the young swinger crowd, but their customer base is aging. Today, the fast-food industry is largely supported by smaller households and by women in the workforce who spend less time at home and have more money to spend than their parents did. People do not decide who makes supper, but rather who picks it up. Per capita spending is highest for people younger than twenty-five, lowest for people aged thirty-five to fifty-four, and high again for people over fifty-five. As a percentage of the total market, the middle age group spends the most. All patrons expect better service and better food. Simply stated, they expect more for their money.

This concept has not completed its evolution, and may never do so. Food services change. Every restaurant has to alter its menu, decor, ownership, or whatever at least once every five years. The public constantly wants something new and different. Visiting a restaurant, be it for pizza, a sandwich, or a gourmet meal, is often more than hunger satisfaction; it is a dining-out experience.

Future fast-food restaurants will rely more on the surrounding area and traffic generators, and less on their own ability to intercept the traffic that is going from one place to another. It will have to generate more patronage from the neighborhood. Menus will offer more variety. Tastes, whims, and new products will come and go. The industry will compete even more within itself. Attractive buildings, speed of service, and nutrition will gain importance. Profit margins will decline as more participants squeeze into the market. Superior management will be key. Theories of cluster marketing and cumulative attraction — restaurants generating trade for each other as well as for themselves — will be further tested. Each will offer something different from its neighbor. At the same time, not all concepts will survive. McDonalds, the pioneer of this industry, and more particularly of franchising, has not produced a winner every time. Yet, it will continue to dominate the fast-food market for many years.

Chains and franchises, together, comprise over fifty percent of all classes of the restaurant market. Fast-food restaurants set the pattern, not only for the remainder of this industry, but for franchising in general.

THE MODEL RESTAURANT

Let us assume the target restaurant is located in the city of Anytown, a Midwest community of 20,000 people, situated midway between two major markets that are 300 miles apart. Transients stop at Anytown and patronize its fast-food restaurants.

Anytown supports a large mixed farming area that produces coarse grains, wheat, corn, beef cattle, and hogs. It also sits in the center of a large oilfield, with the oil industry creating about thirty percent of the local employment. The community's fortunes and growth have varied according to the ups and downs in the oil industry.

The population includes a good mix of young students, working-class adults, and senior citizens. Many retiring farmers have recently settled here. Although the oil industry employs some highly paid persons, Anytown is mainly a blue-collar community.

In overbuilding for an anticipated oil boom that never happened, the city has shown an abnormally high vacancy rate in all classes of real estate. Two years ago, apartment occupancy sank below seventy-five percent, while the retail, commercial, and industrial space vacancy rate approached twenty percent. The thirteen hotels and motels averaged an occupancy rate below fifty percent. Retail store closures and all classes of business failures are above normal.

However, at this time, the restaurants, hotels, motels, and apartment blocks are enjoying a mini-boom. Everything is full. A $1.3-billion oil refinery is about sixty-percent completed. The project's construction phase, slated to last two and a half years, is now peaking, and over 3,000 workers are presently employed. After completion, in about twelve months, the permanent work force will dwindle to 350 people. Since the apartment/hotel/motel vacancy rate was so high, no camp was developed for the workers, most of whom come from out of town. They swarmed into all living accommodations, driving vacancy rates down to zero, a situation that will continue for another year or so. When the construction is completed, however, except for the permanent staff and perhaps some secondary industry still to be created, everything will return to the norm as of eighteen months ago.

Although the subject restaurant lost money during its first year of operation, it has posted sales and profit gains for each of the past two. Yet this current level will not continue. When the construction project closes, the sales volume will plummet. You must not base the restaurant's value on its present level of sales and profit, nor should you project it to increase.

> You must not base the restaurant's value on its present level of sales and profit, nor should you project it to increase.

LOCATION OF SUBJECT BUSINESS AND NEIGHBORHOOD FACTORS

Located on the highway in a community that is a natural stopover between two major markets, the subject restaurant intercepts traffic going from one place to another. In this situation, site visibility, size, and safety and ease of entry and exit are all important. The subject, like all businesses, is also parasitic, drawing some trade from its immediate surroundings. Here, this trade would come from the city itself and the recent construction workers. Consider both the interceptor and parasitic factors when detailing neighborhood and locational influences, especially when projecting future income levels.

The subject restaurant is located on the north side of the highway, towards the east end of the city. The highway, a main internal traffic artery, bisects the city into two halves almost equal in size. The commercial sector is concentrated in the north and west, residential both south and north. The major industrial sections are well to the north, but the incomplete oil refinery is about one mile directly east. This is the first restaurant a traveller meets when entering Anytown from the east.

Immediate highway neighbors are the usual: commercial entities, hotels, motels, gas stations, restaurants, and so forth.

COMPETITIVE ANALYSIS

I will not repeat the requirements of a competitive analysis that were detailed at length in Chapter Three, but do not skimp on this part of your pre-purchase investigation. More businesses fail because of underestimating the competition than for any other single reason.

Most entrepreneurs and developers think that their mere presence will prompt all competitors to fade into the sunset. Quite the reverse usually happens. The competitors do not die, they do not fade away, they get meaner and tougher. (I know I have said it already, but I have seen too many buyers discount this.)

Ideally, the analysis of each direct competitor should detail:

> Most entrepreneurs
> and developers think
> that their mere presence
> will prompt all competitors
> to fade into the sunset.
> Quite the reverse
> usually happens.
> The competitors do not die,
> they do not fade away,
> they get meaner
> and tougher.

- size and type of restaurant,
- seating capacity,
- age and condition of property,
- amount of on-site parking,
- sources of patronage,
- any special attractions or detractors,
- franchise or chain affiliation, if any,
- special theme and/or decor,
- takeout service,
- liquor licence, if any,
- price structure, type and class of menu,
- management qualities,
- levels of service,
- whether the restaurant is for sale or was recently purchased,
- whether any restaurants in the area have recently sold or gone broke,
- whether any competitor plans to expand or renovate,
- newly opened, under construction, and proposed competitors.

When summarizing, always include the subject as a competitor. This way, you can keep better track of it. Always include captive restaurants, such as those in office buildings, in-house cafeterias, golf clubs, private clubs, legions, and caterers.

Because this is solely a demonstration exercise, I have shortened this section to a summary of seating capacity. In actual practice, you should be much more comprehensive in your research.

With a population of 20,000 people, this amounts to one restaurant seat for every four persons. If the lounge seats are included, one for every 2.98 persons. This is well above the national average, which suggests that this small city is restaurated to death, which it is. The off-highway capture, farmers and travellers, accounts for at least fifty percent of the volume of most local establishments. Still, there has been an exceptionally high turnover of restaurants of all types, with some having recently gone bankrupt.

The dangers in not undertaking a comprehensive survey should be more apparent. In this very competitive market, longer-term growth potential is questionable. Volume increases, by anybody, must be at the expense of a competitor. At the same time, do not apply the statistics too broadly. Mark Twain once said there are liars and there are statisticians, and it is hard to tell the difference.

COMPETITIVE RESTAURANTS

	Seating		
	Cafe	Lounge	Total
Primary Competitors, Fast-Food Sector, Includes Takeout Only			
McDonalds	155		155
Hardee's	75		75
Arby's	112		112
Jack in the Box	88		88
Kentucky Fried Chicken	Takeout only		
Total	430		430
Secondary Competitors, Fast-Food Sector			
Taco Time	70		70
Tim Horton Donuts	40		40
Donut Hut	40		40
Donut Factory	40		40
Mr. Submarine	38		38
London Pizza	127		127
Pizza Hut	112		112
Total	467		467
Other Competitive Restaurants			
Hotels	1,029	593	1,622
Service Stations	349		349
Specialty Restaurants	786	299	1,085
Family-style Cafes	1,055	781	1,836
Shopping Malls & Captives	811	97	908
2 private caterers	Nil		Nil
2 Take-out-only Pizzerias	Nil		Nil
Total	4,030	1,770	5,800
Grand Total	4,927	1,770	6,697

SITE CONSIDERATIONS

Never accept without question the word of anyone else regarding the site and what is permitted thereon:

- Confirm the municipal zoning or land classification. Even if the building has existed for several years, it might not comply with all ordinances. If it violates any, you may not be permitted to modernise, renovate, or rebuild after a fire.
- Confirm the site size from a survey or map, or else measure it yourself. Real-estate agents are world-famous for providing incorrect dimensions. They seldom check.
- Consider anything, natural or otherwise, that blocks visibility.
- Consider ease of entry and exit.
- Detail the street surface, sidewalks, and curbs.
- Consider volume and speed of traffic, plus peak periods.

Never accept
without question
the word of anyone else
regarding the site
and what is permitted
thereon…

- Consider topographical conditions.
- Look at encroachments, easements, and power lines.
- What is the potential for flooding?
- Check soil and subsoil conditions.
- Could there be contamination? This is most important on old service-station and garage sites. The buyer is liable for the cleanup cost.

Because of the nature of the business, fast-food restaurant sites must be large, situated on a relatively high-traffic thoroughfare, have good visibility and easy access. The building rarely occupies more than ten percent of the site area and is usually less than one-third of the total value. Even though much of the space would appear to be "wasted" on parking, the owner may make more money by selling hamburgers, ice cream, or chicken from this site than by redeveloping it for a more intensified use. The rule-of-thumb optimum value distribution of eighty percent building to twenty percent land value does not work here. In these situations, real-estate economics take a back seat to the overall earnings capability of the enterprise.

Conversely, and it is common, some fast-food restaurants fail strictly because of location. Not every corner is ideal.

Conversely, and it is common, some fast-food restaurants fail strictly because of location. Not every corner is ideal. Maybe the street is too busy for people to change lanes and enter the restaurant lot, maybe the cars move too fast to enter or exit safely, maybe the site is too small or the visibility is poor or left-hand turns are prohibited. Whatever. If you could earn more money by redeveloping the site, then look at redevelopment. A study that weighs several alternatives could be worthwhile.

THE MODEL RESTAURANT: SITE SIZE & DESCRIPTION

Size

230.0 ft × 127.0 ft. less corner cut off = 29,000 sq. ft.

Description

The site is on the northwest corner of 100th Avenue (Highway 16) and 15th Street, a residential collector street. It sits at the grade level with both avenues, both of which are paved and have concrete sidewalks, curb cuts for access into the site, and concrete curbs and gutters. Drivers can see the site clearly for over one block away if approaching from the west and two blocks from the east.

Paving covers all of the site not occupied by the building. Concrete parking bumpers line the east side against the property line. A four-feet-high chain-link fence marks the rear of the site.

Two flush-to-the-surface catch basins direct excess water to the city storm sewer.

On-site parking can accommodate sixty automobiles.

DESCRIPTION OF THE BUILDING

Fast-food restaurant design aims to obtain the maximum utility in the smallest, cheapest space. These are usually very expensive buildings, far above the square-foot cost of a comparable commercial structure. The entire design caters to traffic flow and maximum efficiency. The designer works to move the greatest number of people through in the shortest time, without appearing to rush anyone — staff or customers.

Due to people's changing desires, restaurant structures must be flexible. Even though their customers turn over, fast-food restaurants still become obsolete. Some franchisors insist on regular upgrading for the premises. All demand a high level of maintenance. All designs must be flexible (so it does not need to be demolished), yet structured for maximum productivity. The menu board, for instance, is usually the focus of the restaurant. Cross-country chains and franchises plan standard, simple, functional, and conservative designs.

Not that many years ago, in northern climates, it was nearly impossible to finance a fast-food drive-in cafe. Lenders argued that business would disappear during a cold winter, and sales during the warmer months would never carry the restaurant through these lean times. They argued that these unique buildings, designed only to sell hamburgers, could not be used for anything else. They also cited the high failure rate of restaurants.

Today's indoor seating has conquered the winter problem. Designs are more adaptable to other uses. In some parts of the United States, a good design can be converted to a branch bank at little cost. The lenders' last argument, the failure rate in the hospitality industry, is still with us and probably always will be, even though some outlets have been fabulously successful.

In some parts of the United States, a good design can be converted to a branch bank at little cost.

THE APPRAISAL MODEL: THE SUBJECT BUILDING DESCRIBED

Type and Size

Freestanding, single-storey, above-average, five years old, 2,688 square feet, masonry structure with a full basement. This fast-food restaurant was constructed to the standard design of XYZ company-owned and -franchised restaurants.

Interior Development

The main-floor restaurant area seats seventy-six customers. The kitchen is divided into cooking and preparation areas, a side-window serving station, a front counter-servers station, janitor storage, and dry storage. Customers' washrooms are located off the stub hallway.

The basement houses the manager's office, a staff room with adjoining washroom, a furnace-utility room, a walk-in cooler, and an unfinished dry-storage area.

Condition of Building

This building is in excellent condition throughout. It was well-built, using above-average quality of materials. It has been well-maintained.

The building complies with the franchisor's requirements, and with fire and health regulations.

No structural deficiencies were noted.

Note to Appraisers: If true, always say that no structural deficiencies were noted — not that there are none. Some could be hidden.

FIXTURES AND EQUIPMENT

When considering any business, the buyer must carefully check the fixtures and equipment, machinery, or furniture. Establish who owns what, as well as what the real-estate price includes. This can be confusing. We recently had great difficulty convincing a client that he could not remove the air conditioning system and sell it separately. Anything that requires a mechanical device to remove — and a screwdriver or a pair of pliers is a mechanical device — belongs to the building. Still, some gray areas are subject to interpretation. For example, a kitchen range is equipment but the range hood or a furnace is part of the building.

Some equipment might belong to a supplier, who offers it for free as long as the store patronises that supplier. Coffee makers, soft-drink dispensers, and reach-in refrigerators — if you see a supplier's name on the equipment, question ownership. Other equipment could be leased or part of a conditional sales agreement.

If you buy a business in a rented building, carefully read — with your attorney if you have doubts — who owns the fixtures and equipment at the end of the lease. The landlord might well walk off with them, despite your having paid the seller a substantial sum for them. Many leases say that all improvements become a part of the premises.

> ...if you see a supplier's name on the equipment, question ownership. Other equipment could be leased or part of a conditional sales agreement.

FRANCHISE AGREEMENT

The restaurant operates under the XYZ franchise, which it holds exclusively for the subject's city and for a five-mile radius from its centre. It grants to the restaurant owner exclusive use of all of the XYZ marks, methods, trade names, procedures, and recipes.

The franchisee must follow the prescribed patterns, merchandising methods, promotions, pricing schedules, and all other procedures as laid down by the franchisor in its manual or as required from time to time.

The term of the franchise is twenty years, commencing July 1, three years ago, and expiring June 30, seventeen years from now. There is no provision for renewal or extension.

The franchise is personal to the owners of the restaurant. It can not be assigned or transferred. If the restaurant is sold, the buyer must reapply for the franchise. The franchisor cannot unreasonably refuse a new owner.

If the restaurant is offered for sale, the franchisor has first right of refusal to buy it.

Franchise and Coop Advertising Fees

Initial Franchise Fee:	$ 25,000
• Service Fee:	
– 1st 10 years	2.50% of gross sales
– 2nd 10 years	Fee to be agreed on, subject to a minimum increase of 2.0%
• National Advertising Fee:	
– All 20 years	1.50% of gross sales
• Administration Fee:	
– All 20 years	1.00% of gross sales
– Fee Total: 1st 10 years	5.00% of gross sales

OPERATIONS ANALYSIS

Consider the subject's operations. Look at the menu, hours of operation, sources of patronage, special attractions or detractions, management and staff, union contracts in effect or contemplated, infractions of health board and fire commissioner's regulations, and anything that will tell you what this restaurant is all about and particularly its position in the marketplace.

NOTES

_____

_____

_____

_____

_____

_____

_____

_____

_____

_____

_____

_____

_____

_____

_____

_____

_____

_____

_____

_____

_____

Chapter 6

INTERPRETING FINANCIAL STATEMENTS
(A Fast Walk Through the Jungle)

THIS is not a manual on accounting, nor does it cover every intricacy of financial statement interpretation. Very qualified people have already written dozens of excellent, affordable books on this topic. Having said that, if you want to know how much a business is worth, you have to understand how to read and interpret financial statements.

In this chapter I will briefly outline what complete financial statements should include, what to look for, and how to make a meaningful diagnosis. If you are not already a skilled accountant or financial analyst, you will at least be better informed by the end of this chapter. I will present only an overview and general references as to how financial statements can help you to place a value on a business.

Warning! I will violate some of the more sacred accounting conventions, but I will elaborate on this as we go along. In the meantime, please note that for the model, I have provided three years' worth of statements and analysis. Frequently only one year is produced, at times two, but never three. Additionally, I am not saying this is how a business should be run. In fact, several entries and allocations directly contravene good management practice. You will hardly ever run into this many infractions in one set of statements. But I repeat: I am talking about business valuation, not the principles of accounting. I want to show you what to look for, the reasons behind many financial statement inclusions and omissions, how to make meaningful interpretations, and leading questions that you should ask.

As a sample, I will use the statements of the model, Big Top Holdings Ltd., operating as ABC Franchised Restaurant. You will find some rationalizations here, plus more in the next chapters, where I will apply the numbers to the actual valuation exercise.

When you appraise any business, certainly before you even hint at its value, you must obtain, read, dissect, and ensure that you understand the financial statements. Too bad they read like gobbledegook for most of us. If you do not understand them, employ an accountant who does.

It is vital for you to be able to pick out the significant numbers and figure out how those numbers came to be. Get as much history as possible; for an established business, you will want statements from the past five or seven years, sometimes even ten, but never less than three. If the owner withholds them, cannot find them, does not have any, says they are confidential, or utters some other flimflam, run like the wind. This is probably a wide-open bear trap, waiting to sink its teeth into an unsuspecting creature. Never believe any nonsense about the statements being prepared only for the benefit of the government tax department, or that income is not recorded, or that the expenses were overstated. If you cannot see it, it is not there. Besides, if the owner lies to the government, he will also lie to you.

In one rare exception, you might give a company a second look even if the seller seems shifty about full financial disclosure. Here, you might think you are scoring a bargain. This is where you can buy the capital assets at far less than market value, or where the business has substantial unrealized potential. A distressed enterprise seldom provides accurate statements, or any at all. So much depends on what the seller wants to accomplish. From experience, I know that every day is Snow Your Friendly Neighborhood Appraiser Day. Potential buyers do not fare any better. So

> When you appraise any business, certainly before you even hint at its value, you must obtain, read, dissect, and ensure that you understand the financial statements.

base your income and expense projections on what you think the business should be doing, but keep your antenna up. All of the red flags are flying, and you are really sticking your neck out. If you are an appraiser, make sure your client knows that you are providing only your own projections, or estimates, not a record of what actually occurred.

HOW FAR SHOULD A CRITIQUE GO?

When a professional appraiser reviews financial statements to come up with a market value, she always asks herself, "How much detail should I provide in this critique?" Although some appraisers are trained financial analysts or accountants, most know only the rudiments of accounting and statement interpretation. If her knowledge is limited, she should appraise only the real estate, rather than estimate the value of the whole business. On the other hand, the appraiser need not write a multi-page dissertation on the strengths and weaknesses of the enterprise, or comment on the capability of its management. In fact, the professional should never venture into this minefield. Such opinions probably will not be accepted within the framework intended. If the review is too critical or too intensive, the analysis might show too much bias. The appraiser's personal likes and dislikes may modify the ultimate values.

I am not saying that an appraiser should not analyse or comment on the statements. Quite the contrary! An appraisal should include a detailed analysis and perhaps a different perspective on many of the allocations. It is just that an appraiser must always clearly focus on the purpose of the exercise and her educational limitations and abilities. Most important, she must never give seasoned opinions and sound business advice beyond her boundaries of knowledge. No buyer, seller, or lender should ever act on such ill-conceived advice.

A WORD OF CAUTION

Throughout this manual, particularly in this chapter, I am going to talk about that dreaded subject: income tax. I may even get stupid and relate some tax rules and how to apply them. Do not take my word for anything in the area of taxation. I am no tax expert, and neither is the publisher, nor do we claim to be. Also remember that tax rules and applications change every other day. Consult your accountant on all matters concerning taxation, and use only the most recent rules, regulations, and interpretations.

We are not tax experts. Verify everything said about income tax.

THE GAAP RULES

The statements represent a business's financial state of affairs at a specific point in time. They record only history and, as with all history, are frequently subject to the interpretation and bias of the accountant and the whims and account-juggling of management. Sometimes the statements are drawn up for the shareholders, sometimes for the bank, and sometimes for the tax department. Financial statements prepared by professional accountants usually meet with the GAAP (Generally Accepted Accounting Principles), but that is not always the best way to report for every single business. Just keep in mind that the financial statements show only

statements…record only history and, as with all history, are frequently subject to the interpretation and bias of the accountant and the whims and account-juggling of management.

results, not causes. Balance sheets do not reflect value, only cost, or cost less depreciation. The recorded actions and reactions of the business are normally historical — and in some cases fictional.

The information needed to determine a business's worth differs substantially from that needed for an in-depth management critique. In business appraisal, you do not have to know how to run the store to find its value. The extent of your analysis will largely depend on your existing knowledge of the enterprise. The additional information that you can extract will depend on your own ability, help from others, and your personal requirements. For example, I can tell you that food expenses in a sit-down, table-service restaurant should range between thirty-five and forty percent of sales. But I will not tell you how to achieve that, or why the present costs might be higher or lower. You will have to look for this information someplace other than the financial statements. It is still necessary, though, to look at the source of all incoming and outgoing funds. You have to verify and explain the origins of all reported sales, expenses, and profit.

> The information needed to determine a business's worth differs substantially from that needed for an in-depth management critique. In business appraisal, you do not have to know how to run the store to find its value.

FINANCIAL ANALYSIS REQUIREMENTS

The minimum financial statements that should be reviewed in detail, and interpreted, are:

- the balance sheet,
- the income statement,
- the statement of changes in financial position,

and where possible:

- any supplementary statements, such as sales and cost of sales analysis, that contain support data for the income and expense summary,

and always:

- a detailed reading and application of the notes to the statements. Always, these notes contain information pertinent to the analysis of the company.

THE NATURAL FLOW: LINKING STATEMENT TO STATEMENT

Accounting statements have a natural flow. All start from the income and expenses as recorded in the cash journals and synoptics of the company, or money that is simply put into or taken out of the cash register. These transactions are summarized on the income statement (formerly called the income and expense statement) and the statement of changes in financial position, terminating on the balance sheet. Then there are the notes that provide source and procedural information, or help the reader to analyse the figures. In double-entry accounting, an entry or its application recorded in one place can always be found elsewhere. All debits and credits must be equal, or balanced. An item appearing on the left-hand side of the ledger must also appear on the right.

CASH VERSUS ACCRUAL SYSTEMS

Every financial transaction and its result, which occurred during the accounting period, is summarized and classified somewhere in the three primary statements: the balance sheet, the income statement, and the statement of changes in financial position.

Some small businesses, not many, particularly ma-and-pa operations, still do their accounting on the old-fashioned cash basis, rather than on accrual. A certain amount of money comes in the front door, the bills are paid, and the remainder is profit. Accounts payable and receivable are kept in a ledger but not recorded as income or expense until received or paid. If, for example, the annual taxes were not paid, no expense for this item would appear. If only a portion were paid, only the amount retired would be recorded. Although the most simple of bookkeeping systems, cash accounting reveals only a small aspect of the transactions. It takes into account only cash flows, which do not correctly show whether the business is profitable or by how much. For this, you need an accrual system, which measures the complete financial performance of the business.

An accrual system would include the annual property taxes as a cost of doing business. If unpaid, the total amount would be recorded as an expense but offset by an accounts-payable entry. If the seller buys something for long-term use, the cost is prorated over the full useful life of the acquisition. For example, if the target business spends $1,500 every third year on staff uniforms, this would appear as a $500-per-year expense. The unexpended portion — $1,000 at the beginning of year two and $500 at the beginning of year three — would be recorded as inventory. Everything is thrown in one big bucket, so to speak, with what is lost one year is recovered in the next.

Sometimes financial statements are inconsistent. A company might flip-flop back and forth between the systems, using cash for one part of the operation and accrual for another. It might record the cost of taxes and insurance on accrual, but supplies on cash. Watch out for radical changes in income or expenses, as well as items that have been mysteriously left out. You will not find this very often in statements prepared by professional accountants, but if it does occur on selected entries, you will see it pop up year after year.

> Although the most simple of bookkeeping systems, cash accounting reveals only a small aspect of the transactions. …you need an accrual system, which measures the complete financial performance of the business.

THE MODEL RESTAURANT: FINANCIAL CONSIDERATIONS

This chapter introduces:

- the balance sheet,
- the income statement,
- the statement of changes in financial position,
- the notes to the financial statements.

The sales and cost-of-sales analysis, which is a normal inclusion will be fully detailed in Chapter Eleven, the Introduction to the Earnings Approaches.

With each statement that follows, a significant point related to financial analysis and determination of going concern value will be raised. Again, this is not a crash course in accounting or business management. No statement represents how an actual business should be run. For example, a good business owner would never reduce non-interest-bearing shareholder loans, and at the same time defer accounts payable and not pay his income tax. But our model, Big Top Holdings Ltd. operating as ABC Franchised Restaurant, is doing so.

I have designed these statements to pique your suspicion. Ask why. Dig deep. Why is the present owner doing certain things? You need to know. Your answer might mean the difference between the business's future success or failure.

In some chapters, I will continue to analyse and dissect the statements of Big Top Holdings Ltd. operating as ABC Franchised Restaurant. At that time, I will refer to specific inclusions, omissions, and concerns, particularly those that will affect the value of the business. Most of what follows complies with the GAAP rules.

THE BALANCE SHEET

This is the summary (or dumping ground) for all recorded assets, liabilities, and the retained earnings, which show the difference between the total assets and the total liabilities. If accounting is a wheat field, the balance sheet is the granary. It stores all the ins and outs of the business for its accounting life. It does not, however, provide the source of either income or expenses, but only summarizes the outcome of the transactions for the period. In other words, it provides the bottom line. The balance sheet presents a snapshot of a specific time, a precise moment on a given day, as though everything were suspended for a brief second. It is the end product of the entire accounting process. This is where the business is at.

Composition of the Balance Sheet

- Left Hand:
  - Assets: Current assets
                     Capital assets
                     Other assets (i.e., investments)
- Right Hand:
  - Liabilities: Current liabilities
                     Long-term liabilities
  - Capital Account:
                     Subscribed capital (paid-for shares)
                     Retained earnings/earned surplus

Assets

Assets fall into two specific categories: current and capital. Current assets can be converted into cash within the next fiscal year. (A fiscal year is a full twelve-month period but it need not start from January 1.) Capital assets (formerly called fixed or hard assets) cannot be converted to cash in the shorter term. Current assets are normally recorded at cost or market, whichever is lower; capital assets at cost, less the accumulated depreciation allowed by the tax department.

Liabilities

A current liability is any debt that must be paid off within the next fiscal year. So the next year's principal requirement on any long-term debt, such as a mortgage or lien, is included. Think about this. If the balance of a long-term liability must be paid during the current fiscal year, it becomes a current liability.

Appraisers take great liberties with current and long-term liabilities, taking them out, putting them back, and taking them out again. We also play innumerable games with other sacred accounting conventions, such as depreciation, short- and long-term debt service, and owner's wages and dividends. Quite frankly, in determining going concern value, we appraisers break many GAAP rules — enough to give most accountants gray hair.

The Capital Account

Under the GAAP rules, equity is classified as the money invested by the owners or shareholders at time of acquisition, plus any additional financial contribution and retained earnings.

Do not confuse this with shareholder's or investor's loans. These loans are cash lent to the company. They are usually fully repayable and considered either as a current or longer-term liability, depending on the repayment arrangement.

With small businesses and closely held corporations, the usual practice is to incorporate what is known as a thin company. Here, the subscribed capital is minimal, and most of the owner's investment is in the form of a shareholder's loan. In the event of windup, shareholder's loans are ranked with all other common creditors, while the owner's equity capital is the very last thing to be returned. With public corporations and stock-market promotions, you will encounter the exact opposite. Capital gains are earned as share values increase. With shareholder's loans, the promoters are entitled to interest only.

Retained earnings, also called earned surplus or retained surplus, are the accumulation of net, after-tax profits that have not been disbursed. In other words, they have been left to accumulate, usually to financially strengthen the company and contribute to its further earnings. Dividends usually come from the retained earnings. For this reason, management salaries and perks may not show up as a company expense.

Together, the paid capital and the retained earnings add up to the tangible net worth of the company, as recorded on the statements. Let me say it again: the company books only show cost or, in the case of capital assets, cost less depreciation, not market value. In a proprietorship or partnership, the capital account will normally be identified as owner's equity.

With small businesses and closely held corporations, the usual practice is to incorporate what is known as a thin company. Here, the subscribed capital is minimal, and most of the owner's investment is in the form of a shareholder's loan.

BALANCE SHEET

Big Top Holdings Ltd. operating as ABC Franchised Restaurant To End of Last Fiscal Year	Last Fiscal Year	2nd Last Year	3rd Last Year
ASSETS			
Current			
Cash	$ 7,456	$ 12,678	$ 3,814
Accounts receivable	10,990	5,247	–
Inventory (Note 1)	20,000	22,500	15,000
Prepaid expenses	4,537	3,628	1,765
Total Current Assets	$ 42,983	$ 44,053	$ 20,579
Capital and Long-term Assets			
Property & Equipment at cost	$ 688,873	$ 679,247	$ 668,685
Less accumulated depreciation	(77,079)	(52,450)	(27,605)
Total	$ 611,794	$ 626,797	$ 641,080
Receivable: Affiliated Co.	45,000	20,000	–
Total Capital Assets	$ 656,794	$ 646,797	$ 641,080
TOTAL ASSETS	$ 699,777	$ 690,850	$ 661,659
LIABILITIES			
Current			
Accounts Payable	$ 29,529	$ 31,043	$ 21,209
Wages Payable	25,000	–	–
Income Taxes Payable	34,555	15,124	–
Current Portion Long-term Debt	50,331	45,164	40,401
Family Loan Payable	50,000	75,000	100,000
Total Current Liabilities	$ 189,415	$ 166,331	$ 161,610
Fixed and Long-term			
Long-term Debt	$ 328,827	$ 374,001	$ 414,402
Less current portion	(50,331)	(45,164)	(40,401)
Total Long-term	$ 278,496	$ 328,837	$ 374,001
Shareholder's Loans	118,585	143,585	143,585
Total Long-term	$ 397,081	$ 472,422	$ 517,586
TOTAL LIABILITIES	$ 586,496	$ 638,753	$ 679,196
CAPITAL ACCOUNT			
Issued share capital	$ 100	$ 100	$ 100
Retained earnings	113,181	51,997	(17,637)
TOTAL LIABILITIES & NET WORTH	$ 699,777	$ 690,850	$ 661,659

WHY WORRY ABOUT THE BALANCE SHEET?

Unless you are acquiring the shares of the target company, and not assets as such, other than providing some support for the final value estimate, you really will not be that concerned about the balance sheet. It plays very little part in the valuation exercise. Your own balance sheet, liquid and capital assets, and debt load, will differ from that of the seller.

Still, you have to get at the numbers and what is behind them. How did the debits and credits sprout up? The balance sheet provides many of the answers. When you read between the lines, or add up, what is — and is not — in the statements, you can make some enlightening observations, such as:

- how the present owner is financing the operation,
- the state of his credit rating, his ability to pay bills,
- how much tax he owes,
- whether he has enough cash to meet contingencies,
- how much you might have to reimburse the seller for prepaid expenses (these seldom appear in the purchase contract),
- the amount of long-term liabilities, some of which you might want to assume.

Specific Questions: The Model Restaurant

Why the build up in accounts receivable? This is basically a hamburger stand, an all-cash business. Does he let friends and relatives run a tab? (These groups notoriously expect free food and service.) Maybe he is extending credit to one of the contractors on the new refinery.

What about accounts payable? Note that he paid off $50,000 of the interfamily loan in the past two years, and $25,000 on the shareholder's loan last year. The cash on hand has also declined. At this same time, he is invested $45,000 in another business. He could be bailing out (also called stripping), trying to get out his cash and investment before the business goes bankrupt. In a bankruptcy, shareholder's loans rank along with common creditors, a long way down the preferred treatment line. Yet although this company lost money during its first year, it was quite profitable during the past two. It should continue to make money. You definitely deserve an honest answer to these questions. Perhaps the owner is experiencing legal problems, marital problems, partnership problems, or difficulty with the city ordinances. Or maybe he just does not want to flip hamburgers. You need to find out.

The accounts payable are greater than the inventory by $9,529, and there is not enough cash to pay them. The owner is financing the day-to-day operation with suppliers' money. A little of this is good business, too much can hurt the owner's credit rating.

RATIO ANALYSIS

Although you probably do not need an in-depth, all-encompassing critique, you should always undertake a ratio analysis. It can help gauge the viability and staying power of a business and identify industry trends, strengths, and weaknesses. It will also detect unusual income or expense items, liquidity, redundant assets, management traits, and often future potential and problems. Sometimes it is just nice to know.

You can extract at least three pertinent ratios from the balance sheet. There could be several others that do not lend much to the valuation exercise, the sale of the business, or the ability of the buyer to make the deal. But these ones detail the owner's ability to pay the bills and continue with the enterprise:

- the current ratio,
- the quick ratio,
- the debt-to-equity ratio.

If a business cannot pay its bills, then creditors apply pressure, which triggers health problems for the owner, which may indicate a failing business, which brings about the desire to unload the whole mess onto some naive soul.

Current Ratio

This critical ratio provides the basic test for short-term solvency. Can the business pay its bills?

The current ratio is the total current assets divided by the total current liabilities, expressed as a factor of so many to one. Lenders used to consider any business with at least a 2:1 ratio a safe risk. Two to one means that two dollars are available to pay every one dollar in short-term debt. Although some quarters still consider 2:1 ideal, this high liquidity is often impractical and might suggest a cash redundancy. Probably a better rule is to have enough cash to pay six weeks' operating expenses. The ratio should be high enough to cushion the business during tough times, cyclical trends, or reversals. These downturns happen to all businesses from time to time.

As a point in passing, although I will play games and adjust the working capital when getting into the earnings value estimate, do not do it when calculating ratio analysis. Calculate it the same way the accountants do.

Big Top Holdings Ltd: End of Last Fiscal Year

$$\frac{\text{Current Assets} \quad \$ \ 42,983}{\text{Current Liabilities} \quad \$189,415} = \text{Current Ratio (4.41)}$$

(number in brackets (___) means negative or loss)

This basically says that for every dollar in current assets, this company shows $4.41 in current liabilities, money that must be paid out during the next twelve months. It has a negative working capital position, trouble paying its bills, and reduced capability to weather any prolonged downturn in business. What is causing this? Theft, poor management, misuse of funds, pressure from outside sources, a failing industry? Although we know, in Big Top's case, that this owner is stripping the company, most times the reason is quite different. That reason could affect the longer-term prospects, and ultimately the value, of the company.

The current ratio was a negative 3.78 to 1 in the previous year, and negative 7.85 to 1 for the first year. While a poor current ratio is common in the start-up year of any business, all three years signify a distinct shortage of working capital.

You might argue that the family loan should appear as a long-term liability, not a current liability. It amounted to $100,000 at the end of the first fiscal year, $75,000 at the end of the next one, and $50,000 at the end of the last year. In the notes to the financial statements, which follow, you will see that this loan is non-interest-bearing and no repayment terms were ever specified. If the agreement were more formal and the terms definite, this loan could classify as long-term. The problem with interfamily loans is that when relatives lend money, they seldom worry about getting it back. But soon, especially if the business starts to take a dive, they are pounding at the door for their bucks. Thus, a loan from friends or relatives is usually considered a current liability.

Without the interfamily loan, starting with Year One, the current ratio would have been a negative 3.24, 2.07, and 2.99 to 1, respectively. Although this is a vast improvement, the company still lacks working capital.

The Quick Ratio (Also known as the Acid Test)

Here, use the same rationale as for the current ratio, except that now you consider only cash, marketable securities, and accounts receivable; divided by the current liabilities. For a day-to-day operational basis, this ratio is probably more important than the current ratio.

$$\frac{\text{Cash: } \$7,456 \text{ and Accounts Receivable: } \$10,990 = \$18,446}{\text{Current Liabilities:} \qquad\qquad\qquad\qquad\qquad \$189,415} = (10.27)$$

The quick ratio shows that for every dollar in cash and accounts receivable, the owner has $10.27 in current debt. This is serious. Creditors are undoubtedly leaning on the seller. He could well be on COD with many. Even so, you must find out why and, before assigning a value, ask yourself if anyone else can really do all that much better.

A number of years ago I was offered a large motor hotel at a fire-sale price: only one dollar down, plus assumption of the debt. Even with the debt, the total price was cheap. The two previous owners had gone bankrupt. I kept asking myself what made me so smart that I could make it where others failed. I did not buy it. The next two owners also went bankrupt.

Debt-to-Equity Ratio

Nowadays, business debt is nearly inevitable, even if means that you just do not pay your utility bill until the due date. Accounts payable is the use of borrowed capital. It is all debt. How much debt can a business incur and still stay afloat? As the secret of being successful is making money on someone else's money, only a poor manager would not borrow from others.

Leverage, minimum equity and maximum debt can work well, compounding the investment into astronomical returns, when the business world is moving upwards. Even highly levered morons look good during periods of rapid inflation. But when the spiral heads down, high debt — specifically the inability to service that debt — turns yesterday's millionaire into today's welfare recipient. In other words, some debt is good, but too much is too risky. Let prudence be your guide.

The principle of leverage is simple. If you buy a property for all cash and the market increases by ten percent, you make ten percent on your investment. On the other hand, if you buy the same property for ten percent down, financing the remainder, and the market increases by ten percent, you double your investment. That is a return of 100%. But if the market declines by ten percent, in the first case you lose only ten percent of your investment, while in the second case you are wiped out.

The debt-equity ratio takes in all total debt, both short-term and long-term; divided by the shareholder's equity or tangible net worth.

As stated earlier, the $118,585 shareholder's loan is considered debt on the balance sheet. Still, for the purpose of valuation, and for this purpose only, you may wish to include anything owed to the shareholders or owners as equity. It is, after all, part of their invested capital. For an accurate picture of capital investment, return on equity, and return on assets in a privately held company, you have to count the money in both pockets, that of the shareholders and that of the business.

> The principle of leverage is simple. If you buy a property for all cash and the market increases by ten percent, you make ten percent on your investment. On the other hand, if you buy the same property for ten percent down, financing the remainder, and the market increases by ten percent, you double your investment.

Big Top Holdings Ltd.

	Last Fiscal Year End	2nd Last Year End	3rd Last Year End
Debt:			
Current Liabilities	$ 189,415	$ 166,331	$ 161,610
Long-term Debt	$ 397,081	$ 472,422	$ 517,586
Total Debt	$ 586,496	$ 638,753	$ 679,196
Equity:			
Share Capital	$ 100	$ 100	$ 100
Retained Earnings	$ 113,181	$ 51,997	$ (17,637)
Total Equity	$ 113,281	$ 52,097	$ (17,537)
Debt-to-equity Ratio:	(5.18)	(12.26)	No Equity

This means that, at the most recent fiscal year end, for every dollar in tangible net worth, or equity, this company had $5.18 in debt. At the previous year end it was $12.26, and in the first year of business, because of a loss, all equity was destroyed. Although this year is an improvement, the high ratio sounds the same alarms raised by the current and quick ratio analyses. This business is undercapitalized. Yet the owners saw fit to siphon a substantial amount of cash from the business and pour it into the interfamily and shareholder's loans, plus invest $45,000 in another business. How can this business withstand a prolonged downward trend or further capital withdrawals? Where is the safety margin?

In an earlier chapter, I discussed at length why business owners sell their shops. Being underfinanced is a principal reason, but you will never hear that from the owner. This you must extract for yourself.

THE INCOME STATEMENT

The income statement (formerly called the profit and loss statement, or income and expense statement) records the business's ability to make sales, control expenses, and generate profit. It summarizes all the business transactions during a stated accounting cycle. Although the income statement commonly covers a full twelve months, or one fiscal year, it can address any calendar period, terminating at the end of any selected day. Many companies use thirteen accounting periods of four weeks each, rather than twelve months. Moreover, it records total income, less the operating and non-capital expenses, and the difference, or profit, during the fiscal interval. Some also detail retained earnings.

While the income statement tells how well the enterprise is doing, it does not account for capital invested in the business, whether it be more equity or loans, share sales, principal reduction on debt, or the purchase or sale of any capital asset. The capital additions, reductions, and changes in owner's investment are recorded on the statement of changes in financial position. A combination of these two statements, income and changes, could be considered as a statement of cash flows. Together, they provide the bottom line.

Prescribed Reporting Order

Sales and Income

- sales and income from all sources, either one sum or categorized,
- cost of sales (opening inventory, plus purchases, less closing inventory),
- gross trading profit (total sales less cost of sales).

Operating Expenses

- fixed expenses,
- variable expenses,
- labor and management costs,
- interest on debt service, long- and short-term,
- capital cost allowances (depreciation),
- total operating expenses,
- income tax.

Net Profit

Statement of Retained Earnings (as applicable)

Usually the income items are listed in order of importance and the expenses alphabetically. It is always best to clearly identify and properly allocate all sources of income. If you cannot see the revenue sources (and this is common), you cannot make any meaningful conclusions, particularly if the business is in trouble.

The same is true for cost of sales. If they are not placed in categories on the income statement (and again, this is common), look for a separate cost-of-sales analysis. By examining the cost of sales and gross trading profit statement, you can compare the subject enterprise with industry standards and the competition.

Fixed costs remain relatively stable year after year. The volume of business does not really affect them. That does not mean they never fluctuate. Property taxes and insurance have a bad habit of creeping upward every year. The accountant will charge higher fees if the business volume, and hence the profit, increases. Variable costs are a direct or measurable percent of sales and income. Still, the line between fixed and variable costs is often thin.

I will talk more about this later, but you should consider the cost of labor and management separately. Here, you will see the greatest concentration of shenanigans on the part of the owner.

In later chapters, I will not consider interest on long-term debt and depreciation as part of the pro forma. At this juncture, as they filter their way through to the balance sheet and the statement of changes in financial position, interest and depreciation are both found in the income statement.

STATEMENT OF INCOME AND RETAINED EARNINGS

Big Top Holdings Ltd. operating as ABC Franchised Restaurant			
	Last Fiscal Year End	2nd Last Year End	3rd Last Year End
Sales & Income	$ 1,623,714	$ 1,273,228	$ 1,167,926
Less: Cost of Sales	757,642	561,493	549,644
Gross Trading Profit	$ 866,072	$ 711,735	$ 618,282
Operating Expenses			
Fixed Costs			
Telephone & Utilities	$ 37,114	$ 36,061	$ 35,227
Property & Bus. Taxes	18,506	21,227	19,074
Insurance, Licences, Fees	10,824	10,846	10,726
Equipment Rent	9,281	7,940	7,940
Total Fixed Costs	$ 75,725	$ 76,074	$ 72,967
Variable Expenses			
Accounting & Legal	$ 5,752	$ 5,358	$ 5,250
Advertising & Promotion	17,065	34,458	35,117
Bank Charges & Interest	4,506	3,166	4,622
Janitor & Maintenance	26,296	24,207	23,309
Office	8,462	7,016	11,273
Repairs & Maintenance	54,306	26,518	9,427
Restaurant Supplies	16,607	17,132	25,872
Travel & Automobile	8,611	6,890	4,867
Total Variable Expenses	$ 141,605	$ 124,745	$ 119,737
Payroll Costs			
Staff Wages & Benefits	$ 476,055	$ 320,358	$ 330,111
Workers' Injury Insurance	5,375	6,996	6,017
Management Salary	45,000	45,000	45,000
Total Payroll Costs	$ 526,430	$ 372,354	$ 381,128
Other Costs			
Long-term Interest	$ 24,196	$ 28,959	$ 34,482
Capital Cost Allowance	24,629	24,845	27,605
Total Other	$ 48,825	$ 53,804	$ 62,087
Total Expenses	$ 792,585	$ 626,977	$ 635,919
Net Before Income Tax	$ 73,487	$ 84,758	$ (17,637)
Provision for Income Taxes	(12,303)	(15,124)	Nil
Net Income	$ 61,184	$ 69,634	$ (17,637)
Retained Earnings			
Beginning of Year	$ 51,997	$ (17,637)	–
End of Year	$ 113,181	$ 51,997	$ (17,637)

THE TRACK RECORD

The value of any existing business, except for some professional practices and service businesses, is based on the underlying value of its tangible assets. That remains the rule, even if some of the following material may tend to convince you otherwise. The criteria is the ability of the tangible assets to generate sales and produce a profit? Let us say you build a multimillion-dollar hotel in the centre of the Sahara Desert. Only one camel train of Bedouins passes each year, and they bring their own tents, pack their own lunch, and do not drink. What is the hotel worth? Nothing! The assets do not hold value by virtue of their existence; they have to be able to earn income. Value is created, not by ownership, but by use.

Analysis of the income statement, as opposed to the balance sheet, has everything to do with the value of the business. The history of sales and profit — that is what makes up the business you are buying. Nothing else matters. Subject to identifiable trends the value of a going concern is always based on the assumption that history repeats itself. So go over the income statement with a magnifying glass. Look for source of income, expenses, profits, return on sales, and return on investment, then compare all this with industry standards. Bear in mind that the distinction between the contributory value of the assets and that of management is often blurry.

Thanks to the hyperbole of brokers, many business buyers wrongly think that they can outperform the present owner. The common line is: "Do not worry about what is happened. Look to the future. Consider the potential." This may be true and good. Still, while you gaze into the future, base your market value estimate on the track record. If you assign a value or bonus for potential that you cannot achieve without sinking more money into the business, then you are paying for, or including in the value, the same thing twice. Consider the following:

> If you assign a value or bonus for potential that you cannot achieve without sinking more money into the business, then you are paying for, or including in the value, the same thing twice.

Sales Volume Analysis

There is a natural tendency for any seller to exaggerate the sales volume and wax eloquent on the areas where no sales are being made, with a detailed explanation as to why not. Here, you really must read between the lines. Follow this old saw: "Believe nothing that you hear and only half of what you see."

Our model, a fast-food restaurant, would naturally operate in a restricted market. With a tightly controlled franchise, that market would be limited further by the product line, consistent pricing, and marketing methods. Although some of these queries might not apply to the model, a prospective buyer of most businesses should ask:

- How is the sales volume recorded? For example, some businesses record sales taxes with the sales, then offset them as an operating expense. Others net out both. The difference, according to the local tax rate, could be eight or nine percent.
- Are sales increasing or decreasing? Why? Is there any identifiable trend? What is influencing sales volume, now and in the future? Why do the customers come here? Or why do they not?
- Is the business increasing by at least the rate of inflation? If not, it is actually slipping backwards.
- Must the business grant extended credit to obtain patronage?
- Must it cut price to obtain patronage? One of our clients operated a gasoline-dispensing facility. Because his price undercut his competitors by about ten cents a gallon, his sales were triple what they should have been. Minor problem: He made friends, but no money, and so he went broke.

- Is the plant too big? A retail store, a manufacturing plant, or any domiciled business might have too much building for its present and projected use. Let me tell you about a hotel I used to own. Of the seventy-five rooms, only forty were ever filled. The restaurant could seat over two hundred diners, but one hundred seats would have been more than adequate. The tavern and lounge were also about twice as large as they needed to be. We could not increase sales, but we had to pay taxes, insurance, utilities, and maintenance on that large, underused building. Because of this, staff costs were too high. This hotel only broke even on operations. It could not service one dollar of debt.
- Do sales ever occur "off the books"? If yes, never consider them as revenue. They literally do not exist. (Accept only what the seller tells the tax department. Believe nothing else.)
- Can the business increase other income? In many types of business, other sales are expressed as a consistent percentage of the total revenue. For example, a hotel's restaurant and lounge sales follow the same pattern as room income. If they are too low, or falling, what is the reason? You might also look at:

  - the ratio of food to bar sales,
  - the average check, and any changes over the past year or so,
  - the average gross margin,
  - the percentage of takeout and/or delivery business,
  - seat turnover, particularly at peak periods,
  - sales volume per square foot,
  - sales volume per full-time-equivalent employee,
  - seasonal sales trends,
  - the gross margin per delivered item,
  - sales capacity compared to sales volume,
  - the percentage of returned items to sales.

> ...return on sales
> is always calculated
> on a cash-flow basis.

Return on Total Sales

This will tell you how well the business is doing as compared to industry standards. Calculate the net profit of the business before debt service, depreciation, or payment of income tax. This is to say that the return on sales is always calculated on a cash-flow basis. (The earnings approaches to market value are based on this, except that in their case the calculation comes after allowance for income tax.) Financing and the physical age of the plant do not affect income, this is the best way to rank the prospect among its peers.

The Model Restaurant	Last Fiscal Year	2nd Last Year	3rd Last Year
Total Sales & Income	$ 1,623,714	$ 1,273,228	$ 1,167,926
Net After-tax Profit	$ 61,184	$ 69,634	$ (17,637)
Add back			
Long-term Interest	$ 24,196	$ 28,959	$ 34,482
Capital Cost Allowance	24,629	24,845	27,605
Income Tax	12,303	15,124	Nil
Net Operating Profit	$ 122,312	$ 138,562	$ 44,450
Percent on Sales	7.53%	10.88%	3.81%

As this income statement does not include rental or debt amortization on the real estate, the profit for the most recent fiscal year is below industry averages, for the second-last fiscal year slightly below, and for the third-last year far below. They should float in the ranges of twelve to fourteen percent of sales. Rental or debt service on real estate normally is between five and seven percent of sales, which would reduce the net operating profit into the range of five to seven percent of sales. You will probably develop the value estimate from a pro forma statement, so this could be important to your valuation process. Any difficult could alarm management, creditors, a potential buyer, and probably a business broker who would not want to land her client in hot water.

Real-estate appraisers always conduct their valuations before tax; business appraisers after tax. If you are using information from different sources, ensure that the basis of calculation is consistent.

> Real-estate appraisers always conduct their valuations before tax; business appraisers after tax.

Other Ratios

You might find merit in some of the following when analysing the operations of the prospect enterprise. Yet most render little, if any, assistance when determining its going concern value:

- To calculate inventory turnover, divide total annual sales by average inventory. This is an excellent tool for management to see how well the inventory investment is performing. Comparisons can be made with industry standards. It can establish the ratio of dead or redundant stock to faster-moving items and help control cost of sales.
- Average collection period, another management tool, ensures that the working capital is working hard. It also urges the company to collect accounts and keep receivables low.

This section is short, but it is not as if I do not have anything further to say on the topic! In Chapter Eleven, Introduction to the Earnings Approaches, I will completely dissect the income statement. At that time, I will also develop pro forma as a part of the going concern valuation of the model business.

STATEMENT OF CHANGES IN THE FINANCIAL POSITION

This is the third of the Big Three statements, which together record all of the operating history of the enterprise for the accounting period.

This summary, also known as the cash-flow statement, details all of the entries that either do not appear on the income statement, or were posted directly from the journals to the balance sheet. That is, capital expenditures, the capital injections by way of equity or debt, and the retirement of the principal portion of the debt. It credits non-cash allocations, such as depreciation.

With the statement of changes in financial position, you can follow the entries year after year to determine the ins and outs, debt incurred, capital injections, repayments, capital purchases, capital payments, etc. The retained earnings or financial position of any company equals the accumulation of cash and assets year after year, which you will find by analysing this statement and the balance sheet.

If business owners pay themselves with dividends, or if the company, rather than they personally, pay the income tax, you will find that information here. This is not always a tax dodge, but instead is intended to show the company profits to be higher than they actually are. Although I will return to this later, for the time-being you need to add together the wages, salaries, perks, staff benefits, and dividends to determine the actual amount paid out. Check the total (not just the recorded wages to staff and management) against industry averages and the rule of common sense.

The following example wraps up with a summation of the changes in the cash position. This same summary commonly ends with "Working Capital at Beginning of Year" and "Working Capital at End of Year." This occurs more frequently for companies with high inventories and accounts receivable. For a more complicated business, or one with inventories or a greater variety of transactions, the analysis of working capital may aid the analysis more than that of cash only.

STATEMENT OF CHANGES IN FINANCIAL POSITION

Big Top Holdings Ltd., Operating as ABC Franchised Restaurant			
	Last Fiscal Year	2nd Last Year	3rd Last Year
SOURCE AND APPLICATION OF FUNDS			
Net Profit from Operations	$ 61,184	$ 69,634	$ (17,637)
Add (Deduct) Non-cash Items			
Capital Cost Allowances	24,629	24,845	27,605
Nonrecurring Income Items	Nil	Nil	Nil
Total Funds	$ 85,813	$ 94,479	$ 9,968
CHANGES IN WORKING CAPITAL COMPONENTS			
Accounts Receivable	$ (5,743)	$ (5,247)	–
Inventory	2,500	(7,500)	$ (15,000)
Prepaid Expenses	(909)	(1,863)	(1,765)
Accounts Payable	(1,514)	9,834	21,209
Wages Payable	25,000	–	–
Income Tax Payable	19,431	15,124	–
Family Loan Proceeds-Repaid	(25,000)	(25,000)	100,000
Total Working Capital Changes	$ 13,765	$ (14,652)	$ 104,444
FINANCING ACTIVITIES			
Shareholder's Loan-Payment	$ (25,000)	–	$ 143,585
Proceeds of Mortgage	–	–	375,000
Proceeds of Equipment Lien	–	–	75,000
Long-term Debt Reduction	(45,164)	(40,401)	(35,598)
Total Financing	$ (70,164)	$ (40,401)	$ 557,987
INVESTING ACTIVITIES			
Advances to Affiliated Company	$ (25,000)	$ (20,000)	–
Purchase of Assets	$ (9,626)	$ (10,562)	$(668,685)
Sale of Shares of the Company	–	–	100
Total Investing	$ (34,626)	$ (30,562)	$(668,585)
INCREASE (DECREASE) IN CASH	$ (5,212)	$ 8,864	$ 3,814
Cash – Beginning of Year	$ 12,678	$ 3,814	–
Cash – End of Year	$ 7,466	$ 12,678	$ 3,814

NOTES TO THE FINANCIAL STATEMENTS

This is where the accountant, or auditor, reveals the source of many of the statement's financial entries. As they help determine the going concern value of the business, often the notes are as important as the statements themselves. How was inventory counted and depreciation measured? To whom are they indebted and what are the terms of repayment? Have the directors lent the company any money, or has the company made any loans to them? Must they continually shell out more money to keep the business alive? What is the issued share capital and the actual investment or equity of the owners? How is the company incorporated?

Most important, the notes draw the reader's attention to any unusual circumstance involving the company itself, the relationship of the owners to the company, or its mode of operation. Often, though, these notes are "sanitized." That is, you will find out only what the owner wants you to know. You need to dig further.

BIG TOP HOLDINGS LTD. – ABC FRANCHISED RESTAURANT
NOTES TO FINANCIAL STATEMENTS
To end of – Last Fiscal Year

The notes that would actually appear are in quotation marks. Of course, they would identify the specific years, not last year or second-last or third-last, as I have done.

All financial statements are preceded by the accountant's engagement letter. This normally indicates the extent of the work undertaken. It usually points out that they have not unearthed anything that would lead them to believe the statements do not comply with the GAAP (Generally Accepted Accounting Principles). Despite exhaustive checks done by most public accountants, a review relies largely on what the client has provided. It does not constitute an audit, and therefore no audit opinion is expressed.

A fully audited statement includes more detailed terms and conditions. If completed by a Certified Public Accountant, or someone of equal qualification, an audited statement can always be trusted as one-hundred-percent accurate. Due to cost, however, small businesses seldom order up this type of statement.

> Despite exhaustive checks done by most public accountants, a review relies largely on what the client has provided. It does not constitute an audit, and therefore no audit opinion is expressed.

Significant Accounting Policies

"These financial statements reflect the following policies."

Inventory

"Inventory is recorded at the lower of net cost or realizable value. Cost is calculated on a first-in, first-out basis."

Capital Assets

"Capital assets are recorded at cost. Depreciation is calculated on the declining balance method using the following annual rates:

Building	3.175%
Fixtures and Equipment	15.0%
Paving	10.0%
Vehicles	20.0%
Motor Home	Nil
Goodwill Amortization	Nil

Assets acquired during the current period are depreciated at 50% of the above rates."

To keep this uncomplicated in the case of the subject company, Big Top Holdings Ltd., the motor home as not depreciated. This is considered as a redundant asset that will be deleted from and reinserted into the schedule of assets as we go along. Application of allowable depreciation will only make the matter more complex than it already is.

In the United States, there is no allowance for amortization of goodwill. In Canada, one can amortize seventy-five percent of purchased goodwill at the rate of seven percent a year on declining balances. Because no goodwill was purchased with the model restaurant, we do not have to worry about its amortization.

Land does not depreciate, so it is carried on the books at all times at cost.

Capital Assets and Capital Cost Allowances (Depreciation)

This is the accumulated total of the capital assets, entered at cost, as initially acquired, as added to annually since the commencement of the business; the capital cost allowance claimed for the current fiscal year; the summary of the total of the capital cost allowances claimed; and the undepreciated balance. Add the cost of each year's additional purchases to the previous fiscal period's total accumulated cost. Depreciation for this fiscal period is subtracted from the accumulated cost total and added to the accumulated depreciation. For the amount purchased, or depreciated, in each individual year, you must review the annual statements, year by year, abstracting from the prior year the difference between the two.

Details of Fixed Assets and Accounting Policies

"Capital Assets and Depreciation

	Cost	Last Fiscal Year Accumulated Depreciation	Last Fiscal Year Net Book Value	2nd Last Year Net Book Value	3rd Last Year Net Book Value
Land	$ 150,000	Nil	$ 150,000	$ 150,000	$ 150,000
Building	349,256	32,222	317,034	327,430	338,167
Equipment	114,439	40,744	73,695	77,073	79,253
Paving	15,178	4,113	11,065	12,294	13,660
Motor Home	60,000	–	60,000	60,000	60,000
Total	$ 688,873	$ 77,079	$ 611,794	$ 626,797	$ 641,080

Details of Depreciation

	Last Fiscal Year	2nd Last Year	3rd Last Year
Buildings	$ 10,396	$ 10,737	$ 11,089
Equipment	13,005	13,610	14,998
Paving	1,229	1,366	1,518
Motor Home	–	–	–
Totals	$ 24,629	$ 24,845	$ 27,605"

In the United States, there is no allowance for amortization of goodwill.

In Canada, one can amortize seventy-five percent of purchased goodwill at the rate of seven percent a year on declining balances.

Hot Tip

Do you want to know what the present owner paid for this business? Of course you do. Any buyer who says otherwise is full of baloney. Add up that first column titled "Cost," deleting any capital items that you know were later acquired, such as the motor home. Also delete any capital expenditures, such as additional equipment, building improvements, or subsequent acquisitions. The additions to capital equipment — fixtures and equipment or real estate — are detailed in the statement of changes in financial position. They came to $9,626 in the last fiscal year and $10,562 in the prior twelve months. Purchases made during the first year of operation will be included with the purchase price of the business, thus distorting the original cost by this amount. This will give you the total of what was initially paid. Here it is: $688,875, minus the $60,000 for the motor home. Total: $628,685, which probably included legal fees and other closing costs. If you can get the opening balance sheet from the first year in business, this same asset-depreciation schedule will provide the exact answer.

To determine how the purchase was financed, go back to that same statement of changes in financial position. Look only at the third-last year. Opposite Investing Activities, you will see where he paid $668,685 for the business. Opposite Changes in Working Capital Components, you will see that he borrowed $100,000 from the family. Opposite Financing Activities, you will see that he obtained a mortgage for $375,000 and an equipment lien for $75,000. An investment of $143,585 appears as a shareholder's loan. Total: $693,585, which suggests that $25,000 was put into the bank.

The Logic of the Depreciation Expense

The US tax department (the Internal Revenue Service, or IRS) allows the cost of any capital asset to be recaptured, or depreciated (accountants now prefer to say "amortized"), over its full anticipated useful life. But predicting how many years anything lasts can only be an educated guess. So the IRS has set up schedules indicating, not the useful life, but the percentage of the initial cost that you can recover each year. Under the Tax Reform Act of 1986, buildings have had a useful life of 31.5 years, cars and light trucks five years, and most machinery and equipment seven to ten years.

> The logic of the US tax law comes from the accelerated cost recovery system. This means a business should recover the cost invested in capital assets by amortizing the cost of the assets over their useful lives.

The logic of the US tax law comes from the accelerated cost recovery system. This means a business should recover the cost invested in capital assets by amortizing the cost of the assets over their useful lives. "Accelerated" means the tax law permits the assets to be depreciated faster than they actually wear out. Most buildings and equipment still have a residual value well after the maximum allowable time. Yet, with time everything eventually wears out and must be replaced. The theory of depreciation maintains that sufficient funds will be set aside to recover the initial cost and replace the asset in due course. Needless to say, very few businesses ever set anything aside for this purpose.

In Canada, the logic and the rules are essentially the same, except for capital cost allowances. Do not apply your US depreciation schedules in Canada, or vice versa.

Long-term Debt

This item details the long-term indebtedness of the company, to whom the money is owed, for what, the security, the terms, interest rate(s), conditions, and any unusual arrangements. Personal guarantees by the owners or shareholders should be mentioned.

"As at the End of the Last Fiscal Year, the company had the following long-term debt:

	Last Fiscal Year	2nd Last Year	3rd Last Year
Total Debt	$ 328,827	$ 374,001	$ 414,402
Current Position	(50,331)	(45,164)	(40,401)
Long-term	$ 278,496	$ 328,837	$ 374,001"

Note: The current liability position is the principal amount to be repaid during the next twelve months. The principal reduction on the income statement is that of the last accounting period.

"Mortgage: First Mortgage to Commercial - Industrial Bank; payable in monthly installments of $4,930.00, including amortized interest at Bank Prime plus 1.50%. The loan is secured by land and building mortgage, assignment of fire insurance, subrogation of shareholder's loans, and general assignment of cash collateral. Personal guarantee of the shareholders.

   Equipment Lien to Jim's Restaurant Supply Inc.; payable in monthly installments of $850.00, including interest at Bank Prime plus 1.50%. The lien is secured by first charge against all fixtures and equipment in the restaurant."

Sometimes the future annual principal due on long-term debt is stated on a year-to-year basis. If the interest rate floats, as here, this is usually omitted because the required principal payments would only be an educated guess.

Due to Shareholders

"The amount due to the shareholders of $118,585 (Last Year – $143,585) is non-interest-bearing. The shareholders have indicated that they may request repayment of this amount within the next fiscal year. Consequently, this amount has been classified as a current liability in the accompanying financial statements."

I have referred to the difference between shareholder's loans and paid-in-share capital. To repeat: a shareholder's loan is recorded as debt. Share capital is equity. Although accountants do not see it this way, business analysts usually consider share capital, retained earnings, and shareholder's loans as equity. Because they are. It simply depends on how the investors put their money into the company. Again, you have to count the money in the company pocket and in the owner/shareholder pocket.

   This heading seldom details the dollar amount of loans outstanding, which is shown on the balance sheet, except in the case of loans to several parties or differing repayment terms or security.

a shareholder's loan is recorded as debt. Share capital is equity. …you have to count the money in the company pocket and in the owner/shareholder pocket.

Share Capital

"Authorized:
- Class A – no par value, voting, participating, non-redeemable, convertible shares
- Class B – no par value, nonvoting, participating, non-redeemable, convertible shares

- Class C – no par value, nonvoting, nonparticipating, cumulative, redeemable, non-convertible shares
- Class D – no par value, nonvoting, nonparticipating, noncumulative, redeemable, convertible shares
  Issued and fully paid: 100 Class A Shares."

Related Party Transactions

In footnotes, the company discloses details of transactions with certain related individuals or corporations. Details of the nature of the relationship and policies applicable to the transactions follow:

"During the last fiscal period the company invested $25,000 and in the previous year $20,000 in an affiliated company. This is an unsecured loan on which there is no interest and no agreed terms of repayment."

Contingent Liability

"Jack's Management Ltd. was given a letter of credit issued by the Commercial-Industrial Bank for $10,000, which is guaranteed by Big Top Holdings Ltd."

Motor Home

"The company owns a motor home that is used for advertising purposes, going to rodeos, community events, etc. No charge for its use is being made to the officers or directors of the company. This motor home, acquired at the cost of $60,000, is not being depreciated."

Other Notes and Miscellaneous Concerns

These always come at the end of the notes. Although intended primarily for the company's banker, and perhaps the tax department, they are still interesting. The effects of each on the going concern value may be somewhat speculative. If buying shares, not assets only, all of the following details are very important:

- details of affiliated companies, parent or subsidiary,
- collateral securities given or received,
- warranty policies on goods manufactured or sold,
- employee pension plans, stock option plans, medical and dental insurance,
- life insurance on owners or directors,
- details of partnership agreements.

ACCOUNTING DIFFERENCES

Some years ago, the accounting profession developed Uniform Standards of Accounting. All accountants and accounting firms were to follow this basis for reporting. (USPAP is supposed to do the same thing for appraisers.) From reading financial statements, it was seldom possible to tell, without being informed, if the client had moved from one firm to another. In more recent years, however, statements and reporting order seem to be varying more and more. Almost all accountants still follow the same general precepts and the GAAP, and they are basically consistent, but now every accounting firm has its own reporting style, particularly in the income and expenses grouping. Probably the only places you will find carbon-copy styles these days are the automobile dealerships. General Motors and Ford specify the accounting procedures and insist that their dealers follow it. For everybody else, it is still all there, but harder to correlate. You should be aware of these reporting differences:

Method of Reporting Inventories

The majority of small and medium-sized businesses report on a FIFO basis (first-in, first-out), rather than LIFO (last-in, first-out). Smaller corporations seldom bother switching methods for income tax postponement, or shareholder reporting. But they might differ in what is included in the inventory. Some might include freight; others may not. Some companies regularly write off stale or dead stock. Others, particularly a troubled firm that is trying to improve its statement for the banker, will carry unsalable merchandise on the books at full cost indefinitely. Although the notes usually say, "at cost or market, whichever is lower," always assume inventory is carried at cost, because it is.

Cost of Sales

This entry probably varies the most from one accountant and one business to another. One cocktail lounge might include mixes with the cost of liquor, another might lump it in with supplies, and another might place it in miscellaneous bar sales. If the lounge and a restaurant are operated together, mixes could appear with kitchen food or kitchen supplies. Maybe it is simply an expense item. Are condiments supplies, or are they food?

Labor and departmental costs, such as sales promotion, supplies, and utilities, would not normally be considered as a cost of sales, yet some accountants do so.

In short, there is no definite pattern. When analysing two businesses, or several years within the same business, you may need to reallocate some of the accounting entries to make them comparable. If you were doing a management critique, you would worry about how the expenses are allocated, but since you are doing an appraisal, all you really want to know is the bottom line.

> When analysing two businesses, or several years within the same business, you may need to reallocate some of the accounting entries to make them comparable.

Management Salaries and Benefits

This is where the management plays games. Maybe my imagination is running wild, but at times it appears that everybody's out to shaft the appraiser (that is me). Sometimes I find management salaries and perks way out of line with industry standards. They are either too high or too low. These differences are often difficult to recognize and even more difficult to comment on, particularly if the owner is paying himself too much. Who has the nerve to say that the owner's spouse is not worth $30,000 a year just for smiling upon the troops from time to time?

You will see one of these scenarios in a private company:

1. Management receives a reasonable and fair wage. (This is common.)

2. The business profits are low because the wage and perks are so exorbitant.

3. The business profits are high as management is receiving a very low income.

So much depends on the owner's intentions, which could be quite honorable. One owner will take a high salary at the expense of the company's profit, and the company will break even at best. Another will draw very little and thereby improve the company's bottom line. If the company is for sale, the owner might want to paint the company as more profitable than it actually is, and will take the second approach.

And consider this:

4. If the salary level and operating profit are both low, the business is probably losing money. Maybe this is why it is for sale.

Sometimes you will see low salaries but large dividends. Management will pay itself one way or another. The method depends largely on whether the individual or the company pays the income tax. When you see this, for purposes of determining a correct net profit, add the dividends to the payroll cost schedule.

When preparing a synopsis, always adjust management income levels to industry standards, or at least to whatever appears to be a fair level of compensation. What could the owner earn if employed by someone else, considering her education, knowledge, experience, duties, and expertise? What the company would have to pay a manager to run the business?

Reporting of Income, Expenses, and Profitability

Here again, you need to make proper financial adjustments and correlations. This amounts to little more than entering the debits, credits, and net earnings consistently.

Contingent Liabilities

These usually appear in the notes to the financial statements, but they might not be recorded at all if the owner wants to hide something. The owner simply keeps them in mind, hoping that they will eventually disappear. Contingent liabilities seldom appear on the balance sheet. The possibility of their existence is one of the dangers of buying the shares, rather than assets only, in a small company.

In all states' and provinces' environmental protection acts have created a host of new problems. Anything that was built or stored on the site, even twenty or thirty years ago, such as gas or oil, could contaminate the property. If you have any doubts, hire a bona fide, fully qualified expert to do an environmental audit. This could cost many dollars, but the investment may well be worth it. You may think you have an ironclad agreement that pins cleanup costs on the seller, but do not expect the seller ever to do it. You may have to pay for cleanup yourself.

Be extra-careful if you are looking at shares in a closely held corporation. You will inherit a whole wardrobe of skeletons, including lots that you did not foresee. If the seller has no money to honor his guarantees, or has left the country, you will be stuck fighting his battle, even if you manage to get out of paying his bills. (Am I being too cynical? I am only telling you this, again, because the seller frequently cannot or will not honor any after-sale commitments.)

A few years ago, I brokered the sale of an oilfield servicing company. The owners insisted that it be no less than a share sale. They said they wanted out nice and clean. They said they were too old to come back or to fight with the tax department. Then I stumbled upon their reason for selling shares, not assets. They were facing a three-million-dollar lawsuit, as a result of a welding accident on one of their propane trucks. An explosion killed the welder and an assistant, injured several others, and destroyed a repair garage. Anyone who would bought their shares would have had to fight the lawsuit. If the buyer lost, she would have to pay the cost of the suit. There was insufficient insurance. I do not know if they ever sold; I gave them back their listing.

In all states' and provinces' environmental protection acts have created a host of new problems.

If you have any doubts, hire a bona fide, fully qualified expert to do an environmental audit.

And Then

Not to discount any of the above, but the key consideration will always be the bottom line, the net after-tax profit. If this is reported on a consistent basis, do not worry so much about the allocations. All you want to know is the most you should pay for a going concern, and to reach this point, you must understand what is and is not there. Only the seller knows for sure, and he probably will not divulge everything. You must be able to separate the wheat from the chaff, what is pertinent and what is not, what can be corrected and what is beyond any owner's control.

CAPITALIZING VERSUS EXPENSING

Watch for capitalizing, rather than expensing, certain cost items. A capitalized cost is added to the schedule of capital assets, while an expensed cost is written off during the current accounting period. A company shows more immediate profit if costs are capitalized but at the same time it takes a bigger immediate IRS tax hit. In the following discussion on machinery and equipment, small items such as cafe cutlery, shop hand tools, and hotel linens will be expensed. Some companies stipulate that any expenditure on building repairs under $25,000 is expensed, over this capitalized. Still, there is no strict rule, and even the tax people do not seem to have specific guidelines.

During the last fiscal year, the target business expensed $54,306 in building repairs and maintenance. To add thirty additional seats along the front and one side, they constructed a $40,000 solarium. Maybe this expenditure should have been capitalized. Repairs in the previous year were half of this amount and in the preceding year still less.

If this item had been capitalized, the building cost in the cost-of-assets schedule (Note 2- Fixed Assets & Depreciation) would have looked like this:

Last Fiscal Year End:	Building Cost	$ 389,256
2nd Last Fiscal Year End:	Building Cost	$ 349,256

Only $14,306 in repairs and maintenance would have appeared as an expense item.

A capitalized cost is deducted from the schedule of capital assets, while an expensed cost is written off during the current accounting period.

NONRECURRING ITEMS

When reconstructing a statement, you must always recast the income statement. First you need to delete nonrecurring income or expense items. These allocations can be quite large and probably do not recur, at least not for a long time. Examples would be the sale of a capital asset, a major liability claim paid or received, a windfall, an abnormal loss, or anything else that falls outside the average day-to-day operations.

REDUNDANT ASSETS

A redundant asset is one that does not earn a return on its capital investment or materially contribute to the company earnings. In the appraisal, it should be either deleted or clearly identified for what it is. If the business does not need it, it is redundant.

Private companies used to put summer cabins, luxury autos, and other owner's toys on the books. Yet they were often totally unrelated to the operation of the business. Now you are more likely to see a vacant tract of land, an underused building, or an idle machine.

Unusual as it may sound, even too much cash can be a redundant asset. One of our clients, who owned a small-town abattoir, carried over $400,000 cash in its current account. They just never figured out what to do with it. It was a redundant asset. This excess cash did not do anything to help the business. (But what a nice problem to have!)

In the case of the subject enterprise, Big Top Holdings Ltd., the motor home is a redundant asset. It is there solely for the pleasure of the owner and friends. Although they tell the tax folks it is used for advertising and business promotion, you and I know better.

MINIMUM NUMBER OF STATEMENTS

You will want at least three years' statements, five if possible, and seven if you can swing it. The more unstable the business or industry, the more years of statements necessary. Sometimes you cannot obtain a detailed historical record of the business, yet any valuation based on less than three years is suspect. You will not be able to explain income and profitability variations or trends in either direction. If definite longer-term trends are variable, or if a single abnormal year could greatly affect the resultant value, then the more annual statements you examine, the better. Many analysts will tell you that five years is the absolute minimum.

In well-established enterprises, especially those that have peaked out, where income and profit do not vary much from year to year, you can probably get by with two or three annual reports. Maybe you will need only one year. On the other hand, in cyclical industries with widely fluctuating income and profit, or definite trend lines, obtain several years. You can never have too much data.

Some years ago, our office was brokering a sawmill operation in northern British Columbia. The five annual statements showed three very profitable years and two that were disastrous. After being carefully coached by the owner, I explained to a prospective buyer that the three profitable years were the norm and the two loss years — created by strikes at the mill — were abnormal. The buyer said I had it backwards. The strike years were normal, the profitable ones rare. Whatever. The point is, if only the three good years had been displayed, the mill might have sold at a much higher price. Conversely, three years of statements including the two loss years would have produced a very low value and sale price. This is a common trap. In an industry as unpredictable as forestry, the buyer should base her valuation, or offer to purchase, on five years' statements at the minimum — preferably seven and ideally ten.

> If definite longer-term trends are variable, or if a single abnormal year could greatly affect the resultant value, then the more annual statements you examine, the better.

UNREPORTED INCOME

This has been said before, yet another area of concern, although not so prevalent these days, answers to several different names, such as sluff, kitty, under-the-table, and side pocket. All mean the same thing: unrecorded income and profits. A seller who assumes you are not a government tax spy, might tell you about such revenues to extract a better price. When this occurs, inform the seller that you will consider only whatever was reported to the government, and nothing else. As an appraiser, I am not interested in hearing about under-the-table benefits or profits that will increase the value of the business, and you should not be, either.

HONESTY IN REPORTING

Dishonesty worries us all, appraisers and business buyers alike. Very few sellers' statements have been audited. The others have been prepared by a wide assortment of persons of varying skills, from professional accountants through to the owner himself. Most are complete and competently prepared. Others provide the bare bones — just enough to satisfy the taxman and at the same time avoid any uncomfortable questions.

In my younger days, I worked for a used car dealer. The owner kept three sets of books. The business was always for sale, and so there was a set always ready for a potential sucker — oops, I mean buyer. Because the owner was afraid of a tax audit, a set was always available for Revenue Canada. The third set, the only correct one, was kept at home. Nobody ever saw it.

Usually, you can safely accept a set of statements prepared by a legitimate accounting firm. Public accountants are professionals, most of whom have made a substantial investment in time and education to build a clientele. Very few accountants will risk their professional reputations, or practices, by submitting incorrect statements, either to their client or to the government. The homemade on-the-kitchen-table variety of income and expense statement is generally suspect. In all fairness, some of these reports could be completely accurate. You just have to make sure that the business can actually produce the revenue and generate the profit that the statements indicate. Moreover, is the information reasonable, logical, and sensible? If you are an appraiser, be certain to inform your client as to the source of the statements and your opinion of their credibility. If the client accepts them, you can also safely do so. Still, to protect yourself further, in your statement of limiting conditions, insert in bold, capital letters that you are using possibly unreliable statements. State it once again at the beginning of your interpretation of the financial statements. And always look to industry standards as a backdrop for revenues and profits, remembering that if its too good to be true, it is. Always ask and positively answer:

Is it reasonable? Is it logical? Does it make sense?

> Public accountants are professionals, most of whom have made a substantial investment in time and education to build a clientele. Very few accountants will risk their professional reputations, or practices, by submitting incorrect statements, either to their client or to the government.

INDUSTRY STANDARDS

These income and expense averages are set by industry peers. They generally suggest certain income, expense, and profitability ratios, which are reduced to common denominators, such as sales per square foot in a retail store, productivity per man-hour in a factory, or consumption of food and beverages per capita by tourists. In many businesses, interdepartmental relationships and balances fit within clearly defined ratios. For example, in service stations, auto supplies are a constant percentage of gasoline sold. The total volume of the business could change year to year but usually the percentage variations between internal departments do not. Variable expenses follow the same pattern. Food costs in each type of restaurant are somewhat stationary. Depending on the type, they vary from about twenty-six percent of sales in a pizza parlor to over forty percent in an elaborate dining room. You can normally define labor costs, and others, as a certain percentage of volume. Deviations from the norm are red flags.

In analysing a going concern, you should hone in on wide variations from industry standards, such as a radical increase or decrease in sales and income, or a drastic change in one department from year to year, or unusual expense items on the debit side of the ledger. Consider industry standards and interdepartmental income and expense distributions and ratios, particularly variable or controllable expenses.

Always bear in mind that every business experiences radical shifts in income, expense, and profitability from time to time. These can be caused by external and/or internal forces, such as management changes, theft, loss of key employees, labor disputes, business cycles, economic and political considerations, changing market conditions, and credit changes. Some are within, others beyond the control of management. Some affect the business for a long time, while others can be corrected quickly.

In some companies, individual departments and their sales should be considered as one or more separate businesses under one roof. Think about confectionery sales and dispensary sales in a drug store, or car repairs and gasoline sales in a service station.

SOURCES OF INDUSTRY STANDARDS

Several statistical gathering companies regularly publish industry standards. To save money, borrow them from your banker or local library. Here are a few sources:

- US Bureau of Statistics and/or Statistics Canada. They carry so many publications on so many subjects, they probably do not even know what is available.
- Prentice Hall Publishing Company. The Almanac of Business and Industrial Financial Ratios. An excellent publication giving income and expense performance details of hundreds of types of businesses.
- Robert Morse & Associates. Annual Statement Studies. Every year this company publishes income and expense ratios on hundreds of businesses.
- Dun and Bradstreet. Several excellent publications provide a wide range of business indicators and ratios.
- Industry associations. Almost every trade and industry, blue-collar and professional, has an association that exists to help its members. Many are pleased to share the statistical data and render assistance. With others, you will have to join or get a member to intercede.
- Trade and industry journals and magazines. University libraries collect these by the ton and are pleased to share.
- Business reports and newsletters from all chartered banks.
- Other federal, state, and provincial statistical publications.

They are out there. Just ask and dig.

INTERPRETATION OF STATEMENTS

For an appraisal, you must identify the sources of income, cost of sales, operating expenses (from which you establish net operating profit), and cash flow. Keep your eyes peeled for anything unusual, such as abnormal entry variances between years, nonrecurring income or expenses, nonexistence of normal expense items (taxes or insurance), or expenses that substantially deviate from conventional industry standards. Using the restaurant example, if cost of food is sixty percent of sales when it should be in the low forties, then obviously something is wrong. Either the bookkeeping is incorrect or some employees' families are being fed at the expense of the restaurant. If labor costs are ten percent, when they should be twenty-five, the owner is not being paid, or he has a large family working for peanuts.

Because of these quirks, you should build on several years' statements to compile a stabilized income and expense summary, use averages, or develop a pro forma. I prefer a pro forma, which tends to level out the income and expense peaks and valleys. If accurately prepared, they will include missed entries and align the greater variations to industry standards, making the appraisal report more authentic. There are really only two areas of concern in this method: reconciling accounting differences that you might not see in the statements; and determining what numbers to use if there are singular abnormal years, particularly income years, or if identifiable trends are developing.

THE LAST WORD ON FINANCIAL STATEMENTS —
FOR NOW

Always remember that all financial statements are designed to satisfy a need of the owner, sometimes a buyer, but never an appraiser. This is not to imply dishonesty, for most times that is not the case, but to accomplish a specific purpose, often to reflect the business in the best light possible. This is what Appraisers call "massaging the numbers." If the company wants to refinance or sell out, the statement portrays high asset values and high profits. If management does not want to disburse dividends to shareholders, the statement portrays a more conservative scenario. If it is time to fess up to the taxman, write all capital assets down to the minimum. Any legal postponement of tax is always the object.

When you determine the going concern value of a business, do not accept everything at face value. Read between the lines. Search beyond the statements. In an appraisal or a to-buy-or-not-to-buy exercise, what is not said or recorded is often more important than what is.

NOTES

_____

_____

_____

_____

_____

_____

_____

_____

_____

_____

_____

_____

_____

_____

_____

_____

_____

_____

_____

_____

_____

_____

_____

_____

_____

_____

Chapter 7

MACHINERY AND EQUIPMENT

IN most small enterprises, except for personal service businesses and professional practices, value is founded on the tangible assets. Only a small percent demonstrate any measurable goodwill, and for many, it can disappear overnight. For this reason, you should always work from the tangible asset base forward. In other words, appraise the capital assets first and consider everything else as surplus. For a liquidation value, all you need to look at is the resale value of the tangible assets. Nothing else matters. These are the tangible assets:

- real estate (land and buildings),
- machinery and equipment, or furniture and fixtures,
- current assets.

To keep these concepts clear throughout this manual, I will regard real estate, machinery and equipment, and fixtures and equipment as capital assets. In this manual, current assets are also considered as tangible assets. When determining the market value of a going concern, you need to add all intangible asset values, particularly goodwill, to the tangible assets.

The going concern value of any business must be considered from the perspective of the principle referred to as "unit in place." It is the sum of the values of all tangible and intangible assets, all working in unison with each other, all coordinated. In this manual, I tend to fractionalize values, placing each into an individual, unrelated compartment, suggesting that going concern value is only the sum of a business's respective parts. In the real world, the categorization is not quite as precise as I will try to have you believe later on.

People buy and sell businesses as composite integrated units, not one piece at a time. Frequently, one element will have little or no value without the others. In a later chapter, for instance, I will assign a specific value to the goodwill portion of the appraisal model. Yet by itself, as no one can sell goodwill without the business, it has no market value. To have value, goodwill must be attached to the tangible assets. Fixtures and equipment valuation follows the same general rule. Equipment value would drop if it were detached from the business.

> People buy and sell businesses as composite integrated units, not one piece at a time. Frequently, one element will have little or no value without the others.

A GLOBAL VALUE

Throughout this manual I will use the terms "machinery and equipment" and "furniture and fixtures." When establishing business value, both mean the same thing, although one or the other applies, depending on the kind of business we are discussing.

Additionally, I will not delve into specifics about any particular type or grouping of equipment, nor the requirements of any particular industry. You will not be a qualified equipment appraiser at the end of all this. Unless you already know a good deal about this valuation specialty or you already have expert knowledge, all you will glean from this chapter is how to apply appraisal techniques to equipment. But we will look at machinery and equipment globally, in total, as a group entity, part of a business, several machines working in concert. I will not tell you how to appraise machines or equipment, one item, or one unit, at a time. We are talking about business appraisal, not machinery appraisal, so I will only touch on aspects of machinery and equipment valuation that affect going concern value.

What you want to know is the machinery and equipment's value in continued use. This implies continued capability to earn income and produce economic benefits, except in a liquidation situation. These assets receive equal treatment with the other tangible assets. The equipment's use must be practical, and the resulting profits are assumed to continue to the end of its remaining useful life.

VALUE TERMS AS THEY APPLY TO MACHINERY AND EQUIPMENT

Market Value

What would the machine sell for on the open market, as is, where it is, with nothing added or removed? I am talking about the price that would be paid to a dealer or supplier, whether it is new or used. This is not liquidation or auction price, book value, nor some artificially concocted trade-in price.

Because market value usually sets the upper limit, it is often synonymous with replacement value. Few would pay more than the price for an equally desirable substitute, assuming no undue delay in making the acquisition, or expense created by the cost of freight and installation.

Book Value

This is the initial cost less depreciation, as shown on the company's balance sheet. The books reflect cost, or cost less depreciation, not value, except if a current value accounting method is used.

Liquidation Value (Orderly Liquidation and Forced Liquidation)

We talk about orderly liquidation value when the income of the company can satisfy only the tangible assets of the business; an earnings increment does not exist. The value must be considered as the price that can be obtained on the open market, one item at a time.

We talk about forced liquidation value if the company's assets are, or will be, sold piecemeal to the highest bidder at auction, or under circumstances of duress. This is never considered market value.

Salvage Value

The machine has reached the end of its economic or productive life. It is now being sold for so many dollars per ton, usually as scrap.

Intrinsic Value

This value is subjective, holding worth over and above its market value or replacement cost. It often applies to machines or processes not easily duplicated. There could be a sentimental or antique value, or a first-on-the-market cachet. Intrinsic value is hard to quantify.

Notional Value

Here, the item holds an assumed market value when no market actually exists. Maybe a single machine is, by itself, functionally obsolete, yet does a great job when banked with others. Some printing equipment fits this description, or any mixture of very old and new equipment, particularly in a highly productive situation. If a single machine were removed and sold separately from the others, it would not bring an equivalent price on the market.

Value in a Box

Few people outside the lumber industry use this colorful term. It means the value of a machine delivered to the place of business, complete with all attachments, ready to be installed, but not yet installed.

GOING CONCERN VALUE

These items of machinery and equipment are not considered individually but rather on a global basis, as part of an operating and profitable business.

Any machine or piece of equipment holds its greatest value when new, installed, and operating, to which could be added a special or intrinsic value if the machine or process cannot be freely duplicated. Price and value are assumed to be equal at this point. The equipment is poised to be used to the max. Moreover, there is less room for quibbling about this price for this equipment at this time.

The equipment's value hits rock-bottom when it is sold for so many dollars per ton as scrap or salvage. In most businesses, you will probably find a mixture of equipment of all ages and conditions. Machines may be new, old, or middling; in excellent condition, poorly maintained, efficient, or technologically obsolete.

Equipment is worth more as part of a going concern, rather than without the business, either as a separate item or with other machines. In many circumstances, the value sits about midway between the new installed cost and the depreciated replacement value. Used equipment usually fetches a lower price on the open market.

When considering fixtures and equipment without the business, as in a bankruptcy situation, or perhaps for a start-up where there is no income, do not attach any intrinsic or subjective additional value. In these cases, you are looking strictly at depreciated replacement cost, or market value, nothing else. For example, you can buy used restaurant equipment almost anywhere for around twenty-five cents on the dollar. If considered as a part of a going profitable restaurant, they are probably worth around fifty percent of new replacement cost. The income-generating capabilities set the upper value, and the depreciated replacement cost sets the lower.

Although I will deal with Figure I, (p. 112) in more detail later, consider, for the moment, Curve C only. The curve implies that the value of machinery and equipment, as a part of a going concern, increases from an orderly liquidation value to its replacement cost as the profitability of the business increases. Even though the machinery (and other tangible assets) earns profits, its value can only rise to the installed replacement cost of any machine. This differs from real estate, where, often with a strong lease, market value can exceed replacement cost.

Any machine or piece of equipment holds its greatest value when new, installed, and operating, to which could be added a special or intrinsic value if the machine or process cannot be freely duplicated.

Figure 1: Elements of Tangible Asset and Going Concern Value Changes

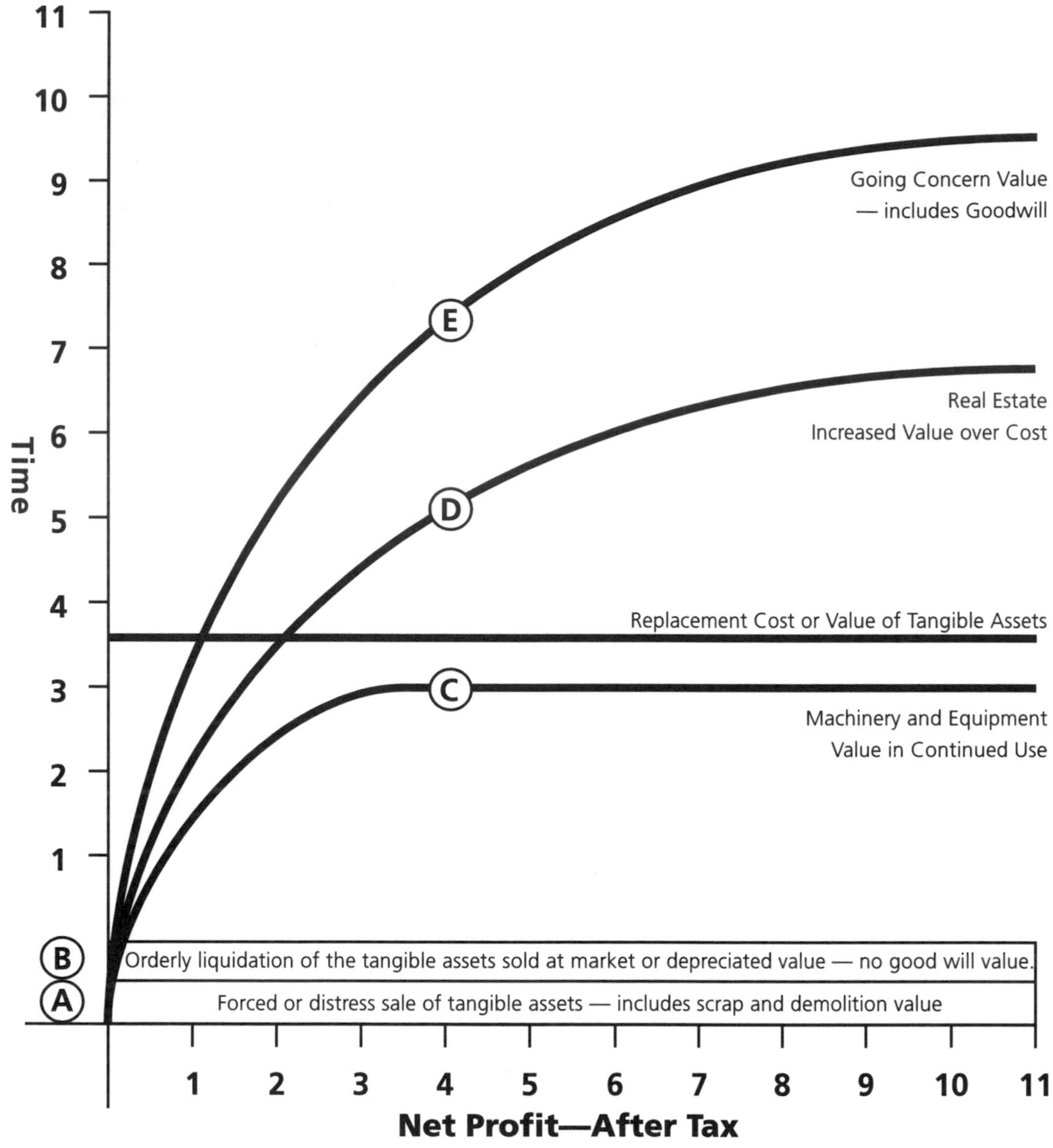

A. The business is losing money. To avoid further losses, the owners liquidate or the creditors foreclose, they dispose of the assets. Assets could be more gainfully employed elsewhere.

B. The business is breaking even. Profit is sufficient to justify the assets investment but no more. No goodwill value if sold as a going concern. No value will be realized over the depreciated or market value of the assets without the business.

C. The going concern value of all tangible assets in place with full utility value realized. The business is profitable and the profits are increasing. Lines flatten as neither profits or value increase indefinitely. The line splits. The value of machinery and equipment can never exceed replacement cost. Because of uniqueness business value in profitable situations or with strong leases or real estate can.

D. This line represents the replacement cost of all tangible assets at market value without the business.

E. The value of a business a going concern. Contains all intangible assets including goodwill. The line flattens. Profits and value stabilize. After a time as redundancy and competition creeps in, the line will curve downward.

CONDITION RATINGS

The American Society of Appraisers rates equipment condition according to physical aspects, with any physical deterioration reducing the value.

Very Good

This term describes an item of equipment in excellent condition, capable of being used to its fullest for its designed purpose, without being modified, and without requiring any repairs or abnormal maintenance at the time of inspection, or within the foreseeable future.

Good

This term describes modified or repaired equipment that is working at or near its fully specified utilization.

Fair

This equipment operates at a point below its fully specified use because of its age and/or application. It needs general repairs and some minor replacements in the near future to bring it back to, or near, its original level of use.

Poor

This term describes equipment that is performing well below its fully specified utilization. It cannot return to full capability without extensive repairs and/or major replacements very soon.

Scrap

This equipment cannot really be used at all, regardless of extensive repairs or modifications. This condition applies to equipment that is been used for 100 percent of its useful life, and also to equipment that is totally obsolete, either technologically or functionally.

DEPRECIATION CONCEPTS

The theory of depreciation for machinery resembles that for real estate:

- physical, curable and incurable,
- functional obsolescence, almost always incurable,
- economic obsolescence, including locational and external.

Yet the application of each type is fundamentally different.

Depreciation is the loss in value caused by the interaction of internal and external forces. Like buildings, equipment deteriorates with age and use. But machines, unlike buildings, can become obsolete overnight if they are upstaged by new technology and other innovation. An owner can expand a building's economic viability by renovating and modernizing. Although a retrofit, or top-notch maintenance, may extend a machine's life, its usefulness has a definite lifespan. An old building might

> Depreciation is the loss in value caused by the interaction of internal and external forces. Like buildings, equipment deteriorates with age and use.

even sell for more than its replacement cost, whereas equipment never will, or if so, only in the most unique circumstance.

Depreciation is often a legal fiction in real estate; in equipment it is a fact of life. Functional obsolescence causes the highest rate of depreciation as new, better, faster, lighter machines are continuously developed — often with a lower price tag and simpler instructions. Look at computers. Depending on use and maintenance, two machines could be identical in age, but one worn out and the other still like new. Use or location can markedly affect value. Does a machine last longer in a desert or on the coast? Which causes more deterioration, sand, or salt and rust? Sometimes economic or locational obsolescence accelerates the value loss — you know, it could be the wrong machine in the wrong place at the wrong time. For example, a sawmill in a highly productive lumber area would be worth a certain high value. But if located in a place without saw logs, the cost of relocating the equipment would force its value way down. It could now be only so much scrap iron lying in the bush, unwanted, unloved, and worthless. You must judge where the equipment lies on the depreciation curve, and how many years of useful life remain.

In-place equipment boasts a higher value because of its usefulness and profitability, and it might even be technically innovative and hold an added special or intrinsic value.

Under the accelerated depreciation rules, the Internal Revenue Service allows depreciation of up to two hundred percent or seven years on declining balances for some fixtures and equipment. Revenue Canada allows depreciation for income-tax purposes on most equipment and machinery at twenty to thirty percent per year on declining balances. Some specialized, high-tech equipment is classified as high as forty or fifty percent.

Actual depreciation from all causes, given normal use and care, usually floats between one-third and one-half of what is allowed by either the United States or Canadian tax departments. That said, you will often see old equipment doing its job longer than anyone would have dreamt. So much depends on initial quality, use, climate, and maintenance. An owner often scraps older equipment because he cannot get repair parts. Sometimes a fully functioning item will be eclipsed by a technological upstart that is perhaps no better than the old one. The owner might continue to run the old one, or else keep it on hand for emergencies. Usually the old equipment is fully paid for or amortized, which can be a definite plus. (I produced the original of this entire manual on an obsolete computer using out-of-date word-processing software. If I had not told you, I will bet you would not have known the difference.)

To restate: The government's allowable depreciation does not represent actual depreciation or loss in value. It is an accounting entry, calculated by a formula that may not relate to market realities. When you examine the books of your target company, do not take book value (cost less accumulated depreciation) as market value, or value in use. They are not the same.

Depreciation is based on all equipment being purchased, either new or used, to perform a certain function as efficiently as possible. This considers initial cost, operating expenses, and intended use or productivity. The company's profit reflects the equipment's capability. We assume that, at the time of acquisition, this equipment provided the best combination of price and value. You can gauge the real worth of any machine by the net present value of the income or profit that can be produced during its remaining useful economic life. As it ages, that value drops.

Actual depreciation from all causes, given normal use and care, usually floats between one-third and one-half of what is allowed by either the United States or Canadian tax departments.

PHYSICAL DETERIORATION

Incurable physical deterioration is the wasting away by time and the elements, while curable physical deterioration refers to problems that can be solved by repairs and maintenance.

Usually, physical deterioration can only be measured by observation. Look at the equipment's age range and condition, but be aware that a good coat of paint can cover many sins. You can determine the age from date stamping, serial numbers, model numbers, owner's records, or similar forms of identification. Condition, well, that is up to interpretation. You cannot estimate a machine's capability or efficiency by simply looking at it.

That said, age is rarely a big deal. Who cares if a hydraulic ram is twenty-five or thirty years old? What matters more is how often it is used, under what operating and climatic conditions, and how well it is maintained.

When considering equipment as part of a going concern, not item by item, think of incurable depreciation as a value loss by all of the equipment, in place and in use, such as all the fixtures in a store, all lumped together according to the general or average age. Curable depreciation applies only to a specific unit, or units, or portions thereof, and the cost of repairs or upgrading to return each to its maximum operating efficiency.

FUNCTIONAL OBSOLESCENCE

You can almost never cure functional obsolescence. A machine becomes functionally obsolete when a new development or newer, better, more productive, and less costly equipment comes along.

In real estate, we would say that functional capacity or efficiency is impaired, maybe as a result of overcapacity, inadequacy, or changes that affect a segment of a property or its relationship with other segments of the same property. It is the inability of the structure to perform its original function adequately.

The same goes for fixtures and equipment, as individual units or as components of a plant system. We are talking about inadequate design or use, compared to the competition or market forces, and the resulting squeezed profits. The cause? Technological change. New, lighter, smaller, more productive, faster, simpler, better-looking machines that are cheaper to buy and cheaper to operate. Like military aircraft, some classes of equipment become obsolete even before fully tested.

Overcapacity is a tricky matter. The item is too much for one business but not enough for two. Standby or replacement equipment would fall into this category.

I will say it again: Replacement cost, installed and operating, sets the upper limit of value; the liquidation stage sets the lower limit. Value in continued use, in a profitable business setting, lies somewhere in between. Depreciation for overcapacity becomes a combination of physical and functional problems, depending upon the equipment, its age, condition, and longer-term intended use.

Physical and functional depreciation almost always overlap. Some believe that equipment only depreciates in the functional sense, never the physical. A machine that is properly cared for could last forever.

A machine becomes functionally obsolete when a new development or newer, better, more productive, and less costly equipment comes along.

ECONOMIC OBSOLESCENCE

You can almost never cure economic and/or locational obsolescence. This is the wrong machine in the wrong place at the wrong time. Nobody wants or needs this machine any longer.

The causes here are totally external, such as the forces of supply and demand in the marketplace. The business owner has absolutely no control. The economic and functional forms of deterioration overlap distinctly. Just think about the products of yesteryear and the machinery that was used to manufacture them. (Hollywood loves to talk about buggy whips. I have no idea why.)

Maybe the raw materials are now too expensive or no longer available. You could blame it on exorbitant labor costs, lack of skilled labor, less demand for the products that the equipment makes, or overall economic, political, and environmental factors. Consider the locational and market forces that affect value, what is coming in and what is going out. Remember the sawmill in the area with no remaining saw logs.

A DEFINITION OF DEPRECIATION

The American Society of Agricultural Engineers defines depreciation this way:

- actual: the change in value of a machine.
- estimated: the change in value as determined by the difference between the purchase price and the estimated future value, both in constant dollars.
- straight-line, declining-balance, sum-of-the-years'-digits: the change in the machine's value, spread over the economic life of the machine.
- obsolescence: the process of becoming obsolete.
- obsolete: the condition of a machine that no longer produces anything, or cannot be fixed because normal suppliers do not carry the parts, or can be replaced by another machine or method at greater profit.

The following graphic delineates the four standard measures of depreciation, starting with the original cost and ending at salvage value.

Figure 2: Depreciation Concepts

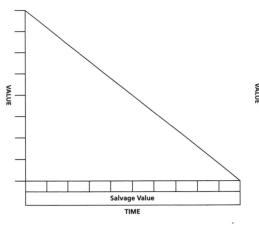

DEPRECIATION – STRAIGHT LINE

An accounting or appraisal function — rarely actually happens. Loss in productivity is seldom at an equal annual rate.

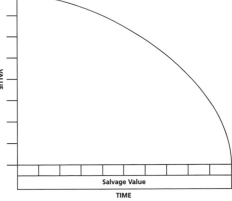

DEPRECIATION – PHYSICAL
(AGE LIFE)

Relatively level at first, then accelerates as the end of its useful life approaches. The machine is wearing out, replacement parts are harder to obtain.

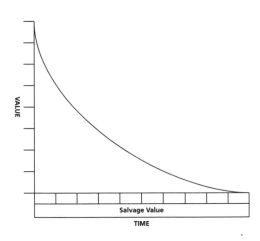

DEPRECIATION – FUNCTIONAL
(VALUE IN USE)

Initial rapid loss in value but then declines. Early replacement by newer and better machines. Develops a high utility value after a certain period.

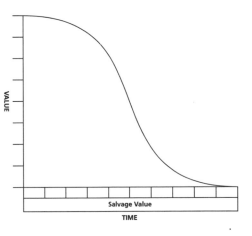

COMBINED PHYSICAL & FUNCTIONAL
(ACTUAL DEPRECIATION)

Relatively level at first, mid life acceleration, then later life lower value loss rate to end of useful life of the machine.

INCORRECT VALUE ASSUMPTIONS

Some common assumptions are incorrect:

- Book value = market value = going concern value.

Company books record cost, or cost less depreciation, but not value.

- On a sale the distribution of values agreed upon between seller and buyer are correct and at the fair market value.

Although these figures are based on the depreciated book values of the seller, they are often the result of negotiations and substantial juggling for the benefit of the tax department. Because income tax on recaptured depreciation tends to rapidly erode any profit on resale, the seller wants to dispose of all depreciated items as close to their book value as possible.

Recaptured depreciation is depreciation that did not actually occur. It must now be reentered, or recaptured. Thus, for the seller's benefit, fixed-asset values should be as low as possible. The buyer wants exactly the opposite, a high fixed-asset base and a minimum amount of goodwill. The buyer's depreciation schedule commences with the allocated dollar values for the assets as agreed upon. Of course, this assumes that the tax department accepts the allocation, which it usually does, unless the allocation is unrealistic. The higher these amounts, the more depreciation allowable to the buyer, thus a lower percentage of future operating profits to be gobbled up by income tax.

Older allocations, however, can help to establish historical values, or to commence a linear depreciation schedule. After so many years, as actual depreciation becomes such a large factor, the difference between what was actual and what was recorded becomes less important. On a larger transaction, a few thousand dollars here or there in the initial transfer consideration loses much significance.

> Recaptured depreciation is depreciation that did not actually occur. It must now be reentered, or recaptured.

- Dollars per room or suite for furniture, fixtures, and equipment in hotels and motels is correct.

No assumption could ever be more incorrect. Furniture, fixtures, and equipment in hotel rooms can be high-quality or absolute junk.

- Standards and industry norms maintain machinery and equipment as a certain percent of total capital cost.

This is as wrong as the previous misconception.

INFORMATION SOURCES

So where do appraiser's get the correct numbers? Well, they consult these sources:

- dealers' and suppliers' catalogues and price lists,
- the company that supplied the equipment,
- a competitor to the company that supplied the equipment,
- industry trade books; red books, blue books, black books,
- published industrial journals, trade journals,

- industry sources; someone else in the same business,
- auctioneers' journals and published sales results,
- records of the company; purchase invoices; the owner.

Caution: Do not always rely on a supplier to be totally objective because she could have a vested interest that would alter the value estimate. She could be angry or pleased about where the owner bought the equipment in the first place. If a local dealer is appraising, say, a fleet of trucks, he may lowball them on purpose, thinking he might acquire some of the units as trade-ins in the future. At auction sales, valuable equipment often brings a very low price while junk commands a premium. And, it appears that everything has two prices: one to buy and one to sell.

COST OF INSTALLATION

No explicit rule exists. You can add this on at cost, discount it, or ignore it. Hardware should normally be added, because it is a part of the equipment. When installation labor's gone, it is gone. In some cases, you will find installation costs capitalized, but in others expensed. You are on your own to sort this one out.

SMALL WARES

Never place any value on small wares, such as hand tools, linens, dishes, or pots and pans. If they have not been written off, and they probably have, do it now. Consider them as expensed items.

Some years ago I bought a motel that had several laundry-room shelves crammed full of sheets, all of which looked good from their neat stacks. The seller's value: $5,000. Fortunately, I placed a zero value. There was not one good sheet in the bunch.

NON-OWNED EQUIPMENT

In many instances, particularly in restaurants and retail stores, you will find fixtures and equipment that do not belong to the business. A supplier owns them, and lets them stay on the premises as long as the business is buying that supplier's merchandise. Examples of this — coffee makers, display racks, confectionery stands, pop dispensers, branded refrigerators — should never be included in the inventory, and definitely not paid for.

EQUIPMENT ON LEASE OR LEASE PURCHASE

The lease agreement will stipulate whether these items should be included in the sale. Some agreements are conditional sales contracts, yet others are actual rental-only agreements. If it is a lease purchase, then place the initial cost plus the capitalized interest on the asset schedule, with the unpaid principal added to the liabilities of the company. Or you can handle it as you would a building mortgage or any other equipment lien. If it is truly a rental agreement, do not include the equipment's value in the assets that you are buying or appraising. Rent will appear as an expense item.

At auction sales, valuable equipment often brings a very low price while junk commands a premium. And, it appears that everything has two prices: one to buy and one to sell.

THE FIFTY-PERCENT-OF-VALUE THEORY

Equipment buyers and sellers employ an unofficial "fifty percent rule," which states that used equipment, on a global basis, is worth fifty percent of its new replacement cost. This average applies to all equipment in a shop or factory or wherever, the old and the new, the modern and the obsolete. That is fifty percent of present, not original, replacement cost. Here is how to do it: Sum up today's cost to buy all of the equipment new. Divide that total in half, and you have the present value.

If the equipment is evenly distributed across an age range, this procedure works well. It is not that good, though, if there is an imbalance. Here is a better rule of thumb: take newer fixtures at two-thirds of new replacement cost, mid-life at fifty percent, and older at one-third. The resultant value still will not be that accurate, but you will have a benchmark for comparing values found by the more sophisticated procedures.

COMMON METHODS USED TO APPRAISE FIXTURES AND EQUIPMENT

There are still only three ways to appraise the value of both real estate and equipment: replacement cost, market, and income.

1. Comparative market data: the price at which you can acquire similar equipment, in like condition and with similar utility value.

   You arrive at the value by comparing the machines or fixtures and equipment with similar types that have been recently sold or are now offered for sale. What would you pay for a duplicate? What would this machine sell for on the open market? Who would buy it? Can it be financed at an equitable rate? How long would it take to sell it? Buyers snap up good used office equipment in a jiffy. Old steam locomotives are a different story.

   The comparative market data method is often a good way to appraise passive real estate. Normally, though, its results are too uncertain for valuing fixtures and equipment in a going concern. But if no intrinsic value is attached, as would be in a liquidation, it is perhaps the only reliable method. For disposal, without the business, or where there is no demonstrated earnings capability, the market price is the only thing that counts.

> The comparative market data method is often a good way to appraise passive real estate. Normally, though, its results are too uncertain for valuing fixtures and equipment in a going concern.

2. Initial cost less depreciation, item by item, one unit at a time: the value found by the cost approach. Perhaps more correctly, replacement cost new, less depreciation, is the sum of the initial cost of the equipment new, including freight, installation charges, and taxes; less depreciation from all sources.

   First, you establish the cost of the machinery new, then deduct accrued depreciation. The replacement cost usually sets the maximum value, bearing in mind the difference between cost and value. Cost is the initial price paid, trended to bring it to the present date, or the price for which substitute equipment is currently available. Value is in place, in use, as a part of a going concern.

3. Income approach to value: Consideration of the machine's ability to contribute to income or profit for a going concern. What revenue will the equipment generate, for how many years, at what operating expense ratio, and what is a fair return on the investment?

Although I appreciate that other writers may disagree, I believe the income approach should be used to estimate the market value of equipment only if an actual lease is in effect or if the machine's productivity can be converted into a rental factor. At times, you can determine market value with a rated output or profit-generating-capability factor. This is usually a cost accounting procedure, not a valuation approach. In so doing, you will have to leap through mathematical hoops to calculate both income and operating costs, including depreciation. The last step is to capitalize the net earnings of the machine(s) into a value estimate. More often this is a method to rate efficiency. This is particularly so when making comparisons, one machine to another or the testing of the performance of several machines operating in series. In most situations, there are too many variables to accurately estimate the market value of equipment by the income or earnings approach.

On the other hand, where productivity is more market-related and can be categorized and accurately expensed, the income approach to value on equipment may have merit. Maybe you could calculate the value of an individual piece of equipment in a specific situation. Note that the same machine might hold a different value in a different setting.

I am not suggesting that you never use the income approach to estimate the going concern value of machinery and equipment. Under ideal circumstances, it is the best and perhaps the only way. Still, you must either be very knowledgable, or very cautious, or both.

THE INDEXING METHOD

Indexing is an effective way to value many types of fixtures and equipment, on a global basis, as a part of a going concern. It works well in the valuation of most types of stationary equipment, store and restaurant furniture and fixtures, desks and chairs, and equipment or machines — that are not subject to technological change, and if they do not suffer from much functional or economic obsolescence. Conversely, indexing is probably the world's worst way to value mobile or rapidly depreciating equipment, machines used in adverse conditions, or those on which the new purchase price is dropping, thanks to advancements or market saturation.

> Indexing is just one method; it is not the only method. In many instances, you can apply better and more accurate procedures, so choose your method to fit the situation.

Indexing is just one method; it is not the only method. In many instances, you can apply better and more accurate procedures, so choose your method to fit the situation.

If you choose indexing, start by abstracting the actual purchase cost of the fixtures and equipment, acquired in each year, for a minimum of the past five years, from the financial statements of the prospect business. Seven or eight past years is ideal. After this, as depreciation becomes such a large factor, the exercise loses all significance. Then you update the annual purchases to their present cost according to an indexing formula. You can find such an indexing formula in a costing manual, such as Marshall & Swift, or simply by using the cost-of-living index. Then you depreciate the present replacement cost on a yearly basis, straight-line, at a predetermined rate. You base the rate on the useful life of the equipment. If it were purchased new, the depreciation rate would be a percentage of the full normal life; if used, then a percentage of the remaining useful years. This is how you obtain a depreciated value for the items purchased in each respective year. The present in-place total value is the sum of the depreciated value of each individual year's purchases.

As usually detailed in the notes to the financial statements, the cost of purchases for each year is the difference between the current year's cost figure and that of the prior accounting period. The first year of the analysis, which would be historical year five, six, or seven, depending on how many past years' statements you have at your fingertips, is the accumulated purchases of all prior years. Because of the depreciation factor, the final value estimate will not be hurt by the lumping together of purchases made in years gone by.

In most retail and service businesses, when globally considered, fixtures and equipment have an almost indefinite lifespan. Many stores intermingle newer, more modern fixtures with items much older than thirty years. For example, technological innovation has conjured many ultramodern, self-serving pricing and measuring devices. Yet display racks, tire changers, and refrigerators have scarcely changed in the past thirty or so years. Considering the differing life expectancies of the various items, fifteen years is a good cross-section in most retail stores, cafes, or service stations, or where a high percentage is stationary equipment. Also, most business put together a policy to continuously replace equipment, because stuff breaks, wears out, is stolen, or becomes obsolete. Quality maintenance can extend productive life almost into perpetuity.

On the appraisal model, ABC Franchised Restaurant, I will base the initial depreciation rate on a fifteen-year, normal, useful life, or 6.67% per annum. Yet I will increase the rate to 10.0% in the goodwill section, as the remaining useful life is shortened for this older equipment.

As in all methods, the indexing formula has definite shortcomings:

- It assumes straight-line or linear depreciation. Fixtures and equipment depreciate unevenly: relatively level at first, accelerating in mid-life, then at a lower rate towards the end of their useful life. Minimum value is scrap or salvage. Although remaining economic life can be estimated by present value methods, it still comes down to where the present value lies on the depreciation curve. Not all items in the same business depreciate at the same rate, as is suggested by straight-line depreciation.
- It ignores the equipment's age, use, and hours of operation. All items of equipment are given equal treatment. All are assumed to be in good working order and used to the max.
- It assumes that the cost of all of the equipment increases at a constant rate. This is seldom true. The price of some types of equipment, such as computers, is actually declining.
- It does not consider technological or functional obsolescence.
- It assumes that the equipment holds no intrinsic, special, or antique value. It treats all items equally.
- Finally, there is the question of the depreciation rate. Estimating full useful life of any type of fixture is often speculative. If the equipment is used, or was made by the client, it is up to you to accurately estimate the average remaining economic life.

THE APPRAISAL MODEL

For the purposes of demonstration, but also considering that the value found will become a part of all other value estimates, I will appraise the fixtures and equipment with the indexing method.

Let us start with the initial cost of the equipment. If a business changed hands some years ago, you can use the value agreed upon by the seller and the buyer. They negotiated this, of course, to put each in the best possible tax position. Still, because depreciation is such a large factor, and because so many years have passed, a few dollars here or there in the initial value, or cost, are no big deal.

The cost of equipment purchases for each subsequent year has been abstracted from the fixed asset and depreciation schedule contained in the notes to the financial statements. This is the initial cost when the restaurant was acquired, plus the cost of purchases during the first year of operation, plus the costs for each year since. Rather than present all of the notes, I will give you, in a moment, the pertinent section from each of the three individual years.

The model restaurant is now five years old. The statements indicate that during the first year, equipment purchases cost $94,251. Further research discovers that $90,000 was included in the purchase price, and subsequent purchases added up to $4,251. And five years ago, when the restaurant was being developed, the equipment purchases cost $100,000.

Now you have a choice. You can either go back five years, beginning with the $100,000 and adding each year's purchases. Or you can start with the present owner's $90,000 acquisition cost, plus the first year's purchases of $4,251. This is not a huge dilemma, but remember that equipment depreciation starts off slowly, accelerates during about eighty percent of its useful life, then levels off towards the end. So starting at the $94,451 makes sense, and it is probably more correct than using 13.33% based on the original $100,000 cost.

Note that (although it has no bearing on the present exercise), no depreciation has been claimed against the motor home in the following schedule. I have done this for the sake of simplification. I keep deleting this redundant asset and putting it back for the purpose of demonstration. In the real world, the investment would be recaptured.

THREE-YEAR FIXED-ASSET COST AND DEPRECIATION SCHEDULE

	Cost	Accumulated Depreciation	Balance
3rd Last Fiscal Year			
Land	$ 150,000	$ Nil	$ 150,000
Building	349,256	11,089	338,167
Paving	15,178	1,518	13,660
Equipment	94,251	14,998	79,253
Motor Home	60,000		60,000
Totals	$ 668,685	$ 27,605	$ 641,080
2nd Last Fiscal Year			
Land	$ 150,000	$ Nil	$ 150,000
Building	349,256	21,826	327,430
Paving	15,178	2,884	12,294
Equipment	104,813	27,740	77,073
Motor Home	60,000		60,000
Totals	$ 679,247	$ 52,450	$ 626,797
Last Fiscal Year			
Land	$ 150,000	$ Nil	$ 150,000
Building	349,256	32,222	317,034
Paving	15,178	4,113	11,065
Equipment	114,439	40,744	73,695
Motor Home	60,000		60,000
Totals	$ 688,873	$ 77,079	$ 611,794

Follow these Steps

1. Establish the starting point or the initial value of the equipment. In this case, I am using the initial cost of $94,251 (3rd last fiscal year).

2. Abstract the annual purchases from the fixed-asset cost schedule. Obtain this amount from the changes in the cost of equipment.

2nd Last Fiscal Year	$ 104,813 − $ 94,251 = $ 10,562
Last Fiscal Year	$ 114,439 − $ 104,813 = $ 9,626

3. Index each year's purchases to bring them up to current replacement cost. The indexing formula is annual inflation recast into a factor as found in most costing manuals. If these are not available, cost-of-living indexes will suffice.

Present replacement cost = initial cost × inflation factor:

4. Base the annual depreciation rate on the normal useful life or the probable average number of years of life remaining.

   This was established at 15 years or an annual depreciation rate of 6.67%.

5. Sum up the in-place going concern value for each year.

VALUATION OF FIXTURES AND EQUIPMENT BY THE INDEXING METHOD

Year of Acquisition	Cost & Additions	Index Factor	Present Replacement Value	Depreciation	In-place Value
3rd Last Yr	$ 94,251	1.05	$ 98,964	20.00%	$ 79,171
2nd Last Yr	$ 10,562	1.03	$ 10,879	13.33%	$ 9,429
Last Yr	$ 9,626	1.01	$ 9,722	6.67%	$ 9,074
Totals	$ 114,439		$ 119,565	$ 21,891	$ 97,674
Rounded to					$ 98,000

The $98,000 value estimate considers it part of a going concern. If this equipment were actually sold on the market, unquestionably the seller would never get $98,000. The indexing procedure has indicated a value of 85% of the original and 82% of the current replacement cost. In an actual sale, without the business, the seller could expect only 30% or 35% of present replacement cost.

If you have more than three years to work with, the value found with the indexing method tends to support the one-third, one-half, two-thirds rule of thumb. As the depreciation factor must be reckoned with, in cases where most of the equipment was bought several years ago, indexing will always produce a lower number. If the purchases were made more recently, there being substantially less depreciation to account for, the indexed value will always exceed fifty percent.

Despite its many shortcomings, indexing is a good method to establish fixtures and equipment value in a going concern, particularly if that equipment is not subject to technological change and if the company accounts help you to establish the original purchase cost. In other words, it works for appraising a retail store or a restaurant. But if technological obsolescence is rampant, or if the depreciation factor is erratic, do something different.

In conclusion, although I have tried to simplify the process, the appraisal of machinery and equipment is usually pretty complicated. I have only detailed the value of equipment on a global basis, as part of a going concern, value in use and in place. Appraising it unit by unit or for sale in an open market is a different kettle of fish. Both scenarios require considerably more expertise and detail than I have outlined here.

A VERY QUICK METHOD

To provide a mere ballpark figure, take the initial cost of the equipment, index it to current replacement cost, then abstract the depreciated book value. The in-place going concern value is about halfway in between.

- Indexed Replacement Cost $ 119,565
- Depreciated Book Value $ 73,695
- Halfway, Estimated Going Concern Value $ 96,630

It is not that far out.

And check the results by asking yourself:

Is it reasonable? Is it logical? Does it make sense?

Chapter 8

RISKS OF AND RETURNS ON INVESTMENT

MOSTpeople buy a business first and foremost to make money. That's my firm belief. I also believe that the underlying value of any business is in its tangible assets. All else is blue sky. You'll hear those conjectures again and again by the time you reach the last page of this book. And now here's something that may or may not be true: the more money an enterprise can make, the more it's worth. It's iffy because subjective considerations play a large part in a sell-buy decision, and because worth is assumed to have an upper limit. At some point you'll say: "I don't care how much money it makes, this company is only worth so much." You'll reason that those high profits, or high return on investment, may not continue indefinitely. The potential for loss might equal the potential for excessive profit.

What you want, apparently, is the highest possible return on your capital, but with safety. You could invest your money and make a good return, or a phenomenal return, or lose some money, or lose it all. How can you measure the opportunity for return, and for risk? When guessing at how much you expect back on your investment, what should you consider?

For starters, let's look at why people make investments and what they anticipate in return. We must consider the trade-offs between obtaining a fair return on our capital and recovering the initial capital itself. It's the weighing of return of the investment and return on the investment.

Return of Invested Capital

At some point during the investment cycle, you'll want all of your initial money back, or at least an assurance that you can get it back. So your first consideration is recapture (what's expected to happen) or depreciation (what already has happened). If you know that you can possibly lose your invested capital, you won't make this investment in the first place, but instead buy something else.

Return on Invested Capital

You must see potential for financial gain on your invested capital — in other words, interest. If there's minimum risk, you might be satisfied with a lower profit potential. But if the risk is high, then you should expect a high rate of return. If the return doesn't offset the potential for loss, then, again, you won't make this investment, but instead will buy something else.

RISK MEASUREMENT VERSUS GAMBLING

Risk-taking and gambling are different, yet interrelated. When you take a business risk, you consider the probability of both winning and losing, usually by degrees. When you gamble, you face either a total win or a total loss. You win the pot or you lose your ante; the horse comes in or it doesn't, nothing in between. In buying a business, gambling can become risk assessment if you hedge your bets.

When you take a business risk, you consider the probability of both winning and losing, usually by degrees. When you gamble, you face either a total win or a total loss.

To measure risk, you consider all probabilities and weigh the likelihood of loss or damage if you follow a particular course of action. If you choose to gamble, you base your game on reckless speculation, betting on an outcome that has an equal chance of not happening, ignoring any possibility of loss, and being shocked when your money goes up in smoke.

In every business purchase, there's risk, and the return on the investment is directly proportional to that risk. You simply have to find the correct balance between an outright gamble and an investment that will provide an astronomical return with absolute security.

As objectives, motives, and penalties vary from one investor and one situation to another, you can never boil down risk measurement to a mathematical process. It's about as exact as gazing into a crystal ball. You spend your nickel and take your chances. Textbook formulas rarely account for changing times and market uncertainties, or else they're impossibly complex. Risk assessment comes down to individual judgment, wisdom, and experience, as well as the quantity and quality of data you can unearth.

In the final analysis, you'll assess the investment as:

- a big gamble, but worthwhile if the chemistry is right,
- quite chancy, but with possibilities,
- a fair proposition, with a 50/50 chance of working,
- having a better than average chance of success,
- a likely winner,
- a near certainty.

BEING PRUDENT

You could, like the servant in a Bible parable, bury your money in the ground. It would be a safe move, but perhaps not a wise one. You'd never get rich this way. Most investors realize that to make money, they have to take risks, and a certain percentage will be poor ones. The potential to make or lose money is always there. Even if you're very wise, you're not guaranteed to choose a winner every time.

The prudent investor will normally choose the best available combination of maximum return with minimum risk. There's always a trade-off. In today's climate, the less speculative, or safe, investment would be Certificates of Deposit (in Canada, Guaranteed Investment Certificates) as sold by US banks and many other financial institutions. Next in line are AAA bonds, preferably those issued by the federal government, followed by cumulative preferred shares in blue-chip companies. These are all passive investments. The investor takes no active role in managing the investment. For the most part, these are classified as midpoint investments, which suggests that others are either safer or riskier. Even AAA bonds benefit, and at times suffer, from cyclical economic swings. And if you want to lose your shirt in a big hurry, remember that the three fastest ways to lose money are fast women, slow horses, and penny stocks.

Alternatively, the active investor wants to exercise more control and take more risk. All business investments, both passive and active, are assessed in relation to the midpoint investment, or the best combination of return and risk normally referred to as the "safe rate."

The prudent investor will normally choose the best available combination of maximum return with minimum risk.

RETURNS, RISK, AND RELATIVITY

Unfortunately, no one has yet found a guaranteed method of making high profits or capital gains with absolute safety. The higher the desired return, the higher the risk of loss. What's worse, most — perhaps all — investments cannot sustain a high profitability ratio for any extended length of time. For any of a host of reasons, exorbitant profits often become excessive losses.

Austin S. Donnelly, in his text *The Three R's of Investing*, suggests that the principal criteria for the making of any investment are return, risk, and relativity:

"**Return**: the overall return comprising income plus capital gain or minus capital loss,

Risk: assessment of the risk of investments, including volatile market fluctuations which can mean that 'good investments' including so-called blue chips are exposed to high risk,

Relativity: assessing the prices and prospects of investments relative to other available investments in deciding whether a particular investment is attractively priced or not under current conditions."[1]

Donnelly says that as a business buyer, or entrepreneur, you should look beyond the simplistic risk/return equation before you buy. You need to compare your prospect enterprise with its alternatives, looking at everything from monetary returns to intrinsic values.

Every purchase or sale results from the weighing of many factors, although the buyer's objectives have no effect on the going concern value of any business. Still, an understanding of investment motivation can help you determine why this particular business was bought in preference to that one. What could a similar business, in similar straits, fetch on the market? Here, you'd look at such stimuli as:

> Every purchase or sale results from the weighing of many factors, although the buyer's objectives have no effect on the going concern value of any business.

- **greed**: the plain and simple desire to have more. This could be linked with ambition, although greed is usually limited to money, whereas ambition often includes power and prestige. Greed is seldom coupled with wisdom, and is thus recognized by the gambling instinct, rather than the investing instinct. A greedy investor, anticipating still higher profits, holds on well after prudent investors have sold. Witness the Bre-X mining scandal of 1997. Less greedy investors cashed in when the share prices were still rising, long before the crash, long before those who hung in lost everything.
- **pride and prestige**: This investor will accept a lower return in exchange for other qualifications or advantages, such as the good old ego trip. This investor likes purebred cattle, show horses, the fanciest office, and the most prestigious title, and is often prepared to sacrifice financial rewards to obtain them. The market is often tempered by this investor's irrationality, or lack of consistency. In such cases, it's difficult to second-guess why a particular business was bought in favor of a more economical or more profitable alternative.
- **fear**: This investor is much more interested in security than in return. She buys Grade A bonds, preferred stocks, and Certificates of Deposit. She steers clear of the racetrack, or else bets on the favorite to show, invariably making twenty cents a race. She never buys penny stocks. Maybe she's just cautious by nature. Maybe she's older and more conservative because she has fewer years to recoup a riskier investment.

- **strategy**: playing the game, feeding from both pastures, making a particular investment for a particular reason, strategic buying, trading off between long- and short-term benefits. This sophisticated investor decides which way to go only after weighing the advantages and disadvantages.
- **intuition**: often more gambling than investing, the desire to be in there first, playing hunches. "I just know something good is going to happen." The greatest rewards, and the greatest losses, are made by those investors who get in on the ground floor, at the grubstake stage of any enterprise. When the operation is well established and proven, almost to the point of being blue-chip, everyone wants in. At this point, however, the risk and the rewards have been largely exhausted.

These principal motivations, and others, influence corporate decisions and thus the capital market. So much for the theory that money has no personality, and that investments are totally governed by the laws of supply and demand, risk and reward. Although the market itself may be quite rational, it is composed of irrational people who make irrational decisions.

INVESTMENT RISKS IDENTIFIED

Donnelly continues by placing investment risks into four specific categories:

1. "**Business risk**: the risk that the business may not do well due to internal factors such as inefficiency, poor management, failure to recognize changing conditions, or external factors such as problems in the industry, the economy or world trade.

2. **Financial risk**: the risk that a company could get into financial difficulties and perhaps fail because of an unsound financial structure. For example, too much reliance on borrowed funds leading to heavy fixed commitments for interest charges, and repayment of borrowed funds leading to intolerable strains in times of weak business conditions.

3. **Market risk**: risk associated with market factors such as market cycles, changes in market fashions, or reaction to previous excessive rises or declines.

4. **Information or accounting risk**: the risk that the investment may not do as well as is expected due to a difference between the true situation and that revealed by the financial statements of listed companies or figures supplied by vendors of real estate or direct business investments."[2]

As I've said before, risk measurement is nothing other than the assessment of risk versus reward. All investors seek the maximum financial gain with the lowest potential for loss. Yet there's no guaranteed method of securing continued high returns with absolute safety. In making the go/no-go decision, the prudent investor must consider:

- **stability**: How stable is the industry in which the investment is to be made? Is it at the inception, growth, maturity, or decline stage of the business lifecycle? What is the probability for survival, growth, and increased profitability? Look at the business's own effectiveness, its place in the industry and community, and competitive factors.
- **opportunity cost**: the comparison of what can be obtained from this investment, as opposed to that one. It's the cost of doing one thing at the

expense of not doing something else. Should I be in business for myself, or should I buy Certificates of Deposit and AAA bonds, and keep my job? Should I buy a hardware store, a grocery store, or a neighborhood pub, or go farming? Businesses for sale always outnumber buyers. The buyer, who at all times has the advantage, must weigh the pros and cons, consider action and reaction, and be alert to the alternatives.

- **hurdle rate**: the minimum acceptable rate of return, interrelated with opportunity cost. It must be virtually guaranteed, before making the investment. Moreover, if a buyer can't be assured of obtaining the hurdle rate, he won't buy, but will redirect his money where the returns are better. Making profit, however, is only one reason why people buy businesses. It still comes down to whether the acquisition meets the objectives and overcomes the constraints.
- **blindness**: the willingness to ignore relevant negative factors. Such investors let their heart win over their head. They won't sell, trade, or move when everything tells them to. They take unnecessary risks for minimum reward, they buy or hold in a declining market.

REAL AND MAYBE MONEY

Real money equals cash returns. It is the amount of the cash flow that can be paid to the owners or shareholders by way of dividends, or the distribution of profits, without eroding the capital base or future income potential.

You can't get your hands on maybe money until the holdings are sold, otherwise disposed of, or refinanced. It can be earnings on reinvestment, profits created by inflation, changes in value on the books of the company, unrealized potential for capital gain, recorded surpluses, and sometimes an accounting allocation.

Total return, also called investment yield, is the total financial gain made by the enterprise, including actual cash flow, equity increase through debt retirement, plus or minus capital gain created by a change of value in the property — that is, both real and maybe money.

Price-earnings ratios, which real estate appraisers call income multipliers, are calculated on the total earnings of a company, regardless of source or distribution to the shareholders. The payment or withholding of dividends is a management decision. The directors decide what percentage of the earned profit should be paid to the shareholders and how much should be retained by the company.

The price-earnings ratio reflects the profit distribution and capital retention, which both affect the market value of the investment. In setting a proper price for any business, the investor should be concerned with both profit and total return. Whether they are distributed to the owners or retained by the company is of little consequence.

When analysing a business, you have to think about both real and maybe money. For the most part, you're going to discount, or capitalize, net earnings based on the actual or real money generated, net after-tax profits. If capital or tangible assets increase in value, except when an actual sale has taken place, that's largely based on maybe money, or at least on those theoretical concepts.

For example, assume that a few years ago the tangible assets of a business had a market value of $250,000. Today, because of increased profits, better management, increased replacement cost, inflation, or perhaps a change of real estate zoning, they are worth $500,000. Yet that increased value of $250,000 is only a paper profit, or maybe money, until the business is sold and the profit realized. Meanwhile, it can't be spent or used for the advancement of the business. Nor can it be abstracted from

Price-earnings ratios, which real estate appraisers call income multipliers, are calculated on the total earnings of a company, regardless of source or distribution to the shareholders.

the company and reinvested, except only by the creation of additional debt, secured by this increased value.

The opposite of this situation is true as well. Recorded losses may not be actual losses at all until the company is wound up, the assets disposed of, and any surplus distributed. For example, all else being equal, neither the quantity nor the quality of corn grown per acre is influenced by the market value of the land. Still, fluctuations in the value of North American farmland over the past several years have created problems for owners and lenders alike.

RECORDED EARNED SURPLUSES

When looking at undistributed earnings or earned surpluses on the balance sheet of most companies (either positive or negative as created by the retention of profits or losses, or by the pay down of debt), you must consider them as maybe money. Neither are realized until the business is disposed of or, if positive, management chooses to withdraw them. In a going concern asset sale, which makes up 95% of small-business sales, the seller will retain them. On a shares offering, they are taken into account during valuation and the transaction. Because of changing circumstances, earned surpluses often constitute little more than a legal fiction that never will be realized by anybody, particularly if unrealistically high book values are recorded.

HIGH GROWTH RATES CANNOT BE SUSTAINED

Very high growth rates and higher-than-normal profits, or those available from alternative investments, can't last forever. History indicates that speculative profits are available for very short periods only. Economists and statisticians say that market volatility, particularly in the stock market, regulates itself. The inherent corrective forces of our economy, mostly the compounding effect of money at work, neutralize these blips. Most investments made during the past forty or so years, generally a period of strong growth, have supposedly generated annual returns of three to three-and-one-half percent. This is a longer-term average that considers the periods of rapid advance and those of equally rapid decline.

An ancient philosophy states: "Where capital is invested and capital is earned, particularly at a higher-than-normal rate, competitive capital will follow." Otherwise stated: you can't beat the odds for long.

> Where capital is invested and capital is earned, particularly at a higher-than-normal rate, competitive capital will follow.

THE EFFECT OF TAXATION

Entire books already deal with this topic, so I won't talk at length about the effect of taxation on investment returns. It behooves the buyer, though, to seriously consider this additional cost of capital or reduction of profitability. A business is appraised after payment of or reserve for taxes. Income tax is regarded as a cost of doing business, treated no differently from cost of sales or labor. Still, nothing is more directly affected than income tax by the games that accountants play, the withholding of tax, reallocation of income and expenses, tax deferment, flip-flopping between ordinary income and capital gain, and so forth. Accountants can adjust, or manipulate, returns on total investment and dividend yields, for the purpose of deferring tax. Cash flows and hence profits are always altered by the payment or deferment of tax, with declared profits directly affecting the resale value of a company as a going concern.

Just in case you missed it the first hundred times I said it:

Business valuations are always made after payment of income tax.

References

[1] Donnelley, A.S. (1985). *The three R's of investing: Return risk and relativity.* Homewood, IL: Dow Jones-Irwin.

[2] Ibid

NOTES

Chapter 9

CAPITALIZATION AND DISCOUNT RATES

Y OU might have all sorts of subjective motives for buying a business: pride, prestige, doing your own thing, being your own person, and so on. But you really buy a business for the objective motive: to show continuing profits, to have something left over after paying the bills, to make money. It always comes down to determining how much you should pay for a company that will generate so many dollars in net profit this year, next year, and each year thereafter. As we discussed in the previous chapter on return and risk, because of the possibility of getting fewer dollars than expected, or none, future dollars are worth less that those obtainable today.

Here is the foundation for investment analysis:

- Receiving today is better than at some time in the future;
- More is always preferable than less.

So the level of return must compensate for the risk and for waiting to obtain a return on and of your investment. The greater the risk and the longer the wait for profits, the lower the price that will be paid for them.

As future profits do not hold the same value as those that would be received today, they are discounted. Their present value, what you will pay to receive them, is reduced proportionate to the risk and the time delay. In any business, as anticipated profits are stretched over several years into the future, the going concern value of the business is the discounted net present worth of all future monetary benefits to be received. You compare this to what you would receive from alternative forms of investment.

Capitalizing or discounting future profits, which form the basis of the earnings approaches to value, are both related to buyer thinking and motivation. You must always be able to measure profits. Thus, these approaches to value are not valid at the forced liquidation stage of any business, or if the breakup value of the assets equals, or exceeds, the going concern value of the business.

THE CAPITALIZATION PROCESS DEFINED

This is the process of calculating the present value of anticipated future income payments, or net operating profits. For a passive real estate investment, this would be cash flows; for a business, it would be net operating profits.

The Real Estate Institute defines the capitalization process as a method of estimating the value of a capital good, such as real estate, through the use of a rate that represents the proper relationship between the capital good and the net income that it produces. In appraising, this usually takes the form of discounting.

Simply stated, it is the process by which future anticipated income is converted into current value.

The valuation formula:

$$\frac{\text{Net Operating Profit}}{\text{Capitalization Rate}} \times 100 = \text{Going Concern Value}$$

...the level of return must compensate for the risk and for waiting to obtain a return on and of your investment. The greater the risk and the longer the wait for profits, the lower the price that will be paid for them.

The capitalization rate, the yardstick by which value is measured, blends return on and return of capital, expressed either as a percentage or a decimal factor. Return on is the bonus for risk and waiting time; return of is simply getting your money back in installments. An annuity capitalization procedure is always assumed, which means that return of is built into the rate. So when you are applying the accounting-formula-derived rates, you use a mortgage constant, which includes a debt service factor, rather than only an interest rate. In the market-abstracted rates, the return of is automatically assumed to be there.

NET OPERATING PROFIT

This is an important term, frequently used. It is simply the profit as recorded on the income statement of your target business, calculated before:

- long-term debt service,
- abnormal or nonrecurring income or expense entries,
- depreciation (amortization or recapture).

THE DISCOUNT RATE AND THE CAPITALIZATION RATE DEFINED

As I will use these two terms indiscriminately, without explanation, I will repeat the standard definitions.

The Discount Rate

This is a yield rate for converting a series of future payments or receipts into present value. It is only return on, not return of, invested capital; in other words, interest.

The Capitalization Rate

This is the sum of the return on and return of invested capital, or in other words, the sum of a discount rate and a capital recapture rate. It applies to any income stream with a finite term over which the invested principal is to be returned to the investor or lender.

All this really means is that a capitalization rate includes invested capital recapture (or depreciation) and/or debt amortization. A discount rate does not; it is interest only.

METHODS TO OBTAIN CAPITALIZATION AND DISCOUNT RATES

The three principal methods are:

1. accounting formula methods, of which there are two:

> The capitalization rate, the yardstick by which value is measured, blends return on and return of capital, expressed either as a percentage or a decimal factor. Return on is the bonus for risk and waiting time; return of is simply getting your money back in installments.

- the weighted average cost of capital, which real-estate appraisers call band of investment or mortgage equity,
- the summation method, which loads the midpoint or safe rate for additional risk and for the wait,

2. market-abstracted rates,

3. the stock market.

SELECTION OF THE CAPITALIZATION RATE

Probably the most difficult part of any valuation exercise is to select an appropriate capitalization rate. Often, even a minute difference will alter the final value estimate by thousands of dollars. The midpoint investment or safe-rate returns fluctuate. The market wobbles with the times, caused by political pressures, the success or failure of lenders with certain types of loans, the changing seasons, what is in and out of favor, the normal market shifts, and other variables that seemingly exist only to confuse business buyers and appraisers.

And, in one valuation exercise for one small business, you can use four different capitalization rates. In all fairness though, the third is not a capitalization rate, but rather a discount rate. You may be faced with:

- a capitalization rate for the real estate.
- a capitalization rate for machinery and equipment. The difference here is that depreciation is much more of a reckoning factor in equipment than it is for a building.
- a discount rate for the goodwill portion of the business on a going concern rather than on a liquidation basis.
- an overall rate where the net earnings of the business are capitalized into an estimate of total value, without subdividing them into the various components of real estate, machinery and equipment, the intangible assets, and goodwill.

Probably the most difficult part of any valuation exercise is to select an appropriate capitalization rate. Often, even a minute difference will alter the final value estimate by thousands of dollars.

Kind of weird, but it is the system and we all have to live with it, at least until some clever soul develops an absolutely guaranteed, foolproof way to determine the exact capitalization or discount rate in any given circumstance. Someday someone probably will. But please be assured, you will not find it in this manual.

THE BANK PRIME RATE

To determine or select the capitalization rate, start with the midpoint or safe rate. All capitalization and discount rates, irrespective of source, method of abstraction, or formulation, originate here. Although you might hear arguments to the contrary, this rate combines the supply of and demand for money, the economic circumstances of the country, and the political forces that theoretically propel the country in one direction or another. All other investment returns, and thus discount or capitalization rates, are derived from this prime bank lending rate. For example, during the past twenty or so years, the prime rate has fluctuated very widely. During these cyclical swings, inflation, the stock market, property values, and most other forms of and returns on investment have swooped and swirled as well.

...investment returns, and thus discount or capitalization rates, are derived from this prime bank lending rate

Capitalization rates have historically been more stable than the bank rate. It seems that in times of rising rates, particularly rapidly rising rates, equity investors are prepared to accept less. Returns to equity decline, not necessarily proportional to the lending rate increase, but sufficiently so that the market rate is more stable than you would expect. Conversely, as lending rates decline, investors consider this to be a time for greater profit-taking. Often, in real estate, as the direct result of longer-term leases and contractual commitments by operating companies, interest-rate variations are further reduced by market lag. Rates of return on commercial real-estate investments and businesses normally lag bank prime rate fluctuations by up to six months, both going in and coming out. Therefore, a market-derived rate, unless the comparable sales occurred yesterday, might not truly indicate what is happening today.

FACTORS INFLUENCING CAPITALIZATION AND DISCOUNT RATES

Capitalization and discount rates for small-business valuations are based on an integration of external and internal factors. By external, I mean forces and influences that are beyond the control of the company's management; by internal, I mean factors that are within the realm of management influence. These are always a synthesis of the three R's of investing: return, risk, and relativity. You make the adjustments according to their interrelationship. These factors include, but are not limited to:

1. the prevailing interest rates of the day, primarily the bank prime lending rate, ease of obtaining credit, and the money market in general. In manufacturing enterprises, particularly exporting, foreign exchange rates, and, more so in larger businesses, stock-market trends.

2. the general trend in interest and money-market rates. Are they increasing, decreasing, or stable?

3. general economic and market conditions. What is the current political climate? How will rates be affected by a change of government, or government policies? Are we in an inflationary, disinflationary, or stable period?

4. local economic and market conditions. What is happening in town? Any new plants opening, any closing, any radical changes to the economy or the outlook? Are we affected by national or local unemployment?

5. conditions in the industry of the target company. What is the economic trend of the industry? Is anything adding or reducing risk for the investor? Do you anticipate any change in the sources of raw materials, or goods and/or equipment suppliers? Are the markets protected?

6. the potential to resell this business. Can you identify potential buyers? Or is this a distress situation that should be wound up?

7. the financial condition of the specific business and its potential for change in either direction. Is this a strong, viable business with good future prospects? Or is the going concern value going down the drain?

8. ease of entrance into this business. In other words, would it be easy for more competition to start up?

Businesses that are easy to enter, because they require either little capital or expertise, are always discounted at above-normal market rates. Is this a romance business that everyone dreams about, such as a travel agency, charter aviation company, or motel? Businesses can be like personal goods, often acquired more on impulse than for logical reasons.

Deodorant or hair-spray commercials on TV probably inadvertently sell restaurants by portraying the very attractive, harried woman, exhausted at the end of an exciting day after serving so many customers, making so many new friends, controlling the service, maintaining order with the chefs and servers, and having so darned much fun. Thank goodness she wore this or sprayed on that! In true life, unfortunately, the romance stops when two of the five table attendants do not show up for the Sunday brunch, one shows up hung over, and the cook does not feel like cooking. (If you think that is an exaggeration, just try scheduling staff in a restaurant. You will find out.)

9. the source of the business's value. Is it the tangible or fixed assets, mostly the goodwill (as in an insurance agency), or the management expertise (as in a professional practice)? The underlying value of any business is proportionate to the value of its tangible assets.

10. adequacy of plant, location, age, technological position, market position, and future potential.

The discount or capitalization rate should be the expected rate of return available from alternative investments when you compare the risk. It must correspond to the needs of the investor climate.

> The discount or capitalization rate should be the expected rate of return available from alternative investments when you compare the risk. It must correspond to the needs of the investor climate.

THE ACCOUNTING-FORMULA-DERIVED RATES

Average Cost of Capital

Also known as the band of investment, the mortgage-equity method, or the weighted average cost of capital, the capitalization rate found by this procedure is a weighted average of the annual constant of the existing or available debt financing and the required equity yield rate, each being a fixed percentage, the total of the two equalling 100% of the rate to be used.

More simply stated, the average cost of capital is the average of the risk rates, weighted between debt service and return on equity.

It is easy to determine details of the availability of debt capital for a certain business, the amount that can be financed, the interest rate, the amortization or repayment period, and the term. Just phone any mortgage company or bank. It is more difficult to establish the equity yield rate.

Truly, I am not trying to confuse you, but I need to add two more terms:

- **equity dividend**. This is the net operating profit only as recorded on the income statement of the company. It is expressed as a cash-on-cash-X-percent return on the equity-only portion of the investment.
- **equity yield**. This is net operating profit as recorded on the income statement of the company, plus equity gain through mortgage pay down, maybe money gained through inflation, or lost through disinflation, and money gained or

lost by any other cause. If it includes capital gain or loss on resale, then equity yield is referred to as the internal rate of return.

Equity yield rates have, in small businesses in the past few years, varied considerably. Businesses in the throes of bankruptcy, or close to it, often show negative returns on the equity portion of the total investment. Yet buyers of businesses or profitable operating entities with strong asset bases anticipate annual returns to equity in the range of fifteen to thirty percent. Actual return depends on many factors. Lower equity returns are translated into lower capitalization rates. These are most appropriate for businesses that are well-located, attractive to lenders, well-managed, and have a history of relatively high or stable profitability ratios. Conversely, higher returns are expected from businesses that present more risk. They could be in a very competitive situation, have a more obsolete plant or facility, or require higher-than-normal management expertise.

Investment analysts and accountants prefer this method. It relies less on historical data. It is less speculative. Unrelated factors and variables are less likely to enter the exercise, as only the equity yield rate is subject to the analyst's personal judgment. Moreover, it is a total rate calculation method that the investment market and lenders understand. Still, the investment community does not separate from the equity yield buildup through debt reduction, nor the gain or loss in value created by inflation or disinflation. These two potential add-ons are accepted as a fact of life and factored into the base rate.

The Formula:

For demonstration purposes, let us assume that a first mortgage can be arranged for seventy percent of the total value of the business, with an interest rate of 8.50% and a twenty-year amortization. The annual constant, the blended interest and principal payment for one dollar, is 0.10414. As payments are usually made monthly, you will use the monthly rate, times twelve. Use the full amortization period, and do not consider a term or balloon date.

The equity yield rate is assumed to be 12.50% for the remaining thirty percent of the total value.

The arithmetic process is:

Mortgage: Annual Constant	$0.10414 \times 70\% = 0.07289$
Equity Yield:	$0.12500 \times 30\% = 0.03750$
Capitalization Rate Total	0.11039
or ($\times 100 =$)	11.04%

The Build-Up or Add-On Method

First, obtain the existing safe or midpoint investment rate from the market, from AAA bonds, Certificates of Deposit, or the like. To this rate, you add a percentage for each additional risk, such as non-liquidity, capital management, demand, and anything else that could apply to that particular situation.

Although this method is taught in every appraisal course and discussed in almost every appraisal textbook, it is seldom used in the appraisal of businesses. It often involves pure guesswork and unprovable suppositions. Further, to this rate you must add an additional percentage for depreciation, the accuracy of which is a subject of its own.

This is the method that James Schilt writes about, and I will talk about his formulas in a moment. In real estate, there are better ways. Still, in the valuation of going concerns, there is some substance to this procedure and to the Schilt theories and guidelines, particularly when the situation warrants a split rate: one capitalization rate for the real estate, and another for the business.

DEWING'S "SUMMARY STATEMENT OF CAPITALIZATION OF EARNINGS"

In 1953, Arthur Dewing, in his publication *Financial Policy of Corporations*, categorized capitalization rates into seven distinct classifications. Since then, so far as I know, no other writer has attempted to repeat the procedure by using more relevant data or broader or different classifications. Several writers, including me, have tried to update the exercise by using current interest rates, but due to rapidly changing conditions, none has been particularly successful. Appraisers, valuators, lenders, and economists still use Dewing's categories, but apply the rates of return expected on the date of valuation. Dewing writes:

> Appraisers, valuators, lenders, and economists still use Dewing's categories, but apply the rates of return expected on the date of valuation.

"It is possible to throw industrial businesses into diverse categories in accordance with which we can form some estimate of the value of a business by capitalizing its earnings. These categories could be described in the following manner:

1. Old, established businesses, with large capital assets and excellent goodwill — ten percent, a value of ten times net earnings. Very few industrial enterprises would come within this category.

2. Businesses, well-established, but requiring considerable managerial care. To this category would belong a great number of old, successful industrial businesses, large and small — 12.5%, a value eight times the net earnings.

3. Businesses, well-established, involving possible loss in consequence of shifts of general economic conditions. They are strong, well-established businesses, but they produce a type of commodity which makes them vulnerable to depressions. They require considerable managerial ability but little special knowledge upon the part of the executives — fifteen percent, a value of approximately seven times net earnings.

4. Businesses requiring average executive ability — and at the same time comparatively little capital investment. These businesses are highly competitive, but established goodwill is of distinct importance. This class includes the rank and file of medium-sized, highly competitive industrial enterprises — twenty percent, a value approximately five times net earnings.

5. Small industrial enterprises, highly competitive, and requiring a relatively small capital outlay. They are businesses which anyone, even with little capital outlay, may enter — twenty-five percent, a value approximately four times net earnings.

6. Industrial businesses, large and small, which depend on the special, often unusual skill of one, or a small group of managers. They involve only a small amount of capital, they are highly competitive, and mortality is high among those who enter the competitive struggle — fifty percent, a value approximately twice the net earnings.

7. Personal service businesses. They require no capital, or at most a desk, some envelopes, and a few sheets of paper. The manager must have a special skill coupled with an intensive and thorough knowledge of his subjects. The earnings of the enterprise are the objective reflection of this skill; and he is not likely to be able to create 'an organization' which can successfully carry on after he is gone. He can sell the business, including the reputation and 'the plan of business,' but he cannot sell himself, the only true valuable part of the enterprise — one hundred percent, a value equal, approximately, to the earnings of a single year.

The summary of categories is not a classification in the sense of clearly defined and marked classes. There are innumerable intermediate stages. These seven categories are in the nature of nodal points in the organization of industry according to the relation of earnings and value. There are many businesses so highly stabilized, so immune to the shocks of industrial depression and incompetent management, that they are worth more than ten times their annual earnings; there may be businesses so peculiar and individual that they are, in the hands of another, not worth even the earnings of a single year."[1]

If using Dewing's rates suggestions as quoted — and he does not indicate whether they are capitalization or discount rates — as a basis for current analysis, you must consider that his categories and opinions are about fifty years old. It seems that in business valuation, anything older than a month is already stale. Although his categories are not definitive, they rationally suggest differing rates for differing risks. They are based on total corporate earnings, not dividends or cash throw-off.

I cannot tell you, unfortunately, whether Dewing based his rates before or after taxes. Back in the 1950s, the taxman's share was not the major consideration it is today, so it is probably safe to assume that the rates are before income tax. Although they provide a guide, do not use Dewing's rates indiscriminately. Accept and treat them for what they are worth, which in many situations may be very little.

SCHILT'S RISK PREMIUMS FOR DISCOUNTING

In 1982, James Schilt developed another theory of determining capitalization rates by categorizing businesses into risk classes. He suggests that each is entitled to a bonus or premium in the rate that is above the risk-free, or safe, rate. Schilt writes:

"As discount or capitalization rates are fairly arbitrarily determined, I have attempted to set forth guidelines for using specific premiums. Beginning with the risk-free rate, a premium would be added according to the risk category, and the sum would be the risk-compensated discount rate."

Schilt's Risk Premiums for Discounting Projected Income Streams

Category	Description	Risk Premium
1.	Established businesses with a strong trade position, are well-financed, have depth in management, whose past earnings have been stable, and whose future is highly predictable.	6 – 10%

2. Established businesses in a more competitive industry that are   11 – 15%
   well-financed, have depth in management, have stable past
   earnings, and whose future is fairly predictable.

3. Businesses in a highly competitive industry that require little   16 – 20%
   capital to enter, no management depth, element of risk is high,
   although past record may be good.

4. Small businesses that depend on the special skill of one or two   21 – 25%
   people. Larger established businesses that are highly cyclical
   in nature. In both cases, future earnings may be expected to
   deviate widely from projections.

5. Small one-man businesses of a personal services nature where   26 – 30%
   the transferability of the income stream is in question.

NOTE: The risk premium is added to the risk-free rate.... . The resulting figure
is the risk-adjusted capitalization rate in use for discounting the projected
income stream. Because of the wide variation in the effective tax rates among
companies, these figures are to be used with pre-tax income."[2]

Schilt's rates, being more modern than Dewing's, although still too broad for most
circumstances, could possibly apply. It would appear that for most situations, although
he does not so indicate, his rates apply only to the business portion of the entity
being appraised. Assuming this to be so, a going-concern value estimate would require
the use of a split rate: one for the real estate and a second, Schilt's, for the business.
In the standard going-concern definition, the business portion includes the machinery
and equipment, all non-real-estate tangible items, and all intangible items. Otherwise
stated, a simulation of the typical rental situation where one party owns the property
and a second the business.

Despite being far too wide in scope for most appraisal applications, the Schilt rates
provide a guide, if only in the most general of terms. Accordingly, as with the Dewing
rates, use Schilt's as a guide only.

MARKET-DERIVED CAPITALIZATION RATES

A market-oriented or market-derived capitalization rate is obtained by dividing the
net operating profit (after payment of, or reserve for, income tax) by the selling price
of the business. It produces a single capitalization rate without distinction as to what
percentage of that rate is interest on the investment (return on) or what percent is
recapture of capital (return of). The rate is abstracted from the transfer of several
similar businesses, by the use of the median, mode, or comparable transactions. (In
both real estate and business appraisal, use of a mathematical average is a no-no.)

The Formula:

$$\frac{\text{Net Operating Profit}}{\text{Selling Price of the Business}} \times 100 = \text{Capitalization Rate}$$

When appraising a real-estate investment, use this method to obtain a
capitalization rate; it best represents what is actually happening in the market. It

> A market-oriented
> or market-derived
> capitalization rate
> is obtained by dividing
> the net operating profit
> (after payment of,
> or reserve for,
> income tax)
> by the selling price
> of the business.

might not work so well for going concerns, because you need an insider to separate the monetary and the intrinsic values in the transaction. Thus, a pure abstraction of a capitalization rate from only the selling price and the reported profitability of any business may not provide the correct answer. As I have said, all transactions are subject to the motivations of the seller and the buyer, as well as price and terms negotiations. If you are appraising, say, an apartment block in a larger community, you can usually find enough comparatively recent sales from which to abstract a market capitalization rate. But how often do you see comparable feed mills, greenhouses, or concrete ready-mix plants offered for sale, let alone including all pertinent data in their sales information?

The other side of the equation, or the reciprocal, is the use of a net income multiplier, rather than an overall capitalization rate. Although multipliers are usually applied only to total sales and income, not after-tax operating profits, you can still use them. Some industries respond better to a multiplier than to some abstract fraction that combines interest and recapture. A business is worth so many times net profit, period. Generally, however, the financial community shies away from multipliers. If you are going to use them, and there is no suggestion that you should not, just do not apply it too liberally.

MARKET RATE WEAKNESSES

Here are the principal weaknesses:

- an insufficient number of similar transactions from which to draw an accurate capitalization rate, the inability to produce a random selection,
- lack of comparability (Are the comparables comparable?),
- insufficient data (an owner who is reluctant to open the books or to reveal the true consideration on a sale),
- some incorrect data,
- accounting differences,
- the assumption of management constancy,
- financing differences, mortgage take-backs, etc.,
- no consideration for future prospects,
- no consideration of the plant's sufficiency or unused capacity,
- age of plant, condition, relationship of the respective values of the different components, real estate, machinery and equipment, goodwill, etc.

You will often hear me say this: when valuing a frequently traded type of business, assuming that proper data is made available, you can obtain capitalization rates from the marketplace. But when these conditions do not exist, and most of the time they do not, or when the market rates vary too widely for any accurate correlation, then you should revert to the more reliable accounting-formula rate-abstraction procedures.

Sometimes, though, you will be able to establish a reasonably accurate market-derived capitalization rate for frequently traded businesses. Much depends on the market sample, the randomness, the similarity amongst the comparable businesses, and the analyst's skill. Individual transactions are subject to unexplainable market deviations, mostly created by seller and buyer motives and unaccountable intrinsic values. To adjust for these variances, you need to refine the market-abstracted rates by a quality comparability process.

> But how often do you see comparable feed mills, greenhouses, or concrete ready-mix plants offered for sale, let alone including all pertinent data in their sales information?

HOW TO ABSTRACT THE MARKET CAPITALIZATION RATE

Consider the sales of five fast-food restaurants, some franchised, some not. All five are actual sales, all fairly recent, and all offering full physical and financial information. Later on, when you calculate the comparative sales value estimate and that of the subject's goodwill, you will break down and use the components of real estate, fixtures and equipment, and goodwill. But not now. At this point, you are interested only in net operating profit and selling price.

Two Notes of Caution:

1. I repeat: When using comparable sales to undertake any of the valuation approaches, always ensure that the comparables used are comparable. Remember our earlier discussions about direct and indirect competitors. In an exercise of this type, use only direct. A store with a fast-food take-out counter is not necessarily comparable to a Burger King.

2. Our model restaurant owns the real estate. If you use a comparable sale that does not, and there is nothing wrong with doing so, make them more equal by separating the comparable's rental, paid on a net basis, deduct it from the expense schedule, and add it to the net operating profit. Property taxes, insurance, utilities, and normal repairs and maintenance are an expense of the restaurant. Only compare like to likes.

Comparable Fast-food Restaurant Sales

	Net Operating Profit	Selling Price	Capitalization Rate
Indicator No. 1	$ 78,000	$ 385,000	20.26%
Indicator No. 2	$ 66,000	$ 430,000	15.35%
Indicator No. 3	$ 142,000	$ 650,000	21.85%
Indicator No. 4	$ 170,000	$ 850,000	20.00%
Indicator No. 5	$ 109,000	$ 575,000	19.96%
Highest Capitalization Rate			21.85%
Median Capitalization Rate			20.00%
Lowest Capitalization Rate			15.85%

WHICH ONE SHOULD YOU USE?

As the five value indicators demonstrate above, the capitalization rates do not acceptably conform. The spread is between 15.35% and 21.85%. So if you take a restaurant that produces a net operating profit of, say, $50,000, then its value is $325,733 at the 15.35% capitalization rate. But at 21.85%, that value drops to $228,833, a difference of $96,900. The correct value should float somewhere between the two extremes, but where?

Except when conducting a regression analysis, professional appraisers seldom use arithmetic averages. Even when it is the most comparable of the comparables, they do not choose either end of the range. The mean takes into account the very high and low values, which tend to skew the final answer. Normally, appraisers prefer to use median values in the final selection of the capitalization rate. Yet you need to weigh it against the best comparable of the group.

The median is the number that is in the centre of the array. Number three of the five, not halfway between the lowest and the highest. Not unduly affected by either the high or the low, tending to dampen the error factor in calculating the rates, it most accurately indicates what an average buyer would pay and an average seller accept for this restaurant. Still, always remember, the average person acts more on subjective than objective motives. Further, this method bases the value strictly on net operating profit. It does not worry about the value of the tangible assets, which form the foundation for the value of all going concerns.

QUALITY COMPARISONS

High capitalization rates produce low values, and low rates produce high values. Median rates are supposed to produce the right number for everybody. Thus, in the above example, using a net operating profit of $50,000 and a median rate of 20.00%, our restaurant is worth $250,000.

Most times, real-estate appraisers use the median rate without further qualification or judgment. In all fairness, most of us spend our lives appraising apartment blocks and warehouses where we see more market conformity and comparable sales than when valuing a going concern. The underlying philosophy is to be able to say, based on the rate produced from each individual sale, "My restaurant is worth so many dollars." When you use several sales, you will notice much more pronounced inconsistency than in the range demonstrated above. If you try to compare one on one, the uncertainty will increase. For example, if your restaurant is high-class but the comparable is dilapidated, or vice versa, the rate abstracted from this particular sale is probably not a fair comparison. So you use the median.

Maybe it is not so bad. Maybe you can consider the obvious differences and accordingly adjust the market-abstracted capitalization rate for each sale. It can be something as simple as a point or two for inferiority or superiority, or a complicated exercise considering points of difference in finite detail. You could include location, ratio of site to building value, building condition, comparison of equipment values, the amount included for goodwill, competitive factors, length of time in business, future potential, etc.

The unadjusted median normally works quite well for a passive investment, such as real estate. Yet frequently for the active business it is simply not good enough to follow the tried formula of selecting the middle number, and leave it at that. Without further qualification, the spread between the highest and lowest is irreconcilable. The theory that the better restaurants always bring the better price, without further qualification, is too abstract. Because the numbers often do not work out, you should narrow the range by assessing the importance of each value contributor's variances. Add a bit to the rate if the comparable is superior to your target business; subtract a point or so from the rate if the comparable is inferior (a higher rate = a lower value).

When using the array of capitalization rate indicators to determine a market value for the appraisal subject, look at the median. But when calculating interest or discount rates for this purpose, use the arithmetic average, not the median. All investors are interested in averaging out. Their concern is the long-term average cost of, or return on capital, not a spot statistical value. Median interest rates in debt servicing, or when studying cost versus return, do not really matter.

High capitalization rates produce low values, and low rates produce high values. Median rates are supposed to produce the right number for everybody.

I have said that working capital must be considered along with all other assets. In almost all sales of going concerns, however, on an assets-only basis, it is not included in the purchase price. Therefore, in the final value estimate, if you developed the capitalization rate without including working capital, then you have to add the working capital to the final value estimate. If you included it when you figured out the market capitalization rates, then it is automatically included in the final value estimate of the subject business.

TERM-OF-LEASE LIMITATIONS

In property leasehold situations, the capitalization or discount rate can be affected largely by the remaining term on the lease. This is in cases where that termination would produce a higher-than-normal rate. For example, assume a normal discount rate of fifteen percent. Your subject has three years remaining on the lease and the probability of renewing it is questionable. You use a discount rate of 33.33%. The exception is if the lease is not an issue: the business can afford to buy the real estate it occupies, could relocate without loss of business or by creating excess costs, or can afford to pay a much higher rent, thus eliminating the possibility of eviction. Alternately, where the lease term exceeds the discount rate, this concern may be disregarded. A fifteen-percent rate equals 6.67 years.

Assume that you are considering a marginally profitable business with six months left on the lease. The discount rate automatically becomes 200%. No ifs, buts, or maybes. In all probability, there was not any measurable goodwill to start with; at this rate, it is dwindled to nothing. The business's breakup or liquidation value might outweigh its going concern value.

Treat this rule with discretion. About two years ago, our firm appraised a drug store owned by five pharmacists. The total sales exceeded $3,000,000 per year. The owners' annual salaries and perks exceeded $425,000, staff wages were above industry standards, cost of sales normal, and the store still showed an annual net profit of about $275,000. The lease had something less than nine months remaining with no renewal negotiations commenced between the druggists and the building owners. By applying the discount rate to the remaining lease term, the earnings of this business would be discounted at 133.3%. It would have been ridiculous to use this rate under the circumstances; no one should ever take such a report seriously.

STOCK-MARKET INDICATORS

Every appraisal textbook and course seems to suggest strongly, almost insist, that you need only look to the stock market to obtain total sales multipliers, relative discount or capitalization rates, price-earnings ratios, and all other measures of value. It is all there, or so they say. This text is different. I am not going to tell you to look there at all; or if you do, be extra-cautious.

In some situations, stock-market indicators could directly relate to the capitalization rates used in the appraisal of small businesses. Like unclassified market-obtained multipliers and capitalization rates, most cannot be applied without further clarification or qualification. The street value of all issued shares of a publicly traded company often have no correlation to its tangible net worth. Yet those same shares are considered as equities. The problem is that the value of a publicly traded share of any company rarely represents a fixed percent of the tangible equity or earned surplus of that company. Usually the market price is a manipulated composition of value and anticipation that frequently changes for little or no reason.

If you cannot see a better alternative, you might find some merit in examining the profitability and price-earnings ratios of specific industries and then correlating them to certain small businesses. But be warned: this is dangerous territory. All of the red flags are flying. For example, if your target company is a larger sawmill, you might successfully compare profitability and share prices with Canadian Forest Products Ltd. or Georgia-Pacific. There is little point, however, in trying to assimilate the Oscar Meyer Meat Packing Company with Schultz's Neighborhood Butcher Shop.

In all fairness, most business valuation texts were written by and for accountants who use what we real-estate appraisers call the back-door approach, by which you discount net after-tax earnings into a single estimate of value, unsupported by other procedures. As the tangible-asset segments form only an undivided part of that total value, they must be extracted later. Additionally, real-estate appraisers rarely conduct share valuations as do the accountants. Because accountants seldom work from the asset base forward, they may find stock-market indicators and share trading prices more relevant.

All else being equal, price-earnings ratios are directly affected by:

- present level of earnings,
- company size,
- risk, both market and political,
- debt-equity ratio,
- dividend yield,
- past growth of company earnings,
- past growth of company dividends,
- expected future growth of company earnings,
- expected growth of company dividends.

But negatively:

- they may reflect an optimism not actually there,
- they may reflect earnings projections that do not materialize,
- they may be paying for earnings before they occur,
- the price-earnings ratio or the stock value may have no relationship whatever to the assets value or to the actual value of the company.

This quotation from the Council of the London Stock Exchange, dated December 1946, is worth repeating:

> "We desire to state authoritatively that Stock Exchange quotations are not related directly to the value of a company's assets, or to the amount of its profits, and consequently these quotations, no matter what date may be chosen for reference, cannot form a fair and equitable or rational basis for compensation."

If you were to examine, over a longer period, the year-end prime bank rates, the five-year commercial mortgage rates, and the long-term bond rates, you would find that they consistently track each other. So there is a strong correlation between cost of debt and return on equity. Whereas the money market demonstrates a high degree of internal discordance, the consumer price index increases, although sporadically at times. This strongly suggests that there is no direct inflationary relationship between the two. Using the cost of living as a criterion, the actual cost of money is decreasing. The various stock-exchange indices show its total lack of relationship to the debt-equity requirements of real estate. This suggests no correlation whatever.

If you cannot see a better alternative, you might find some merit in examining the profitability and price-earnings ratios of specific industries and then correlating them to certain small businesses. But be warned: this is dangerous territory.

I hope I have proved my point. The stock market may provide a reliable indicator for accountants valuing larger or publicly traded companies, but for small businesses, the relationship is practically nil. Although stock analysts and salespeople constantly provide high return figures to prove the worth of stock-market investments, most are based on price-earnings ratios, not dividends paid. To obtain these high returns, and they do exist from time to time, you must own a growth stock, which normally is not blue-chip. And you must sell, not hold.

Before leaving this subject, there is one other consideration: the theory of negative covariance. It suggests that stock and real-estate prices move opposite to each other. When one goes up, the other goes down. I do not want to get into analysing this theory in any depth, but there may be something to it. Without question, the price of stocks is a much more volatile commodity than that of real estate, fixtures, and equipment. It is more subject to the bulls, the bears, the business cycle, economic swings, political decisions, and the fashion of the day. On June 15, 1989, the day after the Beijing student massacre, stock prices on the Hong Kong market fell by twenty percent. Did the companies' asset value decline by this much? Very doubtful, as the market reverted to the original price levels within a few weeks.

Conversely, you should recognize stock-market quotations as a factor in the money market. I have referred to the consideration of alternative investments, the investment climate, and the interaction of the efficient market of which the stock market is a part. Appraisers often have trouble finding enough supportive data. So, if the stock market can help you, use it. Just ensure that you are not comparing apples to oranges. Do not simply provide random quotations to prove something that is otherwise unsupportable. Like an old fiddle, the stock market can produce any sound that you want. At this same time, do not disregard it because it does not fit into some pre-described pattern.

References

[1] Dewing, A.S. (1953). *The financial policy of corporations*. 5th Edition. New York, NY: The Ronald Press Company.

[2] Schilt, J.H. (1982). A rational approach to capitalization rates for discounting the future income stream of a closely held company. *The Financial Planner*, January.

Appraisers often have trouble finding enough supportive data. So, if the stock market can help you, use it. Just ensure that you are not comparing apples to oranges.

NOTES

_____

_____

_____

_____

_____

_____

_____

_____

_____

_____

_____

_____

_____

_____

_____

_____

_____

_____

_____

_____

_____

_____

_____

_____

THE COMPARATIVE SALES APPROACH TO VALUE

FOR the appraisal of residential or small commercial real estate, the comparative sales approach, also called the market data approach, is the all-time favorite. Even for larger properties, the cost and capitalized income approaches draw most of their input data from it. The comparative method is used more often than either of the other two, and by some appraisers more than both combined. With this approach, you directly compare the target with recent sales that are as similar as possible. Listings and properties offered for sale set the upper limit of value.

Here, the underlying principle is substitution. The value found cannot exceed the cost of acquiring an equally desirable substitute that offers all of the same advantages, assuming that there is no undue delay in acquiring it. This principle may have considerable merit when you are looking at small businesses, because the offerings normally outnumber the buyers, but most of the time this method is questionable.

No two properties are identical, but in an active real-estate market, you can usually find a reasonable selection of sold, or for sale, properties with enough similarities to estimate the subject's value with confidence. Active businesses, however, are more complicated. Frequently, they are in the same industry or the same town, yet have nothing else in common. Most of the buyers are subjectively motivated amateurs who seldom bring any consistency to the marketplace. So when you try to compare small businesses, you often wind up comparing apples and oranges, doing a lot of fancy arithmetic, and proving very little.

ONLY REAL-ESTATE APPRAISERS USE THIS METHOD

Accountants, professional business appraisers, and stock-market analysts avoid this method, except when they are using price-earnings ratios to value public companies. Only real-estate appraisers like it, probably because most started by appraising single-family dwellings, where it is still the best procedure.

Despite its many shortcomings, the approach may work in actively traded businesses, such as hotels, motels, cafes, and convenience stores, or in businesses that appeal to first-time buyers. The trick is to find the common denominator. So many dollars per square foot of building, total-sales multiplier standard in the industry, sales per square foot, profitability ratios, potential, or whatever. It might be tough — or impossible — to find any common denominator. Plus you might not be able to ferret out all the information you want, including seller and buyer motivation.

The major problem is that amateur buyers set and control the small-business market, and their emotional, illogical purchases create further waves in an already wonky marketplace. You can look at one business that fetched a certain price, then at a similar business with a totally different price and terms. You just have to do your best to weigh the similar and dissimilar areas between your target enterprise and the comparable. Then you interpret why each business was bought, or sold, for a particular price.

The value found cannot exceed the cost of acquiring an equally desirable substitute that offers all of the same advantages, assuming that there is no undue delay in acquiring it.

METHODOLOGY

First you need to seek out sales of comparable businesses. Next, adjust these sales, based their similarities and differences, toward the business being appraised. For this, you interpret the background information and break down, in detail, the points of comparison.

ELEMENTS OF COMPARABILITY

You must consider the following general and specific areas between the subject enterprise and the comparables. It may be difficult to apply whole dollars or percentages to the general category.

Most often they provide little more than a background, or are used as supportive data. You can usually measure elements that are appropriate only to the business being valued.

General concerns and basic criteria:

1. Are the comparables actually comparable? This may seem silly, but too often I have seen appraisal reports where this is not so.

2. If the target business and the comparable are not in the same specific business, they should at least be in the same industry.

3. Consider the general trend of the industry for the subject and the comparable. Is it growing, declining, or remaining stable?

4. The markets should be comparable. You will not gain much from comparing a cabinet manufacturing shop in Minneapolis with one in St. John, North Dakota.

5. The target business and comparable should be the same general size or at least in the same general category. You must be able to compare their total sales, expenses, operating profits, and future prospects. You might also want to compare them with industry standards and averages.

6. What is the market growth potential for the subject business and the comparable? How does each business's economic environment directly and indirectly affect its selling price?

Specific and adjustable elements of comparison:

1. Look at the interrelationship and breakdown of the capital and other assets, such as quantity and quality of land, buildings, machinery and equipment, age, condition, utility, leasehold improvements, and redundant assets. Did the price include goodwill, inventory, or working capital? If accounts receivable were included, were they discounted?

2. Could any exclusive franchises, patents, trademarks, licensing agreements, long-term marketing agreements, purchase agreements, lock-ins or other special rights, benefits, or counterproductive agreements alter the value of the subject or the comparables?

3. Was it an asset or a share sale? Were any special warranties or conditions attached to the shares? What was the amount of income tax payable on recaptured depreciation, or on capital gain?

4. Were there any special or unusual terms? Any large or abnormal vendor take-backs? There is an old adage in the sale of businesses and real estate: "You can have any price you want if I can name the terms."

5. How long had the subject business and the comparable been established? Were the historical levels of sales and profits stable or variable?

6. How long had the comparable been for sale? If for a longer time, did the buyer discount it to conclude the transaction? On the other hand, if it sold immediately, maybe it was too cheap.

7. Did the comparable have a virtual monopoly in its market, normal competition, or an overly competitive situation? Did new competitors start recently, or others discontinue?

8. Does buyer or seller motivation cause concern? Was the comparable an open market or a distress sale? Would any unusual conditions produce a different selling price under different circumstances?

9. Were there any special buyer circumstances or requirements that would enhance the value of the purchase? Was the buyer a leveraged amateur, an experienced investor, or someone with a special interest?

10. Were there any earnouts? Did the sale hinge on the previous managers, particularly the owner, continuing with the new owner?

11. Did the price and terms depend on the company meeting certain sales and profit objectives after acquisition? Although not common in the sale of a small business, sometimes there is a vendor take-back. That means that the seller helps to finance the buyer, and the principal may be reduced if all that the vendor promises does not come true.

12. Could any pending litigation affect the value or future prospects of the target company or the comparable? Must any long-term product warranties be honored?

13. Do you know the comparable's correct selling price and terms? A title search on a real-estate transfer will normally produce the correct selling price; in businesses, usually the wrong one.

In Canada, and in most American states, the real-estate portion is the only value declared during a property transfer. Although at least part of the fixtures and equipment, goodwill, and sometimes working capital are sold and transferred, too, you will not find these declared at the Land Titles Office in Canada, or the Office of the Registrar of Deeds in most of the United States. So the transfer might show a stated amount, when the business actually sold for considerably more.

In addition to the points listed above, you will undoubtedly compare other items in specific situations. I cannot list every possibility for each situation. There will always be others. Make sure you also account for the background and supportive data detailed in Chapter Three.

ADJUSTMENTS TO MARKET-VALUE INDICATORS

The estimated market value of the subject business, by the comparative market data approach, is a mathematically calculated amount, intended to represent what actually occurs in the marketplace. It weighs the similarities and dissimilarities between the prospect business and the comparables, or market-value indicators.

The complexity of the target concern and the amount of information that can be gleaned from comparable sales will dictate the number and size of the required adjustments. The ideal is to have ten or twelve recent sales, all as similar to the subject in as many respects as possible. Still, more is not always better. Quality is definitely preferable to quantity.

Supposedly, any business's selling price sums up the contributory value of each of its tangible and intangible components. Each component can be individually measured and compared with the same component of any other similar business, then value-adjusted for any differences. This is an adding and subtracting process, item by item, to estimate the most probable market value of the target business. We assume that all similar businesses have a common value, and we are concerned only about their dissimilarities.

Let us say you are valuing a neighborhood dry cleaner. About a year ago, a similar plant in this same general area sold, for assets only, for $225,000. Let us use that sale to estimate the value of your target business.

> The estimated market value of the subject business, by the comparative market data approach, is a mathematically calculated amount, intended to represent what actually occurs in the marketplace.

VALUE BREAKDOWN OF XYZ DRY CLEANER

Sale Proceeds

• market value of the site	$ 25,000
• depreciated value of the building	125,000
• depreciated value of the equipment	75,000
• value of the goodwill	nil
Total Selling Price	$ 225,000

Adjustments can be made by using whole dollars or percentages, individually applied to each difference. Always work towards the subject business. In other words, rate the subject as superior or inferior to the comparable, point by point.

Business Adjustments

- time: the real-estate market has increased by five percent during the past year, (this would not affect equipment or goodwill),   + $ 7,500

- potential: the subject has a better location and thus more potential; it is superior by five percent,   + $ 11,250

- the seller took back a large second mortgage; he would have got ten percent less on a cash sale,   − $ 22,500

- the seller really wanted out; he could have got at least five percent more if not desperate,   + $ 11,250

- the subject is more profitable; add five percent,   + $ 11,250

Capital Asset Adjustments

• subject site is worth $10,000 more than comparable's,	+ $	10,000
• subject building is ten-percent smaller	– $	12,500
• subject building is five-percent superior, for quality, age, and condition,	+ $	6,250
• subject equipment is fifteen-percent superior,	+ $	11,250
• subject has an estimated goodwill of	+ $	25,000
Total of Adjustments	+ $	58,750
Add Selling Price of Comparable	$	225,000
Value of Subject Dry Cleaner, Based on this Sale	$	283,750

When appraising real estate and considering a prescribed time or specific market change, do this first and then factor in all other adjustments. Here, you would adjust the real-estate component by five percent, raising its current value to $157,500. You would base all other comparisons on this. But when valuing a business, unless the market differential is great, this can overcomplicate the exercise. The equipment depreciation changes. Who knows what happens to goodwill? Unless you are looking at something major, I would advise you to stick to the exercise as demonstrated above.

Follow this same procedure, adjusting individual comparables point by point. For the purpose of demonstration, I kept this exercise as simple as possible. In the real world, you would compare many other factors, and the adjustments would be more finite.

Although I broke down the individual components for the comparable, this is seldom available in real life. You will rarely be privy to the composition, terms, motivation, or rationale behind any concluded transaction. Mostly, you will know only the address of the business sold, the price, and the date of sale. The rest is up to your own best guess. This is an excellent procedure in theory, but often a poor one in practice. There are better methods for active businesses.

The market is not a weigh-scale that can scientifically measure, analyse, and correlate every factor in every buy-sell decision. At best, it records the countless individuals' actions and reactions, some based on logic, others based on emotional likes, dislikes, prejudices, and experience.

Moreover, the selling price is not always the key bit of information. What you really want to know is the motivation behind that number. An accurate comparison of two businesses is an elusive thing. Using basic mathematics, you try to appraise them and adjust for differences, with your chance of being correct probably about average.

> At best, [the market] records the countless individuals' actions and reactions, some based on logic, others based on emotional likes, dislikes, prejudices, and experience.

RULES OF THUMB AND MULTIPLIERS

The theory of an income multiplier is that a common denominator applies to all similar properties or businesses. For example, apartment blocks sell for six to eight times rental income, insurance agencies sell for two times annual commissions, grocery stores sell for one-half times sales, and so forth. All common businesses or properties can theoretically be reduced to a multiplier. All others in the same business can be valued by its literal application. It is a real-estate rule of thumb, often taken as gospel. To appraise, all you need to do is find the common denominator, or multiplier, then apply it to the subject.

Sadly, multipliers do not really help in the appraisal of small businesses. Too many areas are left to interpretation, not mathematical exactness. The pure application of a multiplier ignores far too many variables. If several indicators are used, then the

> Sadly, multipliers do not really help in the appraisal of small businesses. Too many areas are left to interpretation, not mathematical exactness.

highs and lows usually vary too much. Due to the shortage of appropriate comparables and the lack of accurate data on each, medians and math means are often suspect.

For example, consider four full-service motor hotels. Each has a revenue of exactly one million dollars. If the strict application of a total-sales multiplier is correct, based exclusively on total sales, all four have exactly the same market value.

Suppose that the first is a new building, well managed, showing a positive growth potential. The second is a skid-row hotel in a very poor state of repair. Although the revenue is the same, the third rents out the restaurant. The fourth is mostly a beverage operation with an annual entertainment cost of more than $100,000. Are all four hotels really worth the same amount on the market? Of course not! Yet an appraisal based on a pure application of a sales multiplier, as some are, would suggest identical values.

A net-operating-profit multiplier, the reciprocal of a capitalization rate, could provide a totally different, yet more accurate answer. The first method accounted for total sales only, without considering how those sales were derived. The net-profit multiplier considers only the bottom line, and that is what business is really all about.

Following are sales data on eleven smaller hotels that were sold during the past several months. As there are definite regional differences in this industry, all are in the same geographical area. The selection is not exactly random, in that all were taken from my files. They were hotels that either my company appraised or for which we have full financial data.

Perhaps a true random selection would provide a slightly different median. As an appraiser, though, I know that most times I have to make do with what is available, not what is ideal.

HOTEL SALES AND MULTIPLIERS

Listed in ascending order, based on date of sale:

Hotel	Total Sales	Net Profit	Selling Price	Sales Multiplier	Profit Multiplier
A	$ 190,602	$ 51,525	$ 310,000	1.63	5.03
B	726,317	150,292	950,000	1.31	6.32
C	370,873	87,087	625,000	1.69	7.18
D	326,239	89,895	475,000	1.46	5.28
E	1,177,765	279,257	1,850,000	1.57	6.62
F	235,679	45,547	310,000	1.32	6.81
G	467,351	118,090	615,000	1.32	5.21
H	1,352,588	162,986	1,250,000	0.92	7.67
I	981,854	123,832	986,400	1.04	7.97
J	377,597	86,048	550,000	1.46	6.39
K	347,249	86,934	425,000	1.22	4.89

High Sales Multiplier	1.69	High Profit Multiplier	7.97
Low Sales Multiplier	0.92	Low Profit Multiplier	4.89
Median	1.32	Median	6.39

To apply the range of multipliers:

1. Total-sales Multiplier

The subject hotel has a total sales and income of $1,000,000.

High value: $ 1,000,000 × 1.69 = $ 1,690,000 market value

Low value: $ 1,000,000 × 0.92 = $ 920,000 market value

Median: $ 1,000,000 × 1.32 = $ 1,320,000 market value

Based on this demonstration, the value of the subject hotel lies somewhere between $920,000 and $1,690,000. But where? Pick a number. It cannot be wrong by more than half of the difference between the two extremes, $385,000.

2. Net-profit Multiplier

The subject hotel has a net operating profit — before long-term debt service, depreciation, or income tax — of $225,000. Assuming a proper ratio for rooms, food, and beverages, this profit level is about right for the average suburban hotel. Also assumed are average industry expenses. More modern hotels that have a higher proportionate income from rooms are generally more profitable. Net income in older establishments, with a higher-than-average percent of food sales, or excessive maintenance or entertainment costs, could be as low as ten percent net on sales.

High value: $ 225,000   × 7.97 =   (rounded) $ 1,793,000

Low value: $ 225,000   × 4.89 =   (rounded) $ 1,100,000

Median: $ 225,000   × 6.39 =   (rounded) $ 1,438,000

If you can choose from a wide selection of comparables, then select only those that are truly comparable.

Use of a net-profit rather than total-sales multiplier did not help much. The range between the high and the low values is still too wide for proper reconciliation. You would expect a better answer by using net profit rather than only total sales, yet it did not work out that well and, frankly, seldom does without fudging the numbers or further refining the comparables.

You might narrow the extremes somewhat by adjusting the hotels' selling prices, or either the total-sales or net-profit multipliers based on other differences. This would include most of the elements of similarity. Or you might find merit in a weighing procedure similar to that used to develop the market capitalization rate. Differences of significance could include the size and economic prosperity of the community, location within that community or district, type of district, and clientele. You could adjust for building size, age, type of construction, quality, and deferred maintenance, as well as for differences in adequacy and condition of furniture, fixtures, and equipment. Do any of the hotels have excess land by way of parking lots, used or otherwise? And so forth.

Such adjustments seldom, if ever, help to provide a more reasonable value range than you had in the first place. If you can choose from a wide selection of comparables, then select only those that are truly comparable. In the eleven sales detailed, some are definitely not appropriate. For example, hotel E is a smaller, ten-year-old, full-service motor hotel in excellent condition in a very good community. Hotel F, located in a very small hamlet, has an old frame building in terrible condition, operated perpetually by some financial institution's receiver.

The median is your best comparison tool, although it provides only an average value for an average buyer who uses average financing to buy an average property from an average seller under average circumstances. The whole exercise becomes self-defeating, does it not? No property and, more specifically, no operating business can ever be considered as average. Each is unique in many respects.

I have shown you that a hotel's value cannot be established by using only a total-sales multiplier as abstracted from the marketplace. Nor can it be accurately used for any other type of business, especially those less frequently traded than suburban hotels. You need more information.

You can never have too many comparables. But you can have too few that are truly comparable.

I do not want to beat the subject of multipliers into the ground, but I just want to give you one other demonstration that relates to the number and selection of comparables, or market-value indicators. Consider what happens to the median, on which most appraised value estimates are based, if all eleven sales multipliers are used, then only the highest seven, and then only the lowest seven. I think this is fair because you will not often find even seven good comparables, let alone use them.

> You can never have too many comparables. But you can have too few that are truly comparable.

TOTAL-SALES MULTIPLIERS

All multipliers are arranged in ascending order:

	All 11	Highest 7	Lowest 7
H	0.92		0.92
I	1.04		1.04
K	1.22		1.22
B	1.31		1.31
F	1.32	1.32	1.32
G	1.32	1.32	1.32
C	1.46	1.46	1.46
J	1.46	1.46	
E	1.57	1.57	
A	1.63	1.63	
C	1.69	1.69	
Median Values	1.32	1.46	1.31

The evidence speaks for itself! Perhaps a different grouping or a more random selection could adversely affect the resultant median multiplier. Let me restate: a sufficient supply of comparable comparables is as rare as hen's teeth. Even more rare is complete or accurate information for those obtained. Therefore, the final value estimate is always suspect.

VALIDITY OF RULES OF THUMB

For the moment, let us be a two-armed economist. On the one hand, multipliers and rules of thumb have been totally discounted, but on the other, they might have a place in determining value. Unsophisticated members of the buying and selling community and, at times, lenders often accept their almost literal application. This suggests that multipliers and rules of thumb might work in certain circumstances.

While every business's sales and income relate to its market value, you should treat multipliers and general rules of thumb as guide posts only. You still need to apply other factors of comparison.

LEVERAGE

Although financing influences price and value, it is hard to nail down a meaningful correlation. Does a buyer pay more, or less, for a business if she can arrange a large loan? In recent years, we have heard plenty about leveraged buyouts, particularly in relation to the purchase, sale, and merger of larger companies. All it means is debt: buying a company with the lowest down payment or contributing the least amount by way of equity. Also included is the outright purchase of a company, then arranging financing by pledging, as security, the assets acquired. There is nothing magical about a leveraged buyout; it is really common. In a corporate situation, the debt can be the issuance of longer-term debentures or high-rate, high-risk bonds; or a public stock offering, although the aim is usually to take a public company private; or a good, old-fashioned bank loan. Leverage is only a fancier way of talking about debt-equity ratios that real-estate agents, business brokers, and appraisers have been calculating for years.

When you buy a book or attend a seminar on how to make a million in real estate, you will hear lots of chat about leverage. Buy an underpriced property with the lowest down payment possible, improve it slightly, then flip it out for a huge profit. Returns on the investment could be astronomical, or so they say. What they do not say — other than how difficult it is to find all those foolish sellers and sucker buyers with deep pockets — is that if the market takes a dive, or if the property is badly managed, then the wheeler-dealer investor can be wiped out overnight. Maybe the old saying is true: "If you ain't got equity, you ain't got nothing."

> ...the old saying is true: "If you ain't got equity, you ain't got nothing."

THE EFFECT OF FINANCING ON VALUE

The standard definition of market value assumes that a going concern will be bought for all cash or its equivalent. Although no one has really defined "equivalent," the term remains. In practice, though, probably less than ten percent of all transfers of businesses or real estate are made for all cash. Purchases are financed by loans from friends and relatives, mortgages, debentures, issues floated on the stock exchange, you name it. Today's society seems to prefer buying with the minimum of equity and the maximum of debt. Spread out the risk, with the other fellow taking the biggest share.

In the real world, you might want to evaluate these financing methods. Compare each transaction with the other and assess its effect on the selling price or market value, price being the easier to discern. Price results from a negotiating process, often the product of a trade-off. Take something off the bottom, add it to the top, reduce the rate of interest, lengthen the amortization period, stretch out the term, and so forth. On the other hand, for the purposes of comparative market analysis, you must consider the adjusted value with the assumption that the sale was made for all cash or its equivalent.

Value could be affected by special financing or a vendor take-back including, but not limited to:

- a low-interest-rate mortgage, such as a second or third mortgage. This would usually be subordinate to available or existing financing. There are two considerations: lower interest rate and availability. Most financial institutions are reluctant to borrow on subordinated mortgages or other instruments, except if the capital assets constitute the major portion of the business value. Borrowing against goodwill is virtually impossible. If and when these loans are made, their interest rates are usually much higher than the market, with reduced amortization and shorter-term periods.

- zero-rate interest. This works exactly the same as a lower-interest-rate loan, exception that the agreement calls for payments on principal only, with interest just on payments in arrears. This form of financing is not that common in smaller ventures but is used by more sophisticated buyers and sellers who want to avoid income tax. If all of the principal is capitalized into the purchase price, it is considered as capital gain, taxable at a lower rate than income on interest.

Both the IRS and Revenue Canada are wise to the scheme. They will often insert the market rate of interest into the transaction and discount the reported selling price accordingly. There is no escaping the taxman.

- a wraparound mortgage, by which the seller receives payments from the buyer, part of which is used to reduce existing debt. This works well if lower-than-market-rate financing is already in place and no one wishes to disturb it.
- mortgage buy-down by the seller. Not as common in businesses as in smaller real-estate properties, it is used at a time of high interest rates when buyers shop around for lower debt-servicing costs rather than total prices. Here, the seller makes a large cash payment against the principal of the mortgage but leaves the outstanding principal unchanged. The effect is to reduce the rate of interest. It would be considered as the reverse of the discount mortgage, the intent of which is to increase the interest rate. By discounting, the amount of money advanced is less than the face amount of the mortgage.
- deferment of a part of the purchase price. A subordinated mortgage is written into the agreement but there are no payments for either interest or principal for a specified period.
- earnouts and equity participation. The business is sold only so much at a time. It can be a two-sided agreement, with payments applied to both equity and debt. A certain down payment is made and the balance is paid to the seller over a pre-agreed period of time. The timing and amount of principal payment, and at times the rate of interest, are determined by the profitability of the business and its ability to pay. By this, the buyer is assured that what the seller said holds true. At the same time, in addition to normally getting a better price because of what amounts to a continuing warranty, the seller can be better protected by keeping a finger on the pulse and can more quickly recover the property, should the buyer not perform.

When the seller is financing the purchase, you should always ask: Who gains the most? Is it the buyer or the seller? The buyer can now get into business, or the seller who can now dispose of an otherwise unattractive enterprise. All of this suggests that price can often result from negotiations. But value should be altered very little, if at all. Therefore, in comparing this sale with that one, you need to reduce these terms and conditions to cash equivalence. That is the value of the completed transaction, assuming an all-cash-to-seller deal.

When the seller is financing the purchase, you should always ask: Who gains the most? Is it the buyer or the seller?

To evaluate the benefits of these deals, you must first determine who received the greatest advantage. Is it the seller or the buyer? Or does the price remain the same, despite the financing arrangement, and both seller and buyer benefit equally?

There is no pat answer, but you may wish to consider these thoughts:

- When selling prices for similar businesses are reduced to cash equivalence, they do not vary quite as much. This brings more logic into interpreting the actions of the marketplace,
- The experts disagree about whether the buyer or seller gains more. You will just have to assess the situation as you see fit,
- The seller often pays income tax only on the money as received, both interest and capital gain. Stretching it out over the longer term may keep her in a lower tax bracket,
- The seller might take back a subordinate mortgage, then require a cash sum but find that the debt instrument cannot be pledged,
- The market rate is the opportunity rate for financing, plus or minus anything gained or lost,
- A low-rate loan or financing from third parties is always regarded as at the current market rate, whether or not that is so,
- Account for the advantage gained by favorable financing only when it affects the negotiations.

In these instances, the advantage is the net present value of the difference in the amount of annual debt service for the term of the advantage. The opposite situation also applies. That is, discounting the price or value for reason of disadvantageous financing that cannot be retired without payment of a severe penalty. Frequently, a seller who genuinely wants to sell and obtain a fair price, will have to help finance the purchase. This is usually done by taking back a mortgage, often subordinated to other debt, for a part of the price. Seldom is any business ever sold for straight cash. The question is: "What are the trade-offs between a high-cost property with an available, large, low-cost mortgage, or another that has clear title?"

To make sense of all this, you need to determine the fair market value for the business. What price would it bring on the open market if bought for all cash or with conventional financing? Use the market-of-the-day interest rate, debt-equity ratio, and amortization period. The question then becomes: "How is the price/value equation affected where the package is nontypical?"

The conventional mortgage market for going concerns has always been hot and cold, frequently expanding or declining. For many, what is a bad deal today could be accepted as blue-chip tomorrow, and vice versa. Most lenders report that they always have money for solid propositions. Yet, for my needs, they seem to have run out yesterday. For the better properties, even with banks and mortgage companies, the rates and terms often differ substantially. At times, it is difficult to tell which deal is preferable.

On the other hand, certain segments continually go begging. For example, have you tried to finance a roadside motel lately? In rural Montana? During periods of rapid inflation, high interest rates, or limited money availability, this method becomes the only means to sell a small business.

You would be wise to spend as much time negotiating interest rates, amortization periods, and balloon dates as you do on the total price. You might do well to pay a bonus to acquire a large, low-rate, assumable loan. Or it might be the worst thing you could ever do. As so few mortgages go the full term, your principal concerns should be about operating within your budget, making the payments, maintaining your business in a profit mode, and being able to live and eat. Sometimes price should be a secondary factor in the buy-sell decision. We are back to "any price you want if I can name the terms."

Privately arranged, third-party financing is seldom considered. You must always assume that money obtained from any source other than seller take-back is at the

> The conventional mortgage market for going concerns has always been hot and cold, frequently expanding or declining. For many, what is a bad deal today could be accepted as blue-chip tomorrow, and vice versa.

current market rate. Any advantage gained by borrowing from an insider is for your exclusive benefit. No buyer has ever said to a seller, "I borrowed all of the money from Aunt Jane to buy your business. Since she is giving me such a low rate of interest and easy payments, I am willing to share in my good fortune by giving you a still higher price." Yet lower-than-market-rate financing, irrespective of source, or a decreased equity-to-debt ratio frequently results in the buyer paying a price that often exceeds value. Usually, the lower the down payment, the lower the rate of interest, and the more liberal the terms, the higher the selling price.

At times you may find the price of a property exorbitantly high but the available financing favorable. Or the price may be dirt cheap but the payments high. Before deciding which way to go, you must analyse each option and its effect on your intended purchase. Work to the point where you obtain the highest rate of interest on your investment and obtain the maximum leverage, but with a comfortable safety margin, then compare. Always remember, though: true value, not price, which is the starting point for comparisons, is always based on the purchase being made for cash, or conventional financing.

Consider three scenarios (all numbers have been rounded):

1. A manufacturing plant. All cash price\value .... $ 2,500,000

    Net cash throw-off before debt service or depreciation .... $ 300,000

    Purchased by:
    Cash down payment .... $ 1,000,000

    First mortgage $ 1,500,000 at market rate of 8%,
        20-year amortization.
            Annual debt service .... $ 150,000

    Cash-on-cash return, 15.0% on equity .... $ 150,000

    Total debt service and return on equity .... $ 300,000

2. The same manufacturing plant, value changed by a below-market-rate second mortgage.

    Purchased by:
    Cash down payment .... $ 500,000

    First mortgage, $ 1,500,000 at market rate of 8%,
        20-year amortization.
            Annual debt service .... $ 150,000

    Second mortgage for $776,000 @ 7.50% interest,
        20-year amortization.
            Annual debt service .... $ 75,000

    Return on $500,000 equity, same yield of 15.0% .... $ 75,000

    Total debt service and return on equity .... $ 300,000

3. The same manufacturing plant, value changed by financing with an above-market-rate second mortgage.

Purchased by:
Cash down payment .... $ 500,000

First mortgage, $ 1,500,000 at market rate of 8%,
   20-year amortization.
      Annual debt service .... $ 150,000

Second mortgage for $415,000 @ 17.50% interest,
   20-year amortization.
      Annual debt service .... $ 75,000

Return on $ 500,000 equity, same yield of 15.0% .... $ 75,000

Total debt service and return on equity .... $ 300,000

Comparative Values of the Manufacturing Plant

Purchased by:

	Case 1	Case 2	Case 3
Amount of first mortgage	$ 1,500,000	$ 1,500,000	$ 1,500,000
Amount of second mortgage	nil	776,000	415,000
Equity	1,000,000	500,000	500,000
Total price/value	$ 2,500,000	$ 2,776,000	$ 2,415,000

The cash throw-off and the percentage return to equity for all three scenarios is identical. Yet the price was boosted by $276,000 by applying a below-market-rate second mortgage, and chopped by $85,000 when the rate was above the market.

Think about it. The underlying value of the manufacturing plant did not change; it is still 2.5 million dollars. Also, if you get locked into a large mortgage with nontypical interest rates, this could create innumerable pricing problems when you come to resell or if you need an operating line of credit from the bank.

I could develop several other scenarios by using different financing techniques and equity yield requirements, shorter or longer amortization periods, balloon dates, and so forth. I could have played with the numbers by maintaining the same equity but reducing the size of either the first or second mortgage so that the payments would be smaller. But I have already made my point: financing techniques affect price, so you need to examine this when you compare recent sales with your subject business.

If you assume that price and value are equal, which they are not, both were increased by up to $276,000 by the use of below-market-rate financing. I say "up to" on purpose. Can you imagine anyone paying another $276,000 for this? Perhaps a little more than the initial $2,500,000, but not this much more. Some studies suggest that only about one-third of the benefit is passed on. So, with this financing, you would probably pay somewhere around 2.6 million dollars for this enterprise. The actual difference decreases because of taxation, the increased risk to the mortgagee created by what appears to be a smaller equity, the psychology of price versus value, and particularly the potential for less capital gain on resale.

With the above-rate financing, would the seller discount the price of the plant by $85,000? Doubtful! Any discount would never be this large. Above-market financing can work to your great disadvantage, so take extra care in negotiating price.

...if you get locked into a large mortgage with nontypical interest rates, this could create innumerable pricing problems when you come to resell or if you need an operating line of credit from the bank.

To calculate the advantage or disadvantage of nontypical financing, the debt-service differential must be reduced to net present value. Although experts disagree about the exact procedure, most prefer to consider only the difference between the amortized payments that would be at the market rate and those as required by the actual mortgage contract. These differences are reduced to net present value by discounting, at the market rate, the difference between the annual payments required. If a buy-down (also called a discount mortgage) is used, you only account for the money advanced, not the face amount of the mortgage. In calculating net present value, you must consider the mortgagor's benefit or loss only for the term of the loan and not the amortization period. If the mortgage has a balloon or term date (a clause stating that the full principal balance is payable on a certain date, before the end of the amortization period), that is the limit of the preference or disadvantage. You must assume that at the end of the term, interest will revert to the market rate.

For example: a subordinate mortgage for $100,000, 20-year amortization, 5-year term:

Market rate	12.50%	Annual debt service	$	13,634
Contract rate	7.50%	Annual debt service	$	9,667
		Difference	$	3,967

Advantage gained by the mortgagor:

Net present value of $ 3,967 per year for 5 years, discounted at 12.50%

$ 31,736

> To calculate the advantage or disadvantage of nontypical financing, the debt-service differential must be reduced to net present value.

So you can pay an additional $31,736 for this business and still be in the same position at the end of the fifth year as you would if you had obtained all of your financing at the market rate. Alternatively, were the market rate 7.50% and the contract rate 12.50%, this would be a $16,050 disadvantage, which should reduce the price of the acquisition by this amount. There was an advantage of $31,736 in the first case, and a penalty of $16,050 in the second, because the discount rate was 12.50% in the first case, and 7.50% in the second.

(You can calculate net present value and/or the discount with a financial calculator or with financial tables that are available in most stationery stores.)

You should break down these nontypical terms and conditions and reduce them to traditional financing equivalency, meaning the value of the enterprise on an all-cash basis, or an all-cash to a conventional mortgage. Still, price/value adjustments are not a single entity, and you should consider them along with all the other factors. What is the financing's direct effect on the transaction and on marketability? What are you looking for? What have you planned for the enterprise over the longer term?

In a nutshell:

- Before making an offer on any going concern, you must reduce the different financing amounts and interest rates, available or assumable, to typical financing. Only then can you measure your true return on assets and know which deal is the best.
- When considering below-market-rate mortgages, gauge who benefits the most. Is it the seller, who obtains a good price and disposes of a difficult business? Or is it the buyer, who takes advantage of a lower-than-market interest rate, often completing the acquisition with less equity? Make sure you are not going to be stuck with a someone else's dead dog.
- Adjust the price only the buyer or seller has a measurable advantage, and then only when it affects the negotiations. Where there is equality, or mortgage-rate differences are minor, you just disregard it.

- With a seller take-back mortgage, you should consider the market rate as the opportunity rate for financing, then add or subtract from that rate the net present value of any advantage or disadvantage.

Last of all, you have to test all discounts or adjustments against market evidence. The experts disagree on how to rationalize and measure the influence of nontypical financing, so be extra-careful not to fall into the trap of textbook exactness but improper market interpretation.

SPECIFIC INDUSTRY STANDARDS

Each type and class of business has its own judgmental criteria. What works for one may not work for another. Dissimilarities in the same industry are the norm. Although I have appraised three or four funeral homes, it has not been my specialty. For the record, and as a good benchmark, the National Association of Morticians suggests the following guidelines for the valuation of a funeral home on a going concern basis:

1. length of time in business in the community,

2. community acceptance: valued by increasing volume or increasing net income,

3. competition from inside and outside the community; past, present, and potential future,

4. funeral home exterior: valued by conformity to the neighborhood, condition of maintenance, parking facilities, location, and visibility,

5. funeral home interior: valued by chapel layout, cleanliness, decor, restrooms, smoking facilities, chapels, embalming facilities, casket display facilities, etc.,

6. location: access by automobile, bus, train, and airport, convenience to churches, main traffic arteries, and access to cemeteries,

7. efficient management: experienced personnel at the door, on the telephone, making arrangements, directing funerals in the office, long-range planning, public relations, and policies,

8. services offered: personal contact and customary items, such as prayer cards, plates, and crucifixes. Comparison to services and facilities offered by competitors.

You could apply the above list, with some minor corrections, to several types of business. Substitute a retail store or automobile dealership for the funeral home. With some changes and extrapolations, the model is still valid.

*...you have to test
all discounts
or adjustments against
market evidence.*

NOTES

_____

_____

_____

_____

_____

_____

_____

_____

_____

_____

_____

_____

_____

_____

_____

_____

_____

_____

_____

_____

_____

_____

_____

Chapter 11

INTRODUCTION TO THE EARNINGS APPROACHES

THERE are three approaches to the estimation of the market value of a going concern: income, income, and income. Agreed, there is the cost approach, which values the capital assets of real estate, fixtures, and equipment. Sometimes you include working capital, most times not. And there is the comparative sales approach that compares the business with similar enterprises that have recently been sold or are now for sale, making adjustments for differences. Still, when the chips are down, when the buck stops, it always comes down to the ability of the business to generate income and earn a profit. If it can't, then you consider going concern value only in relation to orderly or forced liquidation — orderly if there is enough income to support the value of the capital assets, forced if not. Nothing else matters.

To quote Harry Truman, "The buck stops here."

THE EARNINGS APPROACH TO VALUE DEFINED

The going concern value found by the earnings approach is the present worth of all net, after-income-tax profits, which the business is expected to earn during its remaining productive life. Because it's so tough to accurately forecast that productive life, future earnings, and the direct influence of management, we use perpetuity. The capitalization rate is purposely loaded, however, to make the term shorter and more realistic. As in real-estate appraisal, which employs the identical procedure, this method of determining value is based on the principle of anticipation. A buyer or investor expects to earn regular cash profits from the enterprise, plus sustained growth in the capital base. The value of the business is based on the projected amount of those profits and their rate of growth.

VALUATION CRITERIA

Value, as established by an earnings approach, is based on:

- the existing level of cash flows and net profits,
- the probability of the cash flows and profit continuing at or near the present level,
- the rate of return required to justify the investment when compared to alternative investments.

METHODOLOGY

The earnings approaches to value can be divided into two specific categories, from which there are sub-approaches. Although there is the usual overlap, and slightly different calculations to be made, each procedure should arrive at about the same

> …when the chips are down, when the buck stops, it always comes down to the ability of the business to generate income and earn a profit [that creates value].

final value conclusion. In practice, each is only a part of, or more of, the same. They are:

- the assets approaches:
  - the sum-of-the-assets approach,
  - the split rate approach

- the cash flow approaches:
  - the stabilized-cash-flow approach,
  - the discounted-net-profits approach,
  - the net earnings approach (also called debt residual)

FRONT DOOR AND BACK DOOR

The two different earnings approaches could be likened to coming in through the front door or the back door. If both are properly undertaken, both will meet near the same place. That is to say, the end result should be about the same, except that the methods used to get there are different.

The assets approaches, which most real-estate appraisers choose because they like to work from the capital asset base forward, can be considered as the front door. In businesses that are infrequently traded, or where one is not similar to any other, it is the preferable method. You sum up the individual value of each of the business components, the capital or hard assets, all other tangible assets, the intangible assets, and the final element, goodwill, then subtract all liabilities. In the assets-first approaches, you work forward, asset by asset, to establish the total value. Thus the term "front door."

The procedures favored by most accountants and other valuation professionals constitute what we would call the back door. This is the calculation of a single, uncategorizable value estimate, arrived at by capitalizing the net after-tax profits by one overall capitalization rate. In the case of the stabilized-cash-flow approach, the profits are both current and historical; in the discounted-net-profits approach, you look at the projected profits. The value of all elements and contributors to the value of the business are contained within this one going concern value estimate. At this point, you don't break down the specific inputs. If you need to establish each respective element's contribution to the total value, then you must abstract it from that single value resultant. In other words, you first determine the going concern value of the enterprise, then work backward to find the individual value of each contributor. Thus the term "back door."

Some businesses can be valued only by a breakdown or a sum-of-the-assets method. At times, by discounting net profit, the orderly liquidation or breakup value can be greater than the going concern value. For example, many trucking companies still have to make their first dollar, yet have a high investment in mobile equipment. Despite an outward similarity, often there is no correlation between one business and another, even if they are in the same industry. For instance, a sawmill can have:

> In businesses that are infrequently traded, or where one is not similar to any other, [an assets approach] is the preferable method.

- a value for the mill itself, including the real estate, the machinery, the equipment (known in the industry as "the iron"), the working capital, and all other capital assets,
- a value for the timber berths or cutting licences, the quality and quantity of timber in each,
- a value for the established customer base.

The contribution of each to the total would significantly affect the value of a forest products company. Although the ratio of each value contributor from one sawmill to another could vary considerably, the historical profitability of each mill, on a percentage basis, could be similar. Yet it may not be in the future.

For other enterprises, I prefer a cash flow approach, particularly for frequently traded business, those with little investment in capital assets, or where there is a high degree of consistency from one to the next. Insurance agencies, professional practices, and personal service businesses are good examples. Although having a high capital asset base, hotels and restaurants are frequently traded businesses. Except for the benefit of the tax department, you seldom break down the value of the land, the building, the furniture and fixtures, or the intangible assets such as the liquor licence, or a franchise.

Again, you should use the cash flow approach to evaluate actively traded businesses or those that have a high consistency in character, as they tend to set their own market. But if the business is infrequently traded, or differs in character from its peers within the same line or industry, then you need to break it down, asset by asset, to determine its value.

LIQUIDATION VERSUS GOING CONCERN VALUES

Consider the value of a small business from two basic, interrelated perspectives:

Liquidation Value – Orderly or Forced Liquidation

Orderly liquidation value forms the foundation of going concern value, particularly when you use the sum-of-the-assets method. It is the market value of the capital assets only. If you take the position that goodwill is a legal fiction, or nonexistent, which is true in most small businesses, then orderly liquidation value and going concern value are the same.

In the case of forced liquidation, the business consistently loses money and must be sold immediately to meet its obligations. Often this is a distress sale, and you'll pay less than fair value for it.

Going Concern Value
- presupposes that the business is established and will continue, probably from the same location,
- is earning sufficient profits to justify all of its assets; it is producing a satisfactory return,
- has an equitable tangible-asset backing,
- has, or can generate, a goodwill value.

LIQUIDATION VALUES

Sometimes orderly liquidation value exceeds the going concern value. This is despite the company having been in business for several years, and having every intention of remaining. This occurs if the owners could earn a better rate of return on their invested capital elsewhere, yet they continue to operate the company. Many of their assets may be rapidly depreciating, or perhaps they're in a romance-type enterprise, such as:

> …use the cash flow approach to evaluate actively traded businesses or those that have a high consistency in character, as they tend to set their own market.

> Sometimes orderly liquidation value exceeds the going concern value. This is despite the company having been in business for several years, and having every intention of remaining.

- most trucking companies,
- most road contractors,
- most smaller aviation companies (and many larger ones),
- hunting and fishing lodges,
- many restaurants,
- small travel agencies,
- farming,
- writing books on business valuation.

The owners have simply bought themselves a job, which in many instances, is not all that bad. They make friends, not money. Either they're having fun, or else they think things will turn around next year. Usually, particularly in the smaller operations, the owners provide themselves with a livelihood, and at times a pension plan, both important considerations.

In a popular Yiddish story (more fact than fiction!), a business owner says to his friend, "I've been in this business for over ten years, and every year I lose still more money." The friend asks, "Then why do you stay in business?" This owner replies, "How else could I make a living?"

GOING CONCERN VALUES

As I've said before, the going concern value of any business is based on its ability to generate income and profits, especially the probability of those profits continuing. Past operation is the benchmark. When determining the profits to be capitalized into a value estimate, you start with a detailed analysis of the income and expense statement for as many preceding years as are available and applicable. All earnings approaches use these historical statements, analysed and then accepted as is or restructured into a pro forma, subject to certain exclusions.

INCOME AND EXPENSE ANALYSIS FOR THE

ABC FRANCHISED RESTAURANT

Following is the income and expense summary for the past three years of the model restaurant. This essentially duplicates the statement of income and retained earnings, as detailed in Chapter Five. You will note that this is referred to as a summary, not a financial statement, because some entries, both income and expense, are excluded. The intent is to provide a cash flow statement on which to base going concern value.

To identify trend lines more easily, you should use five or more years, and because you'll often develop annual averages, the older years' income and expenses are usually found on the left-hand side.

Items to be Deleted from the Income Statement

Before determining going concern value by any of the earnings approaches, you must adjust the income and expense statement. By deleting the following items, you are not omitting them, but rather just postponing them until another day (as you would defer income tax). You presume that there is no debt (this is actually true now and then, but not often).

Delete:

- nonrecurring income or expense items, such as the sale of surplus assets, a once-in-a-while capital gain, a windfall, etc.
- any income item that has nothing to do with the daily operation of the business, such as interest on deposits,
- new capital investment, debt, or equity,
- interest on long-term debt,
- depreciation (capital cost allowances),
- excess bonuses paid to owners or managers, excess perks,
- the cost of retaining or maintaining redundant assets,
- any expense item that has nothing to do with the daily operation of the business.

Throughout this manual, I've said that working capital is an asset, as much a part of the going concern value as the building and fixtures. But let's be honest about it. Not one seller in a hundred ever includes working capital in the selling price and nothing I say will ever change that. In almost all asset sales, working capital, inventory, accounts receivable, less the responsibility for payables, etc., is extra. The seller retains them, or charges for the transferrable portions, such as the inventory, prepaids, or work in progress. Although I think working capital should be included in the estimate of value, the realities of the marketplace dictate otherwise. Still, as it is an investment, any asset, liquid or capital, is entitled to earn a return and must be accounted for somewhere.

The deletion of interest on long-term debt follows the standard practice. Because you are determining the value of all capital assets through a capitalization process, you assume, for this purpose only, that there's no debt.

Do not include any non-cash items, such as depreciation.

…working capital is an asset, as much a part of the going concern value as the building and fixtures. But let's be honest about it. Not one seller in a hundred ever includes working capital in the selling price and nothing I say will ever change that.

COMPARATIVE SUMMARY OF INCOME & EXPENSES – CASH FLOW BASIS

Big Top Holdings Ltd., operating as ABC Franchised Restaurant

	3rd Last Year	2nd Last Year	Last Fiscal Year
Sales & Income	$ 1,167,926	$ 1,273,228	$ 1,623,714
Less: Cost of Sales	549,644	561,493	757,642
Gross Trading Profit	$ 618,282	$ 711,735	$ 866,072
Operating Expenses			
Fixed Costs:			
Telephone & Utilities	$ 35,227	$ 36,061	$ 37,114
Property & Business Taxes	19,074	21,227	18,506
Insurance, License Fees	10,726	10,846	10,824
Equipment Rent	7,940	7,940	9,281
Total Fixed Costs	$ 72,967	$ 76,074	$ 75,725
Variable Expenses:			
Accounting & Legal	$ 5,250	$ 5,358	$ 5,752
Advertising & Promotion	35,117	34,458	17,065
Bank Charges & Interest	4,622	3,166	4,506
Janitor & Maintenance	23,309	24,207	26,296
Office	11,273	7,016	9,462
Repairs & Maintenance	9,427	26,518	54,306
Restaurant Supplies	25,872	17,132	16,607
Travel & Auto	4,767	6,890	9,611
Total Variable Expenses	$ 119,637	$ 124,745	$ 143,605
Payroll Costs:			
Staff Wages & Benefits	$ 330,111	$ 320,358	$ 476,055
Worker's Injury Insurance	6,017	6,996	5,375
Management Salary	45,000	45,000	45,000
Total Payroll Costs	$ 381,128	$ 372,354	$ 526,430
Total Operating Expenses	$ 573,732	$ 573,173	$ 745,760
Pre-tax Profit	$ 44,550	$ 138,562	$ 120,312
Provision for Income Tax	$ Nil	$ (15,124)	$ (12,303)
Net Operating Income Before Occupancy Cost Long-term Debt Service or Depreciation	$ 44,550	$ 123,438	$ 108,009

STATEMENT OF SALES AND COST-OF-SALES ANALYSIS

This statement, normally contained within the financial statements, or within the notes, exists solely for analysis. It is a management tool used exclusively to compartmentalize the source and cost of sales, the largest single expense in most enterprises, and to determine gross trading profit. At the same time, it's probably a carry-over from years past and older accounting methods. Not that many years ago, we analysed cost of sales almost to the point of being ridiculous. Some still do so. Today's measurement standard is cost per unit of product delivered. For example, some years ago one of my restaurant-owning clients said that he knew the exact cost of delivering each and every meal in his restaurant, every sandwich, every slice of pie, every cup of coffee. I thought this was truly amazing, and said so. Today, I wonder how anyone could successfully run a restaurant without knowing this.

By a detailed analysis of this statement, management can tell what is happening by individual department, which ones pay and where others should be improved. In addition to bringing out the strong points of the operation, it pinpoints where cost of sales is out of line, management and staff faults, loss, theft, waste, and a host of other sins. The statement becomes still more valuable when several years' comparisons are available.

SALES AND COST OF SALES ANALYSIS

Big Top Holdings Ltd. – ABC Franchised Restaurant								
	Last Fiscal Year			2nd Last Fiscal Year			3rd Last Fiscal Year	
Sales	$	1,623,714		$	1,273,228		$ 1,167,926	
Cost of Sales			%			%		%
Food Cost	$	529,846	32.6	$	397,247	31.2	$ 381,912	32.7
Paper-Supplies		74,691	4.7		49,243	3.9	52,539	4.5
Franchise Fee		81,186	5.0		63,661	5.0	58,396	5.0
Promotions		71,919	4.4		51,342	4.0	56,797	4.9
Total Cost	$	757,642	46.7	$	561,493	44.1	$ 549,644	47.1
Gross Profit	$	866,072	53.3	$	711,735	55.9	$ 618,282	52.9

The third-last year was the first full year of operation of the restaurant by this owner. In most enterprises' start-up year, there's uncertainty about what is needed, what to buy, from whom, how to control costs and inventory, etc. A few turn only a tiny profit, if any. During year two, and this restaurant is a good example, management started to get its act together. If they are ever to be profitable, most businesses will break even during this period. By the end of year three, if the business is not showing a profit, the chances are it never will. Although, on a percentage basis, the subject's profit in all three years was less than industry averages, no single cost seems that far out of line. It is just a little here and a little there. The prospective buyer should establish why. Perhaps there is a simple explanation, but on the other hand, it could be a sign of something more permanent or the beginning of a longer-term trend.

Brought about by the current year's 27.5% increase in business from last year, the store had many of the problems of the first year, particularly with untrained staff, creating an increased cost of labor and food. With more astute management, both are correctable.

Analysis of Sales and Income

3rd Last Year:	$ 1,167,926	
2nd Last Year:	$ 1,273,228	Increase of 9.0% from 3rd Last
Last Year:	$ 1,623,714	Increase of 27.5% from 2nd Last

Increase of 39.0% from 3rd Last

First, you must consider the historical sales, to check for changes in either direction, particularly any unexplained wide variations. If last year's sales were higher than in previous years, without exception, every business seller will try to convince you that this is the pattern for future years. If lower, it was an unusual year created by an abnormal, never-to-be-repeated circumstance. If anything, sales will increase each year from here on in because of the increase in the market and your good management. But will they?

The model fast-food restaurant is five years old, purchased by the present owners three years ago. Assuming capable management, and all else to be equal, sales should increase as the new owners become better established, feel more comfortable with the business, and develop their own customer base. There is a peak or levelling off, however, usually referred to as the stabilized year. For most enterprises, this is the third year in business but could be as late as year five. After this, except for major changes to the plant, the market, and inflation, sales and profits have peaked. Where increases are caused by inflation or the market, each competitor shares.

The nine-percent-increase from the third-last to the second-last year, although seemingly high, may not be unusual. Your regional and demographic study told you that this is a growing community and that the restaurant is located on a busy highway halfway between two major markets, 150 miles away on either side. Further examination will soon indicate that the 27.5% increase from the second-last to the most recent fiscal year far exceeds the normal market condition. You will recall from that same regional study that a 1.6-billion-dollar oil refinery is being built about one mile to the east. This project has filled every rental apartment, hotel, and motel in town and caused a boom for services of all types, particularly restaurants. When the project closes, about one year from now, except for the permanent work force, the community will return to near normal. Thus, no matter what the owner tells you, the high sales and income of the past year will not be maintained. The price for this restaurant should be substantially lower than when you were assured of maintaining last year's sales of over $1,600,000, which you are not.

All I'm saying is: never accept rapid increases, or decreases for that matter, in sales and income at face value. Search out the cause, and keep searching until you find it. Never overlook the possibility that the books have been cooked. Seldom are rapid increases caused by either good luck or good management but from some external happening that may not continue. If the sales increase is permanent, additional competition will soon be on your doorstep.

Cost-of-Sales Analysis

As abstracted from the notes to the financial statements in Chapter Six.

3rd Last Year:	Cost of Sales	$ 549,644	=	47.06% of Sales
2nd Last Year:	Cost of Sales	$ 486,493	=	44.10% of Sales
Last Year:	Cost of Sales	$ 675,642	=	47.28% of Sales

When you look at the cost of sales for any business, you must account for two factors: the makeup of the allocation, and how it compares with industry standards. The difficulty is that no two businesses, although in the same industry, seem to report cost of sales on the same basis. For example, in Restaurant A it could be only food cost. In restaurant B it could be for food, paper goods, kitchen supplies, and freight. In C it could also include staff wages and benefits. Are condiments food or supplies? I recently read a statement that included depreciation — prepared by an accountant who should know better. Thus, if you are comparing one enterprise with another, ensure that you are comparing like to like. Sometimes the composition of the cost is broken down in the notes to the financial statement, but often you're on your own.

You need to establish if your target enterprise is reasonably close to industry averages, that is, percentages as recorded by several businesses that do approximately the same thing. They indicate average food costs, average space rental, proper labor costs, advertising and promotional expenses, net profit, etc., all expressed as a percentage of total sales and income. The scheme is that your target should be within close proximity to these industry averages, and if not, something could be amiss. If, for example, food costs are too high, the menu price structure could be too low, you should be changing suppliers, or perhaps some staff members have given themselves a raise in pay. If food costs are too low, although this may be due to low quality, probably the accounting is wrong. There are missed invoices or entries, or some charged to the wrong department. It is usually the other way.

If you find that some costs are rising much faster than sales, particularly food, supplies, and hired services, look for internal staff problems. Someone just may have her hand in the sugar bowl. There are many ways for employees to give themselves a raise in pay. A case in point. Some years ago I bought a hotel that had been operated by a management company. Our cost of meat, vegetables, and laundry was about ten percent less than for the previous owners. And from the same suppliers. Very interesting!

In a family-type sit-down restaurant, food costs should be in the area of 36 to 38 percent of sales. (I never got too excited if they were under 40%.) In a pizza parlor, around 30%; in a fast-food restaurant, 32 to 34 percent; and so forth.

Cost of Food Only – The Model Restaurant

3rd Last Year:	$	381,912	=	32.6% of sales
2nd Last Year:	$	397,247	=	31.2% of sales
Last Fiscal Year:	$	529,846	=	32.7% of sales

Before other considerations, although still well within acceptable parameters, under normal circumstances cost of food should have further declined during the last fiscal year. When you see it increasing for no reason, look for bad management but also look for other explanations, such as cost-of-food inclusions in offsetting accounting entries. Here you will note that supplies are less than one percent of sales. In a fast-food restaurant, paper is usually in the range of five to six percent. Promotional expenses aren't usually included with food costs, but don't rule out this possibility. In the past fiscal year, $71,919 in promotional expenses were included

> You need to establish if your target enterprise is reasonably close to industry averages, that is, percentages as recorded by several businesses that do approximately the same thing.

with cost of sales, plus another $35,117 as uncategorizable advertising and promotion. Since part of the franchise fee is set aside for promotion, an additional expense of $107,000 seems excessive.

One of my restaurant clients has a consistent statement showing cost of food of exactly 36.5%. They also have an unallocated expenses entry that annually varies between six and ten percent of sales. This is where they hide the remainder of the actual cost. I don't know why they record the costs this way. Maybe they're trying to kid someone.

Cost of Labor and Management

3rd Last Year:	Cost of Labor & Management	$381,128	= 32.6%
2nd Last Year:	Cost of Labor & Management	$372,354	= 29.2%
Last Year	Cost of Labor & Management	$526,430	= 32.4%

Based on our earlier information, all else being equal, labor and management costs were three to four percentage points too high in the third-last and second-last years, and six to seven points too high last year. You should ask why. A prevalent cause is inattentive management, but more often it's poor training coupled with improper scheduling. In many businesses, and restaurants are notorious, there is often too much work for one employee but not enough for two. God made everyone hungry at the same time. Thus at noon you seldom have enough staff, but in between meal times, or in the late evening, too much. Poor training is soon evident, in that sufficient staff get in each other's way. Poor coordination between kitchen and servers is a common problem. Another consideration, and I'm not trying to bash unions, is that labor costs in union premises are always two to three points above nonunion stores. Although the unions would argue that productivity is increased, this is not a given. That's all I'll say about unions for now.

How much should management be paid? There is little that distorts the percentage cost of labor more than management paying itself too much, or too little. I always think of the two fellows who ran a car wash in Calgary, Alberta. They constantly complained that they were losing money, but failed to report that each drew out over $100,000 per year in salary and perks. Offsetting this is one of my other clients, who says, "No labor cost. I work. Wife works. Mom works, Dad works, Grandpa works, and my kids work. No labor cost."

Consider what you would have to pay a capable manager who has no interest in the business. Conversely, consider what the present manager-owner could earn elsewhere. Think about the required education and experience, the responsibility, and the expected hours per day. At $45,000 per year, the owner is paying himself a good salary, but not excessive. Except for the unrestricted use of the motor home, no perks or dividends are recorded.

In most restaurants, the combined labor and management cost is in the area of 24 to 26 percent of sales. At this same time, you must account for certain trade-offs. Often one cost is higher than industry averages because another is lower. For example, in a restaurant where all food is brought in prepackaged, pre-cut, and portioned, the cost of food will be above average, but labor costs lower. Where all preparation is done in the kitchen, the opposite will occur: lower food costs but a higher labor cost. So look for a combination of the two.

In many businesses, and restaurants are notorious, there is often too much work for one employee but not enough for two. God made everyone hungry at the same time.

The Model Restaurant

	Last Fiscal Year	2nd Last Year	3rd Last Year
Cost of Food	32.6%	31.2%	32.7%
Payroll Cost	31.4%	29.2%	32.6%
Total	65.0%	60.4%	65.3%

Appreciating the variance from one type of restaurant to the next, the combined costs of sales and labor should be about 60 to 65 percent for the subject.

The real question is: what happened last year? New, untrained staff combined with poor stock control often spells trouble. As a buyer, you will want to make sure that you can correct this.

Consider what you would have to pay a capable manager who has no interest in the business. Conversely, consider what the present manager-owner could earn elsewhere.

FIXED COSTS

These costs vary little from one year to the next and are not a percentage of sales and income. Often it is difficult to compare these costs against industry standards as so few benchmarks exist. Still, examine trends and any radical movement.

* Always count on an annual increase in utility costs. Three to five percent per year is the norm.
* Property and business taxes decreased during the last reporting period. Were they reassessed, was the mill rate lower, or did the owners not pay all of that year's? If you see a very rapid increase in any year they could be playing catchup, that is, paying the arrears. This may also indicate some flip-flop between cash and accrual accounting systems.
* Insurance costs normally do not vary much from one year to the next. If you see a significant increase, it could signal a change of insurers or a penalty for a major claim.
* Why the change in equipment rent? Is this true rent or rental purchase? If a rental purchase or conditional sales agreement, the equipment should be added to the fixture list and the unpaid amount shown as a liability. If true rent, the entry as an expense item is correct. Who owns the equipment at the end of the lease period?

VARIABLE COSTS

Variable costs are normally checked only against the rule of common sense. Here, owners can manipulate the numbers, particularly in charging personal use to the company — travel and auto expense being a good example. (One client flies to Korea every year, paid for by his cafe.) At other times, items such as franchise fees are as per contract.

The main concern is radical changes from one year to the next, especially if they do not move in the same direction or with the same velocity as sales and income. Rapid shifts could indicate problems but could also result from flip-flopping between accrual and cash accounting. Items such as some supplies, uniforms, and cleaning products are infrequently purchased, maybe once every three years, but the cost is totally charged out in the year of acquisition. At other times, with items such as repairs

The main concern is radical changes from one year to the next, especially if they do not move in the same direction or with the same velocity as sales and income.

and maintenance, there is a fine line between expensing and capitalizing. Of the $54,306 repairs made during the past year, $40,000 was for a new solarium. It should have been capitalized.

NET OPERATING PROFIT

When all is said and done, only one figure really counts: the bottom line, net operating profit before occupancy cost, long-term debt service, or depreciation. This is the basis on which, by the earnings approaches, you determine going concern value. In the sum-of-the-assets approach, the net profit amount will indicate any residual value for goodwill. This is a surplus to other demands value, calculated only after you've accounted for the capital assets of real estate, fixtures and equipment, and working capital. The essential consideration, at this point, is to ensure that the value or price to be paid is supported by the net profit, that an adequate return on both sales and assets is provided. More important, can the business, as is, pay its bills, retire its long-term debt, and leave something over for the owner?

FINANCIAL STATEMENT ADJUSTMENTS

Before you commence looking for the business's value, you absolutely must ensure that the financial statements provide the correct answers to the proper questions. If they don't, any value that you calculate will be wrong. Although the statements may be used for financing, it is not in your interest to make a losing business look good. If you're an appraiser, overstatement or optimism will come back to haunt you, guaranteed. Accordingly, the income and expense statements should, as necessary, be restructured to reflect an acceptable balance between industry standards and actual conditions. Forecasts must be based on an accurate interpretation of the market and the laws of probability. You can't just grab numbers from thin air and present them as a true prognosis of what will happen. Difficult as it may be, you must ignore the belief that a new owner can outperform the seller. You must not reflect this optimism in the projections.

For capitalization purposes, assuming that at least five years' statements are available, you must choose one of four income and profitability schedules:

- the average of the past five or more years,
- the average of the past three years,
- the most recent fiscal year only,
- a pro forma statement based on any one of the above, or a combination of all three.

Based on the historical operating record of the company, a pro forma statement is an income, expense, and profitability summary that provides more consistency than you usually obtain from the statements themselves. It deletes nonrecurring income and expense items, levels out the abnormalities, the bumps, and the humps by bringing them more into line with industry standards. It removes non-cash or capitalized items such as long-term debt service and depreciation, and holds itself out to be a true representation of how this business will fare in a normal business year assuming typical but competent management.

[a pro forma] ... holds itself out to be a true representation of how this business will fare in a normal business year assuming typical but competent management.

WHAT TO USE

It's largely a matter of choice, but it is recommended that when:

- sales and profits are both increasing, use only the last year's income and profitability,
- sales are increasing but profits are decreasing, develop a pro forma,
- sales are increasing but profits remain steady, develop a pro forma,
- sales and profits are both decreasing but have bottomed out, use last year's; if they're decreasing but haven't both bottomed out, develop a pro forma,
- sales are decreasing but profits are increasing, use last year's only if the cause, such as a reorganization or discontinuance of unprofitable lines or territories, has been completed; if not, develop a pro forma,
- sales are decreasing but profits remain steady, develop a pro forma,
- both sales and profits remain fairly consistent, use longer-term averages,
- both sales and profits show considerable variance from year to year, use still longer-term averages,
- either sales or profits are variable, particularly if uncoordinated, develop a pro forma statement,
- the past two or three years have been relatively stable, but the prior periods have been either variable or else consistently higher or lower, it's probably best to use the last two or three years only, depending on both the periods of variance and the degree of instability,
- uncertain about what to do, develop a pro forma.

All financial projections
should be in
constant dollars.

CONSTANT DOLLARS

All financial projections should be in constant dollars. Sure, there's a tendency to second-guess the inflation rate and build in what you believe to be realistic, guaranteed increases into the analysis. Somehow, many seem to forget that expenses will increase at the same rate, and the net profit, on a percentage if not total basis, will not change much. No crystal ball is good enough to accurately predict future inflation, and I've never seen a pro forma that predicted a recession. Thus, the exercise becomes redundant. Since it has no point, don't do it. Always assume no inflation.

PRO FORMA TO BE DEVELOPED

To be conservative, we will develop a pro forma income and expense statement. It will form the foundation for the final value estimates in all earnings approaches.

People always wonder whether to use exact dollars or round them off. As they are merely forecasts, and seldom work out to the dollar, round off your numbers. The rounding level will depend solely upon the size of the numbers and the precision you need. For a small boutique, the nearest hundred dollars is probably appropriate; for an international marketer, the nearest hundred thousand may be accurate enough.

Sales and Income

Sales increased 9.0% from year three to year two and another 27.5% from year two to last year. It has been stated that the past twelve months' rapid increase was brought about by the oil-refinery construction project that will be completed in about one year, after which the community will return to near normal. Yet no town ever returns to where it once was. Through the projected population growth and increased highway traffic, future sales should be lower than last year's, but higher than for the second-last year. By how much is pure speculation. In the absence of better information, let's assume that they will be halfway between the two extremes, those of the last two fiscal years.

2nd Last Year:	$	1,273,228
Last Year:	$	1,623,714
2-year Average:	$	1,448,000

It might appear that this number, and this is the number that we'll use throughout, was dragged out of thin air. This is truly tempting because only the future will ever prove you right or wrong. However, the forecast must be supported and justified based on your background and supportive analysis (Chapter Three), the competition, and particularly an astute perception of your market. Never assume that you've built a better mousetrap than the next guy. It ain't so. And of course, always ask, and positively answer:

Is it reasonable? Is it logical? Does it make sense?

Cost of Sales

3rd Last Year:	47.06%
2nd Last Year:	44.10%
Last Year:	47.28%
3 Year Average:	46.15%

Because of past management difficulties directly related to the rapid increase of business, but assuming that all is now under control, you might want to use only the cost of sales as recorded in the second-last year. Still, increased volume does not guarantee increased efficiency and lower unit-production costs. Often it is the reverse. Because we want to be conservative, and primarily because it makes more sense than the use of any single year, or an average, let's go with a cost of sales of 45.0%. This is a reduction from both years one and three, yet takes into account that it will probably be some time before all operating costs are brought into line.

Cost of Sales $ 1,448,000 × 45.0% = (rounded) $ 651,500

Fixed Costs

As fixed costs don't vary proportionate to changes in the volume of sales, you're really just looking for trends here. Are these costs going up, going down, or remaining constant? Many fixed costs can be verified with the licensing and taxing authorities, and insurance agents. If so, use these figures. Remember to look for trends. You are projecting a long time into the future.

Some expenses, such as accounting and professional fees, could be included with either the fixed or variable. Accounting fees usually remain stable, but if your business blossoms, your accountant will want a larger share. As these fees have been increasing each year, I've placed them with the variable expenses. Any radically changing expenses should fall in the variable category, and relatively consistent items should be placed in the fixed category, but it's your choice.

When making projections, such as the feasibility of enlarging the building, adding another line, renovating, or whatever, project fixed costs according to the square feet of area occupied, and variable costs as a percentage of additional sales or income.

Variable Costs

When forecasting variable expenses, look at the history of the business, consider the trend lines, take into account the averages and the peak years, and then apply your best estimate as to what will probably happen. As you know, some things increase, others will remain stable, but nothing goes down. If an item such as uniforms is bought once every three years or so, use longer-term averages; if it's every year, use only the last year's cost. There's no hard and fast rule on forecasting variable expenses. Often it is little more than a combination of interpreting historical evidence, a gut feeling, and crystal ball gazing.

In the following pro forma, I've identified the rationale behind the variable costs suggested.

Labor and Management

3rd Last Year:	Cost of Labor & Management	32.6%
2nd Last Year:	Cost of Labor & Management	29.2%
Last Year:	Cost of Labor & Management	32.4%
3-year Simple Average		31.4%

I'll repeat that for a fast-food operation, the cost of labor and management is too high. This was created by the usual first-year start-up problems and the rapid increase in business, too rapid for the manager and staff to handle properly, in the most recent fiscal period. Still, you'll unquestioningly agree that you are a far better manager than the other guy and will soon rectify the problem areas. I said earlier that when you buy a business, any business, determine the value based on its track record, not on your turnaround possibilities. If you pay for what the present owner did, plus what you are going to do, you are, in effect, paying twice.

Therefore, although we know it is too high, the pro forma cost of labor and management will be the three-year average of 31.4% of sales. The $45,000 management cost was accepted as realistic. Worker's injury insurance is a fixed percentage of payroll. The remainder is staff wages and benefits.

Cost of Labor & Management: $ 1,448,000 × 31.4% = (rounded) $ 454,500

PRO FORMA INCOME & EXPENSE STATEMENT

Big Top Holdings Ltd., operating as ABC Franchised Restaurant
(all numbers rounded to nearest $500)

Sales and Income	$ 1,448,000	
Less: Cost of Sales	651,500	.... 45.0% of sales
Gross Trading Profit	$ 796,500	.... 55.0% of sales
Operating Expenses		
Fixed Costs		
Telephone & Utilities	$ 38,500	.... last year plus 3.0%
Property & Business Taxes	19,500	.... confirmed as correct
Insurance, License Fees	11,000	.... have remained constant
Equipment Rent	9,500	.... just bought new signs
Total Fixed Costs	$ 78,500	.... 5.42% of sales
Variable Expenses		
Accounting & Legal	$ 6,500	.... have been increasing
Advertising & Promotion	29,000	.... same as last year
Bank Charges & Interest	4,500	.... same as last year
Janitor & Maintenance	27,500	.... increase from last year
Office	9,500	.... 3 year average
Repairs & Maintenance	16,000	.... last year, plus 10%
Restaurant Supplies	19,000	.... 3 year average, plus 5.0%
Travel & Automobile	7,000	.... 3 year average
Total Variable Expenses	$ 119,000	.... 8.22% of sales
Payroll Costs		
Staff Wages & Benefits	$ 402,500	.... 27.8% of total sales
Worker's Injury Insurance	7,000	.... 1.5% of total payroll
Management Salary	45,000	.... fixed salary
Total Payroll Costs	$ 454,500	.... 31.39% of sales
Total Operating Expenses	$ 652,000	.... 45.03% of sales
Pre-tax Profit	$ 144,500	.... 9.98% of sales
Provision for Income Taxes	$ 14,500	.... Estimated
Net Operating Income	$ 130,000	.... 8.98% of sales
Before Occupancy Cost		
Long-term Debt Service or Depreciation		

THE FINAL DEVELOPMENT OF THE PRO FORMA

No matter how much care you have taken in preparing the pro forma, it's largely a matter of your personal judgement as to what will happen in the future. You must still compare your conclusions with the actual operating history of the company. Remember: The going concern value of any business is always based on its track record, not on some concocted set of figures that parallel the likelihood of what should happen. At the end of each step, ask yourself and positively answer:

Is it reasonable? Is it logical? Does it make sense?

If at any time you answer "No," go back to where you got off track and start again. The final test is always that of common sense.

You'll base the going concern value of the business almost exclusively on the pro forma that you've just developed.

HISTORICAL CORRELATION

Correlation between the operating history of the target company and the developed pro forma should be done on both a total dollar and percentage basis.

Net Operating Profits

3rd Last Year:	$ 44,450	3.81% return on sales
2nd Last Year:	$ 123,438	9.69% return on sales
Last Year:	$ 110,009	6.78% return on sales
Pro Forma:	$ 130,000	8.98% return on sales

On a dollar net-operating-profit basis, the pro forma does not correlate at all. On a percentage of sales, as it is lower than the best of the three reporting years but higher than the last year, it may not be far out of line. But let's go one step further.

Comparative Sales and Expenses

	3rd Last Year	2nd Last Year	Last Fiscal Year	Pro forma
Sales & Income	$ 1,167,926	$ 1,273,228	$ 1,623,714	$1,448,000
Less: Cost of Sales	549,644	561,493	767,642	651,500
Gross Trading Profit	$ 618,282	$ 711,735	$ 866,072	$ 796,500
Operating Expenses				
Fixed Costs	$ 72,967	$ 76,074	$ 75,725	$ 78,500
Variable Expenses	$ 119,637	$ 124,745	$ 143,605	$ 119,000
Total Payroll Costs	$ 381,128	$ 372,354	$ 526,430	$ 454,500
Total Operating Expenses	$ 573,732	$ 573,173	$ 745,760	$ 652,000
Pre-tax Profit	$ 44,550	$ 138,562	$ 120,312	$ 144,000
Provision for Income Taxes	$ Nil	$ (15,124)	$ (12,303)	$ (14,500)
Net Operating Income	$ 44,550	$ 123,438	$ 108,009	$ 130,000

As the pro forma sales were taken at the halfway point between the last and second-last years, the correlation has substantially improved. Fixed costs, which have changed very little over the historical period, consume a decreasing share of sales. Profits have increased proportionally because of better use of the capital and other assets and increased efficiency. The final test is to consider all of the sale inputs and outgoes on a percentage basis.

Comparative Percentages

	3rd Last Year	2nd Last Year	Last Fiscal Year	Pro forma
Sales & Income	100.0%	100.0%	100.0%	100.0%
Less: Cost of Sales	47.1%	44.1%	47.3%	45.0%
Gross Trading Profit	52.9%	55.9%	53.3%	55.0%
Operating Expenses				
Fixed Costs	6.2%	6.0%	4.7%	5.4%
Variable Expenses	10.2%	9.8%	8.7%	8.3%
Total Payroll Costs	32.6%	29.2%	32.4%	31.3%
Total Operating Expenses	49.0%	45.0%	45.8%	45.0%
Pre-tax Profit	3.8%	10.9%	7.5%	10.0%
Provision for Income Taxes	Nil	1.2%	0.7%	1.1%
Net Operating Income	3.8%	9.7%	6.8%	8.9%

This schedule suggests a strong correlation between the various elements of the pro forma and the actual operating history of this restaurant. Accordingly, it will be used for the development of the value estimates by the various earnings approaches. Remember, though, it's still only a projection, one based on a combination of what has happened and what should happen.

...in most businesses after a period of stability, the curve dips downward. This is caused by equipment wearing out, creating a loss of efficiency with increased cost to operate and maintain.

ELEMENTS OF GOING CONCERN VALUE CHANGES

In the earlier chapter about machinery and equipment, I stated that as the profitability of a business increases, the contributory value of equipment, as a part of a going concern, also increases. Having said that, this contributory value can only very rarely exceed its replacement cost. No one would ever pay more for this machine than for a replacement that's installed and made ready to operate.

This doesn't necessarily hold true for real estate or for businesses. In real estate, because of favorable market conditions or a particularly good lease, the value found by the income approach is often greater than that found by other methods. This can be equally true with a business. As profits increase, so does its value once the orderly liquidation stage has been passed. As **Figure 3** demonstrates, the curve flattens, because high profits cannot be maintained indefinitely.

Although not so indicated, in most businesses, after a period of stability, the curve dips downward. This is caused by equipment wearing out, creating a loss of efficiency with increased cost to operate and maintain. Owners and staff all grow older and bored, markets change faster than management can respond, times change, conditions change, and redundancy sets in. Most times this can be fixed — if it's caught in time. Then the profit line will move upwards again — until the same things reoccur.

Finally, there is a very definite limit as to how much you should pay for goodwill, despite the potential for continued profitability.

Figure 3: Elements of Tangible Asset and Going Concern Value Changes

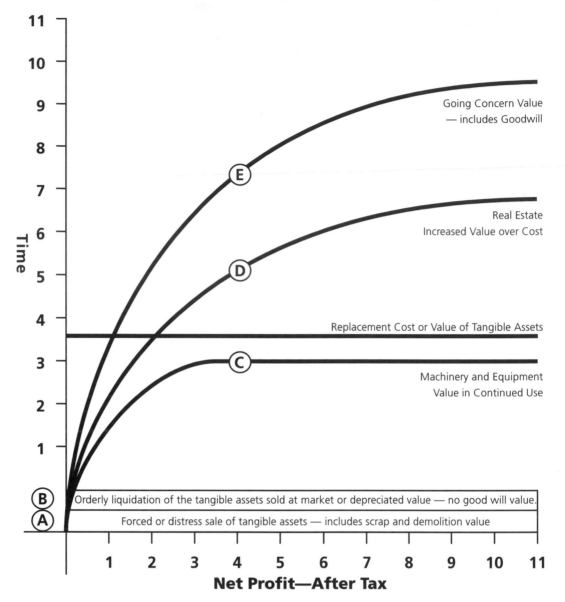

A. The business is losing money. To avoid further losses, the owners liquidate or the creditors foreclose, they dispose of the assets. Assets could be more gainfully employed elsewhere.

B. The business is breaking even. Profit is sufficient to justify the assets investment but no more. No goodwill value if sold as a going concern. No value will be realized over the depreciated or market value of the assets without the business.

C. The going concern value of all tangible assets in place with full utility value realized. The business is profitable and the profits are increasing. Lines flatten as neither profits or value increase indefinitely. The line splits. The value of machinery and equipment can never exceed replacement cost. Because of uniqueness business value in profitable situations or with strong leases or real estate can.

D. This line represents the replacement cost of all tangible assets at market value without the business.

E. The value of a business a going concern. Contains all intangible assets including goodwill. The line flattens. Profits and value stabilize. After a time as redundancy and competition creeps in, the line will curve downward.

Chapter 12

WHAT IS GOODWILL AND HOW DO WE MEASURE IT

IN business appraisal, probably no term is more misused, abused, misunderstood, and misappropriated than "goodwill." Some of my peers and the investing public believe that it does not exist, or if so, cannot be separated from the other value components. It is part of the unit in place, indivisible from the capital assets, and as such it can never have a singular value.

Still, the courts, some lenders, and most buyers and sellers recognize goodwill. Buyers and analysts must not only recognize the reality of goodwill, they must place a monetary value on it.

That value can range anywhere between two extremes. In many small businesses, where the owner has done little more than buy a job, there is no goodwill. It could even be negative if the business is nearing the forced liquidation state, or if it is spent a wad of cash on yet-unproductive product research. But here is an interesting example: In 1987 the Tonka Toy Company of Minnetonka, Minnesota, bought the Kenner-Parker Company for $548 million on a leveraged buyout. Of the price, only $100 million was for assets and $448 million was for goodwill, to be amortized over forty years. This is a discount rate of 2.50%. Goodwill is normally discounted, or amortized, at not less than twenty percent and may be as high as two hundred percent per year.

> In many small businesses, where the owner has done little more than buy a job, there is no goodwill.

GOODWILL DEFINED

Every author, every business person, and every other body has a personal definition of goodwill. Some say it is simply "an intangible asset of a business when the business has value more than the sum of its net identifiable assets." Some break down income-generating capabilities, such as assets, earnings, customer attitude, location, legal protections, excess profits, and personal preferences. You can read lengthy, verbose textbook mush that no one honestly understands, including the person who wrote it.

Probably the best definition, certainly the shortest, comes from an English law case of 1910, wherein Lord Eldon commented: "Goodwill is nothing more than the probability that old customers will continue to patronize the same shop." That is it. Excellent though it may be, Eldon's definition does not help you to place a dollar sign in front of goodwill.

My own definition is:

"The surplus or excess over the value of the capital assets of real estate, fixtures and equipment, any other fixed assets, and the current assets of a business that is ready to operate but without a developed business. It includes consideration of the location and efficiency of plant, the ability of management and staff, and the sufficiency of capital."

It can also be defined as the excess of value over its initial cost, which results from a complete and well-coordinated operation. It is the present value of surplus income after attending to the costs of capital, labor, management, and capital assets.

United States Revenue Ruling 59–60 states in part, "In the final analysis, goodwill is based on earning capacity. The presence of goodwill and its value therefore rests upon the excess of net earnings over and above a fair return on the net tangible assets." The courts have further defined goodwill:

1. "Goodwill is the whole advantage, whatever it may be, of the reputation and connection of the firm which may have been built up by years of honest work or gained by lavish expenditures of money.

2. It is the privilege, granted by the seller of a business to the purchaser, of trading as his recognized successor; the possession of a ready-formed 'connection' of customers, considered as an element in the saleable value of a business, additional to the value of the plant, stock in trade, book debts, etc."[1]

> The presence of goodwill and its value therefore rests upon the excess of net earnings over and above a fair return on the net tangible assets."

WHAT GOODWILL INCLUDES

In most small businesses, particularly those that have no real advantage over any other, goodwill is the value of the intangible assets. These intangibles, or subjective considerations, created by the super profits, or the earnings that more than satisfy the value of the tangible assets at a normally acceptable rate of return on the investment. That normally acceptable return relates to the risk of the venture and the waiting period to have that investment returned.

These intangible assets could include, for instance:

- a superior management team,
- a superior labor force, well-trained and well-skilled,
- favorable agency agreements,
- a secret, special, or innovative manufacturing process,
- an excellent credit rating,
- good customer relations, an established customer base,
- a strategic location not freely duplicated,
- a long-standing, enviable reputation,
- a strong, reliable market,
- quality licences, trademarks, copyrights, patents,
- a favorable franchise,
- identifiable market dominance,
- a weak competitive scene.

Goodwill can take many forms:

Goodwill of Location

Before you consider this seriously, you must determine whether your target business is:

- location-dependent,
- location-independent, or
- location-specific.

A location-dependent business is, above all, convenient to the market base. Its customers live or work within easy walking or driving distance. Advantages may be specific to the location: a dealership, a franchise, or simply a proprietary interest in the traffic that passes its front door. It cannot pack up and move across town without doing permanent damage or starting all over in the new location. Moreover, you cannot transfer goodwill of location to another site. This category would include most drug stores, particularly those situated within medical clinics or buildings, restaurants, all convenience stores, most smaller to mid-sized retail stores, and some service businesses. In this category, you will find any business that would lose a substantial portion of its existing patronage if it were relocated.

You can call it locational advantage. Without doubt, some locations are better than others, particularly for retailing or for any business that relies on walk-in traffic. The measurement of this form of goodwill is tied to the value of the site. A developed key corner will sell or be rented for considerably more money than an inside or back-street lot, yet the replacement value of the building and chattels could be identical. In business, this form of goodwill is linked to profit advantage. You can earn more profit here than there. However, do not mistakenly measure the added value twice: once in the real estate and again in the goodwill.

Most manufacturing plants, distributors, service businesses, and professional practices are location-independent. There is no goodwill of location. The enterprise can be easily picked up and moved, with no loss of customers and clients. With modern transportation and communication, the business might even successfully move to a different part of town, or to a new city, state, or province.

Location-specific businesses are located close to their customers or close to their source of raw materials. I am talking about mines, resorts, and all farms that are tied to the land base. Oilfield service companies are naturally located near oilfields, yet the refineries are near the market.

We are concerned only about location-dependent companies. You cannot assign goodwill of location to a location-independent or location-specific business, which might have goodwill, but for other reasons.

Goodwill of Product or Service

Many businesses have been around for a long time. They have developed an enviable reputation for honesty, fair pricing, good service, quality products, and so forth. Their inherent value is easy to recognize and transfer. Nationally advertised brands are good examples. Although Brand A may not be any better than Brand X, people often automatically shell out more cash for it because its virtues are extolled ten times a day on the tube, it comes in a colorful box, and it is displayed prominently on a store shelf. Who cares who makes it? The product sells itself. This goodwill, however, may take years to develop and can be destroyed overnight. (What ever happened to Schlitz beer? It was the Number One seller for countless years, but scarcely anyone drinks it now.) You must ensure that this goodwill is transferrable before you hand over precious moolah for it. It is frequently tangled up with personal goodwill, which cannot be transferred.

Personal Goodwill

Sometimes a proprietor's friendliness or personality builds up an excellent business reputation. When executives move from one company to another, they often take clientele and trade secrets with them. Are clients loyal to the lawyer who handles their files, or to the legal firm in general? Conversely, is business declining because of location or economic circumstances, or because the staff is rude and the owner cranky?

Can you transfer this form of goodwill? For example, an insurance agency's goodwill is almost always personal. These businesses are built on the agent's persistence and service, seldom on location, and never by discounting premiums. Even though such a sale is really only the transfer of duplicates of in-force, cancelled, and terminated insurance policies, buyers regularly pay between one and two-and-a-half times the annual commissions. A buyer obtains nothing more than a collection of musty files, blank forms, and maybe some office furniture. The buyer is banking on the probability that the same customers will return to the same insurance shop.

On the other hand, a surgeon may have an extensive patient list and very personal, specific skills. She may make a very good living — actually an astronomical return on the investment when you think of her relatively minor expenses for office furniture, diagnostic equipment, and appliances. But because her skills cannot be transferred to anyone else, they have no commercial or goodwill value whatsoever. Personal goodwill must be transferrable and marketable.

Goodwill of Establishment (General Business Goodwill)

This catchall collects all kinds of goodwill, recognizable yet not fitting into a neat little pigeonhole. All goodwill categories overlap somewhat. Does this enterprise beat out its competitors because of its longevity, superior location, better pricing, better management, better visibility, good franchise, or a combination of all of the above? If you can measure any goodwill, it probably comes in all categories. No single value factor is absolute. Good premises, good products, good staff, good customers that pay their bills, and reliable suppliers all contribute. Is this truck stop superior because it serves better food, has sexier table attendants, or provides a better parking lot?

Continuity of Ownership

Any business with goodwill must have continuity of ownership. You cannot have goodwill if a business regularly changes hands, particularly if a succession of owners go broke. In the transfer of any business or professional practice, some goodwill disappears. No buyer has ever retained one hundred percent, although he may increase the business by bringing to it his own clientele and friends. Some customers or clients go elsewhere when a business is sold, maybe because it just is not the same anymore. As goodwill always develops over a longer term, look for continuity and establishment.

The presence of goodwill and its value therefore rests upon the excess of net earnings over and above a fair return on the net tangible assets."

Continuity of Management

This is more of the same, except that it must be good management.

Demonstrated Profitability

The prospect for continued profitability is a must. The value of any business, particularly the intangible value, is the present worth of anticipated future profits. The only reason to buy a business is to earn a living and obtain future profits.

Will the old customers patronize the same shop?

Before putting that elusive dollar sign on the goodwill portion of any business value, consider the company's:

- type,
- history,
- size,
- debt-equity ratio (leverage),
- liquidity,
- variations in historical income and profitability,

- present and future income and profitability potential,
- variability of historical dividends paid,
- income, expense, and balance-sheet adjustments.

INDIVISIBILITY

Although there are exceptions, such as the transfer of some professional practices, and perhaps some franchises, you cannot normally sell goodwill separately from the tangible assets of any business. It is an indivisible part of a going concern and can only be sold as such. Goodwill is recognized only when attached to and part-parcel of a business that is continuously making a profit.

NON-MEASURABLE GOODWILL

Can you see the theme here? Goodwill must be measurable and transferrable. These must be a demonstrated financial advantage or super profits. Sometimes, though, you will see goodwill, but you will not be able to measure it by the traditional procedures.

A case in point: My firm recently appraised a truck box manufacturing and supply company that had been in business for more than twenty years. During that entire time, unfortunately, it hardly ever made money. The two owners were undercapitalized, slightly weak on management, but excellent on technical and personal skills. The profits from the few good years were gobbled up by old debts from prior years. The owners never really got ahead. They made a comfortable living, that is all. Yet in those twenty years they developed an enviable reputation for manufacturing an excellent product, standing behind it, fair pricing, and good service. Everyone liked them and came from well over two hundred miles to patronize their shop. They developed excellent relationships with suppliers and had exclusive, high-quality lines with which they penetrated the market. This excellent business was never very profitable. Thus, by the all standards and measuring methods detailed in this manual, the goodwill of this company was zip.

But was it? I cannot help but think that some goodwill value existed, although no one would ever pay money for it as an intangible asset. A supplier, particularly one interested in vertical integration, or a competitor wanting the facility, the customer base, or the supplier lines, may consider paying a bonus to acquire the capital assets. Without it being identified, any goodwill is obtained. How much more should be paid is anyone's guess. This is where the fastidious rules of business appraisal fall down. In this situation, goodwill can be based only on subjective motivations or values; the objective values are not there.

NEGATIVE GOODWILL

With the possible exception of start-ups in their initial year or so of operation, negative goodwill is not common in small businesses. In the larger companies it more often relates to a process or a product line, or perhaps the cost of setting up a new location, not the entire company. Negative goodwill implies that substantial cash has been sunk into the research and development, advertising, or improvement of a site or product. To date, these costs are only an expense, yet in the future they will probably

> Sometimes, though, you will see goodwill, but you will not be able to measure it by the traditional procedures.

reap great rewards. Today that product or business has a negative value. Accounting-wise it is a loser.

The only way to measure negative goodwill is by discounting projected cash flows. History will not help you.

WAYS TO VALUE GOODWILL

Here are four of the several accepted ways to value goodwill in a small business:

- profit advantage
- discounting of surplus earnings or profits
- excess of value over cost
- abstraction from comparative market sales

Profit Advantage

This is not really an appraisal technique. Analysts use it for feasibility studies, especially when they need to compare investment alternatives. On the other hand, some economists and other professionals believe that profit advantage is the only way to measure goodwill. I will not argue the point, but conventional methods of valuing goodwill do have their shortcomings. Even if you never directly apply the methodology of profit advantage, its principles and concepts are worth considering.

As an example, in retailing, a nationally advertised brand-name product can be sold at a higher price, or in greater volume than an unrecognized competitive product, and so it should produce more profit. Therefore, it has a profit advantage. The value of the advantage is the present net worth, in dollars, of the annual profits that those additional sales or higher markups produce.

You could find profit advantage in a more efficient manufacturing process, an exclusive patent, a sought-after dealership or franchise, an exclusive marketing territory, or perhaps a unique location. It is anything that gives its owner a marketing or manufacturing edge, measurable in dollars and cents.

I will talk extensively about the mechanics of profit advantage in Chapter Fifteen, Valuing a Franchise. The entire rationale of franchising is that the franchisee gains a measurable profit advantage by way of increased sales and lower operating costs.

The Discounting-of-Surplus-Profits Method

This method has several names: the excess profits method, the excess earnings method, the super profits method, and the Internal Revenue Service formula. Originally developed in about 1914 by the IRS and used continuously since then, it is the most popular and probably the best way to value goodwill as a separate entity. It gives the most explainable answer.

Some people criticize it severely, however, because they think the resultant is unreliable. Why? Because you might have to apply two separate capitalization rates and two separate discount rates to carry this method to its conclusion:

- a capitalization rate for the real estate
- a capitalization rate for the machinery and equipment
- a discount rate for the goodwill
- a discount rate for a fractional interest (if applicable)

The critics suggest that good luck is the only factor that will lead you to, at best, one reliable rate, and you will never, ever find four. However, professional appraisers would prefer to make four small rate-calculation mistakes which, when averaged out, should result in an insignificant error factor, rather than make one larger blunder that would nullify any value estimate. It is normally more difficult to select one overall encompassing rate, than to find individual defendable rates that apply only to certain segments of the appraisal subject.

Other reasonable critics argue that the surplus-profits method incorrectly assumes that the value of goodwill can be established as an identifiable entity, separate from all else. Many investors agree. Remember that goodwill is worthless without the tangible assets of the business. This mechanically concocted method works well on paper, but might not be practical. Negative goodwill cannot be measured this way, and some suggest that the whole concept of goodwill is wishy-washy to start with.

Despite the valid criticisms, people will continue to use this procedure until some theorist discovers a better way. One day one will.

The value of goodwill, as established by the surplus-profits method, is the net present value of the excess or surplus earnings, or profits, of the business earned after accounting for all capital and other financial demands. The discounted remainder is the value of the goodwill. To estimate total going concern value, by an assets approach, assuming no other intangible assets, add the goodwill value to the established value of the tangible assets.

Bear in mind that in many small businesses, there is nothing left after you have accounted for all the capital assets, provided an adequate wage for the owners, and maintained orderly debt reduction. In other words, goodwill does not exist. There might be something valuable to sell at the end of the line — in excess of the assets accumulated, equity gain through debt paydown, and inflation — but that is a slim chance. Many pundits will rightly point out that you can expect fair value for either the capital assets or the business, but seldom for both.

I will detail this method of valuing goodwill in Chapter Thirteen, the Assets Approaches to Value.

Excess of Value Over Cost

Financial analysts, particular bankers and lenders, often choose this method of valuing goodwill as a separate entity. Accountants, real-estate appraisers, and other valuation professionals seldom use it, and business buyers usually cannot tell which value increases were created by goodwill or which ones were by something else.

If you choose this procedure, first you sum up all tangible assets, the cost of which is obtained from the actual purchase prices, or the records of the company, usually taken at book value. Then you deduct all the assets' total cost from either the appraised value or, more often, the selling price of the business. Any residual is the value of the goodwill.

Abstracted from Comparative Sales

To perform this method, you need enough truly comparable sales on which you have the selling price and all financial information. These are rare. You cannot extract rates from service garages, hardware stores, abattoirs, or the like, and apply them to a fast-food restaurant. So if you do not have decent comparables, then you need to revert to one of the other procedures. Also, you will find the discount rates all over the map, so you will have trouble reconciling the extremes. You will run across everything from a business that has no goodwill, perhaps even negative goodwill, to a business with little else but goodwill.

...professional appraisers would prefer to make four small rate-calculation mistakes which, when averaged out, should result in an insignificant error factor, rather than make one larger blunder that would nullify any value estimate.

The steps:

1. Establish the selling price of each comparable sale.

2. Deduct the capital assets value from the total selling price. Include in capital assets any working capital that is part of the sale. Disregard working capital that is not part of the sale. The remainder is the value of the intangible assets, which in small businesses is almost always goodwill.

3. Establish the net after-tax operating profit of each comparable sale. Deduct from that net operating profit the amount earned by the capital assets. In this case, these are the real estate and the equipment.

...you will find the discount rates all over the map, so you will have trouble reconciling the extremes. You will run across everything from a business that has no goodwill, perhaps even negative goodwill, to a business with little else but goodwill.

Let us assume that the appropriate capitalization rate for the real-estate segment is 12.5% (9.5% interest plus 3% capital recapture). You obtained this from an accounting formula or market abstraction procedure. For the equipment, we will use 19.5%. The interest rate stays the same, but depreciation becomes a recognizable factor (9.5% interest plus 10% recapture).

The Formula for the Discount Rate

$$\frac{\text{Remainder of Net Profit After Capital Earnings Deductions}}{\text{Established Value of Goodwill by Abstraction}} \times 100$$

- The $\times\,100$ converts the produced decimal factor to a percentage,
- The resultant is a discount, not a capitalization rate.

ANALYSIS OF THE SELLING PRICES OF COMPARATIVE FAST-FOOD RESTAURANTS (all numbers are rounded)

Comparable Restaurant No.	1	2	3
	Component Values		
Selling Price	$ 385,000	$ 430,000	$ 850,000
Real Estate	210,000	285,000	495,000
Equipment	85,000	80,000	255,000
Total Real Estate & Equipment	(295,000)	(365,000)	(750,000)
Abstracted Goodwill Value	$ 90,000	$ 65,000	$ 100,000
	Income and Profitability		
Average Annual Sales	$ 560,000	$ 391,000	$ 890,000
Total Expenses	(482,000)	(325,000)	(720,000)
Net Operating Profit	$ 78,000	$ 66,000	$ 170,000

From the net operating profit, deduct the amount earned by the:

	1	2	3
Real Estate @ 12.50%	$ 26,000	$ 35,500	$ 62,000
Equipment @ 19.50%	$ 17,000	$ 15,500	$ 50,000
Total Deductions	($ 43,000)	($ 51,000)	($ 112,000)
Remainder is to Goodwill	$ 25,000	$ 15,000	$ 58,000
Discount Rate for Goodwill	38.9%	23.1%	58.0%

The final problem is reconciling the discount rates so that you can apply a rate to the surplus earnings of your target enterprise. You are still seeking what an average buyer would pay and an average seller accept, both meeting the test of most probable market value. Thus, once again, revert to the median value obtained from the selection. You may have to adjust the median to bring it more into line with the realities of your subject. In the real world, you will need more than three comparable sales to make the exercise meaningful. I have shown you three only for the purpose of demonstration, so I am allowed some shortcuts. You are not so fortunate. Because of the extreme variation in the discount rates produced, as shown, use at least five sales — preferably more.

References

[1] IRS Ruling 59–60

The final problem
is reconciling
the discount rates
so that you can apply
a rate to the
surplus earnings
of your target enterprise.

NOTES

_____

_____

_____

_____

_____

_____

_____

_____

_____

_____

_____

_____

_____

_____

_____

_____

_____

_____

_____

_____

_____

_____

_____

_____

_____

Chapter 13

THE ASSETS APPROACHES TO VALUE

I have already introduced the front-door and back-door approaches to estimating going concern value. With a front-door approach, you appraise the enterprise asset by asset, both the tangible and the intangible. Their total value equals going concern value. With a back-door approach, you capitalize or discount the net operating profit to establish a single value estimate. If you go about both methods correctly, you should come up with about the same estimate of going concern value.

The two principal earnings approaches to calculate most probable market value are:

- the assets approaches,
- the cash-flow approaches.

Now, and in Chapter Fourteen, I will frequently talk about estimated market value, estimation of market value, and most probable market value. I will always avoid any positive statement about the exact value of a particular business because no one can always produce a number that works in every situation. All that anyone can furnish is a mathematically concocted estimate based on accounting calculations, operating history, statistical references, and (I hope) a qualified yet unbiased interpretation of market forces. The value will be correct in many situations if it is reached with logic, mathematical exactness, and proper procedures. Yet for a buyer or seller, who seldom completely separates logic from emotion, it could be wrong.

Always remember that you will seldom nail down an exact value in the open marketplace. The best you can hope for is an accurate estimate.

The two principal asset approaches to value are:

- the sum-of-the-assets approach,
- the split-rate approach.

Each method is the same, except that the sum-of-the-assets approach lengthens and more clearly identifies each of the value contributors. With both, you sum up the value of the capital assets, working capital, and intangible assets, which in most small businesses is limited to goodwill.

THE TWO ENTITIES:

THE REAL ESTATE AND THE BUSINESS

I know I am repeating myself, but I want to make sure you understand the first step before you launch into a valuation process: You must divide the enterprise into the real estate portion and the business portion. If the real estate is owned and is a part of the package, you must create a hypothetical situation, in which Party A owns the real estate and leases it to Party B. Party B owns everything else and operates the business. When you sum up the value of the two portions, plus any working capital, less long term liabilities, you have an estimate of going concern value.

> All that anyone can furnish is a mathematically concocted estimate based on accounting calculations, operating history, statistical references, and (I hope) a qualified yet unbiased interpretation of market forces.

Sometimes this will not be a make-believe process. You might be considering a business that rents its premises. Or else the real estate, although owned, represents an insignificant portion of the total assets or value. In this event, only the second half of the assets-first, but all of the cash-flow approaches, will apply.

THE SUM OF THE ASSETS APPROACH TO VALUE

The appraisal procedure:

1. Establish the value of the capital assets:
   * real estate,
   * machinery & equipment (or furniture, fixtures, and equipment),

2. Value the working capital (if included),

3. Establish the value of:
   * any other tangible asset,
   * redundant assets (if included),

4. Establish the value of the intangible assets,

5. Detail all long-term and contingent liabilities,

6. Going concern value: 1 + 2 + 3 + 4 - 5 = 6.

THE VALUE OF THE REAL ESTATE

...the comparative sales approach... does not work very well in the valuation of special-purpose properties, such as a fast-food restaurant.

In Chapter Four, I detailed the professionals' ways to appraise real estate, either as an investment or part-parcel to a going concern. I will not restate all that, but will apply the detailed procedures to the model, considering it only as an asset of the business. As fast-food restaurants are seldom sold as real estate only, we will consider only two of the three approaches:

* the cost approach,
* the income approach.

I will not touch the comparative sales approach because it does not work very well in the valuation of special-purpose properties, such as a fast-food restaurant. When properties are sold as part of a going concern, because it is usually impossible to abstract the common denominators and make only objective adjustments, often the exercise's sole merit is justifying the value you wanted to find in the first place.

THE COST APPROACH

With the cost approach, you assume the value to be a synthesis of the physical components of the property. To find the value, you sum up:

* the market value of the land or site as if vacant,

- the reproduction or replacement cost of the building, less depreciation,
- the contributory value of the site improvements,
- the contributory value of any other capital improvement.

For a value of the total capital assets, add to the real estate value:

- the contributory value of fixtures and equipment,
- any working capital.

We are going to cheat a little on terminology and perhaps the GAAP rules. Accountants do not consider working capital as a capital asset — rather it is a concept. Current assets is the capital asset. To make your calculations easier, begin by deducting the current liabilities from the current assets in order to calculate working capital, rather than at the very end as we do with the long term liabilities. Subsequently, where working capital is referred to as a capital asset—trust us and don't sweat the small stuff! It is only a matter of terminology which, for our purposes, is really not that important.

Although the procedure mostly applies to new properties, and does not always indicate market value, the cost approach often plays an important role in the investment decision, especially regarding going concerns, rather than investment real estate. Frequently, a value calculated by the income or comparative-sales approaches may not accurately represent the real estate's value as an integrated entity in the business setting, particularly when you are looking for value in use or value to the owner.

Still, remember that the cost approach provides only an orderly liquidation value. It does not consider the sales and profitability of the business. So a property that houses a successful enterprise has exactly the same value as a property housing a business on the verge of bankruptcy. Also, the measurement of reproduction cost and depreciation, particularly in an older building, is usually just educated guesswork.

COST APPROACH VALUE OF THE MODEL

To come up with a value for the unimproved site, I used market-value indicators; for the building, reproduction cost less depreciation from all sources; and for site improvements, current replacement cost less depreciation.

In Chapter Seven I detailed the value of the fixtures and equipment, in place and part of a going concern. I will use that value of $98,000 throughout the rest of this demonstration.

From the schedule of assets I abstracted the value of the motor home, the redundant capital asset, which we are not depreciating.

Summary of Value Estimates

Market Value of the Site	$	175,000
Depreciated Value of the Building		336,000
Site Improvements		10,000
Real Estate Total	$	521,000
Fixtures and Equipment	$	98,000
The Motor Home		60,000
Total Value Found	$	679,000

Usually, the cost-approach value does not mean all that much. Because it only accounts for the capital assets on an orderly liquidation basis, it estimates only a fraction of the total going concern value. Most often, people use it as a leaning post for other approaches. There may be nothing else, though, so check the resultant against book values, but stay on your toes. Book values reflect only cost, or cost less a formula depreciation — not value. And as I said before, these values are often manipulated to maximize tax advantages for both seller and buyer.

Still, in a location-independent or location-specific enterprise, such as a manufacturing plant, where it might be impractical to work out a property rental amount, the cost approach may be your best bet.

The cost approach only accounts for the capital assets on an orderly liquidation basis, it estimates only a fraction of the total going concern value.

	Book Values		Appraised Value
	Cost	Depreciated Value	
Land, at cost	$ 150,000	$ 150,000	$ 175,000
Building	349,256	317,034	336,000
Paving	15,178	11,065	10,000
Real Estate Total	$ 514,434	$ 478,099	$ 521,000
Equipment	$ 114,439	$ 73,695	$ 98,000
The Mobile Home	60,000	60,000	60,000
Total Book Value	$ 688,873	$ 611,794	$ 679,000

The correlation between the cost and the appraised value is quite good. Still, this business was bought only three years ago. Had it been long ago, this would not have worked out nearly so well.

THE INCOME APPROACH

The value found by the income approach equals the present worth of all net operating income before debt service or depreciation that the real estate will earn over its remaining economic life. Moreover, it is the present worth of all financial benefits.

The technique involves determining the gross rentals and/or income — divorced from the operation of the actual business — which the real estate generates, or could generate, when considered as an investment. From that, you subtract all property operating expenses. By analysing the applicable market conditions, you come up with a capitalization rate that combines interest on investment and capital recapture. You apply that rate to the remainder or annual net operating income. And voila! You have the property value on an investment basis. (That means open-market value in exchange, not value in use or value to the owner.)

Still, in a location-independent or location-specific enterprise, such as a manufacturing plant, where it might be impractical to work out a property rental amount, the cost approach may be your best bet.

The Steps

1. Determine the gross annual rent that the real estate could earn, assuming it to be owned by a third party,

2. From the gross annual rental income, identify and deduct all expenditures that would be chargeable to the property, but not the cost of doing the enterprise's business,

3. From gross annual revenue, deduct all applicable operating expenses to obtain a net operating income (NOI) to the property before long-term debt service, depreciation, or income tax,

4. From the market, obtain an appropriate capitalization rate, or else use an accounting formula to develop one,

5. Capitalize the net operating income into an estimate of the market value of the real estate,

6. To the real-estate value, you add the contributory value of the fixtures and equipment, any working capital, and any other tangible asset. Now you have the total value of the tangible assets.

CALCULATION OF RENT

To calculate the amount of rent the real estate should earn in an open market, you can choose from three methods:

1. Compare it to similar spaces that have been recently rented or are currently held for lease,

2. For a location-dependent business, use a percentage-of-sales factor,

3. For location-independent or location-specific businesses, or one housed in a special-purpose property, or if there are no market comparisons, use a competitive percent return on the investment, with the capital investment amount abstracted from the cost approach value estimate.

In most small businesses, particularly those that are location-dependent, the total sales volume or income produced, assuming a proper profit level, directly relates to the space rental the business can afford to pay.

MARKET AND ECONOMIC RENT: AN OVERVIEW

In most small businesses, particularly those that are location-dependent, the total sales volume or income produced, assuming a proper profit level, directly relates to the space rental the business can afford to pay. Although the lessor thinks of rent as so many dollars per square foot, the lessee focuses on the volume of sales generated within the leased area. Most forms of business and industry have their own guidelines.

You should mainly consider economic rent, not market rent. Market rent is the rent obtainable by the real estate when considering the market. For example, if retail store spaces up and down the street are leased in the general area of X dollars per square foot per year, then a vacant space of similar size and appointments should rent for this same general price. Other than its continuing ability to pay rent, the tenant's viability is of little interest to the lessor. Economic rent is what the business can afford to pay, a percentage of the enterprise's total revenue.

We are concerned with economic rent. No matter how the lease agreement is structured, the rent paid must always be linked with the tenant's profitability ratio. For example: because of its very low markup, yet higher volume, a supermarket can afford to pay only one or one-and-a-half percent of total sales to the landlord. On the other hand, a lower-volume, high-profit jewelry or gift store might not even blink at a rental of ten percent of sales. For the most part, restaurants pay between three and eight percent of total sales for occupancy. (These percentages have declined in recent years.) A restaurant could even pay ten percent in very specific circumstances, such as a well-franchised outlet at a key intersection with a demonstrated profit advantage. At three percent, the restaurateur leases a bare box building and provides all operating requirements, including all leasehold improvements, furniture, fixtures, and equipment. At eight percent, you are looking at a typical hotel, or industrial cafeteria, where the lessor provides everything, including the linen and cutlery. All other equitable rental percentages lie somewhere between the extremes. Industry standards normally dictate the rental range for most business types.

When you determine space rental with a percentage of sales volume, you are appraising management, not real estate. Think of a machine in a factory: If it works twice as many hours per shift, is it worth twice as much money? For the most part, the appraisal of a small business is a valuation of management once the orderly liquidation stage has been passed. In these situations, a tenant's ability to pay rent must balance with the lessor's requirements to justify the real-estate investment. You cannot expect the owner to donate the property for no reason other than having the misfortune of leasing to an unsuccessful enterprise. On the other hand, the tenant should not be penalized because his business is performing better than the industry standard.

The overlap between economic and market rental is not finite. You must consider both, particularly when a business is near the liquidation stage or you are thinking about using the real estate a different way. Or maybe the lessee is very successful and wants a loophole in the contract to avoid paying a rental bonus.

...a tenant's ability to pay rent must balance with the lessor's requirements to justify the real-estate investment.

Always ask and positively answer: Is it reasonable and logical? Does it make sense?

It might not make sense to use a percentage of sales if you have good market data. Yet is it more expedient to conjure a so-much-per-square-foot space rental without market comparisons? Maybe you should consider the subject on an economic basis, which is the usual preference.

Do not accept this as an ironclad rule. In some location-independent or location-specific businesses, space rental has almost nothing to do with productivity or sales. Examples might be, manufacturing and distributing companies, automobile and farm-implement dealerships, auction markets, service businesses, and professional practices. Like all rules, it must be applied with diligence. What works well in a retail store may not apply to an welding shop.

In determining the space rental, look at visibility and identification, convenience to the market, entrance from and exit into traffic arteries, other neighborhood conveniences, parking, compatibility to the neighborhood, and safety. Stores are rated according to price, quality of merchandise, location, service, selection of goods, overall appeal, and fair treatment of its customers.

In many owner-operator situations, when you cannot find reliable market comparisons, use a percentage of sales to establish basic rent.

SOME OTHER CLAUSES

Because of the development of gasoline kiosks and self-serve gas bars, the traditional service station is now somewhat dated. They are still common, especially in smaller communities where the owner might operate the fuel-dispensing facility, sell parts, and rent out the service bays. The owner might even do grease jobs, change oil, install tires, etc. But a mechanic almost always pays rent to the station operator, who may claim a markup on the parts installed. Is this markup considered income or rent? Good question. When buying, examine and judge the situation yourself. The allocation might not even matter. It is all revenue to the owner.

At times, in independently owned service stations, you will find a cross lease, also called "lease-re-lease, same party". The oil company leases the station from the owner, usually on a per-gallon, volume basis, then releases it back to the owner for one dollar per year. The rental paid by the oil marketing company to the station compensates the property owner for providing the marketing facilities and ensures that this outlet continues to "fly the flag." This revenue is always considered income and not separated from the gasoline or other sales. Although legally classified as rent, do not treat it as such.

To ensure that a particular product is prominently displayed in a retail store, a supplier commonly pays so many dollars per lineal foot of display shelf for a stated period. Known in the industry as "push," this income and similar incentives should fall in with other sales receipts. Some agreements, on the other hand, are legitimate space rentals. Supermarkets often lease out large areas to other retailers, such as pharmacists. You can apply the rental income to the business (treated on par with any other form of income) or to the real estate (treated as if the company owns, or holds the property under a master lease, occupies part, and subleases the remainder). It all depends on the structure of the agreement.

CALCULATION OF RENT FROM THE MARKET

Look to the market first. Obtain, as well as you can, the rents charged for similar properties. Consider each property's physical characteristics, not fixtures and equipment, not volume of sales, not profitability.

I have obtained lease information on five fast-food restaurants, all located in mid-sized cities in the western United States. Numbers One and Two are independent, the other three franchised. All five are actual leases and sales, with volumes rounded, not just numbers concocted for this purpose.

Market Comparison No. 1
- Building Gross Area   2,200 sq. ft.
- Annual Rent Net $ 49,500
- Rental per sq. ft. per annum $ 22.50

Market Comparison No. 2
- Building Gross Area   2,200 sq. ft.
- Annual Rent Net $ 60,500
- Rental per sq. ft. per annum $ 27.50

Market Comparison No. 3
- Building Gross Area   2,300 sq. ft.
- Annual Rent Net $ 69,000
- Rental per sq. ft. per annum $ 30.00

Market Comparison No. 4
- Building Gross Area   2,310 sq. ft.
- Annual Rent Net $ 72,000
- Rental per sq. ft. per annum $ 31.17

Market Comparison No. 5
- Building Gross Area   2,400 sq. ft.
- Annual Rent Net $ 72,000
- Rental per sq. ft. per annum $ 30.00

The Model: ABC Franchised Restaurant
- Building Gross Area   2,688 sq. ft.

When comparing existing leases with your target business, account for:

- the time element (older leases might not be renewed at the same rate),
- term of lease (usually the longer the term, the lower the rate),
- quality of the tenant (ranging from local to national AAA),
- location, related to sources of patronage,
- location, related to direct competition,
- neighborhood or area considerations, identifiable trends,
- size of the site, visibility, ease of entry and exit,
- condition of the site, paving, drainage, parking, etc.,
- age, construction, and condition of the building,
- comparative building amenities,
- leasehold improvements (and who paid for them),
- longer-term potential,
- comparability of all leases re: payment of taxes, insurance, repairs and maintenance, etc.
- specific clauses, such as sales renewal options, tax and insurance escalators, percentage override, and radius restrictions.

Although it is a tough call, you may also want to look at motive. How desperate was the lessor? How badly did the tenant want in? Did the parties negotiate successfully? A national tenant with a solid track record always gets a better deal than a local independent.

After weighing all the positive and negative attributes of the five comparative leases, let us assume that the annual market rent for the ABC Franchised Restaurant is $27.50 per sq. ft., net. The term "net" implies that, besides the basic space rent, the tenant must pay all property operating costs, such as taxes, insurance, utilities, normal repairs, and maintenance. The owner pays for property management, structural repairs, and all capital costs.

Annual Market Rental: 2,688 sq. ft @ $27.50 per sq. ft. = $ 73,920

This market rent might not equal economic rent. We did not consider the volume of sales or profitability of each restaurant. The rent is based exclusively on the purchase price, or cost to develop the real estate, and the anticipated return on the lessor's capital investment.

RENTAL AS A PERCENTAGE OF SALES VOLUME

To determine rental based on sales volume, you can choose from two methods:

> The term "net" implies that, besides the basic space rent, the tenant must pay all operating costs, such as taxes, insurance, utilities, normal repairs, and maintenance.

- refer to the market by examining leases and sales,
- refer to published indices and trade journals.

Reference to the Market
These are the same five restaurants discussed earlier. I have arranged them from the smallest sales volume to the highest:

Market Comparison No. 1
- Reported Sales Volume — $ 742,000
- Annual Net Rent — 49,500
- Rent as a percent of sales volume — 6.67%

Market Comparison No. 2
- Reported Sales Volume — $ 975,000
- Annual Net Rent — 60,500
- Rent as a percent of sales volume — 6.21%

Market Comparison No. 3
- Reported Sales Volume — $ 1,150,000
- Annual Net Rent — 69,000
- Rent as a percent of sales volume — 6.00%

Market Comparison No. 4
- Reported Sales Volume — $ 1,350,000
- Annual Net Rent — 72,000
- Rent as a percent of sales volume — 5.33%

Market Comparison No. 5
- Reported Sales Volume — $ 1,800,000
- Annual Net Rent — 72,000
- Rent as a percent of sales — 4.00%

The Model: ABC Franchised Restaurant
- Pro forma Sales Volume — $ 1,448,000

As sales volume increases, the rent percentage decreases, not necessarily proportionally. However, other comparables might not conform to this principle. Still, five is enough to establish a trend. To determine the percentage for the model restaurant, assuming that it is comparable, just slot it into the array.

The above array would indicate an appropriate economic rent for the target restaurant of about five percent of sales.

$$\text{Annual Economic Rent: } \$\,1,448,000 \times 5.00\% = \$\,72,400$$

...statistical gathering houses regularly publish great masses of facts and figures on sales and operational costs for all sorts of businesses. Check out your local library.

Reference to Published Indices

Isn't it wonderful the way some writers say that if you want to find out anything, just look to the market? It is all there, or so we tell you. Analyse this financial statement, dissect that sale, read this lease, crunch these numbers, adjust this, compare that, and everything will work out. There is just one minor problem. We never tell you how and where to get all this good information. Admittedly, it might be tough or impossible to get what you want, particularly if you do not quite know what you are looking for, or where to find it. Even professional appraisers stumble over this with many an assignment. We all rely heavily on information gleaned from other professional appraisers. We are like a bunch of gangsters calling in our markers.

Sometimes we refer to published indices, which produce those industry averages we keep talking about. Several statistical gathering houses regularly publish great masses of facts and figures on sales and operational costs for all sorts of businesses. Check out your local library.

One of the top publications on operating costs, the *Almanac of Business Ratios*, published annually by Prentice Hall, indicates that restaurant rentals run from a low of 3.0% percent to a high of 7.6% of sales. It categorizes by assets, not sales. Although there is no consistency, generally the greater the assets, the lower the rental percentage. As we can safely assume that more assets imply larger restaurants, a higher volume should equate to a lower rental percentage.

At I write, the most recent edition suggests rental at 5.20% of sales if the assets are worth between $500,000 to $1,000,000. This ties in very well with the rental amounts indicated from our analysis of the marketplace.

Using this percentage, which is supported by other statistical publishing houses, the real-estate rental would be:

Annual Percent of Sales Rent: $ 1,448,000 × 5.20% = $ 75,296

Reconciliation

Now you face the appraiser's dilemma. The three different rental amounts cannot all be right, or wrong. Which one to use?

Market Rent:	2,688 sq. ft @ $27.50 per sq. ft. = $	73,920
Economic Rent:	$ 1,448,000 × 5.00% = $	72,400
Percent of Sales Rent:	$ 1,448,000 × 5.20% = $	75,296

This is very tight array, with less than three thousand dollars between the highest and lowest. Probably this is more the result of good luck, rather than good management. Most of the time the indicated rentals are much further apart, in which case reconciliation is very tricky indeed.

Which to use? As with real estate or business value, always go with the one that seems most logical. This is usually the one with the best data. Never, ever average the three. That said, you will usually calculate economic space rental one way, not three, so you need not fret about reconciliation. You might determine the rate by one route, then clarify or support it with a second, but never three. That would be overdoing it.

Let us randomly select the market rental of $27.50 per sq. ft. per year, net.

Annual real-estate rental: ABC Franchised Restaurant
2,688 sq. ft @ $27.50 per sq. ft., net = $ 73,920

This is 5.10% of pro forma sales of $1,448,000, but only 4.55% of last year's recorded sales of $1,623,714. The occupancy cost is reasonable and in line with industry standards. We can safely go with it.

COST APPROACH ABSTRACTED RENTAL RATE

At times, you might need to abstract a rental amount from the cost approach, particularly when the estimation of market or economic rent is more a concoction than a provable amount, such as with infrequently traded, location-independent, or location-specific enterprises. The procedure is to apply a rental percentage to the cost approach value estimate obtained. If you have not calculated a cost-approach estimate, you could, as a last resort, use the initial and depreciated cost of the real estate as detailed in the financial statement.

Cost Approach Value Estimate of the Real Estate	$ 521,000
Book Value: Initial Cost of the Real Estate (rounded)	$ 514,500
Book Value: Depreciated Value (rounded)	$ 478,000

If Using Book Values

You can use the initial cost for a building that is up to five years old. The increased replacement cost of the building and land appreciation would usually offset any depreciation. For an older building, decrease the IRS allowable or taken depreciation by fifty percent. In other words, go halfway between the recorded initial cost and the book depreciated value. The calculation procedure is exactly the same as stated above.

Let us assume that a fair return on the investment, including recapture, is 12.41%. (I will explain this rate later.) This is a restaurant operation, a highly volatile business, domiciled in a building specifically designed for such use and not easily adapted for other purposes.

As Calculated from the Cost Approach:

$$\text{Annual net rental would be: } 12.41\% \times \$521,000 = \$64,656$$

This rent, especially if you used book values, frequently differs considerably from that developed from the market or by using a percentage of sales. This is normal. Often, in going concerns or investment real estate, the cost-approach value estimate does not really relate to its value in exchange on the open market.

Warning: Use this method only when there is nothing else, and I do mean nothing else.

> Often, in going concerns or investment real estate, the cost-approach value estimate does not really relate to its value in exchange on the open market.

EXPENSES TO THE PROPERTY

When looking at leased commercial and industrial real estate, appraisers traditionally make deductions from the Net Lease annual rental income by inserting into the expense analysis items that can be charged to the property. These are costs for the operation of the property only. They have nothing to do with the revenues or profits of the business.

The first is an allowance for vacancy and collection loss, determined by the length of the lease and the strength of the tenant. Whether the property is professionally managed or the owner does it, a property management charge is made. This is the cost of collecting the rents, accounting, advertising, supervising, paying the bills, etc. An expense item is allocated for the cost of property taxes, insurance, and utilities in the event of vacancy. Finally, there is an allowance for structural maintenance. This is the cost of attending to property repairs for which the tenant is not responsible.

Appraisers disagree on whether these costs should be included in the income and expense summary in an owner-occupied situation, particularly if the property is a part of a well-established going concern, the occupancy has not changed for several years, and the business is strong enough to keep going. Should you charge these expenses to the property? Who knows? Are the projected revenue reductions and property costs factual, or do they only satisfy the timeworn tradition that they must be shown?

As I am trying to exemplify a true rental situation, with the property owned by one party and the business by another, they should probably be inserted. The expenses are no more fictional than the rental used, neither of which will ever appear on the company's income statement. Whether they are factual or not, a minimum allowance for the property's operating costs provides some cushion that could be required some day. By capitalizing net income into perpetuity, you can find values and make longer-term projections. Maybe someday the business will go bankrupt and a lender will foreclose, in which case the property would be leased (lenders have no desire to operate restaurants). The value found is the present worth of future anticipated returns, for which today's situation is only a guide. The key words are "anticipated" and "future." The value is, as yet, unproven.

In all of these situations, direct property costs and reserves for future expenses are a composite of what is happening in the marketplace and what is expected to happen. You want to forecast the longer term as accurately as possible. An allowance of three percent for vacancy and collection loss presents a good cross-section between an owner-occupied property and an unrestricted investment property.

The vacancy allowance is totally hypothetical. In a well-established, well-located, owner-operated premise, it should be very low or nil. In a shaky, unadaptable, rented, small-town premise, it could be ten percent or higher.

Property management costs normally range from three to seven percent of effective gross income. That is the total rent stipulated in the lease, or calculated from market references, less the vacancy allowance, or actual rents collected. Five percent is a good average — in fact, the amount charged by most agents.

Operating costs (vacancy, taxes, insurance, and utility cost estimates), which the property owner would pay, are the same percentage as the vacancy rate. Here, they are three percent.

The amount to be reserved for structural repairs depends largely on the age of the building, its construction, condition, the age and condition of the roof, the HVAC (heating, ventilating, and air conditioning), the electrical systems, and any faster-depreciating items. Most appraisers use an annual charge of twenty-five to fifty cents per square foot of total area. If a building is older, of inferior construction, or in poor condition, it should be in the higher range. If new and in excellent condition, then twenty to twenty-five cents per square foot should suffice. Because of unique features and higher maintenance requirements, a restaurant building has a higher rate than an office, apartment, or warehouse. We will say fifty cents per square foot.

SUMMARY OF INCOME AND EXPENSES TO THE REAL ESTATE

Income

Gross Annual Rental Income	$	73,920
Less 3% vacancy allowance & collection loss		(2,218)
Effective gross annual income	$	71,702

> The value found is the present worth of future anticipated returns, for which today's situation is only a guide. The key words are "anticipated" and "future." The value is, as yet, unproven.

Expenses

Management 5% of effective gross			$	3,585
3% of property operating costs estimate				
(taxes & insurance amounts taken from income statement)				
Property Taxes	$	18,506		
Property Insurance	$	10,824		
Utilities, Vacant building	$	4,032	($1.50 per sq. ft.)	
Total	$	33,362 × 3.0% =	$	1,001
Structural reserves: 2688 per sq. ft. @ $ 0.50 per. sq.ft.				
			$	1,344
Total Expenses			$	(5,930)

Net Income to the Real Estate, before Debt Service, Depreciation, or Income Tax	$	65,772

SELECTION OF THE CAPITALIZATION RATE

I have bantered the selection of capitalization rate methods back and forth enough, but I want to say again, that in the asset approaches to value, I prefer formula-derived capitalization rates that can be more properly applied to each individual value contributor. In the cash-flow approaches, the subject of the next chapter, use market-derived rates wherever possible.

Average Cost of Capital

Average cost of capital, known to real-estate appraisers as the mortgage-equity procedure, and by some as band of investment, is a weighted average of the available, or assumable, interest on the debt and the equity-yield portions of a real-estate investment. In other words, it is an average return on the investment, expressed as a capitalization rate, composed of both debt and equity.

In calculating the rate by the average cost of capital, first determine the rate of interest, the amortization period, and the percentage of value that can be borrowed against the property. Take into account the potential for fluctuating interest rates and balloon dates whereby the interest rate could be changed in mid-life.

An alternative method, the equity capitalization approach, uses the present mortgage, not a lender's rate simulation. You might prefer this if the principal sum is high enough, the rate of interest at or lower than that presently obtainable, and the mortgage assumable. The existing debt frequently does not affect property value, however.

As abstracted from the notes to the financial statements:

First mortgage to Commercial-Industrial Bank, payable in monthly installments of $4,930.00, including amortized interest at bank prime plus 1.50%. The loan is secured by a land and building mortgage, assignment of fire insurance, subrogation of shareholder's loans, and general assignment of cash collateral. Personal guarantee of the shareholders.

Balance, end of last fiscal year: $ 353,845.00

This mortgage is not high enough to use. Further, it is on a floating interest rate and carries collateral security. On any sale, the property will probably be refinanced.

For the purpose of valuing the real estate of ABC Franchised Restaurant, let us assume that you can obtain, through the usual sources, a first mortgage to sixty percent of the value of the property at nine-percent interest with a twenty-year amortization period. Although this interest rate may seem high, remember that restaurants are a volatile business with a high failure rate. Accordingly, most financial institutions want a point or two more than for the would charge for a more conventional risk.

Use the annual mortgage constant, not the interest factor only. The intent is to simulate a cash flow to be capitalized into an estimate of value. A mortgage constant is the annual rate for the full amortization period, both interest and principal for $1.00. You can obtain it in an amortization book or figure it out on a financial calculator. Most give or make the calculations on a monthly basis, just like normal mortgage payments. The constant used is annual, calculated monthly, times twelve.

Required equity yield, the net spendable annual income to the property, includes the cash-on-cash equity dividend, plus buildup through debt reduction and gain or loss from inflation or disinflation, but calculated before debt service, depreciation, or income tax. This is both real and maybe money. It considers the return to the real-estate portion of the business from an investor's perspective. Do not forget: This is cash throw off from the real estate, not the operation of the business. In this valuation method, which differs from the cash-flow approaches, the real estate and the business must be kept separate at all times.

The Elwood, Ankerson, and related theories, which date from the 1960s, added another step. Included in the capitalization formula was a sinking fund for equity buildup created by mortgage paydown and a factor for inflation or disinflation. Today, people assume that these pluses or minuses are already built into the overall rate and need not be separately considered.

The essential criteria, in weighing what that return to equity is, or should be:

> This is cash throw off from the real estate, not the operation of the business. In this valuation method, which differs from the cash-flow approaches, the real estate and the business must be kept separate at all times.

- the checkered history of restaurants, which have the highest failure rate of all small businesses,
- the longer-term stability of this particular one,
- the difficulty of operating restaurants, the very high personnel turnover,
- the unique design of restaurant buildings, making many impossible to convert to an alternative use at a reasonable cost,
-
  the building's construction, condition, and remaining useful life,
- the strict requirements of the franchisor, the lack of adherence to which could result in cancellation of the franchise,
- the difficulty of finding a new tenant, should the property be vacated.

All this indicates a fifteen-percent equity yield rate for the remaining forty percent of the capitalization rate total. This is above the AAA bond or midpoint rate, yet below a speculative risk rate. It is a good middle-of-the-road, average rate for this type of property, considering all of the above, including its special circumstances.

Several studies strongly suggest that abstracting small-business equity-yield rates from the market is less accurate than obtaining overall capitalization rates from these same sources. The after-debt-service profit levels simply vary too much from one operation to another. It is impossible to prove any theory, or to obtain enough consistency to interpret what is happening, or should happen, to an individual case with this method.

Capitalization Rate:

Mortgage: Annual Constant	$0.10676 \times 60\%$ =	0.06406
Equity yield; cash on cash	$0.15000 \times 40\%$ =	0.06000
	Rate Total	0.12406
	or	12.41%

Note: In Canada, where interest is calculated semiannually, not in advance, the rate would be:

Mortgage: Annual Constant	$0.10797 \times 60\%$ =	0.06478
Equity yield; cash on cash	$0.15000 \times 40\%$ =	0.06000
	Rate Total	0.12478
	or	12.48%

CAPITALIZED INCOME VALUE OF THE REAL ESTATE

The formula is:

$$\frac{\text{Net Operating Income}}{\text{Capitalization Rate}} \times 100 = \text{Value}$$

Value of the real estate

Net income of $65,772 capitalized @ 12.41% = $ 529,992
                                    rounded to $ 530,000

This is the value that will be used throughout the remainder of this demonstration.

FIXTURES AND EQUIPMENT

An indexing procedure established the contributory, in-place value of the fixtures and equipment, which implies part of a going concern and not an open market sale, at $98,000. I detailed this in Chapter Seven.

The alternative method is to use an income approach. As hypothetical income and expenses were applied to the real estate to determine its value, why not do the same for the equipment? It also earns income. An investor in machinery differs little from someone who buys real property. Both require return on and return of capital. Both similarly assess return, risk, and relativity.

In most circumstances, you can establish a rental factor. You can obtain lease rates, which basically combine required investment return and recapture, from companies that lease equipment. Yet for most going concerns, where fixtures and equipment have primarily a value in use, calculate the replacement cost, less depreciation which is easier to obtain and more reliable for estimating contributory value. In most situations, or where there is a mixture of old and new equipment, it is the more accurate procedure.

Going Concern Value of Fixtures & Equipment: $ 98,000
(The earlier, established, in-place value)

The motor home, owned by the restaurant and retained supposedly for advertising purposes but used by the owners without cost, is a redundant asset. It does not contribute to the company's earnings or profitability. But because it exists and is owned by the company, you must recognize it. Therefore, you continually add it to all value estimates.

Value/Cost of the Motor Home $ 60,000

> The motor home, owned by the restaurant and retained supposedly for advertising purposes but used by the owners without cost, is a redundant asset. It does not contribute to the company's earnings or profitability.

Summary of Values Found by the Income Approach

Real Estate, Capitalized Income Value Estimate	$ 530,000
Fixtures & Equipment, Going Concern Value	$ 98,000
	$ 628,000
The motor home, the redundant asset	$ 60,000
Value of the capital assets	$ 688,000

And always,
where you have
a strong income-approach
or comparative-sales-value
estimate, never use
the cost approach
for anything
except a leaning post.

RECONCILIATION OF CAPITAL ASSET VALUES

The same problem reappears. You now have two value estimates, one determined by the cost approach at $679,000, and one by capitalizing pro forma net operating income at $688,000. They are only $9,000 apart, yet both cannot be correct. Go with the more comfortable one, the one with the most reliable and best input factors. And always, where you have a strong income-approach or comparative-sales-value estimate, never use the cost approach for anything except a leaning post.

Accordingly, we will use the value as developed by the income approach. This could be classified as the orderly liquidation value, in that we have not yet attached any value to the intangible assets. Yet it is not a forced sale value. There is no compulsion to sell.

Going concern value should include working capital, abstracted from the balance sheet for the date that applies to the value. In almost all business sales, however, working capital is not included. Usually the inventory is extra, and the seller keeps the cash, the accounts receivable, and all other current assets. Yet he retains responsibility for accounts payable and any other non-assumed liability. Thus, although I have not forgotten about working capital, I am not going to add it at this time.

VALUE OF THE INTANGIBLE ASSETS (GOODWILL)

The final step in this procedure is to determine, then add to the value of the tangible assets, the value of the intangible assets. In this case, and for most small businesses, this is limited to goodwill. In this approach, goodwill is set out as an identifiable asset. You calculate it with a discount rate or a multiplier, by capitalizing surplus profits that are not required for the normal operation of the business, or to pay for the tangible assets at a normally acceptable return on the investment. You must now account for, or adjust to industry standards, any income or expense item that was missed, deleted, or glossed over, then deduct it from the after-tax net operating profit.

The discounted remainder is the value of all intangible assets, i.e. the goodwill. You deduct from the net profit, or adjust:

Property Occupancy Cost

If the real estate is owned, you must calculate and deduct a fair rental value from the net profit.

If the premises are leased, do not deduct this cost. You will see annual property rental in the expense statement — except if there is a definite leasehold advantage or disadvantage and the owner is paying less or more than market rent and, because of the lease, will continue to do so. In this case, the advantage or disadvantage is the net present value of the financial gain or loss. This is the annual difference between the rent paid and the market or equivalent rental rate, discounted to the end of the lease term.

For example (this has nothing to do with the model restaurant):

Assume market rent to be $25,000 per annum	
Contract Rent (the stated amount from the lease)	$ 20,000
Remaining term on the lease 5 years	

Interest rate 8.50% (Use an interest rate only, not the mortgage constant. This is return on, not of, capital. The lessee has made no direct investment.)

Advantage to lessee:

Net Present Value of $ 25,000 – $ 20,000 = $ 5,000 per annum	
for 5 years discounted at 8.50% =	$ 19,703

This $19,703 is part of, and is to be added to the value of, the goodwill. If a disadvantage (the lessee pays more than the market rental), the calculation method would be the same. The goodwill would be reduced, though, not increased.

Rental on the Subject Property

Property rent is based on the presumption of a net lease if owned, but on the actual lease agreement if not. This is not a duplication. For a rented store, the net profit would have been reduced by the rental amount.

For the subject restaurant, the real estate is owned. Although a property rental was calculated to determine its market value, it was never entered as an expense to the business; by this procedure, it still will not be. Yet the occupancy of the property must be paid for. Here, it is simply a charge against the profit of the business — hypothetical, if you like. The costs of operating the property (taxes, insurance, utilities, repairs, and maintenance) are part of the schedule of expenses.

Annual net rental of ABC Franchised Restaurant	$ 73,920

Leasehold Improvements

The tenant makes these improvements to leased property. Frequently she rents only a bare box, so she pays for floor covering, interior partitions, washrooms, ceiling, lighting, and so forth herself. If you have not retired this investment elsewhere, assuming that this cost is applicable, now is the time. You should amortize the unretired capital investment at the prevailing interest rate over the remainder of the lease term. For this purpose, you must assume that the lease will not be renewed or extended.

For example (this has nothing to do with the model restaurant):

Leasehold improvements, paid for by lessee:	$ 100,000
Remaining Term of Lease:	5 years
Interest rate:	8.50%

Amortization (This time you use the mortgage constant that is, interest and principal, return on and return of. There is a capital investment by the lessee.)

Annual amortization:	$	25,377

The $25,377 would, in this instance, be a deduction against the goodwill. If financed, and the carrying cost is on the schedule of expenses with the total debt service, you can apply only the amortization of the leasehold improvements. Use the charged interest rate and a straight-line recapture rate. If there is no debt service on the expense schedule, assume that the improvements were paid for up front, and treat their amortization as demonstrated above.

Leasehold improvements at ABC Franchised Restaurant:	nil

Amortizations and Sinking Funds

These receive essentially the same treatment as the leasehold improvements: cost amortized over the remaining life of the contract, or that allowable by law, whichever is the shorter. You can depreciate capital investments, such as goodwill purchased, franchises, rights, patents, operating agreements, and the like, under existing Revenue Canada rules at seven percent per year on declining balances, to a maximum of seventy-five percent of cost. In the United States, you cannot write off these acquisitions. Because government rules change, always obtain the most current regulation before you apply it. When it comes to any legal or taxation matter, never take my word for anything.

Interest on Long-term Debt

The value of the real estate was developed through a capitalization process that included return on (interest) and return of (recapture or depreciation) invested capital. The value of the fixtures and equipment was developed by adjusting book values that recognized past depreciation but not future capital recapture. Any other capital assets would also be brought in at current value. For these purposes, you need not consider long-term debt if created to acquire or improve capital assets.

Still, if the long-term debt financing rate is higher than the prevailing market rate, and you cannot refinance it at this time, the excess interest charge would hurt the business. It should be deducted from the surplus profits. Conversely, if the subject has advantageous financing that continues for more than a year or two, then apply a credit for the interest differential. This follows the same logic as for the leasehold improvements. If there is a definite financial advantage or disadvantage, based on its net present value to the end of its term, then discount and include it.

For example (this has nothing to do with the model restaurant):

Current mortgage rate available on the market:	9.00%
Existing mortgage rate on target business:	6.50%
Amortization period:	20 years
Mortgage term/balloon date:	3 years

(The mortgage contains a clause by which the principal balance is due at the end of the third year. Any advantage gained terminates at that time.)

Principal Amount of Mortgage	$	100,000
Monthly payments at the market mortgage rate	$	899.73
Monthly payments on the existing mortgage	$	745.60
Monthly saving	$	154.13
= Annual	$	1,849.56

To establish the value of the advantage, use the existing mortgage rate, 6.50%, to reduce the annual saving to a net present value. The discounting period is only to the end of the mortgage term, not the amortization period. Assume that if the mortgage is not paid out, the interest rate will then be brought into line with current rates.

Advantage, to be added to goodwill:

Net present value of $ 1,849.56 per annum for 3 years, discounted at 6.50%.
$$= \qquad \$\ 4,899.00$$

If the rate is at a disadvantage (higher than the market), assuming no refinancing in the interim, the calculating procedure is exactly the same. Still, use the rate on the mortgage, not the market rate, now 6.50%. This would be a deduction from, not an addition to, the goodwill.

Interest on Short-term Debt

Remember what I have said about including working capital in the final value estimate. Except in very rare cases, it is not part of any sale or purchase package. If working capital is not included, interest on short-term debt is, it is a normal expense to most business. On an income statement, you will frequently find the cost of clearing credit cards mixed in with short-term debt interest. They are not the same and must be separated.

Payment of interest is the penalty for being poor, and the poorer a business, the more interest it must pay. How much of the short-term interest should be charged for this inadequacy? Sometimes all of it is included, and sometimes it is disregarded. To determine which, take into account what would be a normal business operation. Your target company might not be considered normal.

Interest is disguised in some situations. For example, an otherwise prosperous automobile dealer might pay thousands of dollars per year in wholesale finance charges. Vehicles must be paid for the moment they leave the factory. Assuming that this short-term debt does not exist, the company's operating profit picture looks a lot better and its value soars upward. Accountants treat wholesale finance costs the same as other short-term debts, but for the sake of consistency and business valuation, you could consider these high interest charges as a cost of sales.

If working capital is taken to be a capital asset, interest on short-term debt is already included. Treat it exactly the same as interest on long-term debt used to acquire real estate and equipment. Bringing in the interest cost separately, then including the working capital in the asset schedule, would be a double entry. The exception to this would be where there is no working capital, as could happen in service businesses or professional practices. Although working capital is usually not included in the valuation process, you cannot just forget about it. You must account for every expenditure, every asset, and every liability one way or another before reaching the bottom line: the surplus profits. If you removed something earlier, you have to reenter it elsewhere. However, watch that you do not make double entries.

A simple rule: If working capital is out, short-term interest is in. And vice versa.

The target, ABC Franchised Restaurant, has no short-term loans, so you do not have to account for interest.

> If you removed something earlier, you have to reenter it elsewhere. However, watch that you do not make double entries.

Interest on Working Capital

Any business needs liquid funds. The amount depends on the time element and the expenses that must be covered between the purchase of inventory and the receipt of payment for goods sold or services rendered. That requirement normally hinges on the amount of inventory carried and the collection period. In many small businesses, three months' operating expenses, including payroll costs, is standard.

The theory behind charging interest on working capital is that the owners could have deposited the same amount of money in the bank, at the prevailing longer-term interest rate, rather than invest in the business. It should be entitled to at least the same rate of interest. Do not confuse this with interest on short-term debt; the two are quite different. Before calculating working capital, cull out any short-term loans and consider them separately.

The balance sheet of most companies clearly sets out the working capital position, which is simply current assets, minus current liabilities. Accountants consider some entries as a current liability, while an appraiser or buyer would not. Thus, before charging the interest on working capital against the net earnings, you need to deduct those items.

Under the GAAP rules, the first year's interest on any long-terms debt is considered as a current liability. For valuation purposes, it should be treated as a long-term liability. Pin the long-term liability label on any indebtedness, such as a lien or conditional sales agreement on other fixed assets, such as machinery and equipment, even if it is payable in the next twelve months.

Keep your antennae up for accrued wages and salaries payable. To whom are they payable? If truly and genuinely owed, include them. If payable to a shareholder, they may be simply an allocation that accountants make to defer income taxes, rather than actual indebtedness. Carefully examine the origin of the debt, which could be as important as the debt itself.

Depending on circumstances, you can calculate interest on the working capital as recorded in the most recent fiscal period, an average of the past three or so years, or a pro forma average. I recommend that you use the one-year bank interest rate, or a trust company rate for certificates of deposit. This too could vary under differing conditions.

I removed the following current liabilities from the balance sheet:

- accrued wages, owed to the principal shareholder,
- the current portion of the mortgage payable,
- the current portion of the equipment lien,
- the interfamily loan, which bears no interest.

Under the GAAP rules, the first year's interest on any long-terms debt is considered as a current liability. For valuation purposes, it should be treated as a long-term liability.

Statement of working capital as taken from the balance sheets:

	Last Fiscal Year	2nd Last Year	3rd Last Year
Current Assets			
Cash	$ 7,456	$ 12,678	$ 3,814
Accounts receivable	10,990	5,247	–
Inventory	20,000	22,500	15,000
Prepaid expenses	3,687	2,897	1,765
Total	$ 42,133	$ 43,322	$ 20,579
Current Liabilities			
Accounts payable	$ 29,529	$ 31,043	$ 21,209
Income taxes payable	34,555	15,124	–
Total	$ 64,084	$ 46,167	$ 21,209
Working capital	$ (21,951)	$ (2,845)	$ (630)
3-year Average Working Capital			$ (8,475)

When you calculate the average working capital for the three-year period, it is not important if the position is negative or positive. Assume everything to be positive, even if one or two years are negative, or positive, and the other or others the opposite. No matter whether the proprietor or the bank owns the money, it must be paid for. For this purpose, negative and positive working capital are treated the same. If the average is negative, use the actual rate of interest being charged on short-term debt; if it is positive or there is no short-term debt, use the current one-year rate for a certificate of deposit.

One-year Certificate of Deposit Rate:		6.50%
Charge against net earnings		
3-year average working capital of $(8,475) × 6.50% =	$	551

We are concerned with actual depreciation, not allowable formula depreciation.

For this calculation, I used a three-year average. But if you include working capital, use only the current year at the appropriate interest rate as detailed above.

Reserve for Depreciation (Recapture) on Machinery and Equipment

The principal considerations are:

- depreciation as allowed by the government tax department, which is, in effect, a formula depreciation,
- the depreciation that actually occurs.

In my earlier treatise on valuing machinery and equipment, I recited the theories and concepts of depreciation. I hope that I made my point: few, if any, of these allowances ever simulate what actually occurs.

We are concerned with actual depreciation, not allowable formula depreciation. In most small businesses, particularly retail and service types, fixtures and equipment normally lasts fifteen to twenty years, manufacturing or processing machinery ten to fifteen. There is no set lifetime for construction and mobile equipment, or for machinery that is exposed to extreme weather or abusive conditions. There are too many variables.

Examine the equipment and apply a global straight-line depreciation rate based on the estimated total or average remaining economic life. Consider its condition, function, obsolescence, and any inherent value that is not immediately obvious.

In the case of ABC Franchised Restaurant, I used 6.67% per annum earlier to arrive at the in-place going concern value of $98,000. As the equipment is now older and the expected remaining useful life somewhat shorter, I will increased the annual depreciation rate to ten percent, straight-line.

Depreciation on fixtures and equipment:
10.0% × $ 98,000 = $ 9,800

Labor Rates, If Not Equitable

Inequitable labor rates are very common in smaller, family-owned businesses. Although Pa is often considered the manager, Ma and the kids are usually classed as labor. Sometimes they are paid far more than they could earn elsewhere, but usually the reverse is true. The family gets the "pleasure" of working in the business, often for nothing or for very little. Alternatively, some shops' labor costs could be above acceptable standards, but management must pay them. Sometimes below-poverty line wages are paid, creating excessively high staff turnover.

In analysing the business, compare the wages with industry standards. If they are abnormal, adjust them to comply with those standards. Be discreet. Because of a unique situation, the labor costs might merely appear to be out of line.

You usually adjust wages when developing the pro forma income-and-expense operating statement, not now. Still, some analysts prefer to bring labor costs into line with industry standards at this point. The choice is yours.

For the model, ABC Franchised Restaurant, all labor and management costs were adjusted in the pro forma operating statement.

- Staff wages and benefits adjustments: nil

Management Salaries and Benefits

I discussed these entitlements at length in the financial analysis section. I suggested that the income and expense statement be adjusted to reflect industry averages, or what management could earn elsewhere. This considers each individual's education, required skills, hours worked, and responsibility.

In most cases, you make adjustments when you draw up a pro forma statement. The pro forma reflects a more typical operational status. If you have not done this, and the management salary and perks schedule is out of line, adjust it now.

The owner drew an annual salary of $45,000 for each of the past three years. Perhaps this is a bit high for the first year, as this was essentially a start-up operation, but it is in line with industry averages for years two and three. What would this person be paid if working for someone else? What would it cost to employ a manager with equal skill and experience? If it is out of line, it is not that far, so we will not adjust this entry.

- Management wage and benefits adjustment: nil

Other Deductions

Under different or unique circumstances, you may well make other deductions. I presented the above schedule only to illustrate those that are more commonly found in small businesses.

Here you do not deal with redundant assets, long-term, or deferred liabilities, including contingent liabilities. This is also true of any encumbrance against the tangible, which for this purpose, at this time, is considered as being without liability.

You usually adjust wages when developing the pro forma income-and-expense operating statement, not now. Still, some analysts prefer to bring labor costs into line with industry standards at this point. The choice is yours.

Caution: I used depreciation rates, income-tax rates, and other federal, state, provincial, municipal, or other government allowable deductions, depletions, rules, or regulations for illustration only. Always use those currently prevailing in your own jurisdiction. By the time you have finished reading this text, everything that was given to you as gospel, has probably changed.

Summary of Deductions Against Net Earnings

Pro Forma Net Operating Profit Before Occupancy Cost, Debt Service, or Depreciation	$ 130,000	
Deductions From Net Operating Profit		
Occupancy costs (simulated rent)	$ 73,920	The selection of
Amortizations & sinking funds	nil	a proper discount rate
Interest on working capital	551	is the crux
Long-term debt interest adjustment	nil	of the whole matter.
Depreciation on fixtures & equipment	9,800	Although it is essential
Staff wages & benefits adjustment	nil	to determining
Management salary adjustment	nil	goodwill value,
		it is the area
Total deductions	$ (84,271)	most subject
Excess (or surplus) profit for discounting	$ 45,729	to guesswork.

Although not applicable to the model restaurant, in some instances, the deductions exceed the net operating profit. This frequently happens when a company has a low profit ratio coupled with a large amount of rapidly depreciating equipment. We are back to truckers, road-building contractors, and small aviation companies. This may indicate negative goodwill, which cannot be established by this procedure. In this event, the company's liquidation, or breakup, value may exceed its going concern value.

THE DISCOUNT RATE

The selection of a proper discount rate is the crux of the whole matter. Although it is essential to determining goodwill value, it is the area most subject to guesswork. In the appraisal of small businesses, since there are no hard and fast rules, it is more common to guesstimate a discount rate, rather than deduce it scientifically. At this point, all that remains is pure risk, absolute and simple. Everything tangible has been accounted for, all of the capital, liquid, and redundant assets. Even the liabilities were considered, either with the capitalized asset values or with the working capital. At this point we have finished with the tangible assets, and so we move on to the intangible, particularly the management.

This discount rate, which converts the time factor to a percentage, is only return on capital, not return of. All we worry about now is surplus-to-the-operation, after-tax profits. Yet the theory of valuing goodwill anticipates that the return on capital will continue after all capital has been returned. Many theorists and appraisers, probably for this reason, prefer to use a multiplier rather than a discount rate. Perhaps it is confusing to say "a capitalization process using a discount rate." It is easier to explain a multiplier that is X times the surplus profit. And it provides exactly the same answer. You will encounter both.

How to Calculate the Discount Rate

The first method is preferable but the second more common:

- market inferences, rate abstraction from comparable sales,
- plain, old-fashioned common sense.

Market References

In Chapter Twelve, I detailed the procedure to abstract a market discount rate. Except for the following analysis of the selling prices of comparative fast-food restaurants, I will not repeat it. I am introducing this chart a second time only to show you the steps required to obtain the goodwill discount rate. This is a demanding exercise. Unless you are an expert appraiser of restaurants, and few are, it is virtually impossible to obtain enough comparable sales, each with a detailed financial breakdown. Additionally, you have to make several initial assumptions, some of which could be wrong. To obtain the discount rate, you must break out from the selling price both the goodwill value and the pro rata share of the net profit that it earns. To do this, you might almost have to appraise each of the market comparisons in detail. For this reason, many of us just use our noggins and our instinct — plain, old-fashioned common sense, which is also an accounting formula technique.

ANALYSIS OF THE SELLING PRICES OF COMPARATIVE FAST-FOOD RESTAURANTS (all numbers are rounded)

Comparable Restaurant No.	1	2	3
Component Values			
Selling Price	$ 385,000	$ 430,000	$ 850,000
Real Estate	210,000	285,000	495,000
Equipment	85,000	80,000	255,000
Total Real Estate & Equipment	(295,000)	(365,000)	(750,000)
Abstracted Goodwill Value	$ 90,000	$ 65,000	$ 100,000
Income and Profitability			
Average Annual Sales	$ 560,000	$ 391,000	$ 890,000
Total Expenses	(482,000)	(325,000)	(720,000)
Net Operating Profit	$ 78,000	$ 66,000	$ 170,000
From the net operating profit, deduct the amount earned by the:			
Real Estate @ 12.5%	$ 26,000	$ 35,500	$ 62,000
Equipment @ 19.5%	$ 17,000	$ 15,500	$ 50,000
Total Deductions	$ (43,000)	$ (51,000)	$ (112,000)
Remainder is to Goodwill	$ 35,000	$ 15,000	$ 58,000
Discount Rate for Goodwill	38.9%	23.1%	58.0%

Finally, you have to reconcile the discount rates so that you can apply a single rate to the surplus earnings of your target business. You are still seeking what an average buyer would pay and an average seller accept. Once again, you must revert to the median in this selection. In the real world, you will need more than three comparable sales. Here, for the purpose of demonstration only, I have taken some shortcuts. You, on the other hand, must use at least five.

The discount rate is:

$$\frac{\text{Remainder of Net Profit after Capital Earnings Deductions}}{\text{Established Value of the Goodwill by Abstraction}} \times 100$$

- The $\times 100$ converts the produced decimal factor to a percentage,
- The resultant is a discount rate, not a capitalization rate.

The median discount rate from the three comparable sales: 38.9%

Goodwill value:
Excess profit of $ 45,729 discounted at 38.90% = $ 117,555
                       Rounded to $ 118,000

(You could use a multiplier of 2.571 and get the same answer.)

The Rule of Common Sense

People who invest in small businesses expect a return on their risk capital in varying time frames and amounts that relate to the type of business, their personal involvement, and the financial risk. Each industry or class of business has its own criteria. So much depends on the stability of the industry, and how it weathers the normal business cycle, as well as wilder economic swings that could directly affect long-term profitability. It can take as long as five years to get that return in a well-established business or as short as six months in a high-risk, one-person, or service enterprise. The discount rate is that time converted to a percentage factor, or expressed as a multiplier.

Retail businesses are normally in the two-and-a-half-year to four-year return-on-investment category. This suggests a discount rate from a low of twenty-five percent to a high of forty percent. It corresponds quite well with the Schilt formulas, which provide a reasonably good guide to the discount rates applicable to goodwill.

If you had enough comparative sales — and three is not enough for this exercise — you would find that the median for fast-food restaurants would be in the area of 33.33% to forty percent, or two-and-a-half to three times surplus earnings. Non-franchised, sit-down restaurants and those that depend largely on alcohol sales, if they are among the few that develop any goodwill at all, would be in the area of forty to one hundred percent.

For the model, ABC Franchised Restaurant, I have implied a return in three years, discount rate of 33.33%, or a multiplier of three. This considers the type of business, its location, the exclusive franchise, age of the assets, management required, hours required, ease of entry into this type of business, high mortality rate of restaurants, and continuing possibility of competition building on the other corner.

> People who invest in small businesses expect a return on their risk capital in varying time frames and amounts that relate to the type of business, their personal involvement, and the financial risk.

Goodwill value:
Excess profits of $ 45,729 discounted at 33.33% = $ 137,201
                      Rounded to: $ 137,000

Which to use? The same as in all other cases. Go with your most comfortable option, the one with the most reliable information, in this instance 33.33%, as obtained from our best guess.

Value of the Goodwill

ABC Franchised Fast Food Restaurant	$ 137,000

Summary of Values Found A.B.C. Franchised Fast Food Restaurant

Real Estate	
Value of the Real Estate	$ 530,000
Business Value	
Value of the Fixtures and Equipment	$ 98,000
Goodwill value	$ 137,000
Business Total	$ 235,000
The Redundant Asset: Motor Home	$ 60,000
Total Going Concern Value Estimate	$ 825,000

Most of the time, this is as far as you go. The going concern value estimate represents the value of the business on an asset sale.

Still, for a true going concern value estimate, you will sometimes account for these other inclusions and exclusions, although they are normally not part of any sale. This is the added value of the working capital and any other intangible asset not so far included, less all liabilities, including contingent, owed by the company. The final value estimate is not really final without these inclusions.

For the model restaurant, this is only the working capital. There are no other intangible assets and no contingent liabilities. Once again, we violate the GAAP rules by not including the first-years interest on the long-term liabilities. Since you will not assume the interfamily loan and the accrued wages were due to the principal shareholder, they were not included.

The working capital for the last fiscal year was a negative $21,951, which should be deducted from the going concern value.

Going concern value estimate	$ 825,000
Final value estimate ($825,000 less $21,951)	$ 803,049
Rounded to:	
	$ 803,000

Note to appraisers: Be certain to include in your report, at this point, that the working capital amount was calculated as at the date to which value found applies. By the time the report is received, in an active business, it will have changed. The client should know this so that the final value estimate can be adjusted accordingly.

THE SPLIT-RATE APPROACH

Accountants correctly call this the value-added method. The going concern value of any business is the liquidation value, on an orderly basis, of the capital or hard assets,

> The going concern value of any business is the liquidation value, on an orderly basis, of the capital or hard assets, plus the added value of the intangible assets, particularly the goodwill.

This procedure is little more than an abbreviated sum-of-the-assets approach. It could be the best method for someone who is not skilled in interpreting financial statements or is denied vital information required for the longer procedure.

Several times, I mentioned the concept of dual ownership, where Party A owns the real estate and Party B all else, including the fixtures and equipment, and, if applicable, tenant's improvements. On paper, B rents the real estate from A. To properly apply the mechanics of this process, we must once again determine one value for the real estate and one for the business, using a different capitalization rate for each. Thus the term "split rate." If the real estate is leased, not owned, you need only appraise the business portion, which would include any tenant's improvements.

You determine the value of the real estate by the previously described methods. You value the business by a residual process, capitalizing the residual net profit after deducting property costs. This is essentially the same procedure that was used in the sum-of-the-assets approach, except that you do not break down the business components. So you do not deduct interest on working capital, amortization of tenant's improvements, depreciation on fixtures and equipment, sinking funds, inequitable wages or management salaries, or anything else. You assume that any radical departures from industry norms, redundant assets, contingent liabilities, and nonrecurring income or expense items would have been removed or nullified in the pro forma statement.

Professional appraisers frequently break out and capitalize, separate from the other components of the business, machinery and equipment, as well as substantial tenant's improvements. They rightly argue that because of these assets' depreciating nature, they should be capitalized at a higher rate than the more liquid assets. Although this complicates the procedure a bit, if the equipment holds high value or rapidly depreciates, or if improvements are a major capital item, particularly coupled with a short-term lease, each should be treated separately.

The going concern value sums up the values of the real estate and the business. Or it could include three values if machinery and/or tenant's improvements are considered separately. In the sum-of-the-assets approach, we used four rates:

- for the real estate, a capitalization rate of 12.41%,
- or the fixtures and equipment, a depreciation-only rate of 6.67% when calculating value, but ten percent when calculating goodwill. As the in-place value was determined by a depreciated replacement cost method, no capitalization rate was used, but had there been one, it would have been 15.17% or 18.5%, respectively (interest of 8.5%, plus 6.67% or 10% depreciation).
- for the working capital, an interest factor of 6.5%,
- for the goodwill, a discount rate of 33.33%.

In the split-rate approach, you can follow the same procedure, except that now only two rates are required, not four, or else you can obtain the capitalization rates from the market.

THE MARKET-DERIVED CAPITALIZATION RATE

Step 1

Establish the total selling price of the comparable sale. From that total price, deduct the component value of the real estate. The remainder is the value of the business. Let us use the same three sales earlier detailed and the same real estate value.

ANALYSIS OF THE SELLING PRICES
OF COMPARATIVE FAST FOOD RESTAURANTS

Comparable Restaurant No.	1	2	3
Breakdown of Selling Price			
Real Estate	210,000	285,000	495,000
The Business	175,000	145,000	355,000
Total	$ 385,000	$ 430,000	$ 850,000

Step 2

Establish the net operating profit and deduct the amount earned by the real estate. The remainder applies to the business component.

Net Operating Profit	$ 78,000	$ 66,000	$ 170,000

From the net operating profit, deduct the amount earned by the:

Real Estate @ 12.5%	$ 26,000	$ 35,500	$ 62,000
Remainder to Business	$ 52,000	$ 31,500	$ 108,000

Step 3

To establish the capitalization rate earned by the business, divide the remainder of the net operating profit by the value of the business segment.

For Comparable	No. 1	No. 2	No. 3
	$ 52,000	$ 31,500	$ 108,000
	$ 175,000	$ 145,000	$ 355,000
Capitalization Rate	0.2971 or	0.2172 or	0.3042
for the Business	29.71%	21.72%	30.42%

In applying the formula to the model, for the reasons already explained, we will use the median rate of 29.71%.

ABC Franchised Restaurant

Value of the real estate (as before)	$	530,000
Value of the Business		
After-tax net operating profit	$	130,000
Real-estate rental (same as before) consumes of income	$	73,920
Residual to the business	$	56,080
Capitalization rate: 29.71%		
Value of the Business		
$ 56,080 capitalized at 29.71% =	$	188,758
Breakdown of the value of the business		
Already known		
Fixtures & equipment	$	(98,000)
The negative working capital	$	21,951
	$	(76,049)

If the working capital were positive, to establish the intangible assets value, it too would have been deducted from the value of the business.

Goodwill is the remainder	$	112,709
Rounded to	$	113,000

Summary

Value of the Real Estate	$	530,000
Value of the Business (rounded)		189,000
Total Value Found	$	719,000
Add: the redundant asset, the mobile home	$	60,000
Final Value Estimate: by the Split-rate Approach	$	779,000

COMPARISON OF THE VALUES FOUND

Sum-of-the-assets Approach

Real Estate	$ 530,000
Fixtures and Equipment	98,000
Goodwill	137,000
The Mobile Home	60,000
Working Capital (Rounded)	(22,000)
Total Value Found	$ 803,000

The Split-rate Approach

Real Estate	$ 530,000
The Business, which includes	
Fixtures and Equipment	
Goodwill	
Working Capital	$ 189,000
The Mobile Home	60,000
Total Value Found	$ 779,000

The two values correlate reasonably well. The difference of $24,000, or three percent. This is not unusual. Actually, it is much closer than normal. In an actual assignment, you would not use both procedures, thus you would reconcile only between an assets-first and a cash-flow approach, if that.

OTHER PROCEDURES

All non-real-estate tangible assets, including fixtures and equipment, tenant's improvements, working capital, and inventories, are the assets of the business. The value of the tangible assets is the sum of both the hard and the liquid assets. You can obtain this value by either, or a combination, of the following:

- accept book values as correct,
- adjust book values to reflect current or actual values.

You know that book values reflect only cost, or cost less depreciation, not value. You may require them in some circumstances, such as a buyout of another shareholder, or a client wanting to reflect the minimum tangible but the maximum intangible asset, or permission to inspect the premises is denied.

As far as adjusting book values to reflect current or actual values, that is what appraisals are all about. You may use for this purpose the values found by any one of the three standard approaches, depending on the circumstances and the purpose of the appraisal.

As far as adjusting
book values
to reflect current
or actual values,
that is what appraisals
are all about.

Chapter 14

THE CASH-FLOW APPROACHES TO VALUE

"When reading forecasts tied to present rates of this or that, it is well to keep in mind that extending them too far into the future — no matter that they have been valid for several years past — is to presume a continuity of circumstances that never holds for any great length of time ... How about the not-so-long-ago projections for the continuing growth of utilities? Or natural gas, or gasoline and oil consumption? Forecasts that run way out are invariably way off."

Malcolm Forbes

EARLIER, I introduced the concept of the assets (front-door) and the cash-flow (back-door) procedures to estimate market value on a going concern basis. If the data is the same in both cases and correct procedures are followed, they should produce about the same estimate of market value. Some differences, however, are created by disproportionate asset ratios. For example, if the highest percent of the value is capital assets, the resultant produced by a cash-flow approach could be much lower than one produced by an assets approach. Conversely, if a business is composed mostly of intangible assets, the value will be higher with the cash-flow approach. Still, the method does not change the value. What is, is. Bear in mind the difference between value and price. Your task is to interpret the market forces and then choose the best method to estimate value.

The assets approaches can be best described as producing an orderly liquidation value, to which you add the value of goodwill and other intangible assets. You need the continuance of net earnings primarily to justify those assets at a normally acceptable return on the investment. In the cash-flow approaches, you use the opposite tactic. You base going concern value totally on cash flows, more particularly the net profit. There is no automatic breakdown between the value of the tangible and intangible. Thus, for some businesses, an assets-first approach is the only sensible procedure. For others, such as service companies, professional practices, frequently traded businesses, or if the total value of the capital assets is insignificant, it is better to use the cash-flow procedures.

Real-estate appraisers use the cash-flow approaches to estimate market value all the time; they just call it the income approach. In business valuation, we prefer to call them cash-flow approaches, which are simply valuing procedures that capitalize the net after-tax profit. You use one overall capitalization rate, producing a single value estimate, rather than a summation of the individual value contributors, as in the assets-first method. In practice, the cash-flow approach is the same method real-estate appraisers have been employing for years to value income-producing property.

Like all approaches to value, there are limitations. By the very nature of putting everything into one large pot, the cash-flow approaches do not weigh the individual value of the various assets, nor differentiate between the tangible and intangible. For example, Company A has $500,000 in capital assets and Company B only $200,000. If the earnings are the same, as they could well be, using the same capitalization or discount rate, both would have the same going concern value. This does not make sense. Further, the procedure assumes capitalization into perpetuity. But nothing lasts forever. Although some procedures can include a reversionary value, which is the probable future selling price of the business, any such prediction is pure guesswork. Finally, it assumes that the owner can get his hands on all of the net after-

Real-estate appraisers use the cash-flow approaches to estimate market value all the time; they just call it the income approach.

tax profits, which is seldom feasible. As the cash-flow approaches pretend to overcome these deficiencies, you must ensure, before commencement, that this is the best method in this case.

As in the previous valuation approach, you exclude any redundant asset that does not directly contribute to the earnings of the company, only adding it to the final value estimate. You appraise the business as a composite entity, or a unit in place. If you used working capital (which was added on in the sum-of-the-assets approach, but included in the split-rate approach) to develop the capitalization rate, you now include it automatically. If you did not use it for capitalization rate development, you add it later.

Again: When developing a market capitalization rate, where the indicators include working capital in the sale price, then working capital is part of the capitalization rate and part of the total value estimate. Alternatively, if the indicators do not include working capital, and this is usually the case, then add it to the final going concern value estimate, or subtract it if negative.

The cash-flow approaches are:

- the stabilized cash-flow approach,
- the discounted-net-profits approach,
- the net earnings approach (also called the debt residual approach).

THE STABILIZED CASH-FLOW APPROACH

Of all business appraisal practices and procedures, this one is the simplest in theory, the easiest to perform, and, if the input factors are correct, reliable. It best interprets the marketplace. Some theorists say goodwill does not exist, depreciation is a legal fiction, and no one can break down or sum up the contributory value of each asset. One of the strengths of the stabilized cash-flow approach is that it does not try to carve up the business pie, with the largest slice going to the segment that consumes the most capital.

This approach's name implies relatively uniform income and profits, continuing at about the same level as history has demonstrated. With the possible exception of inflation, or disinflation, which will affect income and expenses alike, it does not contemplate any major change in income or profitability for the foreseeable future. Although in theory the value estimate is predicated on the net present value of future profits, in this approach, it is based on past earnings, average or pro forma, at the stabilized level. These earnings, presuming that history repeats itself, are supposedly what the business will earn in the coming years, except for debt reduction and inflation.

> Some theorists say goodwill does not exist, depreciation is a legal fiction, and no one can break down or sum up the contributory value of each asset.

Limitations

This approach works only for mature businesses. Do not use it if the record of income or profits is inconsistent, or expected to be so, or if the business is brand-new, verging on bankruptcy, or on the uptick or downtick. For any of these circumstances, use the discounted-net-profits approach.

Before using the stabilized-cash-flow approach, carefully review the operating history of the company, watch for inconsistent patterns or developing external or internal trends, adjust those entries that could materially alter the final value estimate.

Valuation Principles

The valuation principles, while the same as those that apply to all earnings approaches, are more acute here. You base market value on:

- the existing level of cash flows and after-tax net profits,
- the probability of that profit continuing at or near the present level,
- the rate of return required to justify the investment when compared to alternative investments.

Using this procedure, the value equals the present worth of future net profits, based on history. The discounted-net-profits approach is based on future potential.

The Procedure

1. Establish the stabilized, net, after-tax profits for capitalizing,

2. Establish the capitalization rate,

3. Going Concern Value $= \dfrac{\text{Net Operating Profit}}{\text{Capitalization Rate}}$

Pro forma Net Profit for Capitalization

Using the same pro forma developed earlier (this has not been changed throughout).

Sales and Income	$	1,448,000
Less: Cost of Sales		651,500
Gross Trading Profit	$	796,500
Total Operating Expenses	$	652,000
Pre-tax profit	$	144,500
Provision for Income Tax		(14,500)
Net Profit before Depreciation or Debt Service	$	130,000

The Capitalization Rate

As I have said, it is best to use accounting formula capitalization rates, or built-up combinations of risk and return, if you do not have enough reliable market data or if you need to value components separately. In the cash-flow approaches, use market-derived rates, which more accurately represent the actions of buyers and sellers.

Using this procedure, the value equals the present worth of future net profits, based on history. The discounted-net-profits approach is based on future potential.

Market-abstracted Capitalization Rates

These are the same rates, developed from the same indicators, that I detailed in Chapter Nine.

	Net Operating Profit	Selling Price	Capitalization Rate
Indicator No. 1	$ 78,000	$ 385,000	20.26%
Indicator No. 2	$ 66,000	$ 430,000	15.35%
Indicator No. 3	$ 142,000	$ 650,000	21.85%
Indicator No. 4	$ 170,000	$ 850,000	20.00%
Indicator No. 5	$ 109,000	$ 575,000	19.96%

I did not include working capital when developing any of the above rates.

In Chapter Nine, I talked about quality comparisons. Most times, because real estate is frequently inconsistent, a median rate exemplifies the average price paid and accepted for a given property. With real estate, you can usually find several comparable sales. With small or infrequently traded businesses, it is nearly impossible to obtain enough reliable data to accurately judge value. Consider the above five indicators as applied to the target restaurant.

Pro forma Income of $ 130,000 × (all value estimates rounded)

Highest Capitalization Rate of 21.85% = Value of $ 595,000
Median Capitalization Rate of 20.00% = Value of $ 650,000
Lowest Capitalization Rate of   15.85% = Value of $ 820,000

> You cannot say that, based on one particular sale, which could have a world of differences, your target business is worth so many dollars.

The five sales differ in value by $225,000 between the lowest and highest. Such a jump would be impossible to reconcile. Therefore, you need to apply a quality rating to each of the indicators. You cannot say that, based on one particular sale, which could have a world of differences, your target business is worth so many dollars. To the capitalization rate, you must apply a discount if the individual indicator is superior to the subject, or a bonus if inferior. Higher rates equate to lower values, and vice versa.

Take into account:

- community, area, or neighborhood differences,
- locational differences,
- market size and potential, short-term and long-term,
- competitive factors, present and anticipated,
- franchise and/or market identification, trading advantage or disadvantage,
- differences in the building, such as construction, age, size, appointments, and condition,
- site size, shape, topography, improvements, condition, site visibility, ease of entry and exit,
- ratio of land to building value,
- fixtures and equipment, quantity, quality, relative value,
- the overall quality comparison rating.

You can add to or subtract from the above list, referring to Chapter Three for additional points on market comparability. Just do not make the exercise too horrendous. The purpose, by adjusting the individual capitalization rates, is to make the comparables more comparable. But be careful. As the whole exercise is very subjective, make very small adjustments. You want to interpret the actions of buyers and sellers, not justify some preconceived idea or outcome.

You should compare the quality of each value indicator. Then use the median, as developed from the adjusted indicators, to capitalize the net operating profit of the subject business. In this instance, and again I am taking a shortcut, let us say that the subject is superior to the median rate of all of the comparable restaurants by 1.50%.

Market-derived Capitalization Rate (the median)	20.00%
Superiority rating as above detailed	(1.50%)
Capitalization rate to be used	18.50%

To repeat: If the subject is superior, discount it; if the subject is inferior, increase the rate by the inferiority percentage. (It sounds backwards but that is the way it works.)

And again, since I am in the mood to repeat ideas:

Is it reasonable? Is it logical? Does it make sense?
If not, restart from where you got off-track

The Model Restaurant

Going Concern Value $\dfrac{\text{Net Operating Profit} \quad \$\ 130,000}{\text{Capitalization Rate} \quad 0.1850\%}$ = $ 702,702

Rounded to: $ 703,000

> If the subject is superior, discount it; if the subject is inferior, increase the rate by the inferiority percentage.
>
> (It sounds backwards but that is the way it works.)

Add the redundant asset, the motor home	$ 60,000
Deduct the negative working capital (rounded)	$ (22,000)
Total value estimate, going concern value	$ 745,000

Once again, if working capital is not part of the requirement, do not add it on as demonstrated above; if it is included, because of the capitalization rate makeup, then deduct it.

Value Comparison with Sum of the Assets Approach

Value found by sum-of-the-assets approach: $ 803,000

The value found by the cash-flow approach is $58,000 lower than that found by the sum-of-the-assets. This is not abnormal. If we had used the median capitalization rate without adjustment, the value would have been still lower ($688,000). The inconsistency is created largely by the differing methods in appraising the input factors. With one approach, each factor is capitalized individually; in the other, they are all lumped together. Because of these differing results, most theorists suggest a value range, rather than a specific number. And if most of the value lies in capital assets, then you should use an asset valuation method, which will result in a higher, and more defendable, value estimate than that obtained by a cash-flow approach.

THE DISCOUNTED-NET-PROFITS APPROACH

This approach bases going concern value on what the annual income and profit amounts will be, from now to some predetermined date in the future. These predicted cash flows can increase or decrease. All are capitalized into an estimate of market value at a rate that reflects the risk of the investment.

The stabilized-cash-flow approach, which depends totally on continued, relatively level income and expenses, is ideal for businesses that are stable or have peaked out. The key is stability of income and the probability that history will repeat itself. Conversely, the discounted-net-profits approach presumes to know what will happen in the future. I have often mentioned that analysts cannot accurately forecast the future with their hazy crystal ball. With the discounted-net-profits approach, as if by divine intervention, all becomes suddenly clear and definable.

Limitations

Because of its shortcomings, particularly the inability to accurately forecast the future, most analysts seldom use the discounted-net-profits approach to value small businesses. Lenders generally dislike valuing methods that depend on predictions. Some courts refuse to recognize them if the forecast is material to the case. Most judges prefer time-tested methods, particularly those predicated upon accounting procedures that assume history will repeat itself and the status quo will remain. All forecasts are only as good as the data available, the analyst's ability and experience, and the clarity of the crystal ball.

I am not suggesting that this procedure has no place in the valuation of small businesses, or that it should be avoided. On the contrary, it has considerable merit and is sometimes the only logical approach to value. In some instances, it is as plain as day that the present level of income and profits cannot or will not continue indefinitely. Newer businesses without a track record have nothing but future potential. A business might have recently expanded its size and capacity, launched a new product or process, or experienced something — or expects something to happen — that will improve its fortunes. Alternatively, a new competitor may have just opened across the street, the highway was relocated, the manufactured product is no longer in demand, the business must be downsized, and so forth. A stabilized income and profit level will not exist under these circumstances, and so it would be ludicrous to try to develop a pro forma that assumes stability.

> Lenders generally dislike valuing methods that depend on predictions. Some courts refuse to recognize them if the forecast is material to the case.

Both the stabilized and projected cash-flow methods have their place. Still, only the discounting of projected net profits can consider varying future incomes, positive or negative trends, favorable or adverse events. Use the approach that is best, not the one that is easiest. Just because a procedure does not apply to one situation, does not mean that it will not apply to another. You have to use some kind of model to determine value, the only question is which one?

Length of Forecasts

How far into the future should you predict? In most situations, the shorter the better. As Malcolm Forbes said, "Forecasts that run way out are invariably way off." All predictions are unreliable.

For example, let us consider a plumbing and heating contractor's business. Income and profitability have been relatively consistent, but now this company has secured a large contract that should substantially increase its profits over the next few years. Afterward, unless more contracts come along or the contractor changes her practices, the business will probably shrink to its original size. All else being equal, you should value this company by discounting the potential for future profits. You must consider the present level of profits, the increase created by the timespan of the contract, followed by the probable return to normalcy. This is not too complicated. However, the contractor might choose not to shrink back to the former size. She could bid on and snag another large contract or two or three. As a subcontractor, though, she is at the mercy of the general contractor, who could go broke and leave her holding the bag. Her estimator may have read the prints wrong, or a labor strike could affect her, and a promising scenario could morph into a big loss. On and on it goes.

All you can do is predict what is probable within the given time frame, and apply the risk rate you think is best. In these situations, the appraiser must make certain assumptions, knowing that some will probably be wrong. Thus, final value estimates often vary widely.

Because time-constrained predictions are dangerous, you can see why the courts do not like the discounted-net-profits approach or any value based on forecasts, and why most buyers, particularly the unsophisticated, place little confidence in this method. Still, at times you will have to predict and project. Just ensure that you base your forecasts on substance, not wishful thinking.

Range of Values

Sometimes it makes sense to provide a value range, instead of a single value estimate. Without differentiating between valuing and pricing, and ignoring subjective considerations, there is seldom one number that meets every willing-buyer-to-willing-seller test. To establish a value range, I usually prefer, and rely on, the discounted-net-profits approach. No business is truly stable. They all change constantly.

At times, you are wise to forecast income and profits at three levels: pessimistic, probable, and optimistic. You might even add a fourth: speculative. Thus you build more variables and probabilities into this sensitivity analysis. You can consider varying levels of income and profitability, differing interest rates, reinvestment into further inventory, equipment, or whatever. Although you could insert the same variations into the stabilized-cash-flow approach, the results are not as conclusive.

To make a sensitivity analysis, you usually start by determining most probable market value. From this, you decrease profit by a certain amount, say ten percent, to produce a pessimistic level. You increase profit by the same percentage to achieve the optimistic level, and increase it further if you want a speculative value. Although the results may look interesting on paper, take extra care to make them meaningful. You can determine an almost unlimited range of values by moving around the variable inputs.

Goodwill

Traditional methods for valuing goodwill are generally weak, as we discovered when calculating it with the assets and stabilized-cash-flow approaches. It is seldom possible to isolate goodwill and value it as an identifiable commodity. Assuming constancy, or at least a measurable change in tangible-assets investment over the forecast period, the discounting of future net profits is perhaps the best way to measure goodwill, particularly negative goodwill. It can measure value, with some accuracy, if a company has invested in a research project, expanded operations, acquired a competitor, or developed something that is been a loser so far, but should now become profitable. It also applies to the net earnings approach, which considers all levels of debt service and tax-allowable depreciation, something the stabilized-cash-flow and assets methods do not do.

Capitalization Rate Adjustments

The stabilized-cash-flow approach rarely quantifies varying investment or reinvestment levels in the depreciating assets required to generate cash flows. Yet, in theory, you need to adjust the capitalization rate accordingly. In practice, the

> Without differentiating between valuing and pricing, and ignoring subjective considerations, there is seldom one number that meets every willing-buyer-to-willing-seller test.

procedure automatically assumes that you treat all investments equally. Let us say you select an overall capitalization rate, based on the interaction of market forces and the risk of the venture. There is an overpowering tendency to use this same rate whether the assets are worth $250,000 or $2,500,000. Assuming a constancy of profit percentages, it does not appear to matter if the plant is good, fair, or mediocre. All scenarios are treated equally. Yet they are not equal. On a pure percentage basis, not whole dollars, the future for the two could be totally different. So the current rates should differ, and will vary from year to year as the plant wears out, redundancy sets in, and the risk of the venture changes.

You can adjust a market-abstracted capitalization rate to reflect reality by the same procedure as detailed with the stabilized-cash-flow approach.

The Two Methods

There are two ways to conduct the discounted-net-profits approach:

- the net present value of the variable cash flows,
- the internal rate of return.

Both follow the same general procedure and are based on the present value of anticipated or projected future profits that the business will earn over its remaining life or during the income forecast period.

The net-present-value method forecasts varying income and profit levels for a certain number of years, after which they become consistent as the stabilized profit level is reached. The going concern value of the business sums up the discounted values of all anticipated net profits. These variable cash flows are reduced to a net present value on an annualized basis. To this value, you add the net present value of the stabilized income which, if there is no reversionary value at the end of the forecast period, is usually extended into perpetuity.

The internal rate of return goes further, and it determines return on the investment, either total or equity yield only, rather than market value. In addition to all of the above, it commences with the initial investment, discounts the income stream, then projects the selling price of the business as a going concern at the end of the forecast period. You add this reversionary value to the net present value of the annual profits. Although useful in real estate appraisal, this method is never used to appraise going concerns because no one can accurately predict the value of a business so many years hence. It is still valuable, though, for pricing. You can use it to study feasibility, compare investment alternatives, consider synergy, and weigh potential returns against hurdle rates.

How to Calculate Net Present Value

You need:

- reliable income and profit projections for the forecast period,
- a capitalization rate that accurately measures the risk and is supportable in the marketplace.

The net-present-value method forecasts varying income and profit levels for a certain number of years, after which they become consistent as the stabilized profit level is reached.

Let us assume that an industrial repair shop has a projected after-tax net profit of $51,500 in year one, increasing by irregular amounts to $61,000 in year five, then levelling out at the slightly reduced amount of $60,000 per year as maintenance costs increase and inefficiency becomes more noticeable. (This has nothing to do with the model restaurant.)

We will take an arbitrary capitalization rate of fourteen percent and reduce it to a factor, which is the net present value of one dollar for that year only, expressed as a decimal. The stabilized income flow — the future — is the net present value of one dollar per year, starting with year six and continuing into perpetuity.

NET PRESENT VALUE

Year	Projected Profit	Factor Value	Net Present
1	$ 51,500	0.88719	$ 45,175
2	$ 53,000	0.76947	$ 40,782
3	$ 57,000	0.67497	$ 38,473
4	$ 59,000	0.59208	$ 34,933
5	$ 61,000	0.51937	$ 31,681
Thereafter – per annum	$ 60,000	3.70976	$ 222,586
Total Value Found			$ 413,630
rounded to:			$ 414,000

Although I used a constant rate throughout, which is normal, perhaps the risk rate should drop as the business matures, becoming more stable and less subject to changing times and competition.

We could have done all this in two steps, eliminating the factor by using a financial calculator, or in one step with a computer. I took the scenic route to demonstrate some concepts, principally that the further you project from today, the less value is attached to the money. Although perpetuity, which implies that $60,000 will be received every year, is calculated on the basis of one hundred years, less the years taken by the variable cash flows, leaving a projection period of ninety-four years, the present value is little more than 3.7 times the annual profits. See the interplay of the income stream and the discount rate? Although I used a constant rate throughout, which is normal, perhaps the risk rate should drop as the business matures, becoming more stable and less subject to changing times and competition. In the example, year six saw net profits sag from there on in because of aging and increasing costs. So here the risk rate could have increased. You must properly forecast potential income and the cost of doing business. You need an accurate projection of both profit and risk, not one or the other.

You can use the discounted-net-profits approach equally well to obtain a range of value estimates. You could use varying income and profit levels and discount rates to achieve a sensitivity analysis, particularly when considering synergy.

In conclusion, the procedure is only as good as the analyst, the forecast, and the measurement of the risk.

THE NET EARNINGS APPROACH

This procedure, also known as the debt residual approach or the equity capitalization approach, is almost never used in the valuation of small businesses. It is reserved almost exclusively for the larger enterprises, especially those whose shares are traded on the stock market. But because accountants, security analysts, and some business valuers favor it, it is worth mentioning.

You determine the value of a company by capitalizing or discounting the net profit, after tax, debt service, and tax-allowable depreciation — in other words, the bottom line as per the GAAP rules. You can use either of the cash-flow procedures, but I prefer the discounting of forecasted net profits. You always produce a single value estimate. You can abstract the contributory value of the tangible assets directly from the records of the company, or update them to represent actual value.

The Model Restaurant

As abstracted from the notes to the financial statements:

- first mortgage to Commercial-Industrial Bank, payable in monthly installments of $4,930.00 including amortized interest.
- equipment lien to Jim's Restaurant Supply Inc., payable in monthly installments of $850.00.
- as abstracted from the balance sheet: principal amount owing on long-term debt $328,837.
- equity yield rate, as calculated in Chapter 13 – 1 5.00%

The Calculation

Pro Forma Net Operating Income		$ 130,000
Total Annual Debt Service:	$5,780 × 12 =	$ (69,360)
Residual to Equity		$ 60,640
Value of Equity:	$ 60,640 capitalized at 15.00% =	$ 404,267
Add total of long-term debt		$ 328,837
Total Value of the Enterprise		$ 733,104
Add the redundant asset: The Motor Home		$ 60,000
Less the Negative Working Capital (rounded)		$ (22,000)
Final Going Concern Value Estimate		$ 771,104
	rounded to	$ 771,000

In this instance, the final value resultant correlates reasonably well with the estimates found by the assets and cash-flow approaches, but this is just good luck. If we had have undertaken this exercise in the first or second years of operation, the final value estimate would have been radically different. So do not use this approach unless there is absolutely nothing else, and I mean nothing else. Besides, with the model restaurant, as the mortgage contains a personal guarantee, it would not be assigned. Thus, the exercise proves nothing.

In valuing larger concerns, particularly public companies where a buyer of shares acquires only a minority equity interest, nothing changes except part ownership. The tangible and intangible assets stay the same. Neither the capital base nor the debt is altered because of this stock transfer; the management and staff are still employed. Thus, in the larger concerns, particularly when appraising shares, or in other cases where only a minority interest is bought, it makes sense to use the net-earnings approach. Not so for smaller concerns, most of which sell the assets only, and where management changes and the acquisition is financed.

In valuing larger concerns,
particularly
public companies
where a buyer of shares
acquires only
a minority equity interest,
nothing changes
except part ownership.

Chapter 15

VALUING THE FRANCHISE

WHAT'S IT ALL ABOUT?

WHEN selling any business, the owner will always try to convince the buyer, the broker, and maybe an appraiser that this business is worth much more than any comparable or competitive enterprise. Pushing for the maximum dollar is what the game is all about. Most will babble on about the enterprise's many superior attributes and uncaptured potential. Always, this is for several excellent reasons, one of which could be the holding of a valuable franchise. For this reason, plus all of the others, the buyer is expected to pay a premium, and the appraiser attach an increased value. But does a franchise add value? If so, how much? The answer is yes, no, maybe, sometimes, and all with qualifications.

There is nothing new about franchising, which is the sale or distribution of a product, using someone else's name or trading style. Although they mix franchising and dealerships, the oil marketing companies have been doing it for years. Today, franchises range from the world-famous McDonald's, which is always held up as the standard of excellence, through to neighborhood peanut vendors and housekeeping services. It seems every imaginable product or service business is franchised, or will be soon. Who knows, maybe houses of ill repute will become franchised, or maybe they already are! Franchisors number in the hundreds, franchisees in the thousands. As both change daily and different people count them in different ways, I do not know the exact number of either.

In this chapter, I will not even mention the appraisal model. I only want to make you aware of this prevalent form of business and marketing. Franchising is destined to hog a still larger share of the business pie. Most times, you will find the value of a franchised business the same as for an unfranchised one. Still, the buyer should examine in more detail exactly what is contained in the franchise and accompanying marketing agreements. In practice, a franchise is little more than goodwill under a new name. Its intangible value relies solely on profit advantage.

I have pointed out that uniqueness or exclusivity is one of the cornerstones of goodwill. Frequently, being the only kid on the block with this franchise creates additional value, greater than that earned by the capital assets. Usually a franchise is exclusive; it is granted for a protected territory; it is unique; no one else in the immediate area has the same one.

Is the franchise's added value subjective or objective? Does a franchise hold a definite, separate, measurable monetary worth, or is it just nice to belong? Perhaps we are back to Lord Eldon, only considering possibilities. For sure, goodwill is created by many franchises. But with others, it is not. Like all other forms of goodwill, its incremental value is the added market or sale value of the business enterprise that was created by the franchise, and not by any other cause.

Several articles and books have been written on the subject of franchising. For the most part, they address the needs of, and the benefits to, the franchisor. Success is supposedly a cakewalk — as long as it has the right product or system, proper guidelines for franchisees, and a correctly priced and packaged franchise, the world will beat a path to the franchisor's door. Everybody will want a piece of the action. And best of all, the franchisees will become terribly rich by simply doing the same

> Most times,
> you will find the value
> of a franchised business
> the same as for
> an unfranchised one. ...
> In practice, a franchise is
> little more than goodwill
> under a new name.

thing, following the same procedures, and mixing the ingredients from the secret recipe. That is what the franchisors say, anyway. The truth is that although some excellent franchises are available, many are worthless. Some could make you very rich, while others are little more than scams. Some exist for only one purpose: to make money for the franchisor.

Before putting a dollar sign in front of the added business value created by a franchise, let me enlighten you about what a franchise is and is not. I will also discuss some advantages and disadvantages of franchising, but only from the perspective of the franchisee, and only those that affect going concern value. Of course, there are always subjective stimuli when shopping around for a franchise. What appeals to one buyer may turn off another. Because I cannot measure how these strictly individual considerations affect a price tag, I will not dwell on them. I will also take a few liberties. For example, dealerships, exclusive rights to a line, a marketing or referral system, monopolies on a particular product — are not true franchises, but I will throw them into the franchise pot for you. This is a text on business valuation, not solely on franchising, so I am going to push the envelope a bit. I personally use the exact same method to value franchises, distributorships, and dealerships in the business setting, so I am going to talk about them all at once.

First, though, consider two quite opposite points of view, both provided by knowledgable people. You will have to decide which is more accurate. Both come from the same source, *Smart Money* magazine, a publication of the Dow Jones Corporation.

> ...although some excellent franchises are available, many are worthless. Some could make you very rich, while others are little more than scams.

McDOWNER

When it comes to starting a business, everyone knows that franchises are less risky than setting off on your own. After all, in return for your substantial franchise fees — $45,000 for McDonald's or $25,000 for Mail Boxes, etc. — you will get in on a business that is easy to launch, simple to run, and a proven moneymaker, right? Actually, the reverse is true, according to a recent study. Not only are franchises more likely to fail than regular start-ups, the ones that are successful make less money than similarly successful start-ups.

Timothy Bates, an economics professor at Wayne State University who has tracked Commerce Department statistics, followed the performance of a group of almost 21,000 young companies for four years in the late 1980s. By 1991, 35 percent of the franchises had folded, compared with just 28 percent of non-franchise start-ups. And the average annual profits of those that survived? After four years of operation, franchisees earned just over $14,900 annually, compared with $26,600 for owners of non-franchised start-ups.

That is particularly troubling, since franchises are much better capitalized ($86,500 vs. $29,800, according to Bates's calculations) and have annual sales that are significantly higher ($514,000 vs. $102,400). Plus their owners tend to have more management experience and put in more hours. What gives? One of Bates's theories is that the training and marketing support franchisees receive is not as good as it seems; costs may exceed benefits, Bates says.

Another explanation: Franchisees tend to concentrate on crowded sectors such as retailing and restaurants, where competition is fiercer for all businesses. Most interesting of all, though, is his hypothesis of self-selection: that people who are drawn to franchising may be "particularly risk-averse," he says.

So are franchises a bust? Not necessarily. After all, two-thirds of them do survive. But in light of Bates's data, it becomes even more imperative for potential owners to choose a franchise based on its potential for profit, not its ease of ownership or operation. "Just because you are buying a franchise, that does not preclude you from investigating the business as if you were starting it from scratch, yourself," says Susan P. Kezios, head of the American Franchise Association.

James A. Anderson.
Quoted verbatim from *Smart Money*: January 1995

THE OPPOSITE VIEW

In your recent article "McDowner" (January 1995), the writer seems quite taken by the premise of the so-called Bates Study — namely, that franchises are less, rather than more, successful than non-franchised businesses — though the study has been noted primarily for its questionable methodology, sample size, and conclusions.

Apparent defects in Bates's methodology are many — most significant, perhaps, is the nature and size of the franchise sample. Only 5.9 percent — 431 of 7,270 — of the firms in the study are franchises. This is an extremely small sample, the subdivision of which leads to questions of the statistical significance of Bates's results. According to Dun & Bradstreet's statistical abstract of the US for the years during which Bates measured business growth, his 7,270 firms and 431 franchises represent a mere 0.26 percent and 0.016 percent, respectively, of all new business incorporations during those years. Are those sufficient for marking the kinds of inferences Bates does about franchising?

Every other study of franchising success/failure rates, satisfaction, and growth statistics, conducted by organizations including the US Department of Commerce, Gallup, Horvath International, and Arthur Andersen & Co., among others, has concluded that franchises are extremely successful — more so, in fact, than independent start-ups.

Point in fact, a 1991 study by Arthur Andersen concluded that nearly 97 percent of all franchises opened in the previous five year were still in business, and 86 percent of these franchise operations were under the same ownership. In contrast, a study by the US Small Business Administration from 1978 to 1988 revealed that 62 percent of all new businesses were dissolved within the first six years of operation.

Can all these studies be wrong?

At the International Franchise Association, we encourage all potential franchisees to "investigate before investing." The key, however, is to uncover the facts.

Matthew R. Shay
International Franchise Association, Washington, D.C.
Quoted verbatim from Letters to the Editor, *Smart Money*, April 1995

> You can get pronouncements from learned experts slanted any way that you wish. So much hinges on who picks up the tab.

ACCORDING TO YOURS TRULY

I cited both the article and the rebuttal for two reasons:

1. You can get pronouncements from learned experts slanted any way that you wish. So much hinges on who picks up the tab. With statisticians, it depends on the market sample, how the questions are framed, and particularly on how they are asked. Professional opinions are often rendered in response to a client's instructions. So do not accept everything you hear about franchising, or any other business value component, as gospel.

2. The key is to investigate the franchise yourself. You cannot rely on the franchisor to provide an unbiased or objective market analysis or study. You must constantly ask yourself, "What am I getting for my money? Can this franchise, or the franchisor, do anything for me that I cannot do for myself?"

WHAT A FRANCHISE IS

The International Franchise Association says:

The key is to investigate the franchise yourself. You cannot rely on the franchisor to provide an unbiased or objective market analysis or study.

"A franchise is a continuing relationship between franchisor and franchisee in which the sum total of the franchisor's knowledge, image, success, manufacturing, and marketing techniques are supplied to the franchisee for a consideration."

Alternatively, a franchisee is an independent business person who has a continuing relationship with a franchisor to use, exclusive to all others, the franchisor's products, methods, brand name, or identity.

WHAT IT IS NOT

A franchise is not:

- networking, a multilevel distribution system, or a pyramid. No one makes any money from distributors who buy from a master franchisor, who distribute to others, who distribute to others, who also distribute to others, and so forth down the ladder, or alternatively, recruit people to do essentially the same thing. A franchisee is an independent business person operating his or her own enterprise, often to the exclusion of all else.
- a fiduciary relationship whereby one party is committed to act in the best financial interests of the other. The terms of the agreement, which detail all of the financial and other obligations and responsibilities of each party to the other, are spelled out in the franchise contract.
- a partnership or joint venture. There is no common ownership. Neither party is responsible for the debts or contractual obligations of the other.
- an employment relationship. The franchisor pays no salary and is not accountable for its actions, nor that of its employees, to the franchisee. Nor is the franchisee responsible beyond the requirements of the agreement to the franchisor. Both operations are considered as independent from each other.
- an agency where business people represent large and distant companies on a local level.
- a distributorship or a dealership. Franchisees are not middlemen who buy product from a supplier, then resell it at a profit. It is not General Motors in action in your community.

DEALERSHIPS, DISTRIBUTORSHIPS, AND MARKETING AGENCIES

None of these are really franchises. Yet, like true franchises, they are a marketing force to be reckoned with. Most often they generate additional profits to an enterprise, as well as additional going concern value. Despite the pigeonhole for each specific business model, most owners, buyers, and the general public lump them all together. For example, did you know that each Holiday Inn is a fully franchised hotel, while a Best Western merely belongs to a referral system? Who can tell the difference? Does it matter?

Frequently these dealerships and distributorships form the backbone of a business. Automobile dealerships are an example. Exclusive marketing lines in several wholesale, retail, and service companies substantially contribute to viability and profitability. As with a franchise, exclusivity, premises recognition, and marketing advantage all add value. However, a dealer may hold an exclusive line for a specific territory, but no written agreement, only a verbal representation that if so much product is sold, no other dealer will be appointed. It is pretty tough to attach a specific monetary value to such an open-ended arrangement, where you cannot assign any value to transferability and continuance. It could be lost overnight for some inconsequential reason.

An association identification, generally known as a program, usually organized by a wholesaler, is common in retailing. That means a grocery, hardware, or drug store can be identified by a well-known trade name, with the owner's identity often appearing in small letters. The parent company arranges promotions, produces selling aids, offers buying privileges, and supplies common-to-all brand names. For the most part, it is easy to opt into and out of these programs. There is no joining fee and no cancellation penalty. Few have exclusivity, and when all is said and done, even fewer have any real marketing advantage over unbranded competitors or those who subscribe to, or are affiliated with, a different program. The added value is, in most cases, negligible.

The same holds true for many other kinds of dealerships. Oil marketing companies lease service stations, often at below-market rates, simply to sell their product. There is no franchise fee and no royalty.

> Frequently these dealerships and distributorships form the backbone of a business. Automobile dealerships are an example. Exclusive marketing lines in several wholesale, retail, and service companies substantially contribute to viability and profitability.

PRINCIPAL COMPONENTS AND INCLUSIONS OF A FRANCHISE

A franchise provides:

- an identity, assumed to be readily recognized and respected. The name and trading style, excepting only for those outlets that are owned and operated by the franchisor, is exclusive to the franchisee. It provides the right, within a predetermined area or territory, to exclusive use of the franchisor's trademarks, recipes, and procedures.
- a trading style and format. The franchisor always insists that the franchisee follow, to the letter, a very specific format. This includes selling only the standard product, advertising and signage, pricing, the tested and proven formulas and procedures, and often the size and style of building.

- usually an ongoing supervisory and financial relationship. In addition to collecting a franchise fee, or commencement fee, most franchisors take a royalty percentage of total sales. In exchange for this, they provide an exclusive territory, supervision, and identification. Most franchisors also charge an extra percentage of revenues for joint advertising, the amount varying with the type of franchise and the competition within the industry.

ADVANTAGES TO THE FRANCHISEE

- The chances of failure are substantially reduced. Each week in North America, 15,000 new businesses start up. According to one learned source, more than sixty percent fail within the first five years. By the end of ten years, sixty percent of those that made it through the first five years are also gone. Another study shows that eighty percent drop out during the first six years. Other studies give different figures, but they all say the same thing: the survival rate of start-ups is very low. The relatively few successful business owners — numbering sixteen percent — spend much of their time experimenting with methods, building the business, and subsidizing it through lower profits, longer hours, and loss of family life. Franchising, with its accompanying input expertise, reduces the mortality rate. Most franchisors require sufficient start-up capital, use tested systems, and vend into established, researched markets. The owner/operator spends substantially less time just figuring out how to survive.
- brand identification and recognition, market saturation, and exactness, regardless of location. For example, a Big Mac is a Big Mac, whether you are in Lloydminster, Saskatchewan, or Atlanta, Georgia. The quality, ingredients, prices, and the premises are similar. Before entering the premises, the customer knows exactly what to expect. Originality or deviation from the tried and tested formula is not welcome.
- The parent company provides the market perception and benefits, even though it might be just a collection of smaller independent entrepreneurs, all doing the same thing.
- Start-up help, which is always the justification for the initial franchise fee. This could be of immeasurable value to a new entrepreneur, in particular. The franchisee can often obtain help with site selection, architectural design, settling a building contract, buying equipment, hiring, operating procedures, and accounting and control. The new franchisee might have an army of experts at his beck and call. Also, many franchisors insist that their new franchisees attend their hands-on training school before opening the doors.

...a Big Mac is a Big Mac, whether you are in Lloydminster, Saskatchewan or Atlanta, Georgia. The quality, ingredients, prices, and the premises are similar.

TYPES OF FRANCHISES

- the individual franchise. One franchisee for one location, in one area, at one time.
- the multiunit or area development franchise. The franchisee can operate more than one unit in an exclusive area.
- the master franchise. A franchisee obtains a franchise for a specific territory, then sells sub-franchises. Some real estate franchises are excellent examples.
- the split franchise. A franchisee can hold two or more franchises at the same time, operating all from the same premises. Bottling plants are perhaps the

best example. One plant could bottle and distribute several brands of soft drinks, holding an exclusive and specific territory on all of them.

FRANCHISE BROKERS

A franchise broker — who is not a franchisor or franchisee — earns a commission by selling franchises and could, at one time, represent several in different fields. Some receive a continuing percentage for supervising the franchisee. This is relatively common in the hotel industry.

Do not confuse a broker with a franchise consultant, who is generally an attorney working with accountants and other professionals, to help franchisors set up a franchise system.

CONSIDER THESE POINTS

The objective value of a franchise or distributorship is measurable in dollars and cents. Still, it must be considered as a contributory value, not necessarily a value in the marketplace. The subjective value is the privilege of belonging or of having something not immediately available to others, but it is not distinct or separate from other components of the business.

Value can also be destroyed. If the franchise's added value is only subjective, if considered purely from a business valuation perspective, then it probably does not exist. If it can be quickly ended by termination without cause, non-assignability, non-renewal, failure of the franchisor, or such, then any value will be minimal.

Before paying your first penny for a franchise, either original from the franchisor, or by way of assignment when valuing a going concern, consider those elements that tend to change its value. As many are difficult to quantify accurately, some of the following could be considered as theoretical rather than practical. Yet all affect value and continuance. Ask the questions and insist on proper answers:

1. Are the franchisor and the product recognized as competitive factors in the marketplace? Has this operation demonstrated a measurable growth rate? Are existing franchisees doing well, or is this company a questionable starter?

2. What is the franchisor's reputation? How long it has been in business? How many outlets are included in its marketing system? What are their geographical coverage and market share? Although they are difficult to quantify, establishment and desirability have a value, or at least a price.

3. Does the franchisor have a good marketing plan? Are its products well-recognized and accepted? Does it use modern advertising and promotional methods?

4. Does the franchisor offer good control systems that produce a better-quality product at a lower delivered cost? Does it institute and insist on the use of proven control systems? Do the systems work?

5. Are the franchisor's or owner's sales and profit projections realistic, or based on wishful thinking? Franchisors are first and foremost salespeople. I am not suggesting that they are dishonest; I am merely saying that all salespeople

> If the franchise's added value is only subjective, if considered purely from a business valuation perspective, then it probably does not exist.

are optimists — it is part of the profession. Most projections and forecasts are inaccurate guesses based on limited research and poor background and supportive data. These folks often overlook or play down negative factors. They project inflation and natural market growth to make everyone look good. Sometimes both the analyst and the data are questionable.

6. Does the franchise offer a genuine buying advantage? Do all franchises buy supplies from a central location, or is everybody on her own? For example, a hotel group based in the southern US offers excellent buying privileges to all franchisees, but the advantage applies only to a property located near the head office. A property in North Dakota or Minnesota loses any of these savings in freight costs.

7. When does a new franchisee become profitable? This should be shorter than for a non-franchised store. If not, then why buy the franchise and pay the royalties?

8. Must the franchisee meet a minimum performance standard? Does he lose the franchise or dealership if he cannot meet the quota?

9. Do the front men, those who are supposed to help the franchisee, know what they are doing? Are they trained and experienced?

10. Do the benefits measure up to the royalty charge?

11. Can the franchisee amortize the investment in the franchise by the additional profits it creates during the first contract period? If this cannot be done before the date of termination, renewal, or renegotiation, then the price is too high.

> The value of a franchise increases
> with market recognition and acceptance.
> A brand-new franchise concept holds the least value.
> It then increases as identifiable outlets are established.

The value of a franchise increases with market recognition and acceptance. A brand-new franchise concept holds the least value. It then increases as identifiable outlets are established. It peaks when there is a store on every corner in every town. It was probably tough to sell that first McDonald's franchise. Now buyers line up to pay thousands of dollars for the privilege of using the name.

12. Must the franchisee buy poor-quality, inefficient, or high-priced equipment? Some franchisors make more money selling equipment than they do the franchises. One franchisor, whose name will not be revealed to protect the guilty, is not really in the business of selling his inexpensive franchises. He makes his money by loading up the franchisee with tons of very costly and excessive equipment.

My firm recently appraised one such store. The franchisee sold takeout fried chicken from a small store front. The franchisor sold him high-quality, but very expensive equipment that would have made Colonel Saunders envious. This small store could not use even one-quarter of it. The operator could not make his payments and lost everything.

13. How can either party end the agreement? Can the franchisor terminate for little cause? Can the franchisee opt out? Are there any penalties or buy-back provisions in the event of cancellation or termination? What if the franchisee dies?

14. All franchises are granted only for so many years. How does the franchisee renew or continue after that time frame? What if the franchisor refuses to

renew the agreement, wants to set up in this territory itself without buying out the franchisee, or wishes to appoint another? How is the franchisee protected? More important, how is she compensated?

15. If the franchisor decides to change the theme, signage, or decor of its stores, with the usual mandatory requirements that all do the same, who pays for the change in each franchise?

A popular Canadian fast-food restaurant chain recently radically changed its buildings' design, decor, and finishing. All franchise premises more than ten years old were required to modernize their buildings and equipment to fit this new design. Average cost: $150,000 each. Even though the upgrading has substantially improved the image of the chain and the profitability of each franchise, many franchisees reluctantly had to refinance their stores. Some of them had difficulty raising the money.

16. Can the franchisee relocate the business within the community, or to another town, and retain the franchise? Do any special clauses restrict such movement, assuming it is still within the protected territory?

17. Do any special terms or conditions restrict the franchisee from selling the business to a third party? Does the franchise agreement contain an option to purchase, a first right of refusal, or a clause whereby the franchise is not assignable or transferable under any circumstance?

In some cases the franchise is a personal covenant between the franchisor and the business owner. The contract is in the franchisee's personal name, not that of his company or business. With some, the franchisor just wants to effortlessly extract another inception fee from the next franchisee. With others, the franchisor is genuinely concerned about who will be the new proprietor.

This non-transferability clause is common in licensing agreements. Many cannot be bought or sold and hold no value in and of themselves. When a going concern is sold, the buyer normally maintains the name and trading style, including licences and distributorships, and the privilege of continuing to do business from the same location. The buyer should ensure that any dealerships and distributorships remain. Loss of any could reduce the going concern value. Would you buy a Ford dealership without the right to sell new Ford cars?

> In some cases the franchise is a personal covenant between the franchisor and the business owner. The contract is in the franchisee's personal name, not that of his company or business.

18. Can the franchisor exercise any control over the price or the terms by which the franchisee can sell the business? How would a right-of-first-refusal clause, standard in most agreements, affect any potential sale? Does the franchisor have an option to purchase, at a fair price and on reasonable terms? Can the franchisee sell the franchise, without the business, to a third party?

19. Is the franchisee, while holding the franchise, restricted from engaging in another business, directly or indirectly, competitive or otherwise? Some franchises are so restrictive that the franchisee cannot even have partners, let alone an interest in any other venture.

20. What happens if the franchisor becomes insolvent or is petitioned into bankruptcy? Think about this, because not all franchising ideas are big winners. Carefully examine the repercussions, particularly if you are dealing with a newer franchisor or an original concept. In the past ten or so years, several restaurant franchise/chain operations have gone bankrupt. They left

their sublessees and franchisees with little more than an empty shell and the question as to what to do next.

21. Are competitive products at perhaps better prices available in the area? A franchise, dealership, or distributorship must offer a measurable profit advantage.

22. Is this a master franchisee or sub-franchisor? Would the goodwill hold greater value if you could sell other franchises?

23. What is the breakdown between company-operated and franchised outlets? If the company has trouble selling its franchises and ends up owning or operating most of the stores itself, you should find out why.

24. Is the franchisor in the business of selling franchises, or merchandise? We are back to networking, pyramids, scams, and hanky-panky.

You must do your own investigation. You cannot totally rely on an objective survey done by anyone else. And you must satisfy yourself that the franchise will result in increased profits for the business being considered.

METHODS TO VALUE A FRANCHISE

The franchise's contractual terms and limitations, and its intrinsic and related benefits, contribute to the value, as do the more tangible aspects. Although you cannot accurately measure them by any of the standard procedures, these added values can exist. Subjective factors often add worth to many businesses.

I can measure only objective values. You will have to establish, on your own or with the help of an appraiser, the worth of any subjective factors that apply to your specific case. Objective value, in dollars and cents, can be measured in four ways:

- cost to acquire,
- value added; additional resale value or potential,
- profit advantage. This is the net present value of increased revenues or lower operating costs, or a combination of both, created by the franchise and not by any other cause. Either should result in greater profit. This value, as a distinct entity, is intertwined with and considered part of goodwill.
- SWAG (Scientific Wild-assed Guess), probably the most common method. Most times, though, it's more wild-assed than scientific. It seldom produces a credible answer.

You must do your own investigation. You cannot totally rely on an objective survey done by anyone else. And you must satisfy yourself that the franchise will result in increased profits for the business being considered.

A franchise can also create negative value if a business is locked into a franchise that does not produce more sales or improved profit ratios, is not marketable, and may be a liability. Yet the franchisee has to pay a financial penalty if she opts out early. This negative goodwill does not usually apply to a dealership or distributorship because they are easy to obtain and get out of. It may, however, apply to a program, such as a drug store or grocery store, created by the investment in signage, stationery, house brands, and so forth.

COST TO ACQUIRE

The theory behind this method of valuation, is that if a franchise costs X number of dollars to acquire, then that is what it is worth, no more and no less. This simple procedure sometimes seems logical. You simply sum up the individual contributory asset values and then add the cost of the franchise. You might need to adjust the franchise cost if it varies from one location to another, or has changed at this specific location since inception.

What you need to do is figure out what prompted the franchisor to set the inception fee at this level. Up-front or franchise fees are commonly based on a combination of:

- the goodwill generated by the franchisor's name and reputation The more outlets in the system, the more geographical the diversification, and the greater the brand recognition, the higher the fee. There is a much higher risk to the franchisee if the franchisor is not well-known.
- demand for the franchise. The greater the demand, the higher the fee.
- the size, population, and demographics of the assigned territory. The better the territory, the higher the fee. Aside from all else, the exclusivity of the territory often adds value. Again, that intrinsic or subjective value exists, but it is hard to measure.
- the cost of recruiting the franchisee,
- the cost of training the franchisee,
- the cost of advertising, signs, plans, and other aids to establish the franchisee.

Dealerships, exclusive distribution rights, or marketing agreements often add value to a going concern because they come with the parent company's ready-made reputation, brand identity, market penetration, and goodwill.

THE VALUE-ADDED METHOD

Of the three methods of valuation, this is the simplest in concept, but perhaps the most difficult to calculate. It usually applies best to dealerships, licences, and marketing groups, rather than franchises. Often, you cannot measure the value of a distributorship by the usual means, but only recognize its contribution to profitability. In many situations, you can only perceive, not calculate, any goodwill thus created.

Take an automobile dealership. With all companies, a vendor can sell, trade, or barter the tangible assets, but not the rights to the dealership. Upon the transfer of the business, the dealership automatically reverts to the parent company, and the new owner must reapply to get it back. Who would buy a large service garage that has profited mostly from the sale and servicing of a particular brand of car, without entering into a new agreement with that manufacturer? Although you cannot hang a specific price tag on an automobile dealership, it definitely has a recognized and tradeable value.

Dealerships, exclusive distribution rights, or marketing agreements often add value to a going concern because they come with the parent company's ready-made reputation, brand identity, market penetration, and goodwill. You can usually measure this at source, but seldom at the retail level, where it is an integral part of the business, and not separate from other intangible assets.

You cannot reliably appraise added value without referring to actual market transactions. The procedure is to sum up the value of all of the capital assets and deduct the total from the selling price of the business. Goodwill which would include the franchise's value is the remainder.

PROFIT ADVANTAGE

This is the best way to value a franchise. However, it is almost always reserved for feasibility analysis, particularly when assessing investment alternatives and comparing potential returns against hurdle rates. Still, some economists and like professionals believe profit advantage is the only way to measure goodwill. For sure, profit advantage is the best way to appraise the added or contributory value of a franchise, distributorship, or licence.

I will compare two fictional, identical fast-food restaurants, one franchised and one independent. All else is equal. Neither has any special advantage that is not enjoyed by the other. Let us say the unfranchised restaurant sells $1,000,000 per year in total food and other sales, earning a net operating profit of 12.5%. The franchise's annual sales volume, for the sake of demonstration, is $2,000,000, and its net operating profit, before franchise fees, would be the same 12.5%. I will capitalize the net earnings of sixteen percent to come up with the market value for either restaurant.

Restaurant No. 1: Independent

Total Sales and Income Per Year,	$ 1,000,000
Profitability Factor 12.5%	$ 125,000

Market Value of Restaurant No. 1:

$125,000 capitalized at 16.0% =	$ 781,250

Restaurant No. 2: Franchised

Total Sales and Income Per Year	$2,000,000
Profitability Factor 12.5%	$ 250,000
Less Franchise Fee: 5% of sales	$ (100,000)
Net Income for Capitalizing	$ 150,000

Market Value of Restaurant No. 2:

$150,000 capitalized at 16.0%	$ 937,500

Profit Advantage:

The Value Created by the Franchise: ($937,500 – $781,250)	$ 156,250
Less the Cost of the Franchise	$ (25,000)
Net Total Value Gain by the Franchise	$ 131,250

All else being equal, because of the franchise, Restaurant No. 2 holds an increased market value of $131,250 over Restaurant No. 1. In the real world you could find it necessary to also deduct any additional cost incurred to conform to the franchisor's building design, specialized equipment, operating style, and so forth.

...some economists and like professionals believe profit advantage is the only way to measure goodwill.

Alternative Procedure

You can also calculate it this way, which is a bit shorter and gives the same answer.

Net Operating Profit: Independent	$ 125,000
Net Operating Profit: Franchised	$ 150,000
Increased Profit Per Annum	$ 25,000
Net Present Value of $25,000 per annum at 16.0%	$ 156,250
Less the Cost of the Franchise	(25,000)
Net Value Gain by the Franchise	$ 131,250

Nothing differs from the first process; the input factors are identical. The arithmetic is slightly shortened, though. Each procedure lets you use varying input factors on both sides of the equation, and it does not matter which method you choose.

Undoubtedly, with the increased sales of $1,000,000 per year, Restaurant No. 2 would have greater staff efficiency, better buying power, and other built-in advantages, all of which should increase its operating profit. To keep the exercise simple, though, I omitted these other factors. In a real-life comparison, or when examining only one company, you should account for these benefits.

Last Case

Assume that the franchise is valid for only ten years, after which it is terminated, subject to franchisor buyout, or must be renegotiated. For this calculation, you limit the advantage of the increased profit of $25,000 per year, to the ten-year period, not capitalize it into perpetuity as I did in the examples above.

Then discount, at the same 16.0%, the present value of $25,000 per year gained by the franchise for the ten-year period:

(To make this calculation you need either a financial calculator or a table showing six functions of a dollar.)

Net Present Value of Additional Income	$ 120,830
Less the Cost of The Franchise	(25,000)
Value of the Profit Advantage	$ 95,830

If there is a termination date, no matter what the contract says about continuance, you must always assume that the franchise will end on that date. No matter what the franchisor tells you verbally, never count on the franchise being renewed on identical terms, or without requiring another franchise inception fee.

Although I used the example of a restaurant, I could easily have picked any other franchise, a distributorship, marketing position, or licence. All are calculated by the same procedure.

SENSITIVITY ANALYSIS

You may also wish to undertake a sensitivity analysis, which is a mathematical procedure that keeps asking, and answering: what if? What if the sales volume changes or you do not reach other objectives? What if sales do not increase by the $1,000,000, but only by $250,000 or $500,000 or $750,000? Change the cost of sales. Assume thirty or thirty-five or forty percent, or whatever is the minimum and maximum applicable to the amounts purchased. Test the results using different delivered per-unit costs. Alter the expense and efficiency ratios, as the point of diminishing returns may be reached sooner, or more often, as sales increase. How do these variable results affect the bottom line, and how do they affect the profit advantage, if any, that is created by the franchise?

SENSITIVITY ANALYSIS — VALUE OF A FRANCHISE

In this instance, an independent sporting goods store owner is considering buying a franchise that will make him a local outlet for a national chain. The chain has a good reputation, competitively priced quality products, and meets all of the store owner's qualifications. But will it pay?

The store now has sales of $250,000 per year. Net operating profit — before long-term debt service or depreciation — is 12.50% of sales. After buying the franchise, except for a new name, new signage, and some new product lines, nothing changes. The sensitivity analysis tests the comparative value of the franchise at varying income levels, using the same 12.5% profit margin. The franchise is valid for twenty years.

I will use a discount rate of fifteen percent. This is a fair return of and on invested capital for smaller retail stores.

Case 1: Present Value of Net Profit without the Franchise

Total Sales and Income Per Year,	$ 250,000
Profitability Factor 12.5% =	$ 31,250

Market Value of the Store. Present Value of $31,250 per year for 20 years, discounted at 15.0% =	$ 195,600

Case 2: Present Case Value of Profits with the Franchise

Situation	1	2	3
Total Sales and Income Per Year	$ 350,000	$ 425,000	$ 500,000
Profitability Factor 12.5% =	$ 43,750	$ 53,125	$ 62,250
Less Franchise Fee: 4% of sales	$ (14,000)	$ (17,000)	$ (20,000)
Net Income	$ 29,750	$ 36,125	$ 42,500

Market Value of the Store.
Present Value of Net Profit for 20 years, discounted at 15.0%

	1	2	3
	$ 186,200	$ 226,100	$ 266,000

To Calculate the Added Value (Loss) Created by the Franchise:

	1	2	3
Case 1 Market Value	$ 195,600	$ 195,600	$ 195,600
Less: Case 2 Market Value	$ 186,200	$ 226,100	$ 266,000
Market Value Gain (Loss)	$ (9,400)	$ 30,500	$ 70,400
Less the Cost of the Franchise	$ (20,000)	$ (20,000)	$ (20,000)
Net Business Gain (Loss)	$ (29,400)	$ 10,500	$ 50,400

For a true comparison, you must reduce profits to net present value. If you do not discount the annual profits, you will not obtain the correct answer, but you will still get a good handle on whether the franchise is a wise investment.

Assuming that all else remains constant, you would need additional annual sales of about $160,000, or a total of $410,000, to be at the same point as without the franchise. With anything less, the store is a loser.

Next, you should undertake a detailed market analysis to determine if this is feasible. You may also study cost benefits at the varying levels. For a simple example, I have stuck to the 12.50% operating profit, yet operating costs frequently vary with increased volume. On a percentage basis, they could be more or less. Do you need more staff, larger premises, more advertising, etc., or will the same fixed expenses still hold?

You should also ponder the inability of any business to sustain high profits for indefinite periods. Competition increases and redundancy sets in. Always take into account the value increase created by profit advantage to be for a specified term only, not capitalized into perpetuity as was done in the first and second cases.

This kind of exercise is usually conducted before the business opens. You base all input factors on the area market analysis and the franchisor's hype, projected rather than historical. You need to ask: Will profits increase enough to cover the initial cost of a franchise, pay the continuing royalties, and leave a little left over? Many cannot or just do not. Because of their character and location, businesses often will not generate extra volume with any franchise. Their lower net profit, caused by its initial cost and the royalties, may indicate that the franchise is a liability, not an asset.

> You should also ponder the inability of any business to sustain high profits for indefinite periods. Competition increases and redundancy sets in.

WEIGHING THE ALTERNATIVES

I seem to reduce every procedure to a mathematical formula. Like a franchise hard-sell, where the prospective franchisee need only pour on the secret ingredient and out comes success, I apply a magical formula to conjure the correct number. Yet such exactness exists only in textbooks, not in the real world. Irreconcilable and immeasurable subjective motives frequently outweigh the objective ones — especially when assigning value to a franchise. Therefore, before trying to be so definite, consider how the twenty-two points of consideration (earlier in this chapter) affect that mathematical perfection. Consider the alternatives: How would the business fare without the franchise, or with a different one? Is McDonald's really that much better than Burger King? Does the franchise really add measurable value to the enterprise, or is it just nice to belong, go to their conventions, and fly their flag?

All I have tried to do is show the steps. In the real world, you should — on paper — build a model, showing what you can probably sell and the profit that you can reasonably expect to earn with and without the franchise. Then test this model against several pessimistic and optimistic hypotheses, differing sales levels, matching fixed and variable expenses, changed profits, and diminishing returns. Be honest and analytical. This is often difficult, as all entrepreneurs are eternal optimists. If they were not, none would go into business in the first place. In the end, you have to just cross your fingers and roll the dice. The crystal balls of even the best analysts do not work all that well.

> Is McDonald's really that much better than Burger King?

NOTES

Chapter 16

THE VALUATION OF SHARES

BUYER AND APPRAISER BEWARE

BEFORE you become too engrossed in this chapter, I want to head off at the pass any misunderstandings:

1. I am giving you a bare-bones, very generic overview of shares valuation. I am no legal, accounting, or tax expert, and do not intend to give such advice.

2. This is a guide only, providing a brief idea of what to look for if you venture into these shark-infested waters.

3. You should never even consider buying the shares of any going concern without first obtaining the best legal and tax advice. Not the cheapest, the best.

4. When shares are transferred, significant legal and tax ramifications come along for the ride. Therefore, different buyers could find different values for the same company, depending on how the vendor extracts her money from it.

5. No real estate appraiser should ever feel qualified to undertake a shares valuation after having read only this chapter, or all of this manual — you are not.

6. Most important, and I will shout it in capital letters:

THE ERRORS AND OMISSIONS INSURANCE AS ISSUED BY ALL INSURANCE COMPANIES TO REAL ESTATE APPRAISERS DO NOT PROVIDE COVERAGE FOR THE VALUATION OF SHAREHOLDERS' INTERESTS IN CLOSELY HELD CORPORATIONS.

In other words, fellow appraisers, you are on your own.

Having said all that, I feel I should provide at least an overview of how shares value is calculated.

ASSET AND SHARE SALES

To this point, except for minor references, I have talked about buying assets only. That is because the small-business vendor usually sells the real estate, the equipment, at times goodwill, and the right for the buyer to continue to operate the same business from the same location, frequently using the same name. Very little else is included. The seller normally retains:

different buyers could find different values for the same company, depending on how the vendor extracts her money from it.

- cash on hand and in the bank,
- receivables of all types and classes,
- inventories (generally included, but at extra cost),
- work in progress (generally included, but at extra cost),
- intercompany accounts, payable or receivable,
- any prepaids (some may be assigned at an extra cost),
- assets owned by the company but unrelated to the business,
- all accounts payable,
- all short-term loans and liabilities,
- all long-term and deferred liabilities (some assumptions are common if part of the financing package),
- all loans, to and from the company,
- contingent liabilities,
- unpaid income taxes, including deferred,
- municipal, property, sales, and other taxes liability,
- paid-in-share capital,
- retained earnings or deficit.

When assets only are bought, sold, or appraised, all parties:

- know exactly what is included and excluded, including all assets and liabilities,
- assume ownership and salability of a marketable title,
- presuppose business continuance.

> When transferring
> a business
> by the sale of shares,
> unless specifically excluded,
> everything tangible
> and intangible
> is part of the transaction.
> That is, all of the good
> and all of the bad,
> the whole ball of wax
> except for the vendor's
> body and soul.

When transferring a business by the sale of shares, unless specifically excluded, everything tangible and intangible is part of the transaction. That is, all of the good and all of the bad, the whole ball of wax except for the vendor's body and soul. If the agreement includes earnouts (the owner remaining with the buyer for a pre-agreed time), those might also be part of the deal.

INCLUSIONS AND CONCERNS

In an assets-only valuation, many areas were interesting but not that big a deal. They did not affect the going concern value of the business, at least not very much. That is all vastly different in a shares sale. Everything is part of the package, except for specific deletions from the asset or liability schedule, or agreed-upon limitations.

All parties to the transaction must now be concerned with:

- the actual value of the accounts receivable. Are they all collectible? Must some be discounted? If so, by what percentage? Will the vendor guarantee them? If yes, does he have the money to honor the guarantee if a debtor defaults?
- the actual value of inventory. How much is dead stock? Should the inventory be discounted? If so, by how much? In small business, you need not fret about the various ways to account for inventory, such as LIFO or FIFO. The books will usually say, at cost or market, whichever is lower. In practice, it is always at cost (FIFO). Still, you might have to discount the value, particularly of older or obsolete items.
- Are all accounts payable correctly recorded?
- Are mortgages and liens payable up to date? If not, what is their status? Are any foreclosures proceeding or threatened? This could be material even if

the premises are rented. In some American states, foreclosure nullifies all leases.

- the longer-term liability re: staff pensions, holiday pay, unpaid bonuses, union contracts, etc.
- any management contracts,
- any earnouts that could alter the company's value. An earn-out is: "a compromise between what the vendors believe is their companies' future profit and what the purchasers expect them to be. An earn-out is a way of paying for a company based on its future performance. The purchase price is a combination of an immediate up-front payment plus a number of future payments related to future performance."[1]
- forgivable director's or shareholder's loans,
- any declared but unpaid dividends,
- any shares sold but not paid for. Are any of the shares convertible? Are there any outstanding warrants to buy more shares, particularly at less than fair value?
- Have all income taxes been paid or accounted for, including deferred? Who is liable in the event of a reassessment?
- Has the company taken advantage of accelerated depreciation that may affect its future tax position?
- any grants that are repayable. Are there forgivable loans that may not be forgiven if performance does not meet certain standards?
- redundant assets that may have been overlooked,
- personal property that is to be specifically excluded,
- any lease agreements that worry you,
- any longer-term contracts that may now help or harm the company's performance,
- any unsettled defaults on completed contracts. Are there any continuing performance, repair or replace, or other warranty clauses in any completed or in-progress contracts?
- the status of product warranties, guarantees, and representations? For how many years do the warranties last?
- all legal and other agreements. Are any contracts personal to any director? If so, are they assigned or excluded?
- Can all franchises, patents, licences, etc., be assigned? Usually these are part of the company, but sometimes they are personally owned by a director or officer. Figure out who owns what. Some agreements prohibit any assignment, no matter how it is done.
- Any pending litigation? Any outstanding lawsuits or disputes? Any unpaid judgments? Any writs of execution?
- Is the company solvent? Does it have title to its assets?

You can probably think of several other concerns, depending on the type, size, and complexity of the company. The auditor's report will answer many of these questions. Others will answer themselves. Still, do not ever automatically assume anything. Read the minute book and the articles of incorporation, both of which could provide an insight not provided by the audit. You should verify anything that is in doubt, or suspicious, even if reported upon by a professional accountant or attorney.

Share transfers in privately held companies are complicated. Very few real estate appraisers and still fewer business buyers are trained accountants or lawyers. It is often wise to obtain professional counsel, particularly when considering matters that could have legal or tax ramifications. And in every share transfer or valuation, there are always legal and tax factors.

Share transfers in privately held companies are complicated. Very few real estate appraisers and still fewer business buyers are trained accountants or lawyers.

CLASSIFICATION OF SHARES

In most small businesses, except for the valuation of a fractional interest, do not fuss over the various classes of shares and the privileges attached to each class. Usually it is an all-or-nothing transaction. In some very rare circumstances, however, individual values must be attached to various share classifications. To put it simply, you should first establish the en bloc, or rateable, value of all issued shares. Next, apply bonuses or discounts to each class, based on the rights and privileges attached. That means you need to consider:

- classification of shares (Class A, B, C, etc.),
- whether the shares are common or preferred,
- any warrants attached to preferred shares,
- any letter or escrow stock,
- rights, authority, and privileges of each class,
- priorities in distribution of dividends to each class, including cumulative rights,
- priorities to obtain assets if the company is wound up,
- who can vote and who can not (weighted voting by class),
- right to elect directors or serve as a director,
- any special perks offered to one class but not to others,
- any special right to buy more shares offered to one class or individual(s), but not to others.

> first establish the en bloc, or rateable, value of all issued shares. Next, apply bonuses or discounts to each class, based on the rights and privileges attached.

THIN COMPANY

In small businesses, or privately held companies, most of which are basically incorporated proprietorships or partnerships, founders generally incorporate what is known as a "thin company." Only a very small portion of the owner's capital investment is made by way of shares bought for cash. It is usually only a few hundred dollars. The remainder of their investment is injected by way of shareholder's loans. There are both legal and tax ramifications for doing it this way. The main advantage is that in the event of bankruptcy, shareholder's loans are ranked with the common creditors, while shares investment is recoverable only after all other claims have been satisfied.

Public companies, particularly new issues taking a run on the stock market, are structured exactly opposite. This is maximum investment in shares, with as little as possible of the promoter's capital invested by way of loans to the company. Promoter's equity, and thus subsequent profit-taking, is reflected in share price increases, not in interest on cash advances.

In their initial letters patent, many founders set up various share classes, sometimes to distribute ownership to their families, or to sell employees a piece of the action. These usually are subordinate classes, frequently without voting privileges or any real authority. The privilege of owning part of the company is supposed to be sufficient reward. Sometimes the owner thinks the world will beat a path to his door, all wanting a piece of this soon-to-be-very-prosperous company. In practice, small, privately owned companies seldom sell shares to anyone except an insider.

AUDITED FINANCIAL STATEMENT

Before appraising any company's shares, always insist on an audited financial statement, and do not accept one prepared by a local bookkeeping service. There are too many legal implications and too many areas where failure to disclose could affect the company's value. Never settle for less.

That said, I have never, ever received, or worked with, an audited statement in my work as a business appraiser. Very few small companies have their statements audited. The law and tax people do not force them to do it, and so almost all small and medium-sized businesses settle for a much cheaper, unaudited statement prepared by a public accountant. This is about as fancy a statement as you will ever see.

The company's value applies only to the date of the audit, or to the most recent fiscal reporting period, regardless of when the assets are actually inspected. If the audit is a little long in the tooth, then you must ascertain what changes, if any, have taken place since it was completed.

An appraiser should always insert a special disclaimer into the report, saying that the capital assets, particularly owned real estate and equipment, are assumed not to have changed since the audit (or the end of the last fiscal period). Any changes, debt reduction and working capital changes excepted, should be noted. You should also make it very clear that you worked with an unaudited statement (if this is so).

WRITE-DOWNS AND BONUSES

You, the auditor, and probably the owner, have to decide whether to write down accounts payable and inventories or to apply other discounts, or to award bonuses for funded but not-capitalized-on research and development, contracts, licences, patents, franchises, and the like. There is no hard and fast rule. Much depends on the circumstances.

An appraiser's report should clearly state if the applicable assets and liabilities have been accepted at book value or adjusted, and then give the rationale for any adjustments. If the owner or another, such as an equipment supplier, provided the values, then the report should clearly state this.

OPEN MARKET ASSUMPTION

For most share valuations, you will assume an open and free market, even though that might not exist. Although asset sales occur every day for businesses of all types, share sales of small businesses are much less frequent.

As the shares market is much more restricted than for assets only, you will have to make a choice in share valuations: whether to use a still higher capitalization or discount rate than normal, apply a single overall rate to obtain the final value estimate, or assume an unrestricted market and do nothing differently. This decision is a matter of choice and depends on the situation. There are no strict rules and fewer precedents.

Very few small companies have their statements audited. The law and tax people do not force them to do it, and so almost all small and medium-sized businesses settle for a much cheaper, unaudited statement prepared by a public accountant.

INCOME TAX CONSIDERATIONS

Legally, you cannot avoid income tax, you can only defer it. Like the undertaker, the taxman will get you in the end. Share valuations must reflect:

1. Tax on recaptured depreciation:

   You buy the shares of a company, rather than assets, to lower the initial cost. Because of a low book value but high market or replacement value of the capital assets, you can sometimes buy a company on shares with a minimum of cash investment. The downside is that you assume liability for the future payment of tax on recaptured depreciation. At some future date, unless successful in reselling shares, you must pay this tax.

2. Tax payable or recoverable on capital gains or losses:

   When dealing with capital gains, keep in mind two concepts: first, capital gains tax that is considered a corporate liability; and second, capital gains tax that is the shareholders' personal liability.

   Capital gains tax can be a corporate liability created by an increased value of the assets over their initial cost, realized on a sale, or in specific instances, such as reappraisal or by deemed disposition. It is treated exactly the same as recaptured depreciation. The sole difference is that in Canada, only seventy-five percent of the gain is taxable, at full taxation rates, in the year in which the gain was realized. In the United States, one hundred percent of the capital gain is taxable at rates as high as thirty-nine percent.

   This situation also applies where the company has incurred capital gains or losses on previous transactions and has deferred the tax, or assets bought or sold, with the acquisition or selling costs unpaid. These will appear on the company's accounts, either as a liability or an asset.

   In appraising real estate, you scarcely ever deduct capital gains tax, selling commissions, legal fees, or related costs, from the property value estimate. Ditto for share sales. Once again, tax is not triggered until there is an actual sale of the shares, or a deemed disposition, such as at time of death of the shareholder.

   If you aim to determine a net shares value in the hands of the shareholder, then you should account for potential capital gains tax to that shareholder in the final value estimate.

   In both the United States and Canada, tax deferment by capital losses can only be used to offset tax payable from capital gains.

3. Deferred income tax:

   When appraising most small businesses, you will not worry about this too much. Here, the company claims higher depreciation for tax purposes than what is recorded on the company's accounts. Before totally discounting this entry, you absolutely must ask the company accountant his opinion of the longer-term effects of deferred income tax.

4. Often other tax considerations are pertinent, some to the company, others to the shareholder. These would include but not necessarily be limited to:

   • roll-over provisions,

> When dealing with capital gains, keep in mind two concepts: first, capital gains tax that is considered a corporate liability; and second, capital gains tax that is the shareholders' personal liability.

- assets acquired at less than market value,
- past interfamily or other share transfers, which could be subject to reassessment,
- prior reorganizations,
- shares acquired by the shareholder as a gift,
- valuation day values (1912 in the US, 1971 in Canada),
- transfer of company assets to a shareholder,
- death of a shareholder,
- receipt of stock for unpaid wages or dividends,
- tax-free grants and interest concessions gained.

Remember: in a typical share sale, the buyer acquires all of the assets and all of the liabilities, exactly as they are, specific exclusions excepted. On the positive side, this includes the working capital, but on the negative, the long-term, and the deferred, contingent, or undeclared liabilities. As the balance sheet is acquired exactly as is, it will not reflect any adjusted or appraised values. These adjusted values may be used for internal accounting purposes, or for financing a leveraged buyout. Yet unless the buyer wants to trigger more tax, and no one does, the continued operation of the company must be with an unchanged legal and financial status.

In simple terms, the value of the shares represents the net equity of that company, and that is what you are buying.

> ...in a typical share sale, the buyer acquires all of the assets and all of the liabilities, exactly as they are, specific exclusions excepted.

DISPOSITION CONSIDERATIONS

The sale of a business by shares, not assets, brings up many relative possibilities that I have not yet mentioned. As the seller establishes the value, it can change dramatically, depending on how he chooses to get his money out of the company. Probably the most beneficial way to remove earnings is through the payment of dividends, which at this time would be taxable in the range of eight to thirty percent. Alternatively, he could use roll-over provisions and further postpone payment. If the assets were expropriated, or if a terminal loss occurs, such as a fire, the tax and the share value would both be totally different.

For these and other valid reasons, many appraisers prefer to use an all-inclusive income tax rate of forty to fifty percent. The percentage depends on the amount to be taxed. It varies further according to how the accumulated surplus has been historically treated, the extent of the capital gain or loss, recaptured depreciation, earned surplus, and how the assets are to be disposed of. The vending shareholder wishes to extract as much as possible from the company at the lowest taxation rate possible. At the same time, the buyer wants to acquire the company at the lowest possible price, with the least amount of equity, but will not knowingly enter the untenable position of paying excess tax in future years.

As shares valuation is more complicated and more treacherous than an assets-only transfer, do not be bashful about seeking counsel from accountants and lawyers, particularly those who are more familiar with the target company.

Warning to appraisers: Do not venture opinions or estimate value in unfamiliar terrain. It is the best way to get sued. Ask the trained professionals for advice and take it.

References

[1] Hindle, T. (1993). *Field guide to business terms: A glossary of essential tools and concepts for today's manager/chief contributor*. Boston, MA: Harvard Business School Press.

NOTES

_____

_____

_____

_____

_____

_____

_____

_____

_____

_____

_____

_____

_____

_____

_____

_____

_____

_____

_____

_____

_____

_____

_____

_____

_____

What's it Worth? A Guide to Valuing a Small Business

260

Chapter 17

THE APPRAISAL OF A FRACTIONAL INTEREST

S O far in this book, I've assumed that the acquisition or appraisal would be for a one-hundred-percent interest. Now let's look at a fractional interest, a portion less than the whole. I'll restrict the discussion to share ownerships and transfers, not limited partnerships, undivided interests, or other apportionments. Although the legal requirements may change, the valuation practices do not if you choose another form of business organization.

A fractional interest is defined as:

- any interest that is less that one hundred percent.

A majority interest is the holding of fifty percent of all issued shares, plus one; not fifty-one percent. A minority interest is anything less than this.

In law, there is no such thing as an equal interest. If you own exactly fifty percent of the issued shares, this is considered a minority position.

MAJORITY VERSUS MINORITY INTERESTS

When buying shares in a public stock company, you acquire a partial interest, a specific percentage of the net equity. Although you can control the company with a majority ownership, or some other form of consent, you usually obtain it by acquiring or controlling, by proxy, the holdings of several smaller shareholders. In a public company, to have control, you do not need to own fifty percent, plus one share; you simply need the ability to outvote any other shareholder. The exception to this is where two or more collude to obtain control. Although the rules governing private ownership are less complicated, the rights and benefits accorded a public company shareholding are much the same. In closely held corporations, the minority interest holder may have a small voice, a growth investment, and sometimes a job with slightly more security than otherwise; but legally, little else.

The majority shareholder, special covenants excepted, controls the company. He can make all decisions, elect all directors, and run the company as seen fit. Although some legal protections exist, minority shareholders have few of these privileges and are at the mercy of the majority shareholder.

You would think that in the sale of partial interests, a majority holding would be entitled to a bonus beyond the en bloc value of the shares, while the minority holder's interest should be worth less. In theory, this is correct. In practice, a bonus for the majority shareholder is always questionable. Although sometimes obtained in the transfer of interests in mid-sized or larger corporations, particularly if bought by a special-interest group, a premium is seldom paid to control a smaller company. Yet a minority position is usually discounted.

Fractional interests in closely held corporations are seldom sold on the open market. For a majority interest, the entire business usually goes on the block, unless acquired by an insider (someone who already holds an interest in the company) or an employee. For a minority interest, no secondary or resale market exists. Except for the very rare occasion, only another insider ever buys a minority interest, and

> The majority shareholder,
> special covenants excepted,
> controls the company.
> He can make all decisions,
> elect all directors,
> and run the company
> as seen fit.
> Although some legal
> protections exist,
> minority shareholders
> have few of these privileges
> and are at the mercy
> of the majority shareholder.

never on the open market. So you infer a notional market when you're valuing a minority interest. You assume an open and free market, subject to all of its intricacies, when in fact no such market actually exists.

Some writers argue that the best way to value a minority stock holding in any company, public or private, is simply to look at the stock market. When you buy a specific number of shares in any public company, all you get is a minority interest. However, as I've said, the stock market does not provide an accurate indication of what the share value should be for a closely held corporation, particularly a small business.

CONTROL: THE MAJORITY INTEREST

In small business transfers, an outsider seldom buys a fractional interest. Only on the rarest of occasions is a premium paid for the majority position above the en bloc share value. I don't mean to be contradictory, but in unique circumstances this custom of share value equality digresses. A bonus could possibly be paid for less than a one-hundred-percent position. At times, control, with its privileges, might deserve a premium.

Control gives the power or authority to:

- elect all directors, including yourself, a relative, or a friend,
- hire and fire whom you please, including relatives,
- set your own salary and perks,
- award contracts,
- establish the economic direction of the company,
- establish the investment policies of the company,
- issue new or recall outstanding shares,
- determine the amount and timing of dividend payments,
- liquidate or wind up the company,
- sell that control.

> There are other side-benefits, all suggesting that to effectively manage the company, you must have control. Once obtained, very little legally remains for anyone else.

There are other side-benefits, all suggesting that to effectively manage the company, you must have control. Once obtained, very little legally remains for anyone else.

To have absolute control, you must own all issued shares. This isn't always possible, as some jurisdictions require at least two shareholders. Still, few restrictions specify the minimum number of shares that must be held by the second party. At times, the owner's lawyer will hold one share in trust, thus meeting the legal requirement.

Besides direct ownership, control may also be held by proxies, voting trusts, control though intermediary corporations, trusteeships, etc.

Sometimes you would pay a premium for the value of the control in and of itself. Still, only a special-interest buyer would pay it, and only for a share transfer. Let's say that a majority position provides the buyer with an advantage that couldn't realized by anyone else. Maybe it's a high leverage situation with synergistic values. The highest premium would be for fifty-one percent of the company, as control would be obtained for a lower investment, with the premium declining as ownership increases to one hundred percent. The criterion is: the buyer will derive the benefit. As this differs in every situation, good luck finding any rules or guidelines. There aren't any.

Premiums are steadily dropping as minority holders' rights and benefits are becoming better protected by law and better understood by their owners.

Valuation of a fractional interest is always made on a going concern basis. This assumes continuance of the business and its profits — not orderly or forced liquidation. No buyer will pay any bonus, no matter how small, for the right to liquidate or resell the assets, except for spinoffs on some levered buyouts.

As our discussions are limited to small businesses and closely held interests, not shares in publicly or privately held major corporations, I'll address the following additional criteria very briefly and won't consider them further:

- ownership through another corporation,
- devious or illegal shares ownership,
- control through special arrangements or circumstances,
- blockage,
- special family situations,
- warrants or options for additional shares,
- special restrictions in the articles of association,
- grievances.

VALUE OF THE CONTROLLING INTEREST

The per-share value of a controlling interest can be equal to, more than, but never less than the per-share en bloc value of all issued shares.

If the share value is increased by a bonus for a controlling interest, it must be prompted by added value to an identified buyer with strong subjective motives, or for some specific reason. It is not a fact of the market, nor is it a normal allowance with any significant set of rules, regulations, or legal precedents.

If the share value is increased by a bonus for a controlling interest, it must be prompted by added value to an identified buyer with strong subjective motives, or for some specific reason. It is not a fact of the market…

THE MINORITY INTEREST

On top of your many considerations when appraising any going concern, especially when you're buying shares, you have other points to ponder if you're looking at a minority interest.

Minority share interests are almost always discounted from the en bloc or rateable value. Still, in some rare cases, a minority interest may deserve a premium.

Valuation considerations include, but are not limited to:

1. the size of the block of stock to be valued, the percentage of the total issue,

2. although you might pay a bonus for a majority interest for synergistic or other reasons, minority interests are almost always discounted. The size of the shareholding dictates the amount of the discount. The greater the percentage owned, the lower the discount. The value of a tiny percentage is always greatly reduced, particularly if it's owned by an employee and carries no voting privileges.

3. the book value of the stock and the financial condition of the company,

4. the earning power of the company,

5. the dividend-paying capacity of the company,

6. the history and reputation of the company.

You must distinguish between the salaries and perks paid to the owners, managers, and employees, and the dividends paid to shareholders who have no active role in

You must distinguish between the salaries and perks paid to the owners, managers, and employees, and the dividends paid to shareholders who have no active role in the business.

the business. I've talked about how small-business owners pay themselves. Now I'm talking about dividends paid to shareholders, not wages and benefits. You might increase the discount if the managers pay themselves so much that they leave nothing for the investors. The payment of dividends is always a decision of management. Often it has little to do with the actual earning or paying capacity of the company.

7. goodwill or any other intangible value,

8. recent sales of stock, particularly to outsiders,

9. restrictions on the sale of stock, particularly to outsiders,

10. limitations created by the articles of incorporation,

11. interfamily relationships, which commonly disintegrate almost overnight. Maybe the shareholders themselves aren't fighting. Maybe it's their spouses, or family members totally unrelated to the business, bringing pressure on the individual shareholders.

12. each shareholder's personal strength and direct contribution to the day-to-day operation of the business,

You might think I'm contradicting my earlier comments about equality based on interests. From a purely operational perspective the value could differ from one minority interest to another, even though each owns the same percentage and has identical legal privileges. Much depends on what ownership includes, what goes with the shares. Are you buying out the vice-president of a small company and assuming his position, or are you buying the interest of someone's spouse who was a part-owner in name only? All else being equal, you'd think the vice-president's shares would hold more value. Yet at law both interests' per-share value would be the same.

13. legal statutes and precedents. All concerns must be legal, not personal,

14. the uncertain relationship between the minority and the majority shareholder,

15. minority shares in a closely held corporation must be considered an illiquid investment. There is no secondary market. This differs from the stock market, where every sale and every purchase is for a minority interest. The stock market is really a secondary market, which doesn't exist for shares in a closely held corporation.

16. a minority shareholder may expect excess profits for reason of taking an extra risk,

17. a minority interest could have a nuisance value. Another shareholder could possibly even pay a premium just to be rid of the problem.

Some years ago our firm appraised a five-percent interest in a large automobile dealership for a widow. She had inherited the shares from her former husband, whom she had divorced well before his passing. Some years prior, the dealership's majority owner, in starting up, sold three or four promising young salespeople five percent each for a small monetary consideration. Since then, the dealership had grown to be a very prosperous business. The widow, acting honorably, made several attempts to negotiate the sale of her five percent to the majority shareholder, who made very low offers. Thus the appraisal. He refused to let us inspect the premises or examine the financial statements. We concocted a guesstimate value of the widow's interest in the area of $100,000. At the time, she would have settled for half this.

The owner's final offer was ten thousand dollars, the initial investment plus a small interest percentage.

Over the next two years the widow made a nuisance of herself by frequently going into the dealership and harassing everyone in sight. She threatened lawsuits and asked impertinent questions of the staff at the most inopportune times. She insulted customers, telling many not to buy this or that piece of junk. She was finally bought off for $175,000.

In all fairness, this was not a normal or open-market situation. It was a special circumstance caused by a unique chain of events, not often duplicated. Had the majority owner initially bargained fairly with the widow, the minority shareholding discount would have been in the area of fifty percent. Instead, she was paid a substantial bonus to leave.

The purpose of this yarn is only to show that there are exceptions. A practising appraiser will know, without my saying so, that many an assignment is the exception to the rule. If you're a buyer, there's no such thing as a straightforward deal. Each one has special kinks. Perhaps the exception is actually the rule.

18. the potential for blockage. Maybe there is no major shareholder, but there are several minor players. Two or more shareholders get together to force out a third, or others, or they make life so difficult that the third will sell at any price.

Depending on the relationship among the various shareholders, a special situation could exist, created by proxies, voting trusts, powers of attorney, or some other instrument, where a minority shareholder holds the balance of power. Alternatively, another minority holder could possibly pay a premium to increase her holding, particularly if it transforms her into a majority shareholder.

19. potential for takeover or purchase by another company. Will the synergistic values created by another enhance or decrease the value of the minority interest? It works both ways. This situation is more common in publicly listed companies, particularly if they're involved in a merger, or subject to a hostile takeover.

> A practising appraiser
> will know,
> without my saying so,
> that many an assignment
> is the exception to the rule.
> … Perhaps the exception
> is actually the rule.

LIMITATIONS CREATED BY THE ARTICLES OF INCORPORATION

Other shareholders in the same company always have first call on any shares offered for sale in that company. Most articles empower an existing shareholder to stop the transfer of the interest of any other shareholder to an outsider. This proviso affects the minority holder more than the majority. Frequently each shareholder has first right of refusal to buy more shares as per its present interest. Thus the majority owner can always retain control. Conversely, as a new share issue is distributed to each shareholder proportionate to his existing percentage, a minority interest remains a minority interest. In the case of a 50-50 ownership, where no majority exists, both shareholders must approve any transfer or additional issue.

Most articles contain a second clause whereby the shares of a minority shareholder cannot be sold to anyone other than another shareholder. This limits the market to the other shareholders, who might either be unwilling to buy, or might not wish to pay a fair price.

All shareholders must consent before issuing any new shares of any class to an insider or an outsider.

In most companies, except where all insiders agree to it, the articles of incorporation specifically prohibit the sale of shares to outsiders. Additionally, the statutes of all provinces and most states specify the terms, conditions, and inducements that can be used to sell to outsiders, even when agreement has been obtained.

So there's little or no market for a minority shareholding, unless the entire business can be acquired.

No sale is just an ordinary sale. It would rarely, if ever, meet the tests of the standard definition of market value.

APPRAISAL ASSUMPTIONS

Special rules, guidelines, and restrictions must obviously be observed when appraising a minority interest in any company. Initially, the following assumptions will usually be made:

- The en bloc value of the shares, on which the value of the minority interest is predicated, is on a going concern basis, not a liquidation or a forced sale.
- The value found is based on an amicable relationship between the shareholders. There is no hostility or dissent.
- That capable management will continue.

LEGAL PRECEDENT

Mann Estate v. Minister of Finance
British Columbia Supreme Court
Citation (1974) CTL 222

"Fair market value is the highest price available estimated in terms of money which a willing seller may obtain for the property in an open and unrestricted market from a willing, knowledgable purchaser acting at arm's length.
Where there is a ready market for shares such as the stock exchange provides for its listed shares, the market price, as revealed in regular market quotations, is probably the best but not necessarily the only indication of value. However, where, as here, no market exists in that form, regard must be had to other indicitia of value, other circumstances and other conditions considered."

The key words are: unrestricted market and regular market quotations. Neither exists in the transfer of shares in closely held corporations.

Therefore, in valuing a fractional interest, particularly a minority interest, you must assume a notional market.

> Most articles contain a second clause whereby the shares of a minority shareholder cannot be sold to anyone other than another shareholder. This limits the market to the other shareholders, who might either be unwilling to buy, or might not wish to pay a fair price.

> ...in valuing a fractional interest, particularly a minority interest, you must assume a notional market.

WHAT IS A NOTIONAL MARKET?

This term refers to a suggested or implied market value, one based on the interaction of all parties constituting the same. You are assuming a normal, or open, market condition, when in fact none actually exists.

You can interchange the terms "most probable market value" and "notional market value," except for certain restrictions and limitations. They are to be construed as synonymous.

Notional market value assumes that both parties to the transaction are of equal negotiating ability, both of equal willingness, both have the financial strength to consummate a transaction, and both are informed of all relevant information.

Principal considerations:

- There is no contemplation of a true or open market transaction,
- No actual negotiations between a seller and a buyer are conducted, nor are any contemplated,
- Market buyers are not necessarily identifiable, and in fact may not exist,
- Any speculative or special value to the owner, or to a select buyer, is not considered,
- There are no forced sale considerations, nor any compulsion to sell or to buy,
- Subject to certain limitations, any restrictions on the sale of fractional interests are assumed away,
- Any synergistic value is not considered.

Notional market value is determined by either:

- reference to open market transactions,
- or reference to detailed financial analysis and risk measurement theory.

NONLEGAL CONSIDERATIONS

Let's say that two people equally own the issued shares of your target company. They could be spouses, siblings, friends, parent and child, or what have you. Whenever an active shareholder or partner wants out, or is wanted out, for any reason, consider the following factors. Remember, though, that these are practical — not legal — considerations.

1. Each party's management strength and actual contribution to the operation or management of the business. Are they truly equal, or only assumed to be so?

An outsider must approach this difficult supposition cautiously and tactfully. How do you tell the owner that he's incompetent, or that his wife could do a better management job if he weren't there? Sometimes the differing strengths of the partners are obvious and important. You might consider it when assigning a value to a specific fractional interest. Still, only the bravest would dare openly say so out loud or in writing. If you choose to comment on these differing abilities, or assign unidentical values to identical amounts and classes of shares, as the late Red Skelton always said at the end of each show: "God bless."

2. Do the customers and staff depend on one more than the other(s)?

3. Will the business be materially damaged by the departure of either of the parties? If the stronger partner departs, can you employ a new manager at an equitable wage?

4. Can either of the shareholders finance a buyout of the other's fifty percent? Will the bank accept one, but not the other? Are the considerations different if the purchase is financed internally, or externally?

5. Would either sell to a third party, assuming she could, if it resulted in a dissolution of her interest or that of the other person?

6. Does this particular situation differ from the norm?

THE DISCOUNT FOR THE MINORITY INTEREST

When you're assessing the discount for a minority interest, you'll find that market data, or other reliable valuation guidelines, are in short supply. Except for larger, well-publicized cases, usually American, which Canadian courts often accept as precedents, very few law cases are well-documented. The rationale of the courts is almost never published, so legal precedents are little help. The same goes for most normal market and other indicators, except to indicate discount percentages very broadly. The stock market price-earnings ratios, which are the sale of minority interests, suggest only direction. Yet it's generally recognized that the value of a minority interest should be discounted from the en bloc value of all issued shares.

Both the IRS and Revenue Canada have used lower-than-normal price-earnings ratios in determining the fair market value of minority interests.

The courts specifically, and the market generally, recognize that a lower value is attributable on the sale of a minority holding in a closely held corporation. But it's been left to the appraisers and analysts to say what percentage is appropriate in each situation.

Family members can pay more or less than an outsider. Perhaps the father is selling to his son, wanting the company to remain in the family. Perhaps the family wants to see Mother well-provided-for in her last years. Maybe there are divorces or old-fashioned family squabbles. Each case is unique. The terms for one situation might not work in any other.

The loss, or discount, from the one-hundred-percent en bloc value could range from nil, in an ideal situation, to as high as one hundred percent in a very adverse circumstance.

The assessment of these discounts, and the percentage loss incurred, relate more to convention and textbooks, than to what actually happens in the real world. Most partnership breakups are amicable. If valuation methods haven't been previously agreed to, then the shotgun clause of the buy-sell agreement is enforced. This means the party to whom the offer is made can sell or buy the other for exactly the same price and under the same conditions as offered to him. Although appraisers may suggest that there should be a discount, the sale of most minority interests to insiders, in actual practice, are at one hundred percent of value. Still, as earlier said, since there is no open or secondary market, a notional market must be assumed. Therefore, for the typical arm's-length transfer, a discount from the en bloc value is appropriate.

The tale of the widow who eventually obtained a very substantial bonus for a minority interest must be countered by the following horror story. This fellow owned

When you're assessing the discount for a minority interest, you'll find that market data, or other reliable valuation guidelines, are in short supply.

The assessment of these discounts, and the percentage loss incurred, relate more to convention and textbooks, than to what actually happens in the real world.

exactly fifty percent in a prosperous grocery store in a smaller rural community. His wife absolutely hated the town, his children didn't like the school, and he wasn't particularly fond of the place. There were no business problems, and the relationship with the partner was amiable. One day, the wife said, "Sell the store, or else the kids and I are moving out." The partner absolutely refused to buy and no one else wanted his share. After several months, much consternation, and considerable pressure from the wife, our friend threw the keys at his partner with the traditional salute. The discount on his minority interest: one hundred percent. I'm telling you this atypical story to demonstrate that it works both ways.

Under most circumstances, from what I've seen, a normal discount in an arm's-length transaction would range from twenty to fifty percent. Legal precedents are few and solid market information minuscule, so estimates are usually based on a "shoot from the hip" reaction, rather than on any specific market criteria. A very general rule of thumb is: Discount a fifty-percent share interest by one-third, a twenty-five-percent interest by one-half, and all others around or between these ranges. Again, there are no strict rules or infallible guidelines. A discount percent is often arrived at by mutual agreement between the parties, or established by the judge, not calculated by any particular legal inferences or substantive market data.

Any discount to the value of any minority interest, no matter what you do, will be wrong. But based on all of the writings and all of the jurisprudence to emanate from both the US and Canada, and even Great Britain, you can always challenge another to provide a more supportable discount. They can't, either.

Under most circumstances, from what I've seen, a normal discount in an arm's-length transaction would range from twenty to fifty percent.

NOTES

_____

_____

_____

_____

_____

_____

_____

_____

_____

_____

_____

_____

_____

_____

_____

_____

_____

_____

_____

_____

_____

THE APPRAISAL REPORT

INTRODUCTORY ITEMS

Reporting Format

Although addressed to the professional appraiser, the purpose of this chapter is to show the business buyer what to expect in a professionally prepared appraisal and outline a recommended format. What follows is the reporting style that I've used for many years. I realize that each appraiser has his own guideline; or you may find one that you prefer to mine. Use the one that best suits your reporting style, market, and clientele, but try not to miss any of the following headings and inclusions.

Transmittal Letter

The transmittal letter should contain:

- the date of this letter,
- the name and address of the intended recipient,
- the legal description of the business,
- owned or leased real estate,
- the municipal address, if applicable,
- the name of the owner of record,
- the type, size, and special features of the business,
- the name of any franchise affiliation,
- the final value estimate,
- the date to which the value found applies,
- the name and signature of the appraiser,
- the name and signature of the reviewing appraiser, if any.

Table of Contents

Whether to include a table of contents is a personal matter. It should be included if the report runs on longer than thirty pages. If shorter, such a table might not accomplish much.

Summary of Conclusions and Important Facts

- the purpose of the appraisal,
- the value sought; whether it's a going concern, liquidation, etc.
- the name and municipal address of the business appraised,
- the legal description of the real estate,
- the name of the registered owner, or owner of record,
- a brief description of the business being appraised,
- any franchise affiliation,
- brief details of the real estate lease, if applicable,

- brief details of other leases, if applicable,
- a historical and/or pro forma income and expense summary,
- a summary of assets and liabilities for a shares valuation,
- values found by the:
  - comparative sales approach,
  - assets approach:
    - real estate
    - fixtures and equipment
    - working capital (specify if not included)
    - intangible assets, including goodwill
  - split-rate approach:
    - value of the real estate
    - value of the business
  - cash-flow approach
- the final value estimate of going concern value
- the date(s) to which the value(s) found apply,
- the date of property inspection, if different,
- the name and qualifications of contributing appraisers or others,
- the name and designation(s) of the appraiser,
- the name and designation of the reviewing appraiser, if any.

UNIFORM STANDARDS OF PROFESSIONAL APPRAISAL PRACTICE (USPAP)

Following are the compulsory USPAP requirements of conduct and work performance that set out the minimum standards and inclusions. They have been developed over the past few years by the Appraisal Standards Board of the Appraisal Foundation, a nonprofit group, authorized by the US Congress. It represents almost all of the leading appraisal institutes and associations domiciled in the United States and Canada. The following is abstracted from the 1998 Edition, presented, except as noted, without deletion or annotation.

Most of these comments are not mine, but belong to the Standards Board. As I've already covered all this in earlier chapters, one way or another, I've mostly resisted the temptation to put in my two bits. But because USPAP has really only scratched the surface in developing business valuation guidelines, I couldn't pass up the chance to share some of my worldly advice. Maybe my only personal comment would be relative to Rules 9.2.(b) and 10.3 covering shares, letter stock, etc. If you, as an appraiser, have chosen to wade through these waters, and unless you have special training, be extra-careful. All of the red flags are flying.

USPAP Standard 9 (Business Appraisal Requirements)

"In developing a business or intangible-asset appraisal, an appraiser must be aware of, understand, and correctly employ those recognized methods and procedures that are necessary to produce a credible appraisal.

Comment: Standard 9 is directed toward the same substantive aspects set forth in Standard 1, but addresses business and intangible-asset appraisal."

Author's note: Standard 1 is basically the same as Standard 9, except that it deals exclusively with real estate.

USPAP Standards Rule 9.1

"In developing a business or intangible asset appraisal, an appraiser must:

a. be aware of and understand and correctly employ those recognized methods and procedures that are necessary to produce a credible appraisal;

   Comment: Changes and developments in the economy and in investment theory have a substantial impact on the business appraisal profession. Important changes in the financial arena, securities regulation, tax law, and major new court decisions may result in corresponding changes in the business appraisal practice.

b. not commit a substantial error of omission or commission that significantly affects an appraisal;

   Comment: In performing appraisal services, an appraiser must be certain that the gathering of factual information is conducted in a manner that is sufficiently diligent to reasonably ensure that the data would have a material or significant effect on the resulting opinions or conclusions being considered. Further, an appraiser must use sufficient care in analysing such data to avoid errors that would significantly affect his or her opinions and conclusions.

c. not render appraisal services in a careless or negligent manner, such as a series of errors that, considered individually, may not significantly affect the results of an appraisal, but which, when considered in the aggregate, would be misleading.

   Comment: Perfection is impossible to attain, and competence does not require perfection. However, an appraiser must not render appraisal services in a careless or negligent manner. This rule requires an appraiser to use diligence and care. The fact that the carelessness or negligence of an appraiser has not caused an error that significantly affects his or her opinions or conclusions and thereby seriously harms a client does not excuse such carelessness or negligence."

USPAP Standard 10 (Business Appraisal Reporting)

"In reporting the results of a business or intangible-asset appraisal, an appraiser must communicate each analysis, opinion, and conclusion in a manner that is not misleading.

USPAP Standards Rule 10.1

Each written or oral business or intangible-asset appraisal report must:

a. contain sufficient information to enable the intended user(s) to understand it. Any specific limiting conditions concerning information should be noted.

Comment: Any specific limiting conditions should be noted in the engagement letter as well as in the report itself. A failure to observe this rule could cause the intended users of the report to make a serious error even though each analysis, opinion, and conclusion in the report is clearly stated.

b. clearly and accurately disclose any extraordinary assumption that directly affects the appraisal, and indicate its impact on value.

Comment: This rule requires a clear and accurate disclosure of any extraordinary assumptions or conditions that directly affect an analysis, opinion, or conclusion. Examples of such extraordinary assumptions or conditions might include items such as the execution of a pending lease agreement, atypical financing, infusion of additional working capital or making other capital additions, or compliance with regulatory authority rules. The report should indicate whether the extraordinary assumption or condition has a positive, negative, or neutral impact on value."

Contingent and Limiting Conditions

At this time, there is no standard set of limiting conditions for business appraisal, either approved or recommended by USPAP. Undoubtedly, these will be along in due course. In the interim, I recommend the usual real-estate appraisal disclaimers, as supplemented by special requirements for a small business. Still, if and when USPAP establishes standard disclaimers, you should use them, and not what follows, augmented by the appraiser to fit each unique situation.

In determining going concern value, remember that each business combines tangible and intangible assets. Its value is a mix of the values of real estate, fixtures and equipment, working capital, and goodwill. It's often difficult to separate out each component's contribution to the whole. Rather than photocopy the standard set of limiting conditions and insert it into the report, the wise appraiser considers the potential ramification of each clause and provides the necessary modifications and enlargements.

What follows is more appropriate. Still, the appraiser should bear in mind that this is not intended to be an all-inclusive list. Special situations will require special clauses.

- The name and the incorporated status of the company is accepted as correct. You assume that the company is legally incorporated and properly registered, and is in good standing with the companies branch (or the registrar) in your state or province.

  Annual reporting and continuance requirements vary from state to state and province to province. You'll say that you assume the subject has complied with the requirements of your jurisdiction. If the subject business is a proprietorship or partnership, this clause should be modified accordingly.
- The municipal address and the legal description of the real estate, as stated herein and recorded with the registrar of deeds (or land titles office), is assumed to be correct.
- All personal property included in the business and forming a part of it, is owned by the company, and is, unless so stated, considered to be unencumbered.
- The appraiser assumes no responsibility for anything of a legal nature, including the provisions of any special marketing agreements, franchises, dealerships, or other agreements (as applicable), nor of any other agreement entered into with any other supplier. Legal interpretations, if any, appear

only for the benefit of the reader. They are the personal opinion of the appraiser and are not to be construed as facts at law.

- To arrive at a supportable opinion of value, you must use both documented and hearsay evidence of market transactions. Make a concerted effort to verify the accuracy of this information. State that the information provided is believed to be reliable and correct, but no warranty of that correctness is given or implied.
- The appraiser assumes no responsibility if the income, expense, and other financial statements and information, as provided by the owner(s) and on which the final value estimate is based, are not correct, or if the financial position of the business and company is other than as stated.

     If the financial statements that you use are not audited, and they probably are not, put the above disclaimer in capital letters, not only here but in at least two other places in your report: at the beginning of your comments on the financial statements, and again just before your signature, with the wording modified as applicable.

- Sketches, diagrams, drawings, photographs, etc., presented in this report are included for the sole purpose of illustration. No responsibility is assumed concerning these matters, or other technical or engineering descriptions or techniques or procedures that would be required to discover any inherent or hidden condition.
- All licences, franchises, marketing agreements, dealerships, distributorships, or anything that does or will affect the operation and trading style of the subject, are assumed to be assignable. If any terminate on the sale or transfer of the subject, they are assumed to have been granted to any subsequent buyer at no cost or, at least, a very reasonable cost.
- The appraiser assumes no responsibility for anything of an environmental or toxic nature. This appraisal was made on the assumption that none exists.
- The distribution of values in this report between the various components of the business, real estate, fixtures and equipment, working capital, and goodwill, apply only to the composite entity. Their separate values, as detailed herein, should not be considered as stand-alone values, used in conjunction with any other appraisal, or taken out of context. They may be invalid if so used.
- The party to whom the report is addressed may use it in deliberations affecting the subject business. In so doing, no one should extract portions from it, but should, instead, use it in its entirety.
- The appraisal report is not valid unless it contains the original signature of the appraiser, both on the report and on the certificate of appraisal.

Maps and Photographs

The appraisal should include:

- regional, city, town, and neighborhood maps,
- maps of any proposed roadway changes,
- a site plan. For many businesses, size and traffic moveability on the site is very important,
- several inside and outside photographs.

Whether to put the maps and photographs at the beginning or the end of the report is more a matter of personal preference than of edict. As a general practice, if there are only a few of each, they should be at the front; if several, put them in the addenda. Nothing improves a report more than good maps and photographs, particularly interior photographs.

THE APPRAISAL OF THE SUBJECT GOING CONCERN
Section I: PURPOSE OF THE APPRAISAL AND BACKGROUND INFORMATION

Purpose of the Appraisal and Definition of Value Sought

The purpose of the appraisal must be clearly defined. Depending on circumstances, you could be seeking one of the following values:

- real estate only, value to the owner,
- real estate, fixtures, and equipment,
- going concern value,
- orderly liquidation value,
- forced-sale liquidation value.

USPAP Standards Rule 1.2

"Define the value being considered. If the value to be estimated is market value, the appraiser must clearly indicate whether the estimate is the most probable price:

- in terms of cash; or
- in terms of financial arrangements equivalent to cash; or
- in such other terms as may be precisely defined."

With small businesses, seldom will you appraise shares. In an asset sale, everything included with the transaction, and all that you will value, is clearly identified. This is usually the real estate, if owned, plus the fixtures and equipment, plus the right to continue the business from the same premises, often using the same name. Inventory is almost always extra to the purchase price.

If appraising the shares, you'll also include:

- names and addresses for all shareholders,
- the number of shares held by each shareholder,
- names and positions for all directors and officers,
- each shareholder's position in the company,
- the total number of shares issued,
- the classification of shares issued,
- the voting rights attached to classification of shares issued,
- details of any escrow or letter stock,
- restrictions on sale of escrow or letter stock.

(Including most of this is a good idea even if you're only valuing the assets.)

USPAP Standards Rule 9.3

"In developing a business or intangible-asset appraisal relating to an equity interest with the ability to cause liquidation of the enterprise, an appraiser must investigate the possibility that the business enterprise may have a higher value in liquidation than for continued operation as a going concern absent contrary provisions of law of a competent jurisdiction. If liquidation is the indicated basis of valuation, any real estate or personal property to be liquidated must be valued under the appropriate standard.

Comment: This rule requires the appraiser to recognize that continued operation of a business is not always the best premise of value, as liquidation may result in a higher value. It should be noted, however, that this should be considered only when the business equity being appraised is in a position to cause liquidation. If liquidation is the appropriate premise of value, then assets such as real estate and tangible personal property must be appraised under Standard 1 and Standard 7, respectively."

Identification of Subject Business and the Assets Being Appraised

Detail exactly what you're appraising.

Structure
- the business's full name,
- its corporate structure, legal form,
- the head-office address, if it differs from that of the subject,
- the number of the company's issued and paid-for shares,
- the names and addresses of principal shareholders,
- the names and addresses of directors and officers,
  the owner's name,
- any partners' names and percentages held,
- provide an organizational chart (if you feel that it is appropriate)

Description of the company, intangible assets, and liabilities
- the type of business and product line,
- the number and classification of employees,
- any union agreements,
- the market position and distribution patterns,
- special value contributors, such as ore bodies, timber berths, licences, franchises, and dealerships,
- outstanding warranties or unsatisfied guarantees,
- any contracts that must be continued,
- growth potential,
- inherited or continuing liabilities,
- the relationship with each major customer,
- the relationship with each major supplier.

Description of the capital assets
- the legal description and address of the real estate,
- the details of the chattels included (this could appear in the addenda),
- the details of working capital entries, inventory, work-in-progress, prepaids, and liabilities, if included.

USPAP Standards Rule 9.2

"In developing a business or intangible-asset appraisal, an appraiser must observe the following specific appraisal guidelines:

a. Adequately identify the business enterprise, assets, or equity under consideration, define the purpose and the intended use of the appraisal, consider the elements of the appraisal investigation, consider any special limiting conditions, and identify the effective date of the appraisal.

   b. Define the value being considered.

      i. If the appraisal concerns a business enterprise or equity interests, consider any buy-sell agreements, investment letter stock restrictions, restrictive corporate-charter or partnership-agreement clauses, and any similar features or factors that may have an influence on value.

     ii. If an appraisal concerns assets, the appraiser must consider whether the assets are:

        1. appraised separately; or
        2. appraised as parts of a going concern.

Comment: The value of assets held by a business enterprise may change significantly, depending on whether the basis of valuation is acquisition or replacement, continued use in place, or liquidation.

     iii. If the appraisal concerns equity interests in a business enterprise, consider the extent to which the interests do or do not contain elements of ownership control.

Comment: Special attention should be paid to the attributes of the interest being appraised, including the rights and benefits of ownership. The elements of control in a given situation may be affected by law, distribution of ownership interests, contractual relationships, and many other factors. As a consequence, the degree of control or lack of it depends on a broad variety of facts and circumstances which must be evaluated in the specific situation. Equity interests in a business enterprise are not necessarily worth the pro rata share of the business enterprise value as a whole.
Conversely, if the value of the whole is not considered, the value of the business enterprise is not necessarily a direct mathematical extension of the value of the fractional interests."

USPAP Standards Rule 10.3

Each written business or intangible-asset appraisal report must comply with the following reporting guidelines:

   a. Identify and describe the business enterprise, assets, or equity being appraised.

   b. State the purpose and intended use of the appraisal.

   c. Define the value to be estimated.

   d. Set forth the effective date of the appraisal and the date of the report.

     Comment: If the appraisal concerns equity, it is not good enough to identify the entity in which the equity is being appraised without also identifying the nature of the equity — for example, the number or shares of common or preferred stock. The purpose may be to express an opinion of value, but the intended use of the appraisal must also be stated.
       The report date is when the report is submitted; the appraisal date or date of value is the effective date of the value conclusion.

   e. Describe the extent of the appraisal process employed.

f. Set forth all assumptions and limiting conditions that affect the analyses, opinions, and conclusions.

g. Set forth the information considered, the appraisal procedures followed, and the reasoning that supports the analyses, opinions, and conclusions.

h. Set forth any additional information that may be appropriate to show compliance with, or clearly identify and explain permitted departures from, the requirements of *USPAP Standards Rule 9*.

i. Set forth the rationale for the valuation methods and procedures considered and employed.

j. Include a signed certification in accordance with *USPAP Standards Rule 10.3*.

- *USPAP Standards Rule 10.3* details the mandatory certification inclusions.
- *USPAP Standards Rule 10.4* requires the addressing of substantive matters.
- *USPAP Standards Rule 10.5* covers appraisal review and responsibility.

Lease Details

- Provide a full summary of all details on any real estate leases or rental agreements, if applicable.
- Provide a full summary on any chattel, fixtures, and equipment leases or rental agreements.
- Provide full details of any suppliers' equipment or other non-owned equipment on the premises that is used to conduct the business.

Rights and Interests Appraised

Your clauses under this heading might read something like:

- The fee simple interest of the beneficial owners of the real and personal property, and the rights and interests of the owners to all tangible and intangible assets of every nature, including goodwill, that are or could be considered as a part of this business.
- No consideration whatever was made of any special interest or claim that any party may have in, or to, any of the tangible or intangible assets owned by or connected with this business.
- No consideration whatever was made of any redundant asset, contingent liability, or any asset or liability not herein specified.

Date to which Value Found Applies and Date of Inspection

The date to which value found applies can be the same day as the assets inspection, but for some specific purpose or reason, could be some other date, often historical. Usually, the business is appraised as at the last fiscal year end or financial reporting period.

If you use a date prior to the inspection of the enterprise, you should insert a disclaimer to the effect that there has been no material change in the assets or in the business that would affect their value since that date. If this is not true, and it probably won't be, as working capital changes daily, any differences should be clearly stated and dealt with.

Not a Value of the Shares

Most going concern appraisals are conducted for the assets only, not the shares, nor a fractional interest. To avoid any possibility of misunderstanding or misinterpretation, the report should contain a statement to this effect:

> "This appraisal is made only for the assets and liabilities of the herein-described business that are specifically identified and described. It is not a valuation of the shares of the company or of the interest of the shareholders. No consideration has been made of unstated assets or liabilities, redundant assets, contingent liabilities, or of any holding other than those herein detailed."

If valuing the shares, or a partial interest, you should indicate this in the opening statement, "Purpose of the Appraisal."

Specific Exclusions

You might choose not to worry about this in an assets-only valuation, but if you're appraising shares, the report should now detail any specific exclusions to the asset or liability schedule. In many small companies, both have exclusions, such as redundant assets, personal property used in the business or just stored on the premises, recreational vehicles, or contingent liabilities. Although they appear in the company name, you won't include them in the final estimate of value.

To doubly ensure that they are not missed by the reader, and to prevent misunderstanding, restate the exclusions at least once more, preferably in the valuation section.

If there are no specific exclusions, you can omit this section.

Most Probable Market Value Defined

Depending on the assignment, you may use a real-estate market value definition, or else a going concern value definition.

USPAP Standard Definition – Real Estate

This the most probable price that a property should bring in a competitive and open market under all conditions requisite to a fair sale, the buyer and seller each acting prudently and knowledgably, and assuming the price is not affected by an undue stimulus. Implicit in this definition is the consummation of a sale as of a specified date and the passing of a title from seller to buyer, whereby:

1. The buyer and seller are typically motivated,

2. Both parties are informed or well-advised, and acting in what they consider their best interests,

3. A reasonable time is allowed for exposure in the open market,

4. Payment is made in United States dollars or in terms of financial arrangements comparable thereto,

5. The price represents the normal consideration for the property sold unaffected by special or creative financing or sales concessions granted by anyone associated with the sale.

Going Concern Value Defined

Going concern value is defined by this author as "the most probable market value expressed in terms of money available in the open market for a proven business enterprise that has established patronage, exclusivity or uniqueness, resulting in demonstrated earnings or profitability. It incorporates the value of real estate, machinery and equipment, working capital, and other assets that are in place and operating within, and as a part of, an established business.

It includes the excess of value over cost that arises as a result of earnings capability in a complete and well-coordinated operation. It's the present value of surplus earnings after the costs of capital, labor, management, and real and personal property have been attended to.

The real estate portion includes:

- the land and its improvements,
- the quality and utility of the building,
- the efficiency of plant,
- the location, including access and visibility, neighborhood, and surrounding amenities.

The business portion includes:

- the furniture, fixtures, and equipment (or machinery),
- the management expertise and ability,
- the existing customer attitudes and patronage,
- the stability of earnings generators and their capacity,
- the probability of continued profit.

The definition presupposes that:

- the seller is knowledgable, experienced, and willing,
- a reasonable time is allowed to find an informed, experienced, and willing buyer,
- there are sufficient buyers and sellers to form a market,
- adequate financing is available at equitable rates,
- all parties are informed, and there is full disclosure,
- no party is acting under duress,
- there may be other special values not herein recognized or considered under different or abnormal circumstances"

Note: This definition has not been approved as a USPAP definition.

Legal and Other Encumbrances

Detail any legal encumbrance against any of the tangible assets, such as mortgages, liens, hypothecations, easements, development restrictions, or caveats. If the real estate is included in the appraisal, this is mandatory. Even with a lease, title restrictions could create future problems. It could be important if any encumbrance affects the validity of title or the marketability of the real estate, any asset, or the business itself.

The company's value might differ if any of its assets, tangible or intangible, are not salable. The appraiser must identify any restrictions and limitations. For example, many franchises are personal to the owner of the company. He can't transfer or assign them in any way, even if he sells the shares. You can never transfer a liquor licence. A liquor licence must always be surrendered in any sale, and the buyer must apply for a new one.

If the appraiser is placing a value on shares, she must spell out in capital letters that contingent liabilities, if any, are not being considered. She might never be told about them, and their omission could result in an incorrect value estimate. The appraisal report would be worthless to the client and could return to haunt the appraiser.

The appraiser should always conclude this section by stating that the information conveyed is for the benefit of the reader only. It is not intended to constitute a legal search nor express a legal opinion on the validity of the title, or any claims against the assets or the shares. Attorneys don't appreciate appraisers trespassing on their territory. So don't.

Overview of the Subject's Industry

- What it is, where it is, and how it operates?
- the industry's maturity and new opportunities,
- ease (or difficulty) of entry,
- risks and success variables.

National, Regional and Local Economic Factors and Influences

Competitive Factors

Community Profile

Location of Subject Business and Neighborhood Factors

Reasonable Marketing Time – Demand Analysis

Market value and/or going concern value always assumes a reasonable marketing time.

USPAP Standards Rule 1.2 (b)

"When estimating market value, the appraiser should be specific as to the estimate of exposure time linked to the value estimate.

Comment: Defining the value to be estimated requires both an appropriately referenced definition and any comments needed to clearly indicate to the reader how the definition is being applied."

To satisfy the requirements of USPAP and your client, always include a paragraph or two that highlights the selling potential for the subject business. This would include a reasonable marketing time. The intent is to detail demand for this class of business in general and this one in particular. Some business types actively trade on the market, while others, particularly those requiring a high degree of management skills or capital, go begging. Fast-food restaurants, such as the model, are generally good sellers — among the most marketable small enterprises. People who don't know better think that all restaurateurs make a killing and have nothing but fun managing them. What a shock they get.

If included, detail demand and perhaps lay out marketability criteria, such as typical buyer types, the number of potential buyers, anything that would make the property relatively easy or difficult to sell, special market attractions, financing normally available, typical vendor carry-backs, and so forth. Provide anything to help the reader make a more intelligent decision.

Section II: THE SUBJECT BUSINESS DESCRIBED AND FINANCIAL ANALYSIS

Municipal Zoning – Land Classification

In most cases, municipal zoning or land classification has little to do with the ownership and operation of a going concern. If the premises are leased, still less, except if an occupancy violation could result in lease cancellation or closure. You're concerned primarily with an existing use that contravenes a local zoning bylaw, or in those communities that have none, a violation of any restrictive covenant or limitation-of-use caveat. What happens if the owner wants to expand, modernize, rebuild after a fire, or make substantial changes for some other reason? Is he permitted to do so?

This applies mostly to a business with on-site vehicle traffic, that isn't complying with setback and frontage requirements. Even if no one has ever noticed a problem in the past, that doesn't mean that no one ever will, particularly if the property is sold.

Highest and Best Site Usage

Often a statement of highest and best site use is prerequisite in a business appraisal. At other times, it's there only to satisfy real-estate appraisal convention that it be included in every report. A highest and best, or most probable, land use study is essential in the appraisal of real estate, where the fundamental concept of value holds that under all is land. In businesses, it's usually difficult to compartmentalize the precise contribution of any specific tangible asset to the value of the whole: land, building, equipment, working capital, or whatever. Going concern value is always created by a homogeneous coordination of all elements. You can seldom attach more importance to this or that component.

For example, a key corner, developed for a gasoline dispensing kiosk, a fast-food restaurant, or an automobile dealership, may be considered grossly underdeveloped if appraised strictly for its real-estate earning capability. Some business sites must be large, have good visibility from the road, and provide easy, quick, safe access from and to the traffic lanes. In many cases, the building occupies a mere ten percent of the site area and holds less than one-third of the total real-estate value. Still, the owner may show a better total return on the investment by selling burgers, cars, or gasoline on this corner, than by redeveloping it for a more intensified use. The rule of optimum value distribution of eighty-percent building to twenty-percent land value becomes redundant. In these situations, real-estate economics take a back seat to the overall earnings capability of the enterprise.

Conversely —.and this is common — some businesses fail strictly because of location. Not every corner is ideal. Maybe the street's too busy or too fast for drivers to exit smoothly. Maybe the site's too small or too hidden. If a site could be redeveloped to make more money, as evidenced by the earnings capability of the total investment, you must state this.

Always, you should comment on whether the site is properly developed.

Identify All Capital Assets

Site Size and Description

Description of the Building

This includes:

- its type,
- its dimensions and area, by floor or area,
- the ceiling, roof line, and clear span heights,
- the age of any additions and renovations,
- its probable remaining economic life,
- its construction and exterior,
- its interior development and finishing,
- its condition and any required repairs,
- the design's suitability for this purpose; obsolescence,
- its convertibility for another use.

Fixtures and Equipment

You may want to completely list all fixtures and equipment, or machinery, that are part of the business. Or you might want to comment briefly on their adequacy and condition. Much depends on the size of the business and the client's requirements. The banker might want you to obtain a detailed list, including serial numbers.

Other Capital Assets

Franchise Agreement, Dealerships, Distributorships, Etc.

Provide complete details on any of these exclusive agreements.

Sample Format

The restaurant operates under the XYZ Franchise, which it holds exclusively for the subject's city and for a five-mile radius from its centre. It grants to the restaurant owner exclusive use of all of the XYZ marks, methods, trade names, procedures, and recipes.

The franchisee must follow the prescribed patterns, merchandising methods, promotions, pricing schedules, and all other procedures as laid down by the franchisor in its manual or as required from time to time.

The term of the franchise is for twenty years, commencing on (exact date) and expiring on (exact date). There is no provision for renewal or extension.

The franchise is personal to the principal shareholder of the restaurant. It is not assignable or transferable. In the event of a sale of the restaurant, the buyer must reapply for the franchise. However, the franchisor cannot unreasonably refuse a new owner.

The franchisor has first right of refusal to buy if the restaurant is offered for sale.

Franchise and Coop Advertising Fees

Initial Franchise Fee	$ 25,000

Service Fee:
1st 10 years	2.50% of gross sales
2nd 10 years	Fee to be agreed on, subject to a minimum increase of 2.0%

National Advertising Fee
All 20 years	1.50% of gross sales

Administration Fee
All 20 years	1.00% of gross sales

Fee Total: 1st 10 years 5.00% of gross sales

Provide Detailed Income Summary for the Past Five Years

Indicate that this is a summary, not a statement. If you copy a financial statement word for word, number for number, without giving full credit to the accountant who prepared it, she'll be most annoyed. And if you change her statement, such as by omitting anything, and keep her name on it, suggesting that she prepared it this way, you'll really be in the soup.

What you develop from the accountant's statement is best called a summary. Although you didn't change any income and expense items, you didn't include long-term debt service, depreciation, or income tax. Later on, you'll consider income tax as an expense item, but at this point, it's often better to leave out income tax for easier comparison from one department to another, one business to another, and with industry averages.

- Provide a statement of changes in financial position
- Provide a statement of cost of sales and gross trading profit. For an assets appraisal, you needn't include a balance sheet. If you want to do so, however, place it in the addenda.
- If valuing the company on shares, include a complete set of statements, including a certificate of audit.

Notes to the Income Statement

This is your interpretation of the income statement. Here, you provide your critique of the operation and potential of the business.

- Indicate if the business uses a cash or accrual accounting system. You may also wish to name the accountant who prepared the statements and on whom you rely.
- Explain why income and profits are increasing, decreasing, variable, or constant. Detail trends.
- Detail cost of sales and gross trading profit and how it compares with industry averages.
- Detail fixed costs, referring to any changes that have occurred or may occur.
- Detail variable expenses. Indicate shifts, particularly radical ones, and how they compare with industry averages.
- Detail the cost of labor and management and how each compares with industry standards. Always separate management from labor. If any

shareholders draw salaries without being actively engaged in the business, you should note this. Comment on any radical departures from the norm. For some businesses, such as restaurants, compare the cost of sales and the combined costs of labor and management with industry averages.
- Detail net operating profit before property costs, long-term debt service, or depreciation. Develop percentages for several years back and compare with industry averages. Comment on anything that's way out of line.

You appraise real estate before income tax, and small businesses after tax. Income tax is regarded as an expense item, treated no differently from food, labor, or any other expense item.

Operations Analysis

Now you may wish to comment on anything that you consider vital to the operation of the business and anything that would affect going concern value.

When the reader reaches this point, he should know exactly what this business is all about, its history, mode of operation, trading style, and future potential.

Section III: DETERMINATION OF GOING CONCERN VALUE

USPAP Standards Rule 9.4

"In developing a business or intangible-asset appraisal, an appraiser must observe the following specific guidelines when applicable:

a. Consider all appropriate valuation methods and procedures.

b. Collect and analyse relevant data regarding:

  i. the nature and history of the business;
  ii. financial and economic conditions affecting the business enterprise, its industry, and general economy;
  iii. past results, current operations, and future prospects of the business enterprise;
  iv. past sales of capital stock or other ownership interests in the business enterprise being appraised;
  v. sales of similar businesses or capital stock of publicly held similar businesses;
  vi. prices, terms, and conditions affecting past sales of similar business assets.

Comment: This guideline directs the appraiser to study the prospective and retrospective aspects of the business enterprise, and to study it in terms of the economic and industry environment within which it operates. Further, sales of securities of the business itself, or similar businesses for which sufficient information is available, should also be considered.

In certain circumstances, the business appraiser may also collect and analyse data regarding functional and/or economic utility or obsolescence of the business assets.

Economic obsolescence is a major consideration when assets are considered as parts of a going concern. It may also be one of the criteria in deciding that liquidation is the appropriate premise for valuation."

USPAP Standards Rule 9.5

In developing a business or intangible-asset appraisal, an appraiser must:

a. select and employ one or more approaches that apply to the specific appraisal assignment;

Comment: This rule requires the appraiser to use all relevant approaches for which sufficient reliable data are available. However, it does not mean that the appraiser must use all approaches in order to comply with the rule if certain approaches are not applicable.

b. consider and reconcile the indications of value resulting from the various approaches to arrive at the value conclusion.

Comment: The appraiser must evaluate the relative reliability of the various indications of value. The appraiser should consider quality and quantity of data leading to each of the indications of value. The value conclusion is the result of the appraiser's judgment and not necessarily the result of a mathematical process.

Methods

Detail how you developed the going concern value. You should use at least two methods, so that you can check the results of one against the other. Still, in some situations, one method only will have to do. The rules of correlation are the same as for the appraisal of real estate.

The Comparative Sales Approach

The Sum-of-the-Assets Approach

- Appraise the real estate by one of the three approaches,
- Appraise the fixtures and equipment,
- Appraise any other tangible asset,
- Appraise the value of the goodwill,
- Appraise the value of any other intangible asset,
- Add them all together to arrive at the final value estimate,
- Working capital—in or out?

The Split-Rate Approach

- Appraise the real estate by one of the three approaches,
- Appraise the fixtures and equipment if considered separately,
- Develop the capitalization rate for the business,
- Appraise the business portion, including goodwill,
- Add up the value of the real estate and the business.

The Stabilized Cash-Flow Approach

- Develop the pro forma or stabilized operating statement,
- Develop the capitalization rate,
- Determine going concern value.

The Discounted Net Profits Approach

- Develop the forecast pro forma operating statement,
- Develop the capitalization rate,
- Determine going concern value.

The Net Earnings Approach

- Develop the pro forma or stabilized operating statement,
- Determine the amount of debt and the income consumed by it,
- Develop the capitalization rate for the residual income,
- Capitalize the residual income and add the debt for the going concern value estimate.

USPAP Standards Rule 7 (Personal Property Appraisal)

In developing a personal property appraisal, an appraiser must be aware of, understand, and correctly employ those recognized methods and techniques that produce a credible appraisal.

USPAP Standards Rule 7.1

"In developing a personal property appraisal, an appraiser must:

a. be aware of, understand, and correctly employ those recognized methods and techniques that are necessary to produce a credible appraisal.

Comment: The rule recognizes that the principle of change continues to affect the manner in which appraisers perform appraisal services. Changes and developments in personal property practice have a substantial impact upon the appraisal profession. Important changes in the cost and manner of producing and marketing personal property and changes in the legal framework in which property rights and interests are created, conveyed, and financed have resulted in corresponding changes in appraisal theory and practice. Social change has also had an effect on appraisal theory and practice. To keep abreast of these changes and developments, the appraisal profession reviews and revises appraisal methods and techniques, and devises methods and techniques to meet new circumstances. For this reason, it is not sufficient for appraisers to simply maintain the skills and the knowledge they possess when they become appraisers. Each appraiser must continuously improve his or her skills to remain proficient in personal property appraisal.

b. not commit a substantial error of omission that significantly affects an appraisal.

Comment: In performing appraisal services, an appraiser must be certain that the gathering of factual information is conducted in a manner that is sufficiently diligent to ensure that the data that would have a material or significant effect on the resulting opinions or conclusions are considered. Further, an appraiser must use sufficient care in analysing such data to avoid errors that would significantly affect his or her opinions and conclusions.

c. previously stated as a part of *USPAP Standards Rule 9.1 (c)"*

USPAP Standards Rule 7.2

"In developing a personal property appraisal, an appraiser must consider the purpose and intended use of the appraisal and observe the following specific guidelines:

a. adequately identify the property to be valued, including the method of identification;

   Comment: This guideline is an essential element in all appraisals. An adequate identification of property should accurately describe property as understood within the market.

b. define the purpose and intended use of the appraisal, including all general and specific limiting conditions.

c. identify the effective date of the appraisal.

d. select and define the value to be considered consistent with the purpose of the appraisal.

   Comment: If the value to be estimated is market value, the appraiser must clearly indicate whether the estimate is the most probable price:

   i. in terms of cash; or

   ii. in terms of financial arrangements equivalent to cash, or

   iii. in such other terms as may be precisely defined. If an estimate of value is based on sub-market financing or financing with unusual conditions or incentives, the terms of such financing must be clearly set forth, their contributions to or negative influence on value must be described and estimated, and the market data supporting the valuation estimate must be described and explained.

e. collect, verify, analyse, and reconcile such data as are available, adequately identified, and described, to indicate a value conclusion;

f. value the property by an appropriate appraisal method or technique;

g. All pertinent information in items (a) through (f) above shall be used in the development of a personal property appraisal."

USPAP Standards Rule 7.3

"In developing a personal property appraisal, an appraiser must consider the purpose and intended use of the appraisal and observe the following specific appraisal guidelines:

a. Consider the effect of highest and best use by measuring and analysing the current use and alternative uses to encompass what is profitable, possible, legal, and physically possible, as relevant to the purpose and intended use for the appraisal;

b. Personal property has several measurable marketplaces, and the appraiser must identify, define, and analyse the appropriate market consistent with the purpose of the appraisal;

Comment: The appraiser must recognize that there are distinct levels of trade, and each may have its own market value. For example, a property may have a distinct value at the wholesale level of trade, a retail level of trade, or a value under varying auction conditions. Therefore, the appraiser must consider the subject property within the correct market context.

c. Consider the market conditions at the time of the valuation, including market acceptability of the property as well as supply, demand, scarcity, or rarity;

d. Consider a sufficient quantity of data and any prior sales of the subject within a sufficient period of occurrence to reach a appropriate estimate of value;

e. Consider the cost, income, and sales comparison approaches and their degree of applicability in the valuation of personal property. The selection of valuation approaches to be used should be based on the availability of data and the purpose of the appraisal;

f. Consider the effects on value caused by attributes such as condition, style, quality, manufacturer, author, materials, origin, age, provenance, alterations, and restorations;

g. Identify any real estate, real property, trade fixtures, or intangible items that are not personal property but are included in the appraisal.

   Comment: Additional expertise in real property appraisal may be required in valuation assignments that involve more than personal property.

h. All pertinent information in items a through f above shall be used in the development of a personal property appraisal."

Reconciliation of Values Found

Detail why you preferred one method over another.

Final Value Estimate; Most Probable Going Concern Estimate

Signature of Appraiser

Signature of Reviewing Appraiser (if any)

Names and Accreditation of Contributing Appraisers or Expert (s)

Certificate of Appraisal – The Appraiser

USPAP Standards Rule 10.3

"Each written or intangible asset appraisal report must contain a signed certification that is similar in content to the following:

I certify that, to the best of my knowledge and belief:
- the statements of fact contained in this report are true and correct.
- the reported analyses, opinions, and conclusions are limited only by the reported assumptions and limiting conditions, and are my personal, unbiased professional analyses, opinions, and conclusions.
- I (or the specified) have no present or prospective interest in the property that is the subject of this report, and I (or the specified) have no personal interest or bias with respect to the parties involved.
- My compensation is not contingent on an action or event resulting from the analyses, opinions, or conclusions in, or the use of, this report.
- My analyses, opinions, and conclusions were developed, and this report has been prepared, in conformity with the Uniform Standards of Professional Appraisal Practice.
- No one provided significant professional assistance to the person signing this report. (If there are exceptions, the name of each individual providing significant professional help must be stated.)"

Signature of the Appraiser

Signature of the Reviewing Appraiser

NOTES

_____

_____

_____

_____

_____

_____

_____

_____

_____

_____

_____

_____

_____

_____

_____

_____

_____

_____

_____

_____

_____

_____

_____

_____

EPILOGUE

THROUGHOUT this manual, I could have said more on every topic and technique. I'm not apologizing for this. I can't cover every type of enterprise or provide a valuation method or solution to every conceivable situation. All anyone can do is hit the high spots, outline the common denominators, and describe the more popular procedures. In controversial situations, or where the experts disagree, I've tried to present both sides, the good and the bad, what the financial community likes and dislikes. For many real-world situations, you'll need considerably more in-depth analysis, and more arguments. For appraisers, as the discipline of valuing small businesses grows, as each of us provides valuations on more and different types of enterprises, better methods will be found. And because of increasing risk, decreasing profits, and more businesses being bought by people who shouldn't have, or at outlandish prices, every buyer needs way more astute pre-purchase qualification. Appraisal, while not exact, is not a stagnant science. We all learn, and presumably put into practice, something new each day.

You should read the work of several learned theorists and practitioners in this field. A great variety of excellent texts are available, with new titles being added regularly. Several are written at a much higher technical level than this one. Many delve more deeply into the more technical and theoretical aspects of the science, particularly the analysis of financial statements, and the valuation of shares and fractional interests.

Always remember that pat answers don't exist. No one's ever said or developed anything that provides exactness for every situation. You don't pull appraisal solutions off the supermarket shelf. There are no secret potions for instant and correct solutions. You might approach situations from many angles, using different tactics, and you might reach divergent conclusions that could be foreign, logical, and acceptable, all at once.

Business valuation is, without question, the next field for the practising real-estate appraiser. For the business buyer, it's a must to establish a business's worth before making the initial offer, to ensure that it meets your objectives and overcomes the constraints. Far too many buy blindly, discovering later that they didn't receive what they'd bargained for.

I hope this textbook will boost your confidence. Small-business appraisal isn't all that complicated. You might not even need to learn any new skills, but rather just broaden the basic appraisal sciences that conscientious appraisal practitioners are improving on every day. Most important, I hope that I've provided the groundwork so you can learn still more and become more professional.

Lloyd R. Manning
Lloydminster, Saskatchewan

NOTES

_____

_____

_____

_____

_____

_____

_____

_____

_____

_____

_____

_____

_____

_____

_____

_____

_____

_____

_____

_____

_____

_____

Successful Business Library

A Complete Franchise Solution.

From The Oasis Press®

Understand the nuances of running a franchise or turning your existing business into a successful franchise model. Each of these books offer unparalleled expertise in helping you make the most of operating a franchise in today's marketplace...

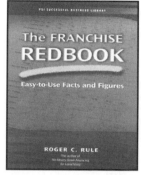

The Franchise Redbook

Easy-to-Use Facts and Figures

ROGER C. RULE

An accurate and user-friendly reference that will help determine your best franchise opportunity. While there are several other reference books available, *The Franchise Redbook* is up-to-date, comprehensive, and by far the easiest to use to determine your franchise options. The organized listings make it easy to weigh the pros and cons of the franchises within your area of interest. Ideal for selecting a franchise, doing market and comparative analysis, preparing a marketing or business plan, preparing contact lists, or doing any other research on franchises.

PAPERBACK $34.95

ISBN 1-55571-484-6
750 PAGES

No Money Down Financing for Franchising

ROGER C. RULE

An essential resource for securing finances and building the foundation to a winning franchise. Broken down into three logical progressions, this book explores every resource available for franchise financing, including many methods that require no money down and explains the vital points that will prepare you in obtaining these goals.

PAPERBACK $19.95

ISBN 1-55571-462-5
240 PAGES

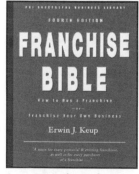

Franchise Bible, 4th edition

How to Buy A Franchise or Franchise Your Own Business

ERWIN J. KEUP

If you are thinking about acquiring a franchise or franchising your own business, this indispensable and recognized guide will tell you how to do it, and save you time and money in the process. You'll learn the advantages and disadvantages of the franchise system and familiarize yourself with the terms and concepts that are essential in operating a franchise today. A recognized, must-read if you are interested in the world of franchising.

PAPERBACK $27.95

ISBN 1-55571-526-5
274 PAGES

TO ORDER CALL 1-800-228-2275 OR VISIT YOUR FAVORITE BOOKSTORE

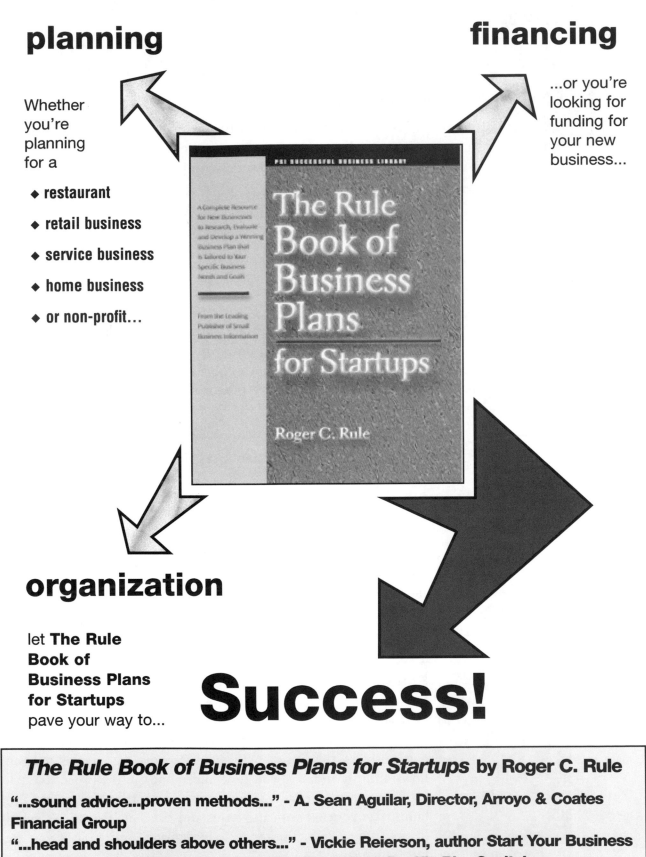

Moonlighting: Earn a Second Income at Home
Paperback: $15.95

Pages: 240
ISBN: 1-55571-406-4

It is projected that half of the homes in America are expected to house some type of business in the next few years. *Moonlighting* takes the idea of starting your own home-based business a step further. It will show you, in realistic and achievable steps, how you can initially pursue a business dream part-time, instead of quitting your job and being without a financial safety net. This confidence building guide will help motivate you by showing you the best steps toward setting your plan in motion.

Home Business Made Easy
Paperback: $19.95

Pages: 233
ISBN: 1-55571-428-5

An easy-to-follow guide to help you decide if starting a home-based business is right for you. Takes you on a tour of 153 home business options to start your decision process. Author David Hanania also advises potential business owners on the fiscal aspects of small startups, from financing sources to dealing with the IRS.

Which Business?
Paperback: $18.95

Pages: 376
ISBN: 1-55571-342-4

A compendium of real business opportunities, not just "hot" new ventures that often have limited earning potential. *Which Business?* will help you define your skills and interests by exploring your dreams and how you think about business. Learn from profiles of 24 business areas, reviewing how each got their start and problems and successes that they have experienced.

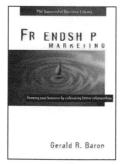

Friendship Marketing
Paperback: $18.95

Pages: 187
ISBN: 1-55571-399-8

If you have every wondered how to combine business success and personal signficance, author Gerald Baron has numerous practical suggestions. After years of working with executives and entrepreneurs, he's found that business success and personal meaning can share common ground. Using dozens of examples, he shows how building relationships is the key to business development and personal fulfillment.

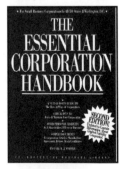

The Oasis Press®
Successful Business Library

Tools to help you save time and money.

Business Owner's Guide to Accounting & Bookkeeping
Paperback: $19.95

Pages: 172
ISBN: 1-55571-381-5

Makes understanding the economics of your business simple. Explains the basic accounting principles that relate to any business. Step-by-step instructions for generating accounting statements and interpreting them, spotting errors, and recognizing warning signs, Discusses how creditors view financial statements.

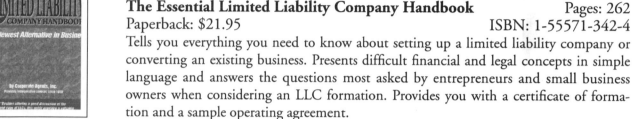

The Essential Limited Liability Company Handbook
Paperback: $21.95

Pages: 262
ISBN: 1-55571-342-4

Tells you everything you need to know about setting up a limited liability company or converting an existing business. Presents difficult financial and legal concepts in simple language and answers the questions most asked by entrepreneurs and small business owners when considering an LLC formation. Provides you with a certificate of formation and a sample operating agreement.

Before You Go Into Business, Read This!
Paperback: $17.95

Pages: 208
ISBN: 1-55571-481-1

Ensures you that the simple things are kept simple, and that the complex things are made simple. It is designed to give the average entrepreneur basic definitions of terms and conditions within industry and the general concepts of running a business. A must for any new business owner!

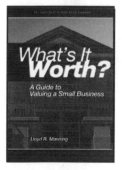

What's It Worth?
Paperback: $22.95

Pages: 234
ISBN: 1-55571-504-4

Determine what your business or investment is really worth. Whether you're buying or selling a business or franchise, this unique guide will quickly show you how to get the best deal. This book is ideal for anyone wanting to purchase a new business, to establish a fair selling price for a going business, or simply to have a better understanding of a professional appraiser's process.

Funding High-Tech Ventures
Paperback: $21.95

Pages: 160
ISBN: 1-55571-405-6

Pursuing a high-tech business has never been more opportune, however the competition in the industry is downright grueling. Author Richard Manweller brings a smart, in-depth strategy with motivational meaning. It will show you how to tailor your strategy to grain investor's attention. If you are looking for a financial angel, *Funding High-Tech Ventures* is the guidance you need to make the right match.

businessplan.com
Paperback: $21.95

Pages: 160
ISBN: 1-55571-405-6

Pursuing a high-tech business has never been more opportune, however the competition in the industry is downright grueling. Author Richard Manweller brings a smart, in-depth strategy with motivational meaning. It will show you how to tailor your strategy to grain investor's attention. If you are looking for a financial angel, *Funding High-Tech Ventures* is the guidance you need to make the right match.

Financial Management Techniques
Paperback: $21.95

Pages: 250
ISBN: 1-55571-405-6

Pursuing a high-tech business has never been more opportune, however the competition in the industry is downright grueling. Author Richard Manweller brings a smart, in-depth strategy with motivational meaning. It will show you how to tailor your strategy to grain investor's attention. If you are looking for a financial angel, *Funding High-Tech Ventures* is the guidance you need to make the right match.

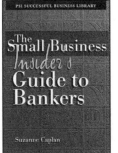

The Small Business Insider's Guide to Bankers
Paperback: $21.95

Pages: 163
ISBN: 1-55571-405-6

Pursuing a high-tech business has never been more opportune, however the competition in the industry is downright grueling. Author Richard Manweller brings a smart, in-depth strategy with motivational meaning. It will show you how to tailor your strategy to grain investor's attention. If you are looking for a financial angel, *Funding High-Tech Ventures* is the guidance you need to make the right match.

OASIS PRESS BOOKS & SOFTWARE

ALL MAJOR CREDIT CARDS ACCEPTED

CALL TO PLACE AN ORDER
— or —
TO RECEIVE A FREE CATALOG
1-800-228-2275

International Orders (541) 245-6502   Fax Orders (541) 245-6505
Web site http://www.psi-research.com   Email sales@psi-research.com

PSI Research   P.O. Box 3727   Central Point, Oregon   97502
U.S.A.